PAPER
GUITAR

PAPER GUITAR

27 WRITERS CELEBRATE
25 YEARS OF
DESCANT MAGAZINE

Edited by

KAREN MULHALLEN

A Phyllis Bruce Book
HarperCollins*Publishers*Ltd

"Introduction" © 1995 by Karen Mulhallen; "Owl and Pussycat, Some Years Later" © 1995 by Margaret Atwood; "Fifteen Notes on the Art of Draftsmanship" © 1995 by Virgil Burnett; "Radar Angels" © 1995 by Catherine Bush; "The Fall of Rome: A Traveller's Guide" © 1995 by Anne Carson; "Martha and The Minder" © 1995 by Pebble Productions Inc.; "A Civil Plantation" © 1995 by Cynthia Flood; "The Lion of Venice" © 1995 by Mark Frutkin; "A Piece of the True Cross" © 1995 by Douglas Glover; "Lisette Model, A Life in Pictures" © 1995 by Katherine Govier; "Seven Poems" © 1995 by Elliott Hayes; "Shouting Saints" © 1995 by David Homel; "Murderous Ways" © 1995 by W.P. Kinsella; "First Sight, A Love Story" © 1995 by Evelyn Lau; "You're Not Gay If You Can Whistle: A True Story" © 1995 by Alberto Manguel; "The Third Miracle" © 1995 by Eric McCormack; "My Night at Valdek" © 1995 by James Miller; "Parts of a Clock, or Asthma" © 1995 by Erin Mouré; "The Translators' Tale" © 1995 by Stan Persky; "A Deeper Theft" © 1995 by Leslie Hall Pinder; "The Yale Chair" © 1995 by Leon Rooke; "'I Roar Through All Creation Like The Wind' . . . (Because I Have No Time To Take Things Slowly) Writing/Mothering" © 1995 by Lake Sagaris; "Title-Page Missing" © 1995 by Josef Škvorecký; "Nightcap" © 1995 by Christine Slater; "Memory-Making and the Stamina of the Poet" © 1995 by Rosemary Sullivan; "A Poem to My Body in Five Installments" © 1995 by Susan Swan; "The Joy of Life" © 1995 by Carol Windley; "Start With A Tree" © 1995 by Eric Wright.

Photographs by Lisette Model appearing in Katherine Govier's "Lisette Model, A Life in Pictures" are courtesy of the National Gallery of Canada, Ottawa. Gift of the Estate of Lisette Model, 1990, by direction of Joseph G. Blum, New York, through the American Friends of Canada. *Frank Sinatra, New York* (c./v. 1939 - c./v. 1944) appears on page 145, *Studio of Armando Reveron, Venezuela* (1954) appears on page 147 and *Rome* (1953) appears on page 150. *Studio of Armando Reveron, Venezuela* and *Rome* copyright © Estate of Lisette Model.

First edition

Canadian Cataloguing in Publication Data

Main entry under title:

Paper guitar : 27 writers celebrate 25 years of Descant magazine

"A Phyllis Bruce book."
ISBN 0-00-647510-8

1. Short stories, Canadian (English).*   2. Canadian fiction – 20th century.   3. Canadian poetry (English) – 20th century.*   4. Descant (Toronto, Ont.)   I. Mulhallen, Karen.

PS8251.P37 1995   C810.8'0054   C95-931376-1
PR9194.4.P3 1995

95 96 97 98 99 ❖ HC 10 9 8 7 6 5 4 3 2 1

Printed and bound in the United States

CONTENTS

INTRODUCTION

This book is a celebration of writers, and of text. Every piece of writing in this volume touches in some way on the process of creation, on its origins, on its motives, on its means. The idea of making is not an abstraction, but has a felt life.

This book is a collection of Canadian writers, many of whom have come from elsewhere, some of whom have gone elsewhere to find their themes. Many have found that here is elsewhere, as exotic as another place. This book is a mapping of territory, the territory of the imagination, and the territory of the world, and the exciting, shifting border-zone where they meet.

As editor of the literary magazine *Descant* for more than two decades, I have worked with the twenty-seven writers in this collection. I asked each to fashion with me a volume which would celebrate art, art-making, the creative process. These are all writers in whom I believe profoundly. With humour and seriousness, together they have created an anthology which marks twenty-five years of the publication of *Descant* magazine.

These fictions, these poems, these essays, these performance pieces, these texts, which are often combinations of many forms, will teach you much about the world, its shimmering sensuosity, its painful contradictions, its beauty spots hovering just on the edge of focus.

I've been thinking about the luxury of editing, of editing this book, and of the years I've given over to the editing of *Descant*. There's an awful freedom about editing. In some ways, it's the surgery of engagement with someone else's text-flesh, the apparent dispassion of nipping and tucking. There's an intimacy like love-making, an entering into the flesh of the other. There's the conversation between equals, in many ways the most ideal conversation which the text-body of the author will experience. You could call it a kind of vice, though its intention is not to harm, but rather never to impinge on the freedom of the other.

I'm attracted to writing which breaks out of its boundaries, its received conventions, which moves outside the limits with which we feel we must live, perhaps for convenience, and perhaps for surety. I am attracted to writing which not only takes us with it, but which stretches us towards it.

A magazine like *Descant* is a record of sensibilities. Separate voices come together under a shelter, the roof of the book. This has been raised by the producers of the book, the craftsmen who design, who edit, who print. All have a hand in the making of the text. You can see the individual markings, the signatures of each over time. And here I reach the point of nostalgia — the humbling fact of the endurance through the co-operation, through the solidarity, of extraordinary people.

Descant magazine's name comes from a poem by the great Irish poet, dramatist, mythographer, cultural critic, nationalist — revolutionary — William Butler Yeats. The poem is called "After Long Silence," and first appeared in a volume entitled *Words for Music Perhaps*.

> Speech after long silence; it is right,
> All other lovers being estranged or dead,
> Unfriendly lamplight hid under its shade,
> The curtains drawn upon unfriendly night,
> That we descant and yet again descant

> Upon the supreme theme of Art and Song:
> Bodily decrepitude is wisdom; young
> We loved each other and were ignorant.

And so Yeats puts the point that song outlives our other passions and yet is fed by them, depends on them, exists because of them.

The magazine has endured for a quarter of a century, our century, our chaotic, war-ridden, intense epoch. And it has changed with the changing currents of that epoch, as have I, who have edited it through that time.

It began as a mimeographed gathering of single sheets stapled together. It began when "young / We loved each other and were ignorant." Those who began have scattered, one is dead, some write still, others have drawn the curtains. But the glory of the enterprise is the glory of the descants which have grown immensely over the years, songs which could not be quelled.

What tunes are sung by the voice as it descants? After I had asked each of the writers to join in celebration of the twenty-five years of the magazine by creating a book, I eventually wrote to each and suggested a leitmotif of art, of the artist, of poesis in its widest sense. My suggestion was not to be prescriptive, but to perhaps stimulate an exchange around a common activity. The passage of time, the power of music, the origins of creativity, the hiding or the revealing of the truth, the revelations of travel, the discovery of the self, the discovery of the other, the weight of history, censorship, freedom, tyranny, and love.

·

We are transformed by texts and by individuals. The text is an agent for change. Human beings change one another. Every writer in this book is an instrument of change. Every writer here has made me re-evaluate the meaning of text. Every writer here is working in the margins, on the frontiers. They will take you there, if you give yourself to them.

What is a frontier? It's the edge of anywhere, a place of freedom and the void. In "A Civil Plantation," Cynthia Flood creates an itinerant Irish schoolteacher, a kind of hedge-master, who carries his books on his back and goes from school to school. In many ways he is preconscious, a nomad of the intellect who goes wherever topography leads him, and yet he is driven by class, and history, and temperament. Is he a coward? I let you judge. But there is some connection between him and the small girl named Amanda, who brings her own class and history and temperament into the arena to lock horns with him.

And Katherine Govier's essay on photographer Lisette Model's life and art will take you to another one of these margins. Model overcame, for a time, family, class, culture, gender, and the doom of history to create new idioms in a major art form of the twentieth century. It was Govier's initial suggestion to me that the theme of this volume might well be art. Her own essay asks us to consider not only Lisette Model, but the impact of one artist on another.

The impact of one artist on another is a sub-theme of Josef Škvorecký's elegant and moving essay on the life and work of composer Antonín Dvořák. For Dvořák gave to the world so many musical themes which have become commonplace that we often don't even recognize where they have come from, that they are Dvořák's creations. Škvorecký argues that perhaps the greatest works are these very commonplaces, which have become so much a part of each of us that they have lost their identifiers — their title-pages — and are ultimately recreated over and over again by everyone who has loved them, and incorporated them into the self.

Inheritance is also the theme of novelist and translator David Homel's essay on the gospel singers in his boyhood, on their ecumenism, on the slippery borders he and they traversed together, and on their lasting effect on the cadence of his own novels. And perhaps Homel's essay is also about their impact, although Homel himself doesn't say so, on his own capacity to cross borders, borders of culture and borders of language.

As I write, I'm moved by the coincidence of geography, by the fact that Stan Persky lives on one margin of Canada, and, like both Cynthia Flood and Carol Windley, has gone abroad for meaning. Perhaps he would disagree, would argue, that it is I the editor with my imperial bifocals who has imposed the idea of margins and centres on the writers of these tales. And he would be right. And wrong. Persky's story, "The Translators' Tale," which overlaps with other stories, self-consciously with that of Conrad's *Heart of Darkness*, and covertly with Thomas Mann, sends searchlights through history, and politics, and human love, and human denial, in a shattering way.

The frontier also brings to mind the work of Leslie Hall Pinder, a Vancouver writer and civil rights lawyer who has spent her life fighting for the rights of native peoples. Pinder has the sensibility and talent of the poet to recreate the world in shimmering bright images, and she has the passionate and determined heart of a fighter for social justice. In "A Deeper Theft," which began as notes and parts of a libretto for an opera on the totem poles of the Pacific coast, she explores both the connection with these artifacts and the impact of these artifacts on the anthropologists who have dealt with them. As she writes, the masks of the Northwest coast aboriginal peoples are with her, inspiring her recreations of anthropologist Wilson Duff, and other figures like Claude Lévi-Strauss and Haida master carver Bill Reid.

Vancouver fiction writer Carol Windley takes her characters first to Wales to the lush countryside, where a painter discovers something she cannot let go. Thirty years later back on the west coast of North America, that very quality is found embedded as well in what might seem like a conventional life. Matisse's painting *The Joy of Life*, which gives Windley's story its title, has been interpreted as a post-apocalyptic scene. What Windley shows is the joy of the here-and-now.

Painting provides a Rorschach in "A Piece of the True Cross" by Douglas Glover. In this story the imagery of the protagonist's paintings constitutes a memory-bank of his family history. Initially the reader decodes the paintings on a superficial but not inaccurate level, but the paintings take on greater and greater richness until the story's climactic ending. Is the protagonist finally liberated from the past, from the burden of history, which he and his sister carry like martyrs? Can any of us finally free ourselves from history? Who would we be without it?

There are of course many sorts of history, but by history in general we mean a record of what actually happened, whether it is a record of what happened to us, to our families, or to others. Several works in this collection are concerned with the way in which history, both personal and public, becomes art.

Timothy Findley's "Martha and the Minder" was written for presentation at a gala for P.E.N. International in 1991 in Toronto, and was performed by Findley, a trained actor, and playwright Judith Thompson. This dramatization is mainly set in a prison, where the prisoner is being held simply for speaking out. P.E.N. is an organization of makers of texts, writers, publishers, and editors, who are fighting against censorship throughout the world. Writer Martha Kumsa, the character of Martha in Findley's text, was imprisoned in Addis Ababa for almost ten years. This is her story.

Eric McCormack's family roots are in the Scottish city of Glasgow. In "The Third Miracle," he explores the interaction of history, family history, biblical history, social history, and legend. The story that he tells is economical and clear. I asked myself as I read it, and reread it: Is this a true story? Could this really have happened? And then I looked back at the epigraph to the tale, from Robert Burton's *Anatomy of Melancholy*, which reminds us that miracles in nature may be observed, but those to do with human beings are most remarkable, are most obscure, are most unrevealable. So I reminded myself of Joseph Conrad's dictum, to trust the tale, and not the teller, and let the matter of history take care of itself.

As Occidentals we often find ourselves turning towards the East, towards the Far East, of course, towards the Near East always, and towards Eastern Europe as the eastern-most extent of the Judeo-Christian hegemony. In "My Night at Valdek," literary critic, curator, and writer James Miller found himself cast ironically as Ishmael, crying in the wilderness, rather than, as he had intended himself to be, as one of the Magi bearing gifts to Prague, the city which is everywhere now acknowledged as the first city of Europe. In his story grounded in the particular, in what actually happened, you will find other stories, many of them mythical, in which the soothsayer is denied.

As I write, the civil war in the former Yugoslavia continues. In February 1994, two years into the war, a mortar shell fired into a Sarajevo market killed sixty-eight Saturday shoppers. One of those killed was a woman selling clock-parts. The shell exploded in mid-air, at chest level. The woman disappeared. Perhaps the woman who had sold clock-parts had dreamt of bread, had secretly laughed. She had wanted to make a bargain with time. Montreal poet Erin Mouré's "Parts of a Clock, or Asthma" insists on the identity between the specific and the work of art.

The text begins as part of the writer's body. It is a gesture out of the body, with the body. That seems such an obvious statement now, in the last decade of the twentieth century, and yet it was not obvious even two decades ago. Three texts in *Paper Guitar* address in very different ways the original site of the work of art.

Artist–fiction writer Susan Swan's work has appeared in *Descant* magazine for more than twenty years. *Descant* published Swan's early performance works, and large chunks of a text which would become *The Biggest Modern Woman of the World*, her mythic novel about the real-life giantess Anna Swan. In her texts, Swan reminds us where it all begins, in the body. "A Poem to My Body" was performed nude by

Swan, in the middle of the night, in a dance studio whose walls were mirrors. Here is Swan's date with her own body.

I first read Lake Sagaris's writing for the *Dis-Ease* volumes of *Descant* magazine, and since then in a host of magazines and journals. As a working journalist, living and mothering in Chile, Sagaris files from Santiago on politics and current events to the English-language press. But she's a remarkable poet as well, with an unerring eye for the resemblances between the apparently dissimilar. Many writers have taken up their pens to contemplate the disjunctions between mothering and creativity. In "I Roar Through All Creation Like the Wind," Sagaris teaches us about their dis-apparent identity.

When I was given Alberto Manguel's short story "You're Not Gay If You Can Whistle," I was sitting high up on a mountain in the Alberta Rockies. Over the years Manguel has constantly reinvented himself as translator, anthologist, essayist, broadcaster, reviewer, arts administrator, literary impresario, and novelist. This story is a departure from his many masks. It is a stripping bare, and yet it addresses the nature of fiction. Manguel takes us back to Buenos Aires, to his boyhood, and forward to the present. The characters are "real," but they are also recreated by the writer.

Why is it that the deepest emotions, our greatest sufferings, are experienced within families? The most tragic effects, the most dramatic materials arise with those who are near and dear to one another. I'm paraphrasing Aristotle, of course, as I write these phrases, for whenever I edit, or whenever I contemplate the nature of texts, it is always Aristotle's texts which I reread, and which I keep by me.

And I found myself turning to Aristotle again, after I had read four very different pieces composed for *Paper Guitar*. Three of them are works of fiction, which take off from and return to the locus of family. The fourth is an essay on the art of biography, but the process of the writing of another's story demanded the exhumation of the subject's past, and meetings with the living members of that family who have survived her.

Christine Slater's "Nightcap" uses the confessional narrator, a middle-aged man, to chart the grisly net of family and neuroses and reputation in which the speaker is imprisoned. It is a portrait not so much of a man who cannot live because he is tied to the past, as of a man who has lived, but who keeps retreating into the past. It's a dramatic monologue which opens up not just the world of his family, but the social and cultural milieu which enchains him as well. There's a sharp satirical edge to this tale, and an energy to the unflinching narrator's voice.

"Radar Angels," an excerpt from Catherine Bush's new novel-in-progress, takes its young protagonist abroad to London in her search for a new self. The story hinges on an improbable event in the Toronto Rosedale ravine, an event which actually happened. This event is personal, but Bush is able to project it against a stage which is international, and which also includes the intense love between the protagonist and her sister.

If anyone ever mistook the voice of a text for the author's very own voice, one witnessing of a Leon Rooke reading would dispel this delusion. For no author better enters into the heads of other beings, speaks with their voices, leaves himself entirely behind, than Leon Rooke. I've been publishing Rooke's crazy stories for years, one of them narrated by a bunch of ants. Only Rooke could have written that story, and only Rooke could have written "The Yale Chair." Its narrator is an Egyptian princess, or at least that's what she tells us, who has married a North American Indian, whose child is born aboard a train. There's a lot of movement in this story, North American trains and Nile riverboats being the chief theatres of the action. And in the midst of the blend of cultures — Egypt, sort of, America, for sure, Canada, sure 'nough, because we do have Louis Riel in the midst of the whole shebang — the inside of the tale is the birth of a baby, and its demise, and maybe its miraculous recovery, and underneath the whole works, of birth, and marriage, and interracial negotiations, and trains, and boats, and love and death, is the wild laughter of the author himself.

I asked Rosemary Sullivan to write an essay for me on the making of her biography of writer Gwendolyn MacEwen (1941-1987). Several years ago, I had heard Rosemary Sullivan lecture on the making of *By Heart* , her biography of the writer Elizabeth Smart. That evening at Harbourfront, as Sullivan lectured on the tasks of the biographer and on the overlaps between the biographer's methods and the artist's, many in the audience, including myself, were moved to tears. Sullivan talked of the tyranny of facts under which the biographer labours, and she showed slides of Elizabeth Smart at different times of her passionate and troublesome life. And there was no doubt that the spirit of Elizabeth Smart was alive in that room speaking through Rosemary Sullivan, and yet Sullivan was not, and is not, Elizabeth Smart. Nor is she Gwendolyn MacEwen. Nonetheless something of MacEwen comes alive in Sullivan's text. She knows it is not the complete person, but something of the extraordinary, passionate, kind, funny, brave, and brilliant Gwendolyn MacEwen, whom so many of us loved and miss, is here in Sullivan's account of her own task. I knew Gwen MacEwen, published her last poems in *Descant*, attended her last birthday party–book launch in her own small Annex backyard, and finally greeted her, and later that evening reached to touch her, as she was carried out of the back door of the Bamboo Club, on Toronto's Queen Street West, from a benefit party for *The Canadian Forum* magazine. That was the last time I saw her. I am grateful to be able to revisit her here in Rosemary Sullivan's essay.

The text as body of desire, as landscape of desire, is exquisitely enacted by visual artist and writer Virgil Burnett's "Fifteen Notes on the Art of Draftsmanship." For the artist is cursed-blessed with double vision, caught "between the evidence of the senses and the illumination of the spirit." Is the body of the draftsman's desire his model's, or the marks he has made upon the page? The draftsman travels, for he believes that the experience of the Beyond will serve his work. Addicted to delineation and solitude, he gives his work away, to the model for whom it was made, or to a child, or to the wind. For it is not the drawing that is important, but the act of drawing.

Perhaps it is also the act of travel, rather than the landscape visited, which is important for the traveller. Not the traveller who creates those humdrum guides that teach us how to excuse ourselves in every language. The real traveller, whose engagement with landscape is vertical, not horizontal. Such a traveller will take us to Rome, at the moment of its fall. But when was that, you ask? Perhaps it was 410 A.D., perhaps today, or yesterday. This traveller will take you to Orvieto. An Etruscan city. A city of artists. There you might find the Signorelli Chapel, with its monochrome scenes from Dante's *Divine Comedy*, with its depictions of the dead who may not be dead, who, like the Etruscans, cast living shadows. The wheres and the whys, the climates and the prices, all useful matters, are to be gleaned from conventional guidebooks, but in Anne Carson's "The Fall of Rome: A Traveller's Guide" we learn life's basic questions and some of the false answers.

I've spoken of the distinctions between history and art, and about the connections between history and art. But I've tried to keep them distinct and to give precedence, in the classical fashion, to art. The contrary movement, whereby art becomes history, is perhaps the nature of myth, the sacred story. This is the process depicted in the excerpt from Mark Frutkin's novel-in-progress about that epic-heroic character Marco Polo. Frutkin's work has often portrayed mythopoeic figures, who are part history and part legend. One thinks of his prismatic long texts, *The Growing Dawn* about the inventor Marconi, or *Atmospheres Apollinaire* about La Belle Epoque and the poet Apollinaire. In "The Lion of Venice," Frutkin portrays the extraordinary conception of his hero, as a union of a human with a non-human. I'll leave it to you to discover how such a man could be conceived.

W. P. " Bill" Kinsella has created many controversial tales of life on the frontier, and in the stadium. *Descant* magazine first published Kinsella's story "Dance Me Outside," which became the title-story in a collection, and more recently a film. *Descant* also published his story which became *Field of Dreams*, the novel and the film. In "Murderous Ways," Kinsella gives us a brief tale of betrayal and of the pleasure in the shooting down of the quarry. It is a tale of revenge. Despite its brevity, its mythos, its plot, is completely appropriate to the characters. A very Aristotelian tale, it is, indeed.

And revenge, its inevitability, its clarity, its completeness, is also what animates Evelyn Lau's tale, "First Sight, A Love Story." Outdoors or indoors, the tales of love on the frontier have a disturbing and appropriate inevitability about them.

I've left my most difficult task for the end of this introduction, for in the course of the making of *Paper Guitar,* one of its co-creators was killed. I had planned to include a conversation between generations, and had asked two writers with a great affinity for one another to talk about art and art-making and their own inter-relationships. The two writers were to be Roberston Davies and Elliott Hayes. The terms of the conversation were arranged, a date was set, a Tuesday in early March of 1994. On the last day of February, a Monday night, Elliott Hayes was killed on the old Embro Road which runs north from Woodstock to Stratford, Ontario. At the time of his death, Hayes's plays were being produced around the world, he was at work on a screenplay and a new novel, and was also literary manager of the Stratford Festival. I've included a gathering of Elliott Hayes's poems from more than a decade, up to the last few weeks of his life. In *A Defence of Poetry,* the

English poet Percy Shelley argues that poets behold "the future in the present," that they are the mirrors which reflect the future in the present. Hayes's poems are mirrors for those "gigantic shadows which futurity" was casting on his own life as he wrote.

Where does art begin, where does it start? "Start with a tree," replies Eric Wright. What kind of a tree? A dead tree. Was it always dead? No. When the narrator was a boy, it was alive, and it was a hiding place. So this is not a story about a tree? No, it's a story about a boy. What kind of a story? What kind do you want? Eric Wright's story is about history and about class, and about the making of stories and about the making of story-makers.

Start with the child, says Lake Sagaris. And with the word and the child. And with the tales told to children, and told by children, and the tales of children. Does the rain peck at the pavement? Who turns the day off? Or on?

Or, take an owl and a pussycat. There's a lot of promise in an owl and a pussy-cat. Check them out, on the same shore, some years later. Now minus "a lot of hair,/or fur or feathers, whatever." The owl sports bifocals now, but he and the pussy-cat, as Margaret Atwood reminds us, "did get prizes." And perhaps they think "something of meaning could still be done."

And so Margaret Atwood, pussycat, and her owl in their "leaky cardboard/gondola" row us out towards "the salty/open sea." There's always the chance that someone may be listening. You're still here, aren't you? And there are twenty-seven inside, playing on their paper guitars, under a full moon.

Karen Mulhallen

Editor's Acknowledgements

Paper Guitar, 27 Writers Celebrating 25 Years of Descant Magazine, has been made possible through the generosity of the authors who created original material for this volume and donated this material to *Descant* as a fund-raising gesture. *Descant* is grateful for the generosity and talent of each of the authors without whom neither the magazine nor this volume would have been possible.

The publishing of *Descant* and this volume owes a great deal to all the co-editors who for twenty-five years have helped put the magazine together, to the designers and printers who have created it with us, especially Tim Inkster of The Porcupine's Quill, Stan Bevington of Coach House Printing, and Gordon Robertson of Gordon Robertson Designs, to the many writers who have grown with us over these years, to the visual artists who have graced our pages, and to the readers who have given us all an audience.

In putting together this volume, my task has been lightened by the loyalty, grace and enthusiasm of the writers, and by my editor Phyllis Bruce at HarperCollins who suggested the project, and supported it in every way, by my co-workers at *Descant* over the years , and by the Office of the Dean of Arts at Ryerson Polytechnic University who provided me with a teaching-assistant during the final editing of the manuscript .

Special thanks to Margaret Atwood for her ongoing support and for the titles of four sections of this book, which come from her poem "Owl and Pussycat, Some Years Later," to Tiff Findley for his ongoing inspiration and support, to Leslie Hall Pinder, Josef Škvorecký, and Virgil Burnett for continuing enthusiasm, to Katherine Govier for theme, care, and text, to Douglas Glover and to Rosemary Sullivan for texts, support, and friendship, and to the others who have always been there, and who have made this all possible: Catherine Bush, Anne Carson, Cynthia Flood, Mark Frutkin, David Homel, Bill Kinsella, Evelyn Lau, Alberto Manguel, Eric McCormack, James Miller, Erin Mouré, Ken Nutt, Stan Persky, Leon Rooke, Lake Sagaris, Christine Slater, Susan Swan, Michael Torosian, Carol Windley, Eric Wright.

I

OUR PAPER GUITAR

ISOLDE OHLBAUM, MUNICH

MARGARET ATWOOD is the author of more than twenty-five books of poetry, fiction, and non-fiction. Her most recent novel is *The Robber Bride;* her newest book, *Morning in the Burned House,* a collection of new poetry, was published by McClelland & Stewart in January 1995. She lives in Toronto.

Owl and Pussycat, Some Years Later

Margaret Atwood

So here we are again, my dear,
on the same shore we set out from
years ago, when we were promising,
but minus — now — a lot of hair,
or fur or feathers, whatever.
I like the bifocals. They make you look
even more like an owl than you are.
I suppose we've both come far. But

how far are we truly, from where we started,
under the fresh-laid moon, when we plotted

to astound? When we thought
something of meaning could still be done
by singing; or won, like trophies.
I took the fences, you the treetops, where we
hooted and yowled our carnivorous
fervid hearts out, and see,
we did get prizes: there they are,
a scroll, a gold watch, and a kissoff
handshake from the stand-in
for the Muse, who couldn't come herself,
but sent regrets. Now we can say

flattering things about each other
on dust jackets. Whatever
made us think we could change the world?
Us and our clever punct-
uation marks. A machine gun now, that
would be different. No more unctuous adjectives. Cut straight to the verb.
Ars longa, mors brevissima. The life
of poetry breeds the lust
for action, of the most ordinary
sort. Whacking the heads off dandelions,
or bats or bureaucrats,
smashing car windows. Though

at least we've been tolerated,
or even celebrated — which meant
a brief caper in the transient glare
of the sawdust limelight,
and your face used later for fishwrap —
but most of the time ignored,
by this crowd that has finally admitted
to itself it doesn't give

much of a fart for art,
and would rather see a good evisceration
any day. You might as well have been
a dentist, as your father hoped. You

want attention, still? Take your clothes off
at a rush-hour stoplight, howl obscenities,
or shoot someone. You'll get
your name in the paper, maybe,
for what it's worth. In any case

where do we both get off?
Is this small talent we have prized
so much, and rubbed like silver
spoons, until it shone
at least as brightly as neon, really
so much better than the ability
to win the sausage-eating contest,
or juggle six plates at once?
What's the use anyway
of calling the dead back, moving stones,
or making animals cry? I

think of you, loping along at night
to the convenience store, to buy your pint
of milk, your six medium eggs,
your head stuffed full of consonants
like lovely pebbles
you picked up on some lustrous beach
you can't remember — my feather-
headed fool, what have you got
in your almost-empty pockets
that would lure even the lowliest mugger?
Who needs your handful

of glimmering air, your foxfire, your few
underwater crystal tricks
that work only in moonlight?
Noon hits them and they fall apart,
old bones and earth, old teeth, a bundleful
of shadow. Sometimes, I know, the almost-holy
whiteness rooted in our skulls spreads out
like thistles in a vacant lot, a hot powdery
flareup, which is not a halo
and will return
if we're grateful and lucky, and
will end by fusing our neurons. Yet,

singing's a belief
we can't give up.
Anything can become a saint
if you pray to it enough —
spaceship, teacup, wolf —
and what we want is intercession,
that iridescent ribbon
that once held song to object.
We feel everything hovering
on the verge of becoming itself:
the tree is almost a tree, the dog
pissing against it won't be a dog
unless we notice it
and call it by its name: "Here, dog."
And so we stand on balconies and rocky
hilltops, and caterwaul our best,
and the world flickers
in and out of being,
and we think it needs our permission. We

shouldn't flatter ourselves: really
it's the other way around. We're at
the mercy of any stray
rabid mongrel or thrown stone or cancerous
ray, or our own
bodies: we were born with mortality's
hook in us, and year by year it drags us
where we're going: down. But

surely there is still
a job to be done by us, at least
time to be passed; for instance, we could
celebrate inner beauty. Gardens.
Love and desire. Lust. Children. Social justice
of various kinds. Include fear and war.
Describe what it is to be tired. Now
we're getting there. But this is much
too pessimistic! Hey, we've got
each other, and a roof, and regular
breakfasts! Cream and mice! For

our sort, elsewhere, it's often worse:
a heaved boot, poisoned meat, or dragged
by the wings or tail off to some wall
or trench and forced to kneel
and have your brains blown out, splattering all over
that Nature we folks are so keen on —
in the company of a million others,
let it be said —
and in the name of what? What noun?
What god or state? The world becomes
one huge deep vowel of horror,
while behind those mildewed flags, the slogans

that always rhyme with *dead*,
sit a few old guys making money. So

honestly. Who wants to hear it?
Last time I did that number, honey,
the audience was squirrels.
But I don't need to tell you.
The worst is, now we're respectable.
We're in anthologies. We're taught in schools,
with cleaned-up biographies and skewed photos.
We're part of the mug show now.
In ten years, bet you'll be on a stamp,
where anyone at all can lick you. Ah

well, my dear, our leaky cardboard
gondola has brought us this far,
us and our paper guitar.
No longer semi-immortal, but moulting owl
and arthritic pussycat, we row
out past the last protecting
sandbar, towards the salty
open sea, the dogs'-head gate,
and after that, oblivion.
But sing on, sing
on, someone may still be listening
besides me. The fish for instance. Anyway
we still have the moon.

ELISABETH FERYN

VIRGIL BURNETT is an artist and writer who lives in southern Ontario most of the time and in France some of the time. He began making "notes" on the art of draftsmanship years ago. An earlier version of those notes was published in *Margin* (London, England) in 1988.

FIFTEEN NOTES ON THE ART OF DRAFTSMANSHIP

Virgil Burnett

I

The draftsman has double vision. He sees everything as both object and emblem. The tension generated by this binary perception provides the motor force and the methodology for most of what he undertakes. It is also the source of grave frustration. Again and again he finds himself wavering undecided between the fact and the sign, between the evidence of the senses and the illumination of the spirit. During the ordeals he endures in this loathsome Between, he often longs for simple solutions, for established rules, for facility. There are even moments when he envies those half-blind people who can see only one thing at a time.

II

With a single line and a fixed point the draftsman draws a circle, a perfect form, perhaps *the* perfect form. By rendering this form he implies, or means to imply, the perfection of the model's breast and of the pupil of his own eye. If he were to draw the same drawing on another day, when he was of a different mind or in a different mood, it might imply the turning of hours and seasons, of sun, moon and stars.

III

With a single line and two fixed points the draftsman draws an oval, an unstable form, enigmatic, perhaps the most enigmatic of all forms. By rendering this form he implies, or means to imply, the awesomeness of his model's sex and the ambiguity of his attentions to it. If he were to draw the same drawing on another day, when he was of a different mind or in a different mood, it might imply an egg, which is just as enigmatic, just as awesome, and the source, perhaps, of even more ambiguity.

IV

The draftsman is scrupulously respectful of his model. He does his best to make her comfortable and to amuse her. Sometimes he succeeds in these endeavours; other times he does not.

It is his work of course that causes the trouble. Certain aspects of it the model finds annoying, even infuriating. Her greatest displeasure occurs when she decides that his fascination with the particular in her makes him insensitive to her entirety, to what she calls "herself as a person." His little obsessions with some curl or mole or dainty fold of flesh, whether white or red, obsessions which seem to him both harmless and necessary, can send her into a rage.

He tries to justify his behaviour by pointing out that he must get to know the bits of her if he is to realize the whole. This argument rarely satisfies the model. She broods and packs her bags. To delay her departure the draftsman quotes poetry to her, Propertius principally and sometimes Ovid, and gloomily predicts that if she goes, he will never work again. Both of them know that this is not perhaps the truth, but the spectre of his impotence without her calms the model and engages once again her interest in their games.

She broods some more and unpacks her bags.

V

There is nothing, the draftsman often thinks, so like pen draftsmanship as tightrope walking. In both one slip must mean disaster.

VI

The draftsman has observed that art rarely thrives in an environment from which animals have been banished. A studio without a pet, he declares, is likely to be as unfortunate as a ship without a mascot, as unfruitful as a coven without a familiar. He does not claim to know why artists require the company of animals but he is convinced that they do. When challenged in this conviction he will cite in its defence long lists of artist–animal affiliations, nor is he timid about naming names: Lion and Keeper, Flush and Floss, Rouge and Scoop and Buffalo . . . . The truth of the matter is he cannot imagine trying to work in a place where beasts are unwelcome. He would as soon live in a house where there was no fireplace.

VII

With closed eyes the draftsman makes an extravagant gesture, draws an arabesque. Still in darkness he hesitates, swaying from side to side, wondering what he has done. He counts to a certain number of private and superstitious significance, then forces himself to confront the mark his unguided hand has made. He squints, scowls, strokes his jaw, pulls his nose. Slowly a shrewd expression composes his features as he readies himself to deal with the random configurations exposed upon his page. Other marks begin to accumulate about it. Patterns develop, systems. A lock of hair appears, then an elaborate *chevelure*. More marks rally, and still more. The hair ceases to be hair as its waves are transformed into waves of water — water seething, churning, becoming a torrent, a maelstrom. The marking continues. From the vortex of the whirlpool rises a ship. The ship becomes a castle, a cathedral, a mountain crag. More and more marks are more and more densely applied in a crescendo of marking until, inevitably, the marks throng the page in such relentless profusion that there are no longer any non-marks between them.

The draftsman puts aside his tool. Exhausted he peers at the blackened page and remembers that someone has called the arabesque the most spiritual of designs. He finds very little comfort in this recollection.

VIII

It has always been the draftsman's aim to imitate reality in his work, imitate it so scrupulously that he invents a reality of his own, one that counterfeits dream.

IX

The draftsman is no mathematician but he has his own arcanum of numbers and his ways of using it. In his system, One is always Two, since it signifies simultaneously a shaft and a slit in which he sees both the phallic rise and the venereal aperture. Conversely he interprets Two as being single and submissive, a digit that seems to kneel. In Three he can find a bosom and a bottom. Four he makes a cupbearer, Ganymede or Hebe, according to his pleasure. Five is death, as in Japan, and a primrose which is another way of saying woman. Six is not so simple as it seems since it can be transformed by inversion. Seven is pain, a crookbacked cripple. Eight fascinates and frightens him for it suggests the most intimate of intimacies, the female fork, the counterpoise of vagina and anus, or anus and vagina, as the case may be. Nine is an echo, imitation, *déjà vu* . . . .

More than is reasonable, perhaps, these calculations contribute to the planning of his machines and ultimately to their construction.

X

The draftsman is a frequent traveller. Although air travel is rapid and land travel is picturesque, he usually prefers to go by sea. He has made voyages in a variety of vessels: black ships, tottering barks, naked hulks, pea-green boats, drunken boats, and even the orchid boat of Li Ch'ing Chao. As a rule these have been orderly excursions. Occasionally, however, he has been taken too far. He never interferes when he suspects that this is happening. On the contrary he rejoices in edges and is eager to surpass limits — certain limits at any rate. The motive for this recklessness is simply that he imagines that experience of the Beyond may serve him in his work when, and if, he manages to return from wherever he ends by going too far.

XI

The draftsman recognizes in himself a furtive impulse, a desire, almost a need, to obscure his thought even while he is in the progress of struggling to reveal it. When he allows himself to be guided by this impulse, he produces works in which his meaning is veiled or obscure, and, unfortunately perhaps, incomprehensible to many. When he ignores it, he produces nothing whatsoever. Although he sometimes tries, he finds no remedy for this dilemma.

XII

The draftsman admits that God is inconceivable to him. This admission bars him from orthodox religious practice and community, but it has not kept him from developing a religious sensibility. In fact his thinking is riddled with religious notions. These may be nothing more than spiritual conceits, but they are constantly with him nevertheless, as constantly, he supposes, as the litanies of the pious are with them. The ever-presence of these ideas, or whatever they are, necessarily advises him in the imagining of his ikons. To it he owes the existence of his Hawk Woman, his Diviner, his Fool, his Exterminating Angel, his Sior Maschera. Even without faith, he concludes, religion has its purposes.

XIII

The draftsman loves black. He tolerates other colours: sepia, ochre, umber, some cadmium reds, some blues, rose madder, green earth, mummy — but he can get along without them. Only black is indispensable. It is the colour of delineation and therefore of fact. As if this were not enough, it is also the colour of the opposite of fact, that is, the colour of nothingness, of the void, of that *hole* of non-being towards which all being tends and for which the draftsman endlessly yearns.

XIV

The draftsman knows that a degree of solitude is essential to his work. Fortunately he tolerates isolation without serious difficulty. There are days when he quite enjoys it, takes positive pleasure in it. He is careful not to depend too much on being alone, however, for he remembers certain other artists who have become entranced by solitude, poor egoists who speak only in monologue, feed on their own dung, and strive desperately to procreate without a partner. Still, solitude is sweet to him. Sometimes he even wonders if loneliness may not be another name for the muse of draftsmanship.

XV

When a drawing is finished, that is to say, when the draftsman has ceased to look at it with the light of inspiration in his eyes, he gives it away. If possible he gives it to the one for whom it was made — his model more often than not. If distance or disaffection or other adversity prevents this, he gives it to a child, for he has learned that children take great delight in draftsmanship and are generous with drawings of their own. If there are no children about, he gives it to the wind.

Appendix I: A Recipe for Making a Drawing

Find a valley between old mountains, not too high or too long or too broad or too dramatic or too beautiful — in other words, a valley that has no pretension to being anything but itself. It should have woods on the height above it, meadows on its slopes, tilled fields and gardens on its bottomland. A few farmers should live in the valley, modest farmers, not too prosperous. There should be a mill, long unused, which can be made into a habitation with a bit of sweeping and scrubbing, painting and patching. New shutters should be provided for the windows, not slatted Persian shutters, of course, but the plain sort with a few silly holes cut in them.

When the mill is more or less in order, find a very large piece of paper. It should not be a standard format, not classical Raisin or Jesus, but a big sprawling surface, two metres at least from edge to edge. Don't worry if it is bent or creased or even torn. Such concerns have nothing to do with drawing.

Take the piece of paper and climb to the very top of the mill, to an attic room with nothing in it but a trestle table. Open the windows of the room so that the landscape and everything it contains may flow in and about the paper.

Then begin to draw. The infinitive "to draw" should be interpreted very loosely. It means, if it can be defined at all in this context, to let things happen to the paper.

For example, marks might be made on it with a variety of instruments, including pens, pencils, brushes, crayons, teacups, jam-spoons, fingernails, trouser-seats, dog-noses, cat-whiskers, mouse-feet, and so on.

If a friend comes into the room and flicks cigarette ash on the paper, so much the better. If another friend comes into the room and spills wine on the paper, better yet. If a child comes into the room, invite the child to play with the paper by drawing on it or by doing whatever he or she wishes to do on it. If a sparrow flies through the room and leaves a small dropping on the paper, rejoice in this event. If a crow flies through the room and leaves a large dropping on the paper, rejoice more vigorously. If an owl or hawk or eagle visits, sing: Hallelujah!

In fact anything that comes in from outside must be encouraged to settle on the paper: dust, pollen, seedlings, insects — any wind-freight at all. Let the sun shine on the paper by day; the moon by night. If there is a storm, accept its raindrops as willingly as the ploughed ground does in August.

Don't worry about finishing the drawing. It will finish itself.

APPENDIX II: ANOTHER RECIPE FOR MAKING A DRAWING

Begin by travelling extensively and rapidly, particularly on the European continent, and more particularly still in France and Italy, countries where the art of the past abounds and has been protected against the ravages of progress.

En route eat and drink lavishly. Sample the specialties and vintages of the most remote regions. Allow yourself to fairly wallow in cream sauces and wine sauces, in light flesh and dark, in barnyard fowls and game, in goose liver and goose fat, in sausages, pâtés, terrines and *rillettes*, in tripes of every sort, in little fishes and big ones, in bi-valves and octopods, in pastas, in cheeses, in sweets of every description.

When your appetite for going and for gourmandise is somewhat satisfied, locate a monument of distinction. An abbey church of the twelfth century is perhaps most appropriate for your purposes because it is likely to be so perfect in form, so austere in decoration, and so exalted in aspiration as to be effectively undrawable.

Give yourself up entirely to this monument. Study it carefully inside and out. Pace its nave and its aisles. Examine its capitals, its tympanum, its cloister, its towers. When you begin to feel sated, as sated as you might after a Burgundian snack of *gougères*, snails, eel in sauce *meurette*, Charollais beef *en daube*, *paillassons*, cream cheese from Alise, Époisse, blue cheese from Bresse, and a *poirat* . . . all of it irrigated, as some say, with the wines of Vougeot, Vosne or Volnay.

When you feel sated, as I say, leave the church and wander about outside it until you find its graveyard, not the cemetery of the monks of the twelfth century, but that of the nineteenth century, which is to say, the graveyard of the local people who lived beside the abbey after the dissolution of the monasteries during the Revolution.

Settle there and prepare to draw. Be sure your back is to the monument. Be also sure that the shadow of the building does not fall directly on you, as it is likely to be a potent shadow.

By preparing to draw I mean take out a little clutch of coloured papers, a fine pen, preferably with a broken nib, and a child's pan of watercolours with a brush or two. Put something on your head if the sun is out. A knotted handkerchief will do.

Draw whatever you see that is least monumental: a rusted gate, a broken pot, some ceramic wreaths, wire mesh, dead flowers.

Again do not attempt to finish the drawing. Leave it for some distant winter month in some distant wintry place, some place as far as possible from the transmogrifying effects of the miasmas of monumentality.

APPENDIX III: STILL ANOTHER RECIPE FOR MAKING A DRAWING

Go to Venice, or some city like Venice. Since there is no city like Venice but Venice, go to Venice.

Equip yourself properly. Be sure to have a portable radio, several broken cameras, an accordion, an eighteenth-century credenza (seventeenth century if eighteenth is not available) or two, a case of fine Russian caviar (Persian caviar if Russian is not available), a supply of sticky buns, a bobtailed cat, a pad of excessively cheap paper, Conté crayon (sanguine, black, bistre), some pens and ink, a gondolier with or without gondola.

Make a public figure of yourself. Get to know everybody. Frequent the artists' restaurants, the artists' bars. Take coffee chez Florian, chez Quadri. Eat pasta and soup at the boatmen's cantinas. Charm everybody. Speak fearlessly, if not faultlessly, in as many languages as you can. When in doubt about some locution, improvise. Speak English in several dialects including "Southern Hostess" and "New York Decorator," speak Italian, Venetian, French, even the smatterings of German, Dutch, Swedish, Farsi and Dalmatian which you may have acquired in bed.

Attend the salons. Participate in the promenades. Participate in the sporting events, even though you may not be an athlete, the religious events, even though you may not be religious, the civic events, even though you may not be a citizen, the political events, even though you may not be allowed to vote. Join the ranks of the demonstrators in their demonstrations, and the workers in their strikes.

Show your colours. Let them be extreme, International red perhaps. Admit to a doctrine, Marxism perhaps, declaim it, flaunt it, and then complicate it with tales implying an almost aristocratic background and education, tales of boarding schools in Britain, Ivy League colleges, long association with the wealthy and the decadent.

Do your drawings in prominent places, all the places you have learned to frequent. Do drawings everywhere.

Draw people, only people. Architecture, even glorious Venetian architecture, may be allowed but only as background, decors. Furniture is only stage dressing. Vehicles, tools, small objects are only stage properties, for Venice is a stage, and drawings made in Venice must be designs for that stage, the stage of Tiepolo, Tintoretto, and Veronese.

Draw people. If your people are predominantly boys and young men of the working classes, temper these predilections with a few girls and women of the working classes. Draw old people, too, and children. Draw tourists, scornfully. Draw dogs and cats, lovingly, as if they were people, even people of the working classes.

And drawing, draw rapidly. If a workman slips and falls from a roof, have him drawn before he hits the pavement.

It matters very little which of your instruments, which ground, or which medium you choose for your drawings, because it is not the piece of paper decorated or dirtied by chalk, crayon, or pen and ink that matters.

What matters in this recipe for making a drawing is not the drawing itself, but the act of drawing, the draftsman's role, and the playing out of a fine drama, the drama of a life lived flamboyantly and entirely, as Tosca claimed to live, for art.

The first of the three recipes for making drawings was given to me by Michel Devrient, a Swiss draftsman who has often lived outside of Switzerland. The second was given to me by Tony Urquhart, a Canadian draftsman who has often lived outside of Canada. The third recipe was given to me by Edward Melcarth, an American artist who often lived outside the United States before his death in Venice. I am sometimes inclined to suspect that the draftsman's natural habitat is somewhere else.

ERIC WRIGHT is the author of the Charlie Salter series of mystery novels, and of *Moodie's Tale*, a comic novel, as well as a number of short stories. He was born in England and came to Canada in 1951. Since 1957 he has lived and worked in Toronto.

START WITH A TREE

ERIC WRIGHT

The starting point is an image of a dead tree, sticking up, multi-branched, from the sluggish surface of a weed-choked river. Just past the tree there is a bridge over the river. The road over the bridge goes past an inn whose grounds slope down to the bank of the stream. Some chairs and a couple of iron tables are set out for anyone who wants to drink outside, but the grass is unkempt and there is no service except at the bar. This is no longer a riverside pub but a roadhouse, noisy with gambling machines and a jukebox.

It wasn't always like this. Sitting alone at one of the tables an oldish man remembers the time, fifty years before, when the river ran clean, and punts could be hired to dawdle on the stream. The posts sticking up out of the river now are the last remnants of the landing stage where twenty boats were once moored, waiting to be hired by the lovers who came to dally of an afternoon. The boatman was a young boy, twelve years old, the same who now sits, remembering.

He remembers the freshly painted chairs and tables, the umbrellas, and beyond the lawn, some apple trees fringing a large vegetable garden, and a greenhouse. There was a gardener then, who stored the russet apples in the boathouse, now full of discarded furniture and appliances.

"Change and decay in all around I see" might be the story, then. The wanderer revisiting a scene of his childhood, when he, the young poor brother of the landlord's wife (herself risen above her station) tasted middle-class living; the simple contrast between the schoolboy and the man; the memory of the pastoral world, when he and it were young, contrasted with the blight that has replaced it. (On the bank beyond the dead tree, a rusted perambulator sticks up out of the mud.) The man remembers a tune that his sister played over and over again on the gramophone, a popular tune adapted from a Mozart sonata. But he can't recall the tune now because of the racket of the jukebox.

But before he can begin to find the details for his narrative, another image occurs, that of Roberto, the houseman, a Spaniard, a doctor, a refugee from Franco's victory, mopping the floors of an English tavern. Roberto is kind to the boy, offers to teach him Spanish, but the boy is no scholar though he looks like one. One day Roberto declines to mop any more. He's a refugee, yes, but he's a doctor, too, so he's going to town to try to find work in the hospital. The boy is witness to Roberto's last act, the breaking of the mop over his knee.

Since then the old man has learned about Roberto's world, read his Orwell and his Hemingway, visited Catalonia, stayed in Roberto's province of Asturias (home of some of the bloodiest opposition to Franco), absorbed Roberto's history as literature. This is not the story, though. The memory of Roberto is more formal than emotional, a detail for another story one day.

But a different war began after Roberto's was lost, the boy's. He too was a refugee — evacuee, they called it — sent into the country to escape the bombs of Franco's friends, lucky to have a "rich" sister to take in the boy, though not his seven or eight brothers and sisters. Now the man remembers, not an image, but the sound of a stick of bombs, c-c-crumping closer and closer, straddling the inn near where the boy lay masturbating on some cushions in the apple-fragrant boathouse, then continuing across the fields. The contrast, then, between the peaceful Berkshire countryside and the rain of death? Hardly. One of the bombs killed a cow, but that was reported, not experienced. Afterwards, the boy went looking in the field for shrapnel souvenirs.

Concentrating now, the images popping, the old man sees the river clear of weeds, without dead trees, and the boats at the landing dock, and the boy, himself, in charge. The boats can be hired for a shilling and sixpence the first hour, a shilling an hour thereafter. Two or three pounds a day. The boy has never seen so much money, so casually handled. Perhaps this is it.

He is one of a large family living in Kennington in a tenement built by a brewer out of the profits of selling stout to the poor. The family originated in Lambeth (don't call it the slums, though: they are fiercely respectable); the tenement is a step up for them. One brother is in the army, and another in the merchant navy. The boy's oldest sister, twenty years his senior, has done well for herself through her marriage, and now wants to do something for the youngest boy, give him a taste of a better life, make him ambitious. And what a taste! His own bedroom; his own *bed!* He feels like William, his favourite fictional character. His sister gives him a lesson (where did *she* learn?), a lesson on how to eat a boiled egg genteelly (cut the top off, don't pick away at the shell, eat the top last), buys him some underwear, has his hair cut properly. Practically a young gentleman. Then, to occupy him, she gives him the management of the boat rentals.

The boy from Kennington, of course, routinely steals anything not nailed down. He did not steal the rent money from the teapot on the kitchen dresser at home in Kennington because he would be caught and very nearly killed, but anything outside the house was fair game. The boat rental money was ripe for stealing, as his brother, trailing along with his mother on a flying visit from London one day, points out. This same brother belonged for a time to a junior house-breaking gang. Two members were caught and sent to Borstal and suspicion flickered over his brother's head, but nothing was proved. The thrashing he got inside the house once the police had disappeared set him straight, though.

So the boy has access to uncounted income from boats. Does he steal some? Does he ever consider *not* stealing some?

He begins in a grey area, by keeping quiet about his tips, honestly gained, but he thinks he might be suspected of enlarging the tips from the boat rental money, laundering the boat money, as it were. The tips come from the young men who have dallied with their girls under the willows round the bend in the river past the railway arch. If the afternoon goes well, they will owe the boy three shillings and sixpence, or even four and six, and out of contentment or panache they sometimes give the boy the sixpence change from two florins or two half-crowns. The boy learns to be slow with the change, encouraging them to leave it behind.

A sixpence buys a lot, all the sweets he wants, but caution is necessary, once he has decided to keep quiet about the tips. His sister sells chocolate and potato crisps in the pub and he must take care not to be caught eating anything that he might be thought to have stolen from the pub. Ice cream is safe, as is licorice, sherbert and the loose sweets sold from large glass jars. Any chocolate he buys he eats on the way home from the sweetshop.

On a warm day in June, the boy takes the next step. Five boats are hired by a party of young blades and each other's sisters. His sister and her husband have gone to London, leaving the pub in charge of the woman who helps out on Saturdays. The boy chalks up the time the five boats move off, and when they return, collects the money, walks twice round the garden to make sure no one is watching, wipes out the record of the fifth boat and puts fourteen shillings in the cigarette tin where he keeps the day's take, pocketing the three and sixpence, to be hidden later in the actual, real, hollow tree on the other bank of the river.

The hoard grows until there are two or three pounds in the old oak tree, more money than he had ever imagined. Now he has to spend it. Only two desires lie close to his heart. One is for a large Meccano set. He owns a starter set, with enough wheels and tiny girders to make a model handcart, but the set came with a leaflet picturing what could be done with a giant set: gantries, windmills, trucks — the possibilities were unlimited. But it is out of the question; he could never account for it. Not so his other passion, postage stamps, philately. He has a tiny collection, bought with hoarded half-pence, mostly German inflationary issues, printed in the millions. He lusts, not after penny blacks, or cape triangulars, but for the gorgeous mint samples of the British colonies, the king's head in one corner of a beautiful picture of a giraffe (Kenya, Uganda, and Tanganyika), and all the other works of art from Africa, the Caribbean and the South Seas.

Then, in the small market town nearby, he finds a dealer and begins to buy. One by one he brings them home and fixes them carefully in his stamp album. There is no need to show them to anyone yet; he can do that later at home, on the street where he lives. For now he can enjoy gloating over the little Stanley Gibbons album he keeps in the cardboard suitcase under his bed along with the lead soldiers, the propelling pencil he found in one of the boats, and the army badges. (Perhaps this is the real story, his poverty, but memory instructs the old man that he never felt poor at the time.)

And then, one day, the stamp dealer asks him his name, and he knows this is the end. "William Brown," he lies.

"Where's all the money coming from then, William?" The stamp dealer with a look invites his hovering wife to listen.

"My paper route."

"You're not from around here. You're a Londoner. You don't have a paper route."

The boy looks out the window, thinking. "That's my dad," he says suddenly, and is gone.

For three days he lives in the fear that the dealer will appear at the inn, but he never does. No quiet trap is set with a marked half-crown. And no one has been watching his regular visits to the old oak tree, etc. This is how it happens:

The boy continues to divert some of the boat takings into the hollow tree out of habit, but less systematically because the hoard is growing and he does not now know what to do with it. Then, one day, the fair comes to town and he is given a shilling by his sister to visit it. It has been a quiet day on the river and all he has in his pocket is another sixpence. Of course, it occurs to him what a good time he could have at the fair with the hoard from the old oak tree, but the gardener is deputed to look after the boat rentals for the afternoon, so he has no excuse to cross the river before he catches the bus to the fair.

He is surprised how quickly his pocket money disappears. Two rides, a go on the shooting gallery, and a coconut shy, and he has only three pennies left. He pauses by a round tent that invites him to roll his pennies down a wooden slot in the hope of winning more. He does, and on the second try his penny drops on a winning square. The Gypsy lady in charge deals him six pennies and moves on. The booth is large and busy, and the Gypsy has to circle around the inside, picking up the losing pennies and paying out the winners. The boy rolls down another penny and wins six more; he does it again, and again, and again, until he is breathless. There is a tiny warp in the surface of the table just beyond his wooden chute, and if his penny reaches this warp, travelling at the right speed, it falls over into the square. The boy wins eight times, and then, deliberately, under her eye, puts the penny too high in the chute and loses. He leaves the concession for a while, throws some more balls at the coconuts, but nothing compares with winning pennies.

When he returns, another Gypsy has taken over and the boy is able to win another four shillings before he has to lose to avert suspicion. Now he develops a system, winning a couple of times, going for a walk, returning to win again as soon as his chute is free. Soon, both pockets are crammed with big copper pennies, and the attendant in charge of the tent with the slot machines changes some of them for him, and most of the rest the boy spends on rides, shooting ranges, and games of chance, until he is sated, and walks home with a story to tell.

He arrives back at the inn, passing through the Private Bar to get to the living quarters behind. His brother-in-law is behind the bar, talking to a customer. His face is grim. "Mary wants to see you," he says. "In the kitchen."

The customer turns round and the boy nearly swoons when he sees the face of the stamp dealer. It is the end. But the man merely says, looking at him slyly, "Who's this, then?"

"Mary's brother. Staying with us for a while."

"Has he got a name?"

"Derek."

"Lucky boy, living in a pub." The dealer takes a swig. "Interested in stamps, son?"

"Not much."

"I thought you collected them," the brother-in-law said, holding up the flap of the counter to let the boy through.

"Used to. Don't now."

The dealer smiles, picks up his change, winks at the boy. "Cheerio," he says, and leaves.

"She's waiting."

The boy slips through, light-headed with relief at the dealer's mysterious loyalty, and runs through to the kitchen where his sister is waiting with the woman who helps out on Saturdays.

"Come here," his sister says. "Turn out your pockets." She says it sadly, kindly. No Mrs. Gargery, she.

Now it seems as if the dealer has shopped him after all, as is natural. The scene in the bar had been a tease, a cat-and-mouse scene, while all the time the dealer knew what awaited him in the kitchen.

His sister points to the kitchen table to show him where to put the contents of his pockets.

"Don't have to," the boy mumbles.

"You want me to tell Mum?"

Threat enough. He empties his two pockets; he still has a dozen pennies, and several of the shillings that he had changed back. A pile the size of a man's fist. His sister looks at the money in misery. The face of the woman who helps out on Saturdays is shining.

"Where'd you get it?" his sister says at last.

"Won it."

Head-shakes.

"I'll ask you again. Where'd you get it?"

"Won it."

She has used up the threat of telling his mother when he complied with the first request. It wouldn't be fair to use it twice. She tries shame. "Don't tell lies," she says. "Don't *lie.*"

Remembering this, the old man is suddenly shaken with anger. *Everybody* lied to the authorities, of which she is now a part. His sister knew that. She'd been part of his world once. She had had no right to load her new middle-class morality on him.

"I'm not lying. I won it."

The woman who helps out on Saturdays says, "They don't let you win. Only once or twice p'raps. Our Fred lost six bob on that roll-the-penny game." She gleams at his sister, encouraging her to go for the kill.

"You took it out of the boat money, didn't you?"

"No. I won it."

And then he sees that she needs a confession. A little brother who steals is one thing, a thief and a liar is too much. It was time for a guilty plea, and some bargaining.

"Some of it was tips," he says.

"Not that much." She looks at the pile on the table. "Elsie here watched you all night. You went on all the rides."

"Spent a fortune," the woman said.

So it was this rotten cow. *She* is the Mrs. Gargery. The dealer had kept quiet, after all.

"Some of it probably *was* tips," his sister offers. "Not all of it, though, was it?"

"Not all of it, no."

"Some of it was boat money, wasn't it?"

He is silent.

"Make him say," the woman who helps on Saturdays says. "Go on."

"That's all right, Elsie," his sister says. "Leave us alone now."

"Make him say," the woman repeats as she goes through the door.

"Don't tell Mum," the boy says, when they are alone.

She shook her head. "What are we going to do with you, then?" He feels her yearning across the space between them. They have never touched; you didn't in this family. "Will you promise never to take the boat money again?"

"Oh, yeah." Then, suddenly, "I don't want to look after the boats any more."

"You can still look after the boats, but . . ."

"I don't want to."

"What do you want to do, then? Help the gardener?"

And then it came. "I want to go home," he says, and as he says it he does, go home, back to bread-and-margarine, back to the other liars and thieves he hung around with on his street, back to a world of crime and punishment he understands. "I want to go home," he says again. "Let me go home."

She nods. "P'raps that's best. Don't say I sent you, mind. If I take you up to London and put you on the right tube, can you manage?"

"Course I can." They used to ride all day on the tube for a penny, changing trains. He hates her treating him as a kid. Then, to be certain, he repeats, "Don't tell Mum."

And she nods, on his side. "She'd kill you. What'll we say? You got homesick?"

"That'll do. In the morning, then?"

She sniffs and looks down at her hands.

"Don't cry, Mary," the boy pleads. "It's not *your* fault." But he can't cross the gap between them.

You can start anywhere. Set down an old man looking at a dead tree, sticking up out of a weed-choked river. Go from there. See what happens.

DAVID HOMEL was born and raised in Chicago, and now lives and writes in Montreal. He is the author of three novels: *Electrical Storms*, *Rat Palms*, and *Sonya & Jack*.

SHOUTING SAINTS

DAVID HOMEL

The paradox of gospel music hit me for the first time in the auditorium of Gainesville High School, down in north Florida. The Dixie Hummingbirds were there to bring the word to the people. The Birds, those eternal gentlemen of the road, had started out in the late 1930s in that same flat Florida town. They not only sang holy, they appeared to live that way, too — something of a distinction in the trade.

They began their program with "Jesus Is the Light of the World." Not only was their version perfectly skilled in its harmonics; it was incredibly daring, showy, pyrotechnic — a piece of virtuosity. Almost frivolous. Yet it elicited a holy laugh of recognition from the audience.

I didn't know what to think. Their version seemed to attract too much attention to itself, and to its singers, to be much good as praise. It was too beautiful to serve the Lord. It was a form of competition with His creation. The paradox had me feeling uneasy.

But it certainly didn't heavy up the air in that hall as far as the rest of the audience was concerned. After that introduction, the Hummingbirds got down to their usual business, which was wrecking the place for the Lord (gospel argot for delivering a rousing performance).

The paradox of "Jesus Is the Light of the World" stayed with me. In the end, it won me over permanently to gospel music which, I have come to see, has in it all the good enigmas that the act of making art should contain.

Actually, my conversion to the form occurred years before that, before I even dreamed that one day I'd get to consider such lofty, important issues. I spent those sexually anxious years known as adolescence in La Grange, one of the old suburbs of Chicago. The old suburbs had been around since the Civil War, maybe before, but they really started percolating after the Chicago Fire of 1871. Once the ashes had cooled, the city fathers decided: *Enough's enough,* no more wooden buildings in our town, they're too prone to burning, and when one burns, they all burn. Wood is cheaper than brick, or at least it was back then, so the people who wanted to build those cheaper wooden houses simply moved out past what was then the city limits, and proceeded to create architectural anarchy. Long live the rugged individualist!

Most of Chicago is built on swamps, and the La Grange neighbourhood is no exception. So it just seemed natural to the white folks there that the blacks would want to live in those swampier areas, where the bugs were thicker, and the diseases they bore more prevalent. No one asked the blacks, of course, but anyway, that's what they ended up with, and seeing that things weren't likely to change, soon they began pitching their A. M. E. churches on that land.

In French, the word *âme* means "soul," which does justice to what the acronym stands for: the African Methodist Episcopal church. It was there, on Sunday evenings, that I first heard gospel singing. In the days before Dr. Martin Luther King was murdered, there was more curiosity than hostility towards a good-hearted white boy in those neighbourhoods, and I was free to linger by the church door and listen to the singing, and imagine what it would be like if I could sing like that, or believe like that, or be like that.

I lingered there, but I did not go in. Not that I wasn't invited in. You will never find more hospitable folks than the ones in and around a gospel event. At the

Hummingbirds' program, it was automatically (and rightly) assumed, even in that racially polarized town in the 1990s, that I was there to make worship, and not stand around with my hands in my pockets. But back in La Grange, I didn't cross the threshold of the A. M. E. church because I was intimidated by all that believing. It was more than simply not having the same beliefs those people had. The inhibition ran deeper. I doubted myself. I doubted I could possess the mechanisms of, and the capacities for, belief.

I've felt the same way around the more orthodox members of my own home religion. Every morning at the corner kosher bakery in Montreal, I have to run this gauntlet. The *payess* flying, the sombre, grave, concentrated foreheads, the lamenting over the need to make change from a two-dollar bill on a $1.85 double rye loaf, the suspicious stares reserved for those of little faith like myself. It's enough to give you a feeling of inadequacy. Not of the spirit *per se*, because the spirit cannot be measured, but concerning the outward signs and convictions of belief.

I was right to hesitate at the threshold of the A. M. E. church. Back then, anyway. Since then, I've worked my way back towards the primitive roots of worship and belief. The love of gospel enters here; that music helped me achieve the gift of belief. I've understood that belief comes from art — from music, in this case. I've understood that through shouting, through self-escape, comes belief.

Self-escape? Yes, ma'am! It is the cornerstone of art, for the artist and the audience alike. For in these pages, we could very well substitute the word "novel" for the words "gospel music."

If there's one figure from the Bible whom the gospel singer can look to for inspiration and method, it's Jacob. Forever wrassling and tussling for a blessing. Deceiving his blind father for a blessing. Wheeling and dealing for a blessing, buying and selling and trading. Anything for a blessing. Even prevarication — a fancy word for false witness. The gospel singer is on the edge of this precipice. On the edge of antinomian conduct. He will use the beauty of his voice, he will show off. He will clown around, he will make a spectacle of himself to get closer, momentarily, to his God.

Jacob, "the supplanter," according to the etymology of his name, is given great coverage throughout the Holy Book. Apparently, the Book admits and supports the fact that one's quest for belief and blessing can bring the quester into some pretty rough neighbourhoods, morally speaking.

Antinomianism, a dictionary word if there ever was one (but a common enough practice in our lives), is among the paradoxes and pleasures lurking around gospel. According to the idea, those who inhabit Grace, those who are struck by the Light, are exempted from the moral laws of this fleeting world. The false Messiahs, who have come along to entertain and mislead holders to the Hebrew and other traditions over the centuries, were (are) great antinomians. According to them, when the end of the world as we know it comes, if you are among those in the know, among the believers, you will be able to do whatever you want, because all petty moral laws will have lost their currency. That makes sense; when the Messiah comes, everything will be turned upside-down.

There is a strong antinomian strain to gospel, too, that has gotten some singers into big trouble (Sam Cooke is one, as we'll see). If you inhabit Grace, as the singer must, if you are moved by the Lord, if you can wreck a church and lay out its congregation in the aisles (more wonderful gospel-trade argot), if you can lead to the conversion and sanctification of many, doesn't that put you a little above common moral strictures?

Of course it does. Besides, what man or woman can give so much, can sweat pounds off an already meagre frame, and not expect some compensation down here on Earth? "The virtue thing," the great Rebert Harris of the Soul Stirrers called it, lamenting its relative absence. "The life" is how those people living it refer to it.

If you sing for the Lord, and excel at it, then for certain select times, you are above His interdictions. Many of us practise the antinomianism of perfect moments. Lovers are superior to the world when they inhabit the blindness of love. In Russia, as I found out firsthand, drunks are allowed any sort of public foolishness because they are said to be in a kind of childish state of grace.

I've seen such things happen. Brilliant epiphanies on the Sea Islands, along the Atlantic coast of Georgia. Underneath the striped canvas of the tent show, the Lord's music was being played, all day long and into the night. Meanwhile, back behind the devil crab concession, the Dark One was lurking. I was pulling for both sides, knowing that one can't live without the other. It so happened that behind that devil crab concession was a package store. Those who had just enjoined us to take the high road to glory were now washing down their spicy crabs with bourbon and beer. I thought

I heard someone praise the virtues of a meaty thigh — and that wasn't a crab thigh either. But where was the contradiction — hadn't the singers earned this reward?

The gospel singer sings for the Almighty. He — or she — sings for himself. Therein lies the age-old battle. No matter what they say, nobody wants to be God's voice on earth. No messenger wants to be slave to the message. The great Georgia writer Harry Crews wrote a book about that, and he wasn't the first. Healthy human pride makes that impossible. Nobody wants to be a clear channel through which the word flows. Gabriel, when he came down to bring vision to the prophets who turned out to be so damned reluctant, discovered this fact. Unworthy as they were, the prophets embarrassed themselves — and probably Gabriel, too — by rolling around in the dust with their hands over their eyes, refusing to accept the gift of prophetic vision. They didn't want to carry the Lord's word. Gabriel crossed his arms, he tapped his feet impatiently in the sand. Come on, get up, accept it, no one's ever been able to say no.

The prophets were only doing the human thing. Who wants to have all that responsibility? Look at Moses. He demanded proof. The Lord teased him with miracles. There was a bush on fire. There was a voice. Moses looked everywhere but at the bush. You can't blame him. "Here am I," the Lord had to specify. "That's okay," Moses said, reacting to the news that he would soon be doing the Lord's business by leading His people out of slavery, "but what if they don't believe me?" As proof, the Lord showed him a miracle, the brazen serpent thing. "Show me another one," he urged the Lord. He liked a good story. He liked spectacle. A *shtik*. And so a people was born.

The gospel singer says he's singing God's word. And he, or she, is. But what about that twitch of carnality? What about the skinniest member of the Dixie Hummingbirds with the thinning conked hair who jumped right off the stage in the Gainesville High auditorium and started in preaching at extremely close quarters to a group of handsome ladies in their finery? Each one of their hats was more colourful than an azalea bush in full spring flower. You can't tell me he was only in it for the Almighty.

The gospel singer needs that hip-shake. After all, the music rose out of a land that gave us a ladies' softball team in the South Carolina wetlands called the Low Bottom Pirates, and I don't think they were talking topography. You've got to get the faithful in. You need spectacle. Since God's word hasn't changed all that much since He first issued it, all that can differ is the telling of it. A little like novel-writing. How many ways can you tell the same plot? Besides, you won't be able to convince any-body of your intimate knowledge of the subject at hand unless you've been down. Been level to the ground. Sinned. Otherwise, your word has no authority. A child can speak from a position of undimmed, unsullied virtue. No one wants to listen to a child. Innocence has no authority. I am not going to convince you that I've eaten dirt until I unlock my jaws and you see the gravel chips stuck in between my teeth.

Belief enters through carnality. Belief enters through the body. That's the crack where God's light comes in (to paraphrase that great popular Montreal theologian, Leonard Cohen).

The gospel singer's carnality speaks of his or her authority. But it also reminds us of the danger, ever present, of backsliding. There is a palpable suspense in the air at great gospel programs. Will the singer, carried away by his performance, fall over the edge? Will art, personal pride and that good old-fashioned taste for big leg triumph over the Lord's interdictions, right there in His own temple?

I've witnessed it. Usually it starts like this. Instead of "Jesus," it's *"Baby!"* A snake crawls up the candlestick, nestles in the chalice, waits for you there. And a very confident snake it is.

The vocabulary of gospel is tremendously seductive, and it informs and gives light to the southern school of novel-writing, including my own *Rat Palms. Glory* is a euphemism for "death." And the heaven that lies beyond, or so we hope. *God troubles the waters.* Drinkers use the same expressions to refer to the mix into which the intoxicant of their choice is liberally splashed. When a singer makes the audience shout through his performance, he shouts *someone:* "He shouted the ladies in the front row." This kind of language goes out of the church hall and into the community. Every day, you can encounter people on the street or in the fields, some illiterate, who sound exactly like the Old Testament. That's the only book they know, the only style that's available for them to emulate. It's always startling to stop by a fruit stand at the end of the day and hear two people who sound exactly like Isaiah and Jeremiah, arguing over whether a scuppernong is a grape or a plum (it's a grape, by the way, in the muscat family).

The glorious, image-filled, yet strangely abstract language of King James helps us feel what we must feel in order to participate in gospel. We have to feel our Saviour as we serve Him. We are brought out, we are turned around, we are kept, our change is imminent, we're going to wait on it. For a few precious seconds, we are totally under the control of another, we do not have to choose, we have been chosen, inhabited. That's what I call self-forgetting; that's what I call love!

Anyone from the Hebrew culture, no matter how much he or she has forgotten, no matter how little they may have learned in the first place, will find comfort in the retelling of the old gospel tales. Anyone with a feeling for the Passover — the passing out of bondage into freedom with a little help from the mighty tool-box of miracles — has to dig gospel. For who reading the lines at the Passover service could claim that he doesn't need a little liberation, and a little help in attaining it?

Though, sometimes, I have to admit, the singers do get it wrong. Moses didn't really write the Ten Commandments, the way the Dixie Hummingbirds say he did in their song "The Final Edition." And there's no shortage of kitsch. How about Sister Wynona Carr, who compares the Old and New Testaments to a baseball game? Even someone who loves the game has to pause and reflect. The relief pitcher who finishes up the Big Game in the ninth inning is — you guessed it — John of the Revelations, the last book in the Book.

And there's plenty of clowning, cutting the fool. You've got to tickle the audience, get them in, keep them there, make them come back. During a particularly strenuous show, the Five Blind Boys (the ones from Alabama, not Mississippi), being way past retirement age and still shouting, are wrestled into their chairs by their handler for a well deserved rest. But the spirit won't let them stay there. They keep popping up, rushing to the microphone for one last holler or shout or entreaty. The handler sprints over and escorts them none too gently back to their chairs. And since the Blind Boys really are blind (not all blind singers really are), the handler has an unfair advantage, and we in the audience hate him for it. The message is clear: the Boys are inhabited by the spirit, no handler is going to keep them down, and as such they *are* the spirit, too. Maybe they stole that *shtik* from James Brown — though, if there was any stealing, it would have been the other way around. After J.B. worked himself to death, and was nothing but a streak of sweat and hair tonic on the floor, his handlers would come and gently lower a cape over his exhausted form. But no! James Brown was up and hollering again! He couldn't help himself, the spirit was in him. And the crowd went absolutely wild.

What do you expect? Plenty of shouting saints were minstrel artists and blues singers before they got sanctified. There's bound to be a certain cross-over. Singing, prophesying, selling barbecue at a penny a bone, getting ugly for the Lord. But woe unto the gospel shouter who's actually caught red-handed (or red-tongued) singing the blues. His soul will be dropped by the church like a smoking, sulphurous hot potato. Ask the Staple Singers about that.

At first, some of us may have trouble figuring out what all that clowning around is about. But remember the Hummingbirds and their pyrotechnical virtuosity in "Jesus Is the Light of the World" — too showy, too much emphasis on the artist's perfection, not enough on the perfection of the Eternal One. But that's gospel, that's its paradox. The Book says you can't serve two masters. I don't know; sometimes I think I've seen it done.

During that same program, another paradox struck me, but it, too, turned out to be superficial. The Birds were wrecking the church, and many were the hearts that were rejoicing. People, men and women alike, were falling out for Jesus. Possessed, in other words, and doing the kind of things you do when you are possessed. When it came time for a richly deserved intermission, the Birds mopped their brows with clean white handkerchiefs, politely thanked the audience for listening (half of them were just picking themselves up off the floor) and said they'd be right back for a little more church. Then these same folks, so recently possessed, filed out to the lobby for iced tea. The same people who, a few minutes earlier, were so joyful they couldn't keep on their feet, were now discussing their gardens, and what they were going to put up for the winter and how their sons and daughters were doing at school. The usual things any of us might talk about with our friends or next-door neighbours.

What can you say? The spirit is always there, imminent. Your life would be unlivable if it inhabited you all the time. Constant possession is tantamount to illness. But when it does come, it's a gift. The rest of the time you get by as best you can.

The gospel service puts belief — or, better yet, possession — within reach of every member of the congregation. For a Hebrew, that radically democratic side strikes a chord. The rabbi is a learned man, respected as such, but he's not necessarily any closer to the Almighty than anyone else. In gospel, everybody can shout. In fact, you're encouraged to. You're even encouraged to try and out-believe the preacher and the singer (usually one and the same person), though the competition will be tough; he (or she) is a professional, and you're not.

But whatever you do, you must be sincere. These people can sniff fake spirituality a country mile away. Shouting is a release of the self by the self; without it, life would be intolerable. What with the great competition for belief and its outer manifestations, there's bound to be a few false shouters, a few poseurs in the crowd. But woe unto them, for a church has a keen nose for their ilk. They will be cast out quicker than the devil. In fact, public insincerity of belief is worse than an honestly wrought sin, no matter how low-down it is.

Since it's the doorway to virtue, gospel is tremendously competitive. But more than the public acknowledgement of virtue is at stake; there is money and fame, records to cut and concerts to give. And, for those who wish to sample it, "the life." The wine and women that come with song (though the prospect of gospel groupies does seem a little unlikely). But the weapons in this competition are different from those in most contests.

Who can speak most convincingly about the pain of his mother's death? Who can be most possessed? Who's the most spiritual, who can believe the hardest, the deepest, the most showily and, simultaneously, the most sincerely? Who's the shoutingest?

The vocabulary says it all. So-and-so is a well known church-wrecker. So-and-so laid out the slain in the aisles. A certain quartet took over the town and shook down the houses for a week. There have been deaths recorded — real deaths. Large dignified ladies have thrown themselves out of the second balcony and haven't always landed right. You can't get any more committed than that. Others have passed on over into Glory out of sheer happiness in the middle of a song.

This is serious business. This is no place for the ambiguous heart. This is no place for asexual, post-modern cool. This is where the human voice is at its most authentic, one of the last outposts where you can hear it in all its pleading glory, where it can still move you over the edge. Novelists, take heed!

Let us name some of the great singers. Archie Brownlee. Ira Tucker. Rebert Harris. Dorothy Love Coates. Alex Bradford. Sam Cooke. And the great groups. The Hummingbirds, the Soul Stirrers (in their many incarnations, including with Cooke), the Swan Silvertones, the Mighty Clouds of Joy, the Five Blind Boys from Mississippi and Alabama, the Pilgrim Travelers. And the choir leaders: James Cleveland, Shirley Caesar. And all the others we've forgotten here. Let us praise them.

Wait a minute! Did you mention Sam Cooke back there? Could you possibly be referring to the Top-Twenty sporting of tunes like this one, tunes that made a lot of cash for a lot of miscreants, tunes about "my baby" who loves to "cha-cha-cha"? Or was it *this* Sam Cooke who lamented that he was "a poor pilgrim of sorrow"? Somebody call somebody sanctified and let's get this whole thing sorted out once and for all!

Of course, there is no sorting it out. Sam Cooke was both those people. He was the hinge that swung between the sacred and the profane in popular music. Like the founder of gospel who died in 1993, Thomas Dorsey, he pulled both ways, he was pulled both ways, by the devil and the Lord, and he wanted to reconcile the two in his voice. He failed. He died in the process, at the age of thirty-three, shot to death. For his attempts, he's earned a place in American popular theology.

I wonder whether there's any way *but* failure and destruction for the man or woman tries to harbour both impulses in the instrument of his voice.

Thomas Dorsey chose. He was able to choose. He loved the music of "the life," but he was also deeply religious. He managed to reconcile the two by choosing virtue, and praising it in a new brand of music that contained a spicy mix of blues, which had previously been restricted to the devil's domain. Then again, it was easier for Dorsey than for Cooke. The pressures and stakes were lower for Dorsey. There was less money floating around; pop music hadn't yet become an industry with its less-than-reputable captains. You could stay in your little "race" corner and make enough to live on.

Those options weren't available to Sam Cooke. After he left gospel for pop, then tried to return to the church, even for a Soul Stirrers reunion, he was shouted off the stage for being non-Christian. The ante had been upped between the forces of light and the forces of darkness.

Then there was the issue of his good looks. He was just too clean and pretty. Even when he was still singing straight gospel, the black bobby-soxers would crowd the front rows at the Apollo in New York to hear the program. Maybe his beauty was his undoing.

Then again, some say it was politics that eventually got him killed. Politics and money. A lot of that story has gone untold. Since it's an American story, there's bound to be a conspiracy. Some say it was the Mafia. White folks who thought Cooke was getting too uppity because he wanted to hold on to his publishing; he wanted to retain copyright and the cash that goes with it. You know how those writers are about copyright! Some say it was the right wing; they arranged the hit because they were worried about him going into politics, and about what a politically aware black man with his charisma could do to the electoral process. (The same rumours were bandied about, albeit less successfully, after Otis Redding's death in a plane crash.) Others held to a theological explanation. Murder was Cooke's just reward for having deserted the church.

But not all believers wanted to subscribe to that explanation with its vengeful god.

We'll never know what really happened. The official version — one that has never been successfully contradicted, it should be said here — was that Cooke was shot to death by the landlady while forcefully pursuing a stripper in a hotel of ill repute. It's very possible that the facts were just that banal. Here was a man who was besieged by women, who had a $30,000 car in the parking lot, and who died chasing a $30 whore. It just doesn't make sense. Maybe that's what happens when you try and reconcile the unreconcilables in your voice.

If so, then we writers are in a world of trouble.

My appreciation to Anthony Heilbut, whose book on gospel music put the background behind the singers I've always listened to.

ROSEMARY SULLIVAN was born in Montreal, where she studied at McGill University. After studying in England she taught at universities in France and at the University of Victoria and is currently Professor of English at the University of Toronto. Sullivan is the author of *By Heart: Elizabeth Smart/A Life*, which was nominated for a Governor-General's Award for Non-Fiction, as well as two collections of poetry, *Blue Panic* and *The Space a Name Makes*, which won the Gerald Lampert Award. Sullivan is also the editor of six anthologies of poetry and prose, including the Oxford anthologies *Poetry by Canadian Women* and *Stories by Canadian Women*. Rosemary Sullivan lives in Toronto.

Memory-Making and the Stamina of the Poet

Rosemary Sullivan

The last time I saw Gwendolyn MacEwen was in the spring of 1987. We were crossing Harbord Street in the rain talking about a mutual friend who had just married a criminal. The prison wedding had been a lead item on the national news and we were joking about the longevity of the demon lover still alive at the end of the twentieth century. "Why," Gwendolyn asked me, "do we love the dark?" Her eyes — everyone remembered her eyes: almond shaped, crystalline blue, so preternaturally large in her small face — were laughing. I had thought it a light moment. I watched Gwendolyn head towards Robert Street — she was a lonely figure, hunched down in a brown wool coat. I had wanted to follow her, but the moment passed. She seemed so autonomous — I hadn't wanted to invade that privacy. Six months later she was dead. It seemed inconceivable.

And then the story surfaced of her last appearance in public at a November poetry reading at the Bamboo Club on Queen Street in the middle of a Toronto blizzard. I hadn't gone. She had collapsed on stage too drunk to read. A friend leaned over to help her up. "Don't touch me," Gwendolyn screamed. She was carried out crying: "Don't touch me." Gwendolyn who had been so dignified, even decorous. It seemed inconceivable.

> When someone lifts us
> He lifts in his hand millions of memories
> Which do not dissolve in blood
> like evening.
> — Nelly Sachs, "Chorus of the Stones"

Gwendolyn MacEwen was that extraordinary creature, a fully independent, creative woman. I want to know what unwound her life as she bashed forward with such energy and so I have decided to write her biography. To me biography is an elegiac art, a form of revenge against life for the impossible fact that a life can disappear so easily — all that energy, passion, humour that constitutes an individual can one day simply stop. But how can I recover Gwen?

I have doubts, of course, about biography. Is biography a form of betrayal, an invasion of the secrets of a writer's life, when the work should be allowed to stand for itself? Is it, as some say, simply a form of voyeurism, the biographer a professional burglar breaking into the house and riffling through hidden drawers? But for me biography is not about secrets. It is a different kind of search. One is asking: what is a life? Why was this particular life lived as it was? We feel the need instinctively to turn a life into something intelligible that we can reflect on.

Why not simply write a memoir? But that wouldn't do. I don't want a portrait of Gwendolyn simply as I knew her. I want the whole puzzle — not solved, of course, but unlayered so that the mystery of what it was to be Gwendolyn can be experienced, even if that experience is partial, only an interpretation.

But what is it to be involved in the nitty-gritty of a life? Gwendolyn had expected a biographer. She left instructions to her sister in her will to set aside certain papers for her biographer. Yet she didn't talk much about her life. She said her life was all there in the poems, and I am discovering that it was, but encoded. I am going to have to string all those glorious poems back to their literal roots in life. Am I undoing something in the process?

Gwendolyn was a house with many rooms. As a friend, you were invited into the one that most suited you, while the others remained secret simply because you lacked the key. What did people know of Gwendolyn? Michael Ondaatje called her the last of the bardic poets, a poet who took all risks for the poetry. "I remember her reading at the Saint Lawrence Centre in the mid-seventies," he told me, "reciting the poems from *The Armies of the Moon* by heart. It was the first time I had the sense of the poet as a public person. She was giving herself to the public. It was the voice of the bard." Only a few people knew that she was a genuine autodidact. One day at Western Tech she got up in frustration in the middle of a chemistry lab and walked out, just a couple of months shy of completing her high school matriculation. She taught *herself* Arabic, Greek, Hebrew and French and translated the work of writers in each of the four languages. When one thought of Gwendolyn, one thought of magicians, arcana, Egypt, the Trojan Horse, demon lovers, cryptograms, riddles, ellipses. I remember her phoning and asking what I knew about Nostradamus.

Once Gwen said: "A poet doesn't have to be a myopic thing in an attic or a basement; he or she might well be a dynamic human being, truly involved in the gutsy aspects of life." No one was gutsier than Gwen; few were as funny. She could do scathing limericks on *Paradise Lost* or write of being eighteen and slipping out to the Wah Mai Café on Queen Street whenever she could evade her aunt's watchful eye. When the cops raided and began to haul in the prostitutes, they asked about the kid in the brown corduroy jumper. She told them she was training to be a writer: "I'm just a page now but one day I'll be a book." And I say to myself — I need to tell this life because no one, beyond that eccentric circle who still reads poetry in this non-poetic age, knows Gwendolyn's work. And even among them, there were only a very few friends who knew the real cost of what it meant to be Gwendolyn, knew what lay beneath the gutsiness and bravura.

I sit before a photograph of Gwen's childhood home. Once it stood at 38 Keele Street, but it no longer exists, torn down to make room for a subway. I have to stop and think about homes. The homes of our childhood are more than domestic architecture. They are mental spaces that define the power dynamic of the world we enter unwittingly; they will surface repeatedly in our dreams and we will reconstruct them throughout a lifetime. Even Gwendolyn's *home* is a riddle to be decoded: on the first floor were her Aunt Margaret and Uncle Charlie, immigrants from Poplar, the poorest district of working-class London; on the second, Gwen's family; on the third, children from the Protestant Foster Children's Home, cared for by Aunt Margaret, who came and went over the years. But two stayed. All these people will have to become real for me.

We believe the roots of a lifetime are hidden and entwined in childhood. A biography begins its archaeology there. The first person I must speak to is Gwendolyn's sister Carol. Powerfully but matter-of-factly, she tells me that they moved into 38 Keele just before Gwen was born because her mother was schizophrenic and couldn't be trusted alone with her children. She crafts for me, out of broken memories, a mother who disappeared into hospital at regular intervals of fifteen months. As a child Carol didn't know why she left — it was a secret that mother was mad, and everybody protected you from that secret. And I think, for a child, secrets are more deadly than the truth — a secret turns a childhood into a puzzle of lost and missing pieces. Carol's role was to protect her sister from the truth: "You're not old enough. Don't ask."

In a dream journal she began to keep in her late twenties, Gwendolyn preserved the first page for a single entry: "Recurring dream from the age of four to nine: 'Dream of a giant key floating through dark skies like a space ship; silent, heavy, v.[ery] slow — fearful, reminiscent of army blimps.'" This was the image, as she remembered it, that occupied her mind throughout her childhood. The world was threatening, a locked secret; it required a key to open it, but the key was inaccessible. Was it the adult Gwendolyn who coloured the image in military metaphors? The image began to haunt her childhood in 1945 when all the world's metaphors would have focused on war. What was the dread secret that threatened the skies of Gwendolyn's childhood? I will make the leap, assuming the secret was her mother's madness. Gwen's dream stopped at the same time as an experience Carol recounts to me, one that altered her own version of the world.

I am entering the lives of real people. Carol sits across from me in her small kitchen in Barrie, Ontario. Eight years older than Gwendolyn, she is a photocopy of what Gwen would look like now. Carol took an opposite route into life: she is pragmatic; she brought up five children, virtually, it seems, on her own. She has worked as a union organizer. She is skeptical about the idea that life is mysterious — it is a power structure that resists you — but she has the candour, the directness of a woman who has invented herself against the odds. She is telling me something that is profoundly painful, but she feels, if I am to write about Gwen, I must know this. I must have the whole story.

In 1950, her family moved to Winnipeg. She describes to me one night when she and Gwen were sleeping in the upstairs bedroom in their house on Dominion Street. Carol awoke to hear screaming—her father was calling her name. She raced downstairs. The screaming came from the bathroom but the door was locked on the inside. Finally the door was flung open. There was blood everywhere. Her mother held a razor in one hand — she had cut her throat and blood was pouring from the wound — and she was trying to slash her husband. His arms were already badly cut. He screamed to Carol to call the police. Carol remembered Gwendolyn racing down the stairs; her one thought was to stop her from getting into that bathroom. She remembers calling the police and taking Gwendolyn upstairs. When the police arrived, her mother was subdued and taken to hospital.

Carol has recounted this in a halting voice full of pain. "This is not easy for me," she says. What did Gwendolyn see that night, she wonders. She is fairly sure she did not see into that bathroom. But if she did not see, she had come closer to the disaster than she had ever been before; her childhood world had been irrevocably shattered. By Gwen's own account, this was when the dream of the key ended.

There is Marion, one of the foster children on the third floor, who spent most of her childhood at 38 Keele. Her story shifts the mystery of Gwen's home through yet another permutation. We sit in Ottawa on her living-room couch before a photograph album. She points to a beautiful young woman in her twenties — she is refined and delicate and is wearing an elegant dress. Beside her is a child — I notice the eyes: eager, expectant and happy. "That is me," Marion says. "The other is my mother. Why are we so well dressed? What went wrong if we were so well dressed?" At the age of seventy, she still knows little about that woman. Marion's childhood disintegrated when her mother suffered a mental breakdown in her early twenties and was sent to Whitby Mental Hospital. (With life's ironic capacity to weave coincidences, she and Gwendolyn's mother would be there together in the 1940s.) There is a sense of collusion between myself and Marion, an excitement. Why has she offered me this candour? It comes from a love of Gwen, an astonishment that, out of that childhood, she would have constructed such a powerful life for herself. There is an urgency to Gwen's story — a sense that secrets distort; the having-to-keep-hidden is what does the damage.

I need to know Gwen's mother, Elsie. I cannot leave it as a simple statement in a biography: "The poet's mother suffered periodic mental breakdowns." What does that mean? What shattered Elsie's life? There are files, I learn, and with the assistance of a lawyer and Carol, who is Gwen's literary executor, I gain access to them. I track Elsie to the Queen Street Mental Health Centre where she died in 1982. I know that on such a trail a biographer enters dangerous territory. Will this be another sensational case of the biographer raiding the secrets of the psychiatrist's couch? That is not my intention, nor is it what happens. The Elsie I discover moves me deeply. I will know her in ways her children couldn't since they never saw those records.

I read a doctor's summary of her mental status:

Elsie has been the youngest in a large family who allowed her to remain dependent on others so that she never attained an emotional maturity and always requires a great deal of reassurance. Her exaggerated ambitiousness with her inability to stand her failures and her inner insecurity make her situation intolerable . . . She evades her responsibilities and when taken from them she reacts in a healthy way. She is just a typical neurotic person who has lost her courage, inner security and self-confidence.

I find an effort of sympathy for Elsie among the pages of these files, but little help. What was so different about Elsie's history? A youngest child, lost at the back of a family, indulged and dismissed. A woman of "consistently superior intelligence" (she passed most of her hospital tests at the Superior Adult Level I) who was terrified of the dark and had nightmares in which she sank into a terrible abyss until her sister pulled her back. A woman who wondered if she would ever be normal. Elsie was typical, and so was her family. There was violence in that family — there was anger. These lives are not fictional and there is no comfortable sense of closure, all the loose ends tied, solving the puzzle of a life.

We want to see madness as located in a defective personality. We feel more comfortable if we can find an explanation for it in the personal chemistry of the individual. But what if madness is simply located on the extremes of the spectrum of normalcy, and therefore very much tied into our social structure? After her mother's death in 1982, Gwendolyn began work on a poem called "The Black Tunnel Wall." She remembered her mother telling her of her experiences as a child during World War I. On nights of the full moon when the German zeppelins were cruising the sky with death, the family had sought shelter from the bombs in a local tunnel. Elsie remembered that black tunnel with terror. In a poem about her mother called "The

Black Dogs of War" Gwen asks: "So you still believe these children are individually insane?"

On one of my visits to Barrie, Carol hands me a sealed envelope, on the back of which Gwendolyn has scrawled her name in large childish letters. Carol tells me it contains the pencil with which Gwen wrote her first poem at age ten. We do not open it. She also tells me that Gwen changed her name. The family had always called her Wendy, but at age twelve, she insisted that her name henceforth would be Gwendolyn. She told them she thought one day she might be important and Wendy was not the name of somebody important. Carol always remembered this as Gwen's explanation.

Art was a way to make life make sense. It required training, discipline, love. And Gwen had an astonishing mind, perpetually in gear. I build the story from clues left behind: I go to libraries to find city directories — all the addresses Gwen lived at are under her name in those mangy books. I find her letters in writers' archives across the country, echoes of that lost voice. I consult the Mormons in Salt Lake City for genealogy — they keep files on all of us so that we can be identified by our histories when we pass to the other side. I phone Edinburgh, searching for Gwen's father. I write hospitals for files. And I track down all the witnesses who shared, however peripherally, in this life. The story grows — how Gwen after leaving school roamed the back streets of High Park until she found a small *chaider,* or Hebrew school, and walked in asking them to teach her Hebrew — if she was to know the Bible, the Zoar, the Gnostics, she must read their language. I find letters to and from her father, a man whose life had begun with such promise and yet who died of alcoholism. Margaret Atwood, who had been Gwen's friend, gives me their correspondence, two young female mavericks confronting the world together at a club called the Bohemian Embassy. I begin to watch magic shows. Gwendolyn loved magicians. "Poets are magicians without quick wrists," she said. You enter a life and it takes you over. It is as real as most things get.

Now I am searching for a lost lover. When I began he was a figure in one of Gwen's last poems. She imagined him lost to her somewhere in Cairo. I know only his first name, Salah, and a vague story that he was studying for an M.A. in chemistry at McGill University when she loved him in the late sixties. Margaret Atwood remembers a handsome young Egyptian, educated, sophisticated. I phone McGill's department of chemistry. All the old files were burnt in a fire in the seventies. But I find a woman who is willing to search for a lost lover who has a mysterious first name. It has something to do with nostalgia — we have all had lost lovers — and with the fascination we feel for memory, for recovering the broken-off pieces of the past. We find a likely name. I am phoning the Egyptian Embassy in Ottawa. We are all searching — I am told I might advertise in the *Cairo Gazette*. When I do find Salah, I discover he has been living all these years in Montreal. It takes the usual number of days to gather my courage to phone him. Who am I that I should walk into his life carrying his past? But I do phone. There is a silence. "Yes, I am the one who knew Gwendolyn. I knew she had died. How did she die?" I will visit him soon, wondering what it will be like to bring to this man a piece of his life that had gone missing.

The loneliness of being Gwen cannot be reduced simply to her childhood. That would be too easy. Rather that childhood was responsible for Gwen's stance — her anger at a modern world that takes so many casualties. Gwen believed that all our values are upside-down and have to be reinvented; that our souls need to be cured — of violence, of hypocrisy, of the lust for power. She wanted to subvert the norm, to change us. I would speculate that part of the pain at the end of her life was knowing how impossible such a task is. Poetry, she realized, changes nothing. Poetry didn't even afford her a living. (When she died, Gwendolyn left her family her writings, a battered fold-up bike, and a bank account which, after her last withdrawal, contained $2.02.) Poetry had not even brought her the love she was looking for. I think that despair caught her for a moment. Could her life have gone another way? She had plans for other books.

Every life is a puzzle and the art of biography is a decoder's art. Reading another's life, we search for our own. To think of biography as the exposing of secrets is to misconstrue the art. Recently I was invited to be on the radio program *Morningside* to discuss biography. One of the other interviewees was Andrew Motion, and talk turned to his biography *Philip Larkin: A Writer's Life*. Peter Gzowski was disturbed that Motion revealed Larkin read pornography. Shouldn't that have been a secret buried with him in his grave? "But is that such a dark secret?" I asked. "You could have found that pornography in your father's bedroom." As I saw the blanched look on Gzowski's face I was immediately sorry I hadn't said "the pornography I found in my father's bedroom." I remember as a child, sneaking down to the master bedroom to look at it: titillated, excited, appalled. The point that Motion was making was about British society in the fifties — how sad and inadequate the intimacy in families was — how the society was pervaded by a pernicious racism, classism, sexual repression, misogyny. Larkin had tried to rise above that in his poems — few have written so well about male loneliness and emotional crippledness — even if he backslid into it in his life. The writer can only be a product of his or her society like the rest of us, whatever critics say to the contrary. Biography is not just about the writer, it is about all of us.

When I was growing up I was still being told that great literature was written by men, men who were different in kind from normal people, geniuses on another plane. "Literature is not life," I was told. As if the writing were like those cartoon bubbles that float in space over the heads of caricatures. The work had been cut off and floated in hyperspace without any connection to the man who wrote it. Those works were called "well-wrought urns," autonomous artifacts sealed in air-tight rooms and the space had a name: immortality. It was not a space that admitted many women writers.

But any writer knows that literature comes out of the guts of the writer. All one's emotional intelligence and all one's lived experience are poured into the making of a novel or a poem. The real distinction is that a book or a poem is not autobiography. In the work, the writer orchestrates his or her own vision; in the life, he or she is slapped around as much as the rest of us by life's vicissitudes. A writer's life, I would say flatly, is a story of an individual in a cultural context in a moment in time. That seems to me rather simple.

A biography matches what we do to our own lives. We live our lives as stories, examining them, interrogating ourselves, trying to make them an intelligible whole. Like the novel of a good writer, we do not will our own plot. It evolves moment by moment out of accident, contingency, intuitive leaps — how many writers have said that if they knew where the plot was going they'd get bored and give up. We believe there's something that's consistently us, call it our personality, our character, that strings the story together. We believe this identity we call ourselves is shaped by deep structures in our minds laid in childhood, by the intrigues of our culture shaping our thinking, and by our own desire. We are willing to accept that the self is infinitely complex but we are not quite willing to give it up.

To mirror that complexity is all a biographer tries to do: offering an hypothesis about how a writer's life was lived. Biography is a thought experiment: this life was lived; can it be told? It is, of course, a madcap exercise — collapsing a life into three hundred or so pages. Why attempt it? Because you believe in writers and writing.

Biographers are devoted to memory. They put a shaft in time, still the flux for a moment, struggling for insight. And the point is, only insight gets us through.

Will my biography of Gwendolyn be *true?* The novelist Timothy Findley has told me that in his book *Headhunter*, Gwendolyn is the source for Amy Wylie, a character who fights against the destruction of birds at the end of this plague-ridden decade: he has offered her as the embodiment of the truly civilized human being. At least I know the woman I want to arrive at, the courage, intelligence, and stamina it took to be Gwen.

Gwendolyn MacEwen published twenty books, including *Julian the Magician*, Macmillan, 1963, *A Breakfast for Barbarians*, The Ryerson Press, 1966, *The Shadow-Maker*, Macmillan, 1969, *King of Egypt, King of Dreams*, Macmillan, 1971, *The Armies of the Moon*, Macmillan, 1972, *Mermaids and Ikons*, Anansi, 1978, *Noman's Land*, The Coach House Press, 1985, *Afterworlds,* McClelland & Stewart, 1987, and *The Poetry of Gwendolyn MacEwen*, 2 vols, Exile Editions, 1994.

II

BORN WITH MORTALITY'S HOOK

CAROL WINDLEY's collection of stories, *Visible Light* (Oolichan Books), was nominated for the Governor-General's Award for Fiction in 1993 and for a B.C. Book Prize. Her stories have appeared in literary journals, including *Descant* and *Event,* and in *Best Canadian Stories* (Oberon Press), in 1985 and 1993, and in *The Journey Prize Anthology* (McClelland & Stewart). A new story will appear in *The Malahat Review* this year. She lives in Nanaimo and works for the Vancouver Island Regional Library.

THE JOY OF LIFE

CAROL WINDLEY

Once, in Wales, a man named Felix Curtis spoke to Alex about the "persistence of vision." He was quoting Ptolemy, he said, but he was also speaking of his own view of individual immortality. Did she understand his gist? Yes, she said, although she was, at the same time, trying to hear what Désirée and Robin were saying to one another. Well, look, Felix Curtis said, an image, a scene, a particular face, captivates the mind. For the peace of the soul, this image must be preserved. But perhaps she was not interested?

"Oh, yes," she said. "I am. I'm very interested."

It was a summer night, and it was raining and a coal fire was burning in the hearth. These images, of the fire and the room with its restless shadows along the walls and its more or less static occupants were to remain in Alex's mind over the years, persistently, just as Felix Curtis and Ptolemy before him had said. If that was what the phrase "persistence of vision" meant, and she supposed it was.

***

In a small art gallery located about a block and a half up from Pier 69, on the Seattle waterfront, on a fine afternoon in early September, thirty-eight years later, Alex stands in front of Désirée's painting of the picnic. Unharmed by time, looking, in fact, as if the paint has just been freshly applied, as if the artist has just put down her brush and wandered off for a moment of respite, its grandness astonishes Alex. Such effort, she thinks; such a task. Light positively shines out of every object: the purple lupins and the blue delphiniums, the slate roof and narrow green front door of the house. The painting shimmers in the still, cold air of the gallery. Alex waits for a suitable response to occur within her. She waits receptively, as if the painting is an icon she is praying to. What she wants, she thinks, is a powerful surge of memory, an elegiac, romantically vivid memory of that time and place, which is to say, the verdant front garden at Grove's End, in West Glamorgan, Wales. In June 1957.

Désirée's painting of the picnic looks something like this: a luminous thin blue wash of sky above green hills and sharp grey mountains, and in the foreground a garden, and in the garden, spread out on the green grass, a plaid rug with a group of people carefully disposed on its surface. Désirée, who can't bear, ever, to be left out of anything, has painted herself in next to Robin Pritchard. Her hand is touching the edge of Robin's shirtsleeve, as if she has just thought of something she wants to say to him. Loren, Désirée's daughter, is resting her hand lightly on the back of a small brown dog with a tail like a feather duster. Alex, in the painting, is seated, her legs tucked under her. Like the other figures she appears solid, solemn, yet also languorous, somnolent and strangely blind, her downcast eyes merely suggested by violet shadows. No one, except possibly for the dog, who has a friendly, eager expression, is smiling.

Alex stops next in front of a painting of a young woman leaning against a tree in a grove. Oh, I don't want to see this, she thinks. She keeps looking, however. The woman in the painting is her. And yet it is not her; she didn't ever look that cowed, that miserably meek, surely? Not even when she was young and unhappy and far from home. Désirée altered her face, pinched it in, made her features elongated and neurotic; sulky. (Alex has nurtured, over the years, a small nagging fear that this was done spitefully.) In the painting, she has her arms full of quickly gathered lupins and daisies, which she remembers as being dusty with pollen and rank smelling, as if pulled out of a swamp. At the dark centre of each flower was a restless corona of small black insects, some of which had tried to creep up her bare arms. Désirée was mixing paints on her palette, absorbed, businesslike, mixing the paints and then squinting at Alex, sizing her up.

Alex remembers how, while she was posing for this painting, a shiny green beetle with long delicately jointed legs plopped onto a leaf right in front of her face. There she was, pressed up against the rough, raw bark of a tree, a woodland nymph undergoing a painful metamorphosis into a more rudimentary, natural state. While all she truly wanted, or so she remembers thinking, was to go back to the house for a nice hot cup of tea. She felt awkward and alternately too hot and too cold, and Désirée had skilfully caught all this. She had portrayed with great precision the splotches of colour on Alex's cheeks, the agitation in her eyes, the thirst in her throat, and turned it all to advantage: she had made Alex look as if she were about to run away or go mad or make, suddenly, a strange appalling confession. (Which, in Alex's case, would go something like this: I am enthralled with a man, another woman's husband. I dream of him. I have carved his name into the trunk of a tree in this very grove. I carved so finely, with such precision, that no one will ever discover it, least of all you, Désirée.)

An idea had come to her, Désirée then said. When she was painting someone, it seemed to her that she understood that person better than anyone else did. Better, in fact, than the subject understood himself, or herself. For example, everything Alex thought and felt was clear to her, *at that very moment.* "I see all your most secret thoughts," she said, and Alex said, "Then you know I'm getting hungry and I want to sit down for a while." She rubbed her forehead, erasing any errant thoughts. "No one can read minds," she said.

"Oh, you'd be surprised," Désirée said, unperturbed. "You'd be surprised at what I can do."

Désirée's art has the power to supplant memory, Alex now realizes. Or at least to recast it. When she looks at these paintings, she is seeing the past through Désirée's eyes, not her own. Alex thinks the daisies were crawling with insects; she thinks she felt the tree pressing into her back. She thinks she saw a beetle on a leaf. How far can she trust such evanescent minutiae? Not very far, she decides. She can't even be sure if she looked like the young woman in the painting: petulant, cross, pale with fatigue. It is Désirée's memory, not hers, that is present in each painting, like some kind of fixative applied across the surface. This is the artist's power, solely, Alex thinks, as she stares at herself, the self she may or may not have been thirty-eight years earlier.

In 1957, Alex and Désirée, and Désirée's daughter Loren, then four years old, travelled to Wales, so that Désirée could stay at Grove's End, which was a kind of retreat, or refuge, for artists, owned by a man named Felix Curtis. This Felix Curtis — Alex was never comfortable calling him either Felix or Mr. Curtis — had set up Grove's End as a place where artists of all kinds, painters, writers, poets, could go in order to live and work in peace, without distractions, for a certain amount of time. Alex can no longer remember how Désirée came to hear of Grove's End, but she does remember her passionate determination to go there. Désirée saw it as her salvation, the only possible place where she could be quiet and think what she wanted to do and, best of all, paint every single day.

"I want you to come with me, though," she said to Alex. "I can't leave Loren behind, she's too little. Tom wouldn't know what to do with her. And anyway, he has to work." Tom was Désirée's husband. "It's the only solution, Alex. You have to come. And it'll be like a holiday for you, you'll see."

Once she was there, once they were all settled in at Grove's End, Désirée did indeed begin to work. She studied painting from great huge books Felix Curtis supplied her with; she went out in the morning and sketched in charcoal; she experimented with watercolours; she did as she pleased. And because this was also meant to be "like a holiday," she planned picnics, like the one she was later to paint.

On that day, Alex remembers — and she does remember this, it is her own memory, she is sure, not Désirée's — Désirée woke up early and ran downstairs in her dressing gown to put a chicken in the oven to roast. Then she ran back upstairs and rapped sharply on Alex's bedroom door, and on Robin Pritchard's bedroom door. "Come on, you two, I need help," she called out. "I need a picnic brigade, on the double." By the time Alex dressed, and got Loren dressed, and the two of them went down to the kitchen, Désirée was baking scones. She put Alex to work chopping up boiled potatoes for potato salad and preparing the devilled eggs. Loren insisted on helping too, so Alex let her kneel on a chair at the table so that she could sprinkle paprika on the eggs. Robin Pritchard came downstairs and poured himself tea and sat at the table and moaned, "It's dreadfully early, isn't it? I am not at peace with this hour of the day, Désirée."

"What a shame," Désirée said. "It is the best time." In passing, she touched the back of his neck with her hand, leaving a floury mark. She never missed a chance, Alex thought, marvelling. Her own hand, stirring sugar into her tea, was only a few inches from Robin Pritchard's hand, but she would never, never. However, if she did, if she felt like being bold, as bold as Désirée, she could well imagine the sensation: a fine tingling warmth along the skin, as far up as the wrist. A hotness, in her face, betraying her. Désirée never blushed; her head was not foolishly transparent, like Alex's.

Later, Désirée swept a plaid wool rug off the couch in the sitting room and went outside to spread it on the grass. Robin Pritchard had, by this time, gone back upstairs, to work on his poems. Désirée had dressed in a skirt and a sleeveless blouse and had darkened her mouth with red lipstick and put on gold hoop earrings. She smoothed the rug over the grass, which was, as Alex could feel through the soles of her shoes, damp and more than damp in places, soggy. It had been raining, for days.

"It isn't really a lawn, is it?" Désirée said. "It's more of a bog. Never mind, the sun is warm."

Although not apparent in Désirée's painting, a white mist, caused by the sudden warmth of the sun on the wet ground, had been rising from the grass that day. It made Alex think of souls, the souls of the wildflowers, perhaps, rising towards heaven. (Being at Grove's End made her think in such foolish, poetical terms.) The effect of this mist, gauzy and indeterminate, was lovely, as was the softly filtered sun in the grove of ancient oak trees — there really was a grove at Grove's End. Robin told them that one of the ancient Welsh gods, none other than Gwydion, the god of the arts, he believed, slept curled around the roots of the trees and would one day awaken and make everyone at Grove's End immortal. Robin lay on his back with his head propped up on his arm and smiled up at Désirée. That morning, he told her, he had written two fine long poems. Later, he would read them again, he said, and discover — to his sorrow — that they were rubbish.

Désirée opened the wicker basket and began taking out the chicken, still warm, unfortunately, she said, and bowls of salad and the devilled eggs, also not quite cold enough and crimson with paprika. ("What lovely red eggs!" she said to Loren.) She unwrapped a fragrant loaf of crusty bread, and passed it to Robin, who immediately tore off a piece and began eating it. When the dog, a great scrounger who had managed to insinuate himself into the picnic, began to whine, Robin broke off a few more pieces and tossed them to him. Loren then wanted to do the same.

"The bread is for people, not dogs," Désirée told her. "You're setting a bad example," she said to Robin, reaching over and swatting his hand. He said, "Ah, but the child is enjoying herself, aren't you Loren, *bach?*" He gave Loren a piece of the loaf so that she could feed the dog. "Watch that the doggie doesn't nip your fingers," Alex said, a small, sensible warning, that, for some reason, annoyed Désirée. "Oh, you, you're always looking for the worst to happen, Alex," she said, unfairly, Alex thought. And then, even more unfairly, she added: "You must stop that. It's a bad habit."

If Robin Pritchard had not turned up at Grove's End, nothing would have happened, Alex believed. Nothing, that was, other than a great deal of talk about art and lots of walks in the mountains and the valley, and getting used to the custom of a high-carbohydrate tea at four o'clock, with sausage rolls and ham and mustard sandwiches and, occasionally, rice pudding as a treat for Loren. But Robin Pritchard was inevitable, Alex could see, or at least came to believe. He was a Welsh poet, a dark figure straight out of Welsh bardic history. "Ah, Robin Pritchard," Felix Curtis said. "He's a marvel, is Robin Pritchard. Not a word of a lie, now; he's devilishly good. Nearly as good as Dylan Thomas himself."

Alex and Désirée did not meet Robin Pritchard at Grove's End. They came upon him in a bookshop, quite by chance, one wet afternoon in July. The name of the bookshop was Madog's Corner, and the poet, about to read from his own work, was in the middle of saying, "Madog, impartial protector and defender of all manner of poets, those significant and those highly forgettable. How suitable the name is, is it not? This lovely bookshop, preserve of the wild-eyed poet. A sacred grove, yes, most sacred."

There was a shuffling of feet and backsides on chairs and an appreciative wave of self-conscious laughter.

He looked, Alex thought, more like Rupert Brooke than Dylan Thomas. He had thoroughly wicked, enchanting eyes, large, luminous, richly brown. His thick black hair curled over his high white forehead. She watched him while pretending oblivion, browsing through the cookbooks. Désirée, on the other hand, was plainly intrigued. Her eyes were bright, her lips parted in the slightest of smiles. Alex tightened her grip on a book of Welsh recipes. Loren, who was with them, tugged on her coat sleeve.

"Yes, yes, in a minute, love," she whispered to the child.

She watched Désirée taking books from the shelves, opening them, shutting them, putting them back.

"I want to go," Loren said, pulling on Alex's arm.

"Yes, we will go," Alex said. "We are going, right now."

It was warm in the bookshop. Loren's face was flushed and her nose was running. Alex glanced at the women in their navy blue macs and tweed skirts perched on folding chairs in front of the poet. It seemed to her that there were two groups of women in attendance, of different ages, one middle-aged and attentive, the other young, dreamy, full of smiles, equally attentive perhaps, but more to the poet's fine eyes than to his words. Very cleverly, by not taking a seat, by appearing not even to listen particularly, Désirée avoided joining either group. Alex was amused by this. Désirée simply leaned over one of the women while Robin Pritchard was reading and casually plucked a copy of his book from a stack on the table.

"Excuse me," she said softly, holding her hair away from her face. Wordlessly she paid for the book, tucked it under her arm, and then walked out of the bookshop with Alex and Loren trotting after her. They went down the street and got into Felix Curtis's grey Hillman Minx, which they had borrowed for the afternoon.

"Well. I am full of admiration," Alex said to Désirée. Désirée smiled and bumped a front wheel up over the curb. "Whoops. Daydreaming," she said. She pulled out into the road and shifted gears. "I beg your pardon, Alex?" she said. "What are you talking about now? Admiration for what?"

And then, later that same day, Robin Pritchard appeared in the dining room at Grove's End, his hair hanging in his eyes and dripping wet, his shoes, which he had removed and was holding in his hand, soaked. "Good evening. Excuse me. I walked. Where shall I put these?" he began, and Felix Curtis, from his place at the head of the table, said, "Robin. Dear boy. Welcome, welcome. Put them on the radiator, that's a good man, and do, please, join us. Have a cup of nice hot tea."

Désirée said, "Pour Robin a cup of tea, Alex."

Alex had been buttering bread fingers for Loren to dip into her soft-boiled egg. She wiped her hands and poured a cup of tea. It was black, and not very warm. She handed it to him. All roads evidently led directly to Grove's End. All poets, writers, artists, stonemasons too, for that matter, she shouldn't be surprised, ended up here. Felix Curtis, patron of the arts, gathered them in and found them a warm pile of straw.

Robin Pritchard said, Hadn't he seen Alex and Désirée earlier, in the bookshop? "With your little girl," he said to Alex, and, before she could correct him, Désirée began saying how much she'd enjoyed listening to him. "I bought your book, by the way. I'm going to read it tonight," she said.

"I think we will have to persuade Robin to give us a private reading," Felix Curtis said. "For our personal enjoyment." He was feeding his dog scraps of meat under the table. The dog's jaws kept snapping shut with loud cracks, like breaking crockery.

"It would be an honour," Robin Pritchard said, smiling at Désirée and turning his teacup around in its saucer.

Seven of Désirée's paintings in this exhibition in Seattle were completed during that summer at Grove's End, and are actually referred to, in a pamphlet Alex picked up at the front door, as "The Grove's End Paintings." There are also some pencil sketches from the same time, and a few oil pastels of Loren, which are Alex's favourites, and which, it seems to her, really ought to belong to Loren.

The pamphlet also points out that, sadly, Désirée didn't produce a great deal in her brief life, her tragically short life, and Alex thinks wryly that, Yes, that was true enough, Désirée's life was brief, but not, she thought, tragic, and, if she hadn't produced a great deal, it had as much to do with her unfortunate habit of tearing up or otherwise destroying her work if it didn't please her as with anything else. In fact, the wastebaskets and dustbins at Grove's End were always brimming over, and not only with Désirée's discards. Artistic dissatisfaction was greatly in vogue, it seemed to Alex, in 1957. No one ever seemed especially pleased with what was accomplished, and in fact there was always some writer or poet striding manically around the low-ceilinged rooms or else sitting slumped, greatly despondent, in an armchair.

At Grove's End, Désirée said to Alex: "Oh, God, sometimes it comes crashing down on me. The realization that I'm not an artist. I don't know what I'm doing here. I'm surprised I haven't been sent packing. Alex, I'm a dabbler. Horrid word. But that's what I am. A dabbler."

"Oh, Désirée. You know that's nonsense," Alex said automatically. She said again, with more enthusiasm, "You are definitely not a dabbler." She sat down and picked up some sewing. She was mending the hem in one of Loren's dresses. Loren was sitting on the floor, taking the apron off a doll in Welsh national costume that Felix Curtis had given her. It occurred to Alex that she had learned to absorb

Désirée's rages and doubts as placidly as if she were a pool of water, the same pool into which Narcissus had stared with such devotion, with such need. This was her role in life; it was a role she had willingly taken upon herself, immersed herself in: Désirée needed her, Loren needed her. But perhaps she was the one being too intense, too analytical. Perhaps she was simply *here*. She squinted, trying to thread her needle.

"Are we going home, then?" she said, knowing what the answer would be, and Désirée, purged by now of her distress, replied, calmly, "Oh, I'm not ready to give up yet. It's just that it's so hard. You wouldn't believe how hard, Alex."

Alex and Désirée had been friends long before Désirée married Tom. They had been wild young things together, intent on experiencing everything possible, as quickly as possible — for why else were they alive? Désirée had said — including fast cars, cigarettes, hard liquor, haunting love affairs with virtual strangers. At least, they had dreamed of these things. Mostly, they had driven up and down the coastal highways of the Pacific Northwest in Désirée's battered red MG. And then they began making detours in order to call in on Désirée's friend, Tom, who owned a garden nursery on several acres of former farmland in Washington State, overlooking Puget Sound. She wanted to paint here, Désirée said. She wanted to try to capture the fog shrouding the opposite shore, the way it was reflected like a milky stain on the water. And then the sun suddenly breaking through and turning the rain-drenched air to gold and silver, the finest elements.

Désirée kept saying, jokingly, that Tom was perfect for Alex. He was quiet, home-loving, honourable, oh, yes, a truly honourable individual, with a firm abiding *innate* love for the soil, the family, the community, his country. "A real square," Désirée had said, laughing. "*Exactly* your kind."

He was. She had to agree. He was indeed her kind. She liked Tom very much. This did her no good, however; she could see he didn't notice her, certainly not in the way he noticed Désirée.

It's you he likes, Alex said, and Désirée said, Well, too bad. She wasn't interested, she said. She was never going to be serious about anyone; she was never going to get married. Once a woman married she really didn't have anything of herself left over. Désirée had, just that year, discovered that it was art that mattered to her. She was wedded to her art. Oh, yes? Alex said. Was it possible, Alex sometimes wondered, that Désirée believed the things she said? Did she even hear what she was saying?

They spent a lot of time that summer hanging around the nursery. They offered to help out. They learned to pinch back the growing tips on geraniums, and to transplant tender young seedlings from flats into pots, and at the same time they watched Tom as he worked at the far end of the greenhouse. He was tall, lean, with fine, light-brown hair, and the slightest limp, acquired not in the war (he had enlisted several months before the war's end, on his eighteenth birthday), but from an injury to the ligaments of the knee in a football game the previous fall. They knew that he liked fried chicken and vanilla ice cream, and preferred coffee to tea. He admired — how was this possible? Désirée and Alex laughingly asked each other — John Foster Dulles. He thought Doris Day was "cute." "Well, she is cute, I suppose," Désirée said. "Cuter than John Foster Dulles, anyway."

"Ask him if he has any snapshots of himself we could have," Désirée said. "No, you," Alex said.

"No, you," Désirée said.

The thing was, artists had to experience every single thing that life had to offer, Désirée began to say. Why should this or that way of life be considered superior? she wanted to know. The true artist was able to make use of everything, she said. Besides, she certainly didn't want to turn into an old maid with dried paint under her fingernails and one of those beret things stuck on her head.

When Désirée married Tom, Alex was her bridesmaid. And exactly a year later she was godmother to Désirée's daughter, Loren Alexandra. On the day of her baptism, the baby lay stiff as a china doll in Alex's arms. Then she took a great gulp of air and began to shriek. She cried all the way home from the church, and continued to cry for a good part of every day, and night, from then on. Alex walked up and down with her; she patted her back and tried singing to her.

Désirée stared at the baby helplessly; when Loren cried, she also wept. She cried more helplessly than the baby. "Babies do cry a lot," Alex said. "But they get over it."

"No, they don't," Désirée said. "They just go from one thing to another. I think she's coming down with a cold now. I don't know what to do with her, I just don't." Désirée used to throw herself down on the floor in the living room after Loren had finally fallen asleep. She would say that she couldn't survive. "I'm so tired," she said. "I'm so tired I just want to die." Tom took her seriously. "Don't say that, you have everything to live for," he would say, trying to pull her up from the floor.

Leave her alone, Alex wanted to say. Leave her alone; she'll get fed up with herself. Instead, she offered to stay and see to the baby during the night, and Désirée would say, "Oh would you Alex, are you sure you don't mind?" "I truly don't mind," Alex had said. "I truly don't."

Alex was good with babies, even babies as ornery — that was Tom's word — as her godchild. Alex was patient, and able to get by on very little sleep. She enjoyed helping out when needed. This was what she told herself. And she tried very hard, with all her will, not to covet what Désirée had. The truth was, when Alex had first seen Loren, only an hour or so after she had been born, her heart had — as they said — melted. She had lightly, reverently, brushed her fingers across the baby's head, along the side of her face. In the shape of her eyes, the dimple in her chin, the fine brown hair, she was a small replica of Tom. She had to force herself to hand the baby back to Désirée. "Be careful, don't drop her," she had actually said. What was happening to her? she had thought in dismay. She wanted this baby and she wanted Tom and she wanted Tom's house, a splendid white house with green shutters at every window, and she wanted the flowering cherry trees, and the view of Puget Sound, and the salt smell of the sea and the soft grey fog manifesting itself all at once in place of the clear sky. Yes, let her be honest: she wanted all this, and at the same time she felt horribly ashamed and impatient and angry with herself. She kept thinking, But what shall I do?

Loren was four years old, that summer at Grove's End. Désirée enrolled her in a Montessori kindergarten in the village, and then sent her off every morning with Alex. The teacher, Mrs. Clara Fradkin, spoke of herself, to Alex, as being exceptionally devoted to children, to their development and happiness. Loren and the other children called her "Mama Clara," and happily followed her around the schoolroom like ducklings. Loren, who even at the age of four cried easily and often, as if this was, for her, the most natural form of expression, cried when it was time to go home.

"This is the exact opposite of what usually happens," Mrs. Fradkin said severely, removing Loren's hands from her skirt. "This is a very unusual situation. Do you have good rapport with Loren?" she asked of Alex, who explained once again that she was not the mother, she was only a friend, a close friend.

"I'm an aunt, really. I'm Aunt Alex, aren't I, Loren?" she said.

Loren buried her face in the folds of Mrs. Fradkin's substantial skirts. Mrs. Fradkin wore black cloth slippers and print dresses under voluminous aprons and her plentiful grey hair was twisted in thick braids around her head.

"Perhaps the mother should come for Loren," she said to Alex.

Alex agreed. She thought Loren would like very much to have her mother come to the school, and she also imagined that Désirée would be delighted to see this schoolroom, with its long wood tables and its easels and paint pots and flowers in jam jars and its scarred wood floor. And surely, if Désirée caught sight of Mrs. Fradkin, she would immediately reach for her paintbrush. She would, Alex imagined, have Mrs. Fradkin sit with her feet in a bucket of steamy water, eating apples. Or knitting, with a fluffy cat asleep on her lap. She would have her sit in the cold blue light from an uncurtained window, reading an antique leather-bound book. The wrinkles in Mrs. Fradkin's intelligent and sensible face would be accentuated. The mole beside her upper lip would be preeminent. Alex, seeing this painting in her mind, became quite excited. She wanted to pick up a brush and begin work on it herself.

"Loren's mother would come for Loren if she could, but she is always very busy," Alex explained, trying to grasp Loren's hot damp hand in hers and discreetly disentangle her from the teacher. "She is at Grove's End," she added, because she suspected that Mrs. Fradkin would have heard of Grove's End, but Mrs. Fradkin, unimpressed, merely said, "I think the mother should at least on some occasions call for the child. It is the child that matters, after all."

"Mrs. Fradkin does not approve of you," Alex later told Désirée.

"The club is always looking for new members," Désirée said. "Let her join. It's not exclusive, believe me." She was drinking a glass of red wine. She had a letter from Tom in her hand, and she waved the sheets of paper at Alex. "He wants me to come home," she said. "He misses me. He's offering to take me somewhere wonderful if I come home now, this minute. Mexico, Jamaica." The letter slid from her hand to the floor.

"I would love to go to Jamaica," she said. "Some day. I just don't like it that he puts conditions on everything. *If* I come home now, he says. If I'm a good girl. Well, to hell with that." Then she said, "Robin is taking me to Pembrokeshire, to see the town where he lived once. Where he had a house. Or his parents had a house. I think it was before the war. I meant to ask, would you mind looking after Loren while I'm gone?"

"No, I wouldn't mind," said Alex, not meeting Désirée's eyes.

"We could take her along, but I'm sure she'd be bored. So this would be a better arrangement, wouldn't it?"

"Oh, yes," Alex said. "I suppose it would."

"I know what you're thinking," Désirée said. "You're thinking that I'm terribly wicked to be going anywhere with Robin. Aren't you? Be honest, Alex."

"Oh, Désirée, I don't know," said Alex. "It's up to you, isn't it? I mean, I don't mind, I'm happy to look after Loren."

"I don't want you to judge me. Oh, Alex, I want some happiness out of life. Not always later, later. Not that I wasn't happy before. I was. I think I was. But this is different." She picked up her wineglass and took a drink. "I just don't want you to think badly of me." Then she put the glass down again and wrapped her arms around her knees and smiled at Alex, a sunny smile, full of complicity, as if they were girls again, students cutting classes, preparing for another adventurous journey in Désirée's red car.

On the kitchen wall at Grove's End there was a copy of a painting by Henri Matisse: *The Joy of Life*. It was a scene of nude figures lying around in what seemed to Alex a post-apocalyptic garden. Her first impression was that the figures had, in a sense, all turned their faces to the wall. They had finished with life; now they were preoccupied with what they could learn through their senses, through the tips of their fingers, or by gazing for timeless moments at the closed lids of their eyes. In her opinion, at least to begin with, the painting was immoral, or did she mean amoral? She tried to explain this to Désirée, who said, "Oh, Alex, you are an old fuddy-duddy."

Désirée took the print down from the wall and wiped a cobweb from the backing. She propped it up closer to the window and studied it avidly.

"Well, I don't care for it," Alex said. "I don't think I like the colours. They're harsh."

"You know, it's not about life," Désirée said. "It's not really about the joy of ordinary life. It's about the joy of art, I think. It's about the sheer joy that can be attained through art. Through the simplicity of art. Which is, oh, I don't know, seeing with perfectly innocent eyes. Does that make any sense?"

Look how delicate the figures were, how insubstantial, she then said. And then above them were the great massed dream-shapes of the trees, and the clouds, and the sea.

"It's decadent, though," Alex said. "How can you see decadence through inno-cent eyes? It's strained, in a way. As if the artist is reaching for something he can't quite grasp."

"Perhaps that is what painting is all about," Désirée said. "Perhaps that is where the joyfulness comes in. Working at something so hard you almost die of it." She smiled gently, as if Alex couldn't be expected to understand, or to share in this vision of art. Sometimes it seemed to Alex that everyone at Grove's End gave her the same look. It made them all feel superior, she supposed. She didn't care. She knew she wasn't an artist, or a poet. The only reason she was here at all was to look after Loren while Désirée worked. There had been trouble about this at first: Felix Curtis had told Désirée he was very sorry, but, no, there wasn't room for a friend and certainly not for a child. He said this in a letter, before they left America. I can't come without my daughter, Désirée had written back. Felix Curtis had replied immedi-ately, by telephone. He had said he would make room for Désirée's daughter and for Alex. He would sleep in the garage, if necessary. On the floor in the garage. When she finished talking to him, Désirée had said to Alex, "I think he's mad."

When they arrived at Grove's End, Felix Curtis immediately presented Loren with the Welsh doll. Alex had thought, in surprise, Why, how sweet of him. He was older than she had expected, and slight, dark, with odd, almost unnaturally large, flat, glistening eyes. He kept a tin of toffees especially for Loren on the mantelpiece. "Would you like a sweetie?" he would say. "Only one, that's a good girl. You don't want to spoil your tea."

In the evenings at Grove's End, everyone gathered around Felix Curtis. They would wait (there were generally three or four writers or painters staying there at a time), seemingly mildly amused at their own eagerness, for Felix Curtis to say some-thing tantalizing or provocative. And he, obviously relishing the moment, would lean back with his pipe clamped between his teeth and his dog curled at his feet. (There was a watercolour of Felix Curtis, done by Désirée, in this exact pose: fire-light flickering across his face, his eyes darker than ever, more lustrous, a cartoon-ishly ardent assembly crouched at his feet in the murky orange light, and in the recesses of the room shelves of books, paintings askew on the walls.)

Not long after Robin Pritchard arrived at Grove's End, he told Alex and Désirée that he firmly believed Felix Curtis was a reincarnation of Madog ap Maredudd, manifesting all over again that mighty warrior's special fondness and regard for poets. "Madog and Felix. They are one and the same, in my opinion," he said. Désirée said she didn't know about Madog ap Whatever-his-name-was, but she certainly felt that Felix Curtis was her salvation. She worshipped him. He was like a religious figure to her, she said. A priest, a saint. Once, he had casually informed her that he was actually given to visions, religious visions, angels and demons, in spite of the fact that he was not religious in an orthodox sense. It was something in his brain that caused this, he had said: a bit of loose wiring.

"Now, let me put this question," Felix Curtis was saying. "Can we afford art? What are we doing, when we indulge ourselves with our personal, narrow 'artistic' interpretations of history, of nature, of humanity?" And what, he wondered, did art have to do with memory? With the psychology of memory? With the "persistence of vision?" He winked at Alex: Now there was a question, he said to her. And here was another: How did the artist deal with the strictures of bourgeois life, which as everyone knew hampered and even destroyed more promising careers than did any other factor?

Hah, Alex thought. She had just finished washing up a sink full of dirty dishes which had been ignored by everyone else. What about the strictures of Bohemian life? she wanted to ask. But Désirée was agreeing feverishly.

"Yes, yes," she had said. "That is exactly what happens. I'm sure that if I hadn't come here, I would have simply stopped painting."

"I don't believe that," said Robin. "I don't believe that for a moment." He was perched beside Désirée, on a hassock. He had helped himself to a toffee from the tin on the mantelpiece and was slowly unwrapping it. Désirée was half-reclining in a chair, her head back, her legs crossed, one foot swinging. She was wearing sandals and a blue dress, and her hair, which she hadn't had cut since coming to Wales, was held in place with one of Loren's hair ribbons. She put out her hand and Robin caught it in his and as they smiled at each other Alex felt, fleetingly, a disturbance, rather like an electric shock, pass through her, and, she imagined, through the walls of the house. And at the same time she saw the look of surprise, of recognition, on Felix Curtis's face, followed at once by a quick, pleased, and even proud smile, as if he were saying to himself, Well, it is all happening just as I planned, after all.

One day when Alex went to pick up Loren, Mrs. Fradkin told her how much she, and the children, enjoyed Loren's songs.

"Her songs?" Alex said.

"Indeed, yes. Loren invents the most lovely little songs. She sings them for us. But you must know this. The songs are little ballads about Loren's daily life, the things that happen to her. She sings about you. And about her mother. She sings about a little brown dog that likes to eat bread."

Alex bent down and began helping Loren into her sweater. Her cardigan, Loren called it, in her new, shy, quick Welsh voice. "I didn't know you liked singing, Loren," she said to her. "Is it a secret? Are you going to sing for me and Mummy when we get home?"

Loren shrugged herself out of Alex's grasp. She wanted to do up her own buttons, she said. She knew how: Mama Clara had taught her.

Alex took Loren straight from the school to a greengrocer's where she was able to use the telephone to place a collect call to Tom. This was an arrangement she and Tom had made, without Désirée's knowledge. Of course, he also heard from Désirée, but Désirée often forgot to call, and when she did she didn't seem interested in talking about practical matters, according to Tom. He wanted to know if she was really working, if she was finding that she could spend more time painting now than she had at home. And she wouldn't tell him, not sensibly. Also, he couldn't make her tell him when she and Loren, and Alex, were coming home.

Alex telephoned at about two in the afternoon, when it was early morning in Washington State and Tom was still at the house. (It took some time for the call to be completed, and while she waited she tried to picture Tom sitting at his kitchen table with a cup of coffee, his eye on the telephone, but instead she saw him striding happily through the glassy humid air of the greenhouse, up between flats of recently misted plants.)

As soon as Alex heard Tom's voice, she pressed the phone to Loren's ear.

"Say hello to Daddy," she prompted in a whisper. Loren became too shy to speak. Her eyes lit up and she smiled, but she wouldn't say a word.

Alex took the phone back and told Tom that evidently Loren was a singing star. "She's never sung a note of music in my presence, but this Mrs. Fradkin says she makes up whole songs, long stories set to music. Today at school, she made a puppet out of a hanky. It has wool hair and button eyes, one red and one black. She won't let go of it for a minute."

"That sounds like Loren," Tom said. And then he said, "Has Désirée said anything definite to you about coming home?"

"I'm not sure," Alex said. "I don't think so." This was on a Friday afternoon, when Désirée was in fact at Grove's End packing an overnight bag for the weekend trip to Pembrokeshire with Robin Pritchard. She thought: I could tell him where she's going, what she's up to. I could say I had to tell him because I'm concerned about Loren. I'm genuinely worried that Loren will find out that her mother behaves like a perfect slut, and that she has no respect for herself or for her marriage. Also, there's a certain amount of creeping about, doors opening and closing, up on the second floor at Grove's End, in the middle of the night. Secret (supposedly) kisses on the stairs. Cosy whispers behind partly closed doors. She stared at a glass jar full of pink rock candy beside the cash register. She was mute. She was shaking with rage. She knew she wouldn't say anything. She couldn't. Ever.

"Do you want to try talking to Loren again?" Alex said. She put the phone against Loren's ear. Loren pressed her puppet against her mouth and scrunched her face up in concentration. "She likes listening to you, but she doesn't want to say anything," Alex then explained to Tom. "She isn't going to sing, either, I guess. Maybe she's going to turn out to be a poet." She waited, as if Tom was going to be able to read some kind of coded message from this. Poet, get it? Robin Pritchard? A weekend in Pembrokeshire?

"And how are you doing?" Tom asked.

"Oh, fine, thank you," Alex said. "I'm looking forward to coming home. It's nice here, but I get homesick every now and then, to tell you the truth."

This art show Alex is attending is being held in a large warehouse-like room that had obviously once served as a dance studio. There are other people here, a few, women mostly, standing transfixed in front of the paintings, murmuring to each other. Alex has overheard one young woman saying that Désirée's paintings are beautiful, perhaps too beautiful: sentimental. "Well, definitely beautiful, but not sentimental, I wouldn't say," her friend says, pointing at the picture of Alex languishing in the grove of trees. "She looks scared, to me. Lost. Makes you wonder what happened to her next. Maybe she was running away from some creep. Her husband or boyfriend or something. I bet that's what's supposed to be going on there."

The ceiling is very high and there are practice bars along the walls in places, beneath the paintings. The wood floor feels elastic under Alex's feet. Loren took ballet lessons once. Alex had wanted Loren to have everything: dance lessons, birthday parties, a bed with a white lace canopy, dolls, pretty dresses. Perhaps all this had been intended as compensation, but she didn't think so. Her feelings for Loren have never felt ambivalent to her, or marred by guilt, or a sense of inadequacy: she really does think of Loren as her daughter.

On the plane coming home from Grove's End, Alex had tried to distract Loren by drawing stick figures. She tried to draw the Welsh doll, but it ended up looking like Mrs. Fradkin with her limp print dresses and her pinafores. Her mouth, a smudged pencil mark, spoke clearly enough to Alex: It is always better if the mother comes home with the child. Loren had tucked her hand inside her cloth puppet and pressed its mismatched button eyes against the window, so that it too could look out on the empty grey sky above the Atlantic.

Alex sits down on a bench, facing Désirée's paintings. Now that they are at a distance from her, she feels a little less overwhelmed, although the figures in the painting of the picnic seem to have assumed colossal proportions. They dwarf the sky, the garden, the house. They tower, strange, surprised, wonderful, above Alex. Why, she wonders, did Désirée choose to do this particular painting on such a vast scale? All of Désirée's paintings, the ones here in this gallery, are possessed of such vividness, indeed such urgency, that Alex finds herself feeling oddly enervated. She wonders if Désirée hovers, an unseen but discernible presence in the room. Or, perhaps Alex's sudden discomfiture is simply a result of not being used to art shows. It is true that she and Tom don't ordinarily visit art galleries. They do go sailing a lot. They love gardening. They read. Anyway, she didn't even tell Tom about this show. In fact, the only reason she's here at all is that Loren phoned to tell her about her mother's paintings. "I hope you can come down to see them," she had said. "I think it would be awfully sad if you missed them."

It suddenly occurs to Alex that she's put a lot of energy into her life. In a way, she has been the real artist. Or sculptor, perhaps. She's worked with stone, with the immovable weight of time and circumstance and personality. She has achieved one perfect work of art; that is, she's managed to get what she desired, what she most desired, which is Tom and his handsome white house overlooking Puget Sound. She has been married to Tom for thirty-two years. And she is very happy. She has three grown children, including Loren, who is now forty years old, a teacher, inspired, perhaps, by the early example of Mrs. Fradkin.

Loren has already been here, to see Désirée's paintings. "They're utterly amazing," she said. "Imagine how hard it must have been for a woman to work as an artist in the 1950s. My mother must have been an incredibly determined woman to have accomplished so much. And brave." Had she known how brave she was? Loren has asked Alex.

In 1957, when she and Loren had finally arrived home from Britain, Tom had been waiting for them. Alex had impulsively, gently, put her arms around him, in the manner of Mrs. Fradkin comforting one of her baby ducklings. She and Tom were courteously silent with one another; the one subject of consequence between them at that time was Désirée, who had chosen to stay behind. How could they possibly speak of her, how could they mention her name, when they both knew that she was in an openly adulterous (that was the way people talked in 1957; that was the word they used) relationship with Robin Pritchard?

Désirée wrote to Tom asking for a little more time. She kept saying, "Don't give up on me." Tom read portions of these letters to Alex. And then he tore them up.

I'm afraid, Desiree wrote to Alex, *that if I come home I won't be able to paint and I won't be happy ever again. I have to take my chances here. I know that you, at least, will understand.*

Alex had her own ideas, her own fears, and has them still: that Désirée unwittingly made herself noticeable to one of those incandescent jealous gods, the kind with a keen eye for anyone who dares to set herself apart. Désirée, hiking in the mountains of Snowdonia with Robin, became lost. Or rather, both she and Robin became lost. It began to snow. It was early spring, the weather cruelly changeable. There had been a snowstorm, in fact, only days before. Robin decided that he would go on alone, as fast as possible, in the hope of sighting the shore of a certain lake, which he thought would help him to get his bearings. Désirée, tired of waiting, had tried to make her own way down the mountain. She walked, Robin theorized, until it became dark and she was simply too tired to go on. She found a place to rest, and in resting, was overcome.

Alex knows all this because Robin wrote to her. He wrote her several letters, heartbroken and strangely lyrical, full of descriptions of snow and frost. Alex felt as if she were reading a fairy tale.

How can she believe that Désirée's life ended in the monochromatic white noise of a snowstorm, all colour and warmth drained from the world around her? Of course she can't. She prefers to think of Désirée (and why shouldn't this be true?) living under an assumed name in a comfortable cottage somewhere in the Welsh countryside, her vision clear, unclouded, persistent. At the end of each day she cleans the paint from her brushes and sets them neatly aside. The air smells of linseed oil and turpentine and lilac. (A lilac tree grows outside the window, Alex is quite sure.) Désirée has given away every single thing that mattered to her so that she can work in peace. She paints from pure memory, her colours light and clear. Outside her cottage is a grove where Welsh gods, all of them bearing a strong family resemblance to Felix Curtis, sleep curled at the roots of ancient trees, clutching in their arms the latent gift of individual immortality.

The idea comes to Alex that she and Désirée have shared a life between them. This idea slips perfectly, unexpectedly, and very clearly into her mind as she studies, perhaps for the last time, Désirée's paintings. It is, Alex thinks, as if she has carried on all these years inside the life Désirée set aside. She is a practical, and, she hopes, graceful custodian. Linked, she and Désirée have managed to discover joy, more even than, separately, they deserved, its strength and radiance, its sheer power running through the delicate yet reliable veins of one singular form.

DOUGLAS GLOVER is the author of three story collections and three novels, including the critically acclaimed *The Life and Times of Captain N.* (Knopf/McClelland), hailed by *The Chicago Tribune* as one of the best books of 1993. Glover's story book *A Guide to Animal Behaviour* was nominated for the 1990 Governor-General's Award. His stories have been frequently anthologized, notably in *The Best American Short Stories* and *Best Canadian Stories*.

A PIECE OF THE TRUE CROSS

DOUGLAS GLOVER

I

My sister Darla was struck by lightning the summer we bought the house on Block Island.

She wasn't killed, and now, twenty years later, she is married to an investment banker named Tad and has two healthy sons. She complains of deafness in her left ear and a residual ache in her left elbow and shoulder. She is apprehensive when storms approach. She claims sometimes to see auras around people's heads. A lot of people claim to see auras, but I generally disbelieve them. Darla, I believe.

I was thirteen that year, and the world seemed an ineffably sad and lonely place to me. Our father had founded a chemical company with plants in Georgia and Louisiana. He had come from the South, those were his roots, but he had never taken us back for so much as a visit. Summers we usually went to Nantucket or

Provincetown — until we bought the old Waring place on Block Island. I spent my falls, winters and springs at a boarding school in the Berkshires.

I was standing at my bedroom window watching storm clouds advance over the sound when the lightning struck our house. More distant bolts were etching maps in the sky. I had just spotted one that looked so much like the Mississippi River I could pinpoint where the family fertilizer factory stood, down by the delta.

I imagined the delta heat and humidity; I imagined elderly black men with floppy-eared dogs sitting before ramshackle clapboard houses, spitting and nodding to me as I rode by on my bicycle; I imagined fishing for catfish in the bayous on long mosquito-filled evenings. But I failed to notice at once that the Mississippi of my imagination had struck dangerously close to the house. It hung there a moment, illuminating everything in a brilliant chiaroscuro, until the clap of thunder broke over my head.

Almost at once a second clap erupted through the ceiling of my room. A ball of fire, the size of a tennis ball, hovered over the metal bedstead, then split in two and travelled along the frame and across the painted plank floor before climbing the pipes of my bedroom sink. With amazement and delight, I watched it recombine and spiral into the sink, disappearing down the drain hole. With a loud pop, the sink suddenly exploded away from the wall, dangling free on its pipes, a cloud of plaster dust mushrooming up from the floor.

From elsewhere in the house, there came the sounds of splintering glass and wood. On the floor below, Mother began to scream, filling me with irritation and dread.

I was so confused I could only turn again to the window to watch the play of light and dark on last year's dead leaves swirling above the broken stone walk, the skewed croquet pins in the lawn, and the dying elm tree next to the mysterious octagonal carriage house with the revolving floor and the garret apartment where St. John Waring's mistress had once lived in luxury and car fumes.

Just below, the gardener's elderly black Lab, Sukey, raced her sinister shadow, her tongue lolling in fright, past the juniper bushes.

Then, hearing Father's grumpy, short-winded imprecations and his heavy feet on the stairs, I finally ran to the hall doorway and peered out. The house was dark, the electricity having failed when the storm began. Lightning struck again, bursting white from the hall-end window. The pungent odors of smoke and singed hair penetrated my nostrils.

I saw Mother standing at Darla's door, her face a pale mask of horror, her mouth open, everything white and black.

The old Waring place was to be our summer home from then on.

The Warings, who had once been very rich, built the house with the intention of establishing a permanent family seat on the model of the old English country home, a refuge and retreat for succeeding generations of Warings stretching into the millennium. But Grace Waring, the widow, had closed the house after St. John's death, mostly because of that mistress and her bitter memories.

When she died, a son sold the estate for taxes and for a time it had served as a tuberculosis sanitarium, hence the metal bedsteads and the chipped enamel wash-basins in every room.

The basement and attic concealed more macabre vestiges of those sad years: kidney-shaped bedpans and spit dishes, musty cardboard crates of patient records, bales of blank admission forms, a pyramid of unexposed X-ray film, the frame of the old X-ray machine, and neatly stapled files of invoices (for fresh vegetables from the local farmers, a keg of nails and a dozen copper pipe elbows from the hardware store in the village, gas and per diems for a doctor's trip to a medical convention in New Haven — homely things oddly unconnected with thoughts of death).

These parts of the house were considered closed-off by my parents, who seemed to have gotten an idea from their real estate agent that doors had been nailed up or bricked over, that whole wings had been condemned (this is why, they congratulated themselves, they had been able to buy it so cheaply), though, in fact, Darla and I wandered in there for days on end, alternately chilled and fascinated by each grisly discovery.

The last owners before we moved in, the summer the lightning struck Darla, were a French-Canadian family called the La Douceurs, a madcap bunch, by all accounts, who, when they abandoned the place, left behind a large assortment of beach furniture, a roomful of fake Japanese screens bought at a sale when the 1967 world's fair closed in Montreal, a fieldstone and concrete shrine on the front lawn with a statue of the Virgin Mary in a niche, and their grandmother's ashes.

We only learned about the ashes a week after our arrival when Mr. La Douceur telephoned from Quebec City in a panic.

Mother sent me racing upstairs to a room marked Linen where, in a back corner of a wall cabinet, I found a copper urn about the size and shape of a bowling pin. The urn smelled vaguely medicinal, as did almost everything in that house. The ashes made the sound of sand shifting.

When I looked up there was a stranger, a gaunt young woman, wrapped in a sheet, like a mummy, I thought, standing in the doorway watching me. She had black eyebrows like bits of charcoal, and wide, feverish eyes that gazed at me with startled affection. When she saw that I saw her, she smiled slightly, wearily, it seemed, then turned and vanished down the hall. Clumsy with the weight of the La Douceur family ashes, I ran to the door, but the woman was nowhere to be seen.

Reluctantly, I returned to the wall cabinet where, just as she appeared, I had noticed something hidden on the shelf behind the urn. I reached up and fished out a clear plastic plaque with a jagged splinter of wood embedded in it. On the plaque backing, behind the splinter, there was an illustration of the Sacred Heart. Turning the plaque over, I found a legend printed in Gothic script: A PIECE OF THE TRUE CROSS.

Later, when I told Darla about the woman in the white sheet and showed her the relic, she seemed unsurprised.

Darla was two years older than me, and it was about this time that she tried to have sexual intercourse with me in one of the eight bathrooms distributed amongst the upstairs bedrooms. This was our one and only attempt at physical intimacy, and it was unsuccessful (to be precise, I did not attain complete erection, and my bladder sphincter relaxed out of nervousness just as I entered her vagina, causing us both a good deal of embarrassment).

Mr. La Douceur arrived a week later alone in the family station wagon to retrieve his mother's ashes, sweaty, self-important and evincing little embarrassment at forgetting such an important item. Though there were several Japanese screens in evidence (Mother having decided she liked them as an interior decoration for breaking up the vast spaces and sight lines of the living room), he did not mention them. And he drove away quickly without a nod to the Virgin Mary.

Once a year Father had the basal cell cancers removed from his nose and forehead, his face becoming a pattern of red skin and flesh-colored bandages. ("Quite a sight," Darla would say.) The last time I saw him was at the opening of a show of my paintings at Verna Walter's gallery in Soho when he came through the door with his face bandaged, wearing a dinner jacket and carpet slippers.

Offering him a glass of champagne, I whispered huffily, "You always have to make yourself the centre of attention."

He blinked but did not reply, though I believe he understood what I meant, the whole depth and breadth of my lifelong accusation.

He was blind by then and chronically depressed. He wore thick spectacles and read, with difficulty, with the aid of a magnifying glass. This blindness contributed to his death three years ago when he spilled something in a lab and the whole Louisiana factory went up. What was left of him could have fit easily in Madame La Douceur's urn.

I have his glasses, though.

Mother was mesmerizing, energetic, directionless and hysterical. When I was sad, Mother tore her clothes. When I was angry, Mother punished me. She was forever exhorting me to *do* things with the accent and enthusiasm of a girls' school field hockey coach (a tone I notice Darla suddenly acquired when it came to raising her own sons).

I would never have skied, played softball or ice hockey, sung in the St. John of the Apostle's choir (where I was fondled, pleasantly enough, by one of the lay brothers named Peter McNab), gone out on dates, or learned to paint, if it hadn't been for Mother. I wouldn't have lived without her, Darla says, meaning "lived" figuratively.

Yet when my father died, she became a spent force.

Now, like me, she lives in the city. Once a week she telephones to ask what she should do, redecorate the living room or buy new china, go to Jamaica or take a tour of English pubs?

"Sell the old Waring place," I say.

But, like me, she never does anything.

Both my parents refused to see ghosts or anything else unusual about the summer house, or themselves for that matter (I was twenty-five before I realized there was nothing normal about my upbringing). They thought it was a sign when Darla did not die of lightning bolts. A miracle, Mother said, with her usual melodramatic flair.

I remember the three of us converging on Darla's door, the odors of singed hair, dry rot, and ancient dust (since house dust is mainly sloughed-off skin cells, Darla and I assumed we had been breathing dead TB patients the whole summer), and the sounds of glass breaking, clapboards tearing themselves from old square nails in agony, and Mother's muffled shrieks.

Darla lay amidst her smouldering bedclothes, the hair on one side of her head burned down to the scalp, her window frame smashed in and dangling from the wall, shards of glass glittering on the floor and blankets every time the lightning flashed. Her left breast was bare, the nightdress torn or burned from her, and her nipple stood black and salient against the whiteness of her skin.

She looked like a queen of the dead, with her startled eyes, the black-and-white strobing of the lightning, the terrible music of the breaking glass.

Unable to see, Father stumbled forward with his arms outstretched (his magnified eyes peering everywhere, trying to identify who was a friend and what was dangerous).

Mother flung herself at his neck, crying inanely, "Oh, darling, I'll save you. I'll save you. Don't go near her."

Pushing past them, cutting my bare feet on the glass, but feeling nothing, hypnotized by the beauty of the scene and the sense of strangeness, I touched Darla's forearm where it lay across her belly, half-expecting it to be cold in death, half-expecting it to jump with high voltage and drop me in my tracks. It was only then, in a flash of lightning, that I saw she was still breathing and that in her hand she clutched the La Douceur relic, the plasticized piece of the True Cross.

II

I am thirty-three now. My private life is a disaster.

A year ago I gave Mother's Irish claddagh ring, the one my father gave her on their engagement (signifying love, friendship and loyalty), to a twenty-year-old leather boy who let me masturbate him in a peep show on 42nd Street. I did not know his name but believed, apparently without foundation, that we were in love.

For four years, I shared my loft and bed with an aspiring poet from Cleveland named Vicky Wonderlight, and though we kissed and cuddled and masturbated each other, we never made love (to be fair, this must reveal as much about Vicky's capacity for intimacy as mine).

I design and build museum exhibits for a living (growing up in my family, I had become accustomed to making old dead things the centre of my life), travelling around the country, sometimes sojourning for weeks in comfortingly anonymous motel rooms while I do my work.

Nights, I linger in my loft (now all my own) painting huge canvasses that look, at first, almost preternaturally black. Yet, when held under a bright light, they come up in a dozen hues of electric blue-white and red.

The subjects are all the same, a naked man (self-portrait) falling in space. Around him swirl a number of objects, ash urns, thick wire-rimmed spectacles, croquet pins, old Daimler automobiles (of the kind that St. John Waring used to park beneath his mistress's apartment), iron bedsteads and enamelled bedroom sinks, choirboy vestments and lightning bolts and tennis ball–sized balls of light that dance upon his fingertips.

Always half-hidden somewhere in the chaotic background there is an object that resembles a plaque of clear plastic containing a splinter of wood (like a lightning bolt) to signify the miraculous quality of life, our slim hope of redemption.

These naked male figures are like ghosts. You can see through them, and their faces wear hurt expressions of puzzlement and nostalgia.

Darla always claimed to remember nothing of her near brush with death by electrocution. A doctor examined her, gave her a sedative by injection, and closed her eyes with his fingers. She slept for three days, and when she awoke she was deaf.

The deafness lasted a month, and then gradually abated — though for years Darla was haunted by mysterious pops, grindings, clangs and echoes. My mother and father never noticed, except insofar as they grew irritated with her inattentiveness. I managed to cover for her most of the time, answering their questions, giving her furtive hand signals and exaggerating my lip movements when I could get away with it. Alone, we seemed to communicate telepathically. By touching hands and pointing, or looking into each other's eyes, we knew at once each others' most complicated thoughts.

Mother cut Darla's hair so that the singed areas did not seem so obvious. Though, for several weeks, Darla drew stares when she ventured into town on grocery-buying trips.

Because of her deafness and the hair, and a certain timidity caused by her fear of storms (at first she had only to look up at a clear sky to be overcome with terror), she grew to depend on me completely.

One day I found her in the bathroom next to my room, naked, stinking, and moaning, covered with her own faeces which she had retrieved from the toilet and rubbed on herself. I cleaned her up and helped her to bed, where she slept an afternoon away, only to appear for dinner, clean and fresh-smelling, silent and inattentive.

That summer I lost my virginity to the gardener's son, Billy Dedankalus, a pale, thin young man who was terrified of the ghosts (though he had never seen one). I think now that I was in love without really knowing it. Sometimes I think that this was the one great love of my life, the pattern for all the rest. For Billy quickly fell in love with Darla and left me with my memories.

In the days following Darla's accident, while she was still confined to her room, I began wandering in the gardens, sometimes following the aging Sukey on her habitual rounds, or in the abandoned hothouses where old Dedankalus, the gardener, kept a few beds for starting vegetables and a collection of rare cacti, huge in red earthenware pots, on the rough wood tables.

At first silently and at a distance, I watched him work, admiring the ritualistic precision with which he dug, planted, weeded and pruned. Soon I began to help, working alongside him with my sleeves rolled up and sweat rolling down my flushed cheeks.

He was a lean, sinewy man, with a sun-browned, cadaverous face and thin, white hair cropped close like a convict's. He carried a rifle, wherever he worked, to shoot stray cats, groundhogs and rabbits that threatened his plantings. His intensity and off-hand cruelty both repelled and fascinated me.

He had first worked there as a boy, assisting a Japanese gardener the Warings imported from the city to lay out their estate. He had helped put in a pool where fat-cheeked goldfish swam and where the La Douceurs' Virgin Mary now stood contemplating her feet. Behind the house where the shore dunes met the lawn, there were dwarf cedars Dedankalus had learned to trim and bind into agonized shapes, now run mostly wild, or dead.

During the years the place had been used as a hospital, he had turned the ornamental flower beds into vegetable gardens. His greenhouses forced hothouse tomatoes and melons for the dying patients. Now he tended the place mostly out of love, or the memory of love.

Neither of my parents knew what a superb gardener he was; they only complained about the cost (though he charged for part-time work and supplemented his income doing odd jobs and caretaking for several other summer residents).

Darla joined us when she was out of bed, not because she loved gardening, but to be close to me. She was pale and, with her singed and cropped hair, looked touched in the head. She would sit at the edge of a flower bed, pulling up tufts of grass and watching. Sometimes, she would wander away a few yards and stare at the ocean or one of the contorted cedars that separated the grounds from the sandy shore dunes.

Dedankalus was kind to her because (this is what I believe) she reminded him of the patients who had once lived in the house and similarly spent their wan convalescence watching him garden.

It was on one of these hot working days, while Dedankalus and I sweated in the rock garden below the back patio, that Billy came home on leave from the army base in Georgia where he was stationed. He was twenty-two, fearful of ghosts, in awe of and hating his father. He wore jeans, a dirty T-shirt, a wallet on a chain and down-at-heel cowboy boots.

These memories are painful, let me tell you.

And I would not write them out this way except on the advice of my therapist who has come to understand that I cannot speak about what I feel but that I can hint at it in my art or in a diary that will be destroyed, in letters that will not be sent, or in stories that will not be read.

The secret self is the real self, and I make my paintings difficult to understand because I am afraid that what I really have to say will be met with apathy and stony silences, or a sigh and a quick change of subject. This would be devastating — so I make difficulty the subject of my paintings. The images adumbrate a soul whose unique activity is concealment. It is highly adept, it has made an art, a whole aesthetic out of concealment, while yearning, aching, straining for some other connection.

"Why did you let them rob you?" asks Darla.

I don't know what she means.

I am the empty man, I have no feelings left because my habit of concealment has hidden me from myself.

When I started therapy, she said, "This will do you good only if you don't turn it into another technique."

Remembering Billy makes me think of Vicky — the truth is I fell in love with both of them because they rejected me. In bed at night, Vicky would hiss at me in the dark, "Faggot! Queer! Shit-lover! Art-fraud! How many times did you take it up the ass today?" and I would spurt come on my pajamas, weeping and melting at the same time.

Then she would come by herself, shouting "Mamma? Mamma? Save them! Can't you save them?"

What she meant by this was a mystery.

That summer, working with Dedankalus, watching his rough hands delve in the soil and fondle the tender plants, watching him casually raise his rifle to kill small animals (so cold and stiff within minutes), observing him unzip his pants and urinate in the junipers, being aware of the ghosts, or the sense that always there was someone watching, and that so much was hidden, I began to have sexual feelings that seemed unconnected with any particular person.

I began to masturbate out of doors, hidden in the dunes, or in the old sanitarium morgue, imagining someone tall and lank and beautiful coming upon me like that, stripping and joining me on the dune grass or the loose cool soil or on the padded gurney.

One day Billy did find me, or (and this is what I think) perhaps he had been watching me all along and only chose then to reveal himself. I pulled up my shorts and started to weep with embarrassment. When I tried to run away, he grabbed my shirt, tearing a button off, and laughed.

It was strange to see him laugh, a combination of a grimace and a sneer. I could see the self-loathing in his face, the strange compulsion to do the worst thing, to seek danger, to put himself in jeopardy. His carelessness propelled him into some zone of freedom, and our sex became a composition of fear, violence and abandonment.

It was Billy who told us stories about the men and women who haunted the rooms of the old house, about the doomed patients, old and young, or the young nurses recruited with danger pay to care for them, and who, as often as not, fell stricken with the same disease and died on the premises. About the babies born to patients lonely for love, babies born with the disease, who died almost at once, buried without names. About the doctors who lived in cottages in the village, their uproarious, drunken parties, their balls, their black-tie bridge tournaments.

It was Billy who told us about St. John Waring's mistress and her apartment over the garage and who also showed us the machinery beneath the garage floor that turned the cars around.

Nights, Billy told us, his father had trundled the plain pine coffins from the morgue and buried them in the lonely, unmarked graves. It was the memory of this time, of all the anonymous dead, that had rendered him so inward, silent and cruel. The gardener had a recurring dream, that he awoke tied up, wrapped in a sheet, cradled in the frozen earth. A gaunt, skeletal man with red cheeks and shining eyes bends over and beckons him.

Old Dedankalus had finally married one of the patients, that was the romance of Billy's life. She was a fortyish, unmarried Italian woman from New York who had come to the island to die. No one had ever visited her, so Dedankalus had brought her fresh vegetables and flowers smuggled from his hothouses. When she was allowed outside, he would wheel her invalid chair to the row of contorted trees, explaining about the shapes and the Japanese gardener.

She had died a week after Billy was born, and Dedankalus had dug her grave.

Billy showed us her admission forms, her death certificate and, most chillingly, her autopsy report. He even had a chest X-ray, showing the lesions and scars on her lungs, the enlarged heart, the tangle of arteries like the contorted limbs of her husband's trees.

His mother, Billy believed, haunted the house, and whenever I or Darla came across one of the ghosts (in time, it seemed, we saw them as often as real people — they grew to accept us and went about their business as though we weren't there), he would cross-examine us, hoping that we had spotted her.

I never told him about the woman in the linen closet the day I found the piece of the True Cross. With those eyebrows and the pale, gaunt cheeks, they could have been twins.

The worst is that this will go on and on without changing, that my father's heavy, depressive presence and Mother's melodrama will define me to eternity. I am happy only when I can lose myself in my paintings, which are really nothing more than elaborate messages, as Darla says, to the world outside.

It is as if the paintings are myself, and I am this oddly constructed and inept instrument for expressing them. Yet I also stand in the way of my paintings; yes, it is I who obstructs, inhibits, corrupts and deforms them.

For me, the task was always to liberate myself from love.

III

Darla telephoned me at my loft a week ago.

This was twenty years to the day (I checked the wall calendar next to the phone) since she and Billy tried to elope, stealing his father's car and driving as far as the ferry landing before my father and the gardener caught up with them.

"Why did you let them rob you?" she asked. Perhaps, I thought, she is only asking herself, though she seems to have everything any normal person could desire.

Hearing her voice, I remembered Father, Billy and Vicky and all the other losses and betrayals that seem to make up my destiny.

One day Billy said to me, "The minute someone tells me they love me, I start planning my escape as if he had taken me prisoner of war."

"I didn't say I loved you," I pleaded, but by then it was too late.

Sometimes out of loneliness I would crawl into bed with Darla in the mornings, and she would be fully dressed, the ankles of her jeans damp with sand and dew from the dunes.

Sand everywhere.

Darla had finally talked Mother into letting us sell the Waring place. She wanted me to drive up with her to meet the real estate agent, who was, it turned out, a cousin of Dedankalus.

She went on in a tone of voice I found surprising but also oddly familiar, a tone that was at once breathless and frightened.

Without pausing, she told me that Tad had gone into a corporate drug rehab clinic near Lake Placid, that Lonny, her youngest, her baby, was having nightmares, horrid dreams of dark men cutting off his genitals and throwing him off buildings, that her own life was falling apart. She had had two abnormal pap smears in a row, and was scheduled for a biopsy. No one else knew.

After a moment's hesitation, I said yes, remembering the way she looked in the weeks after the lightning struck, her pale vacantness, her cropped hair and the out-sized clothes she borrowed from me or Billy.

I said I would pick her up with the boys in the morning. We would make a family outing, complete with a picnic lunch and seafood dinner at Renaldo's on the ferry pier. I would pack the picnic, she should bring the wine from Tad's cellar.

"Don't pretend," she whispered. "You can't even take care of yourself. This terrifies you."

I hung up, wishing she did not know me quite so well.

I thought, these things that happen to us have no cause or reason. It is as though we are not real at all but being written by some ghostly hand. There is no presence, only a vast nostalgia and, on every page, just the shadow of something which never appears and is never named.

I could not paint any more, just stared and stared at my canvas, a black vortex of images, falling boys, a bloated face covered with moth-like twists of gauze, Japanese screens, bowling pins, a jagged crucifix of light, a girl with blazing hair, Billy Dedankalus slumped in his chair with his rifle propped against his forehead, the way we found him, and myself as a grown man, standing to one side, watching in horror.

That night the black dog visited, by which I mean that I dreamt of Sukey, the gardener's aged black Lab. Waking, I heard the distant rumble of a thunderstorm, an occurrence which, for obvious reasons, always sets me on edge. Though it was three a.m., I tried to telephone Darla and kept getting a recorded message telling me to hang up and dial again.

We made the trip in silence.

I asked Darla once when Tad was coming back and then tried to remind her of Mr. La Douceur and his mother's ashes. But she was lost in thought, her fingers working nervously at her pocketbook. She was wearing jeans and one of her husband's checked workshirts. Her hair was done up at the back in a ponytail — such informality has long been completely out of character for her. The boys, in the back seat, seemed crabby and tired, and promptly fell asleep before we left the city.

Ray Dedankalus, the cousin, met us at the ferry dock and drove with us to the house, stopping for hamburgers along the way.

Darla maintained her reserved silence, staring out the passenger window. I could not help wondering if, somehow, she were reliving those long-ago events. After all, she had driven this road with Billy the night they tried to escape, only to be dragged back from the pier in Old Dedankalus's car. Billy had ridden just ahead of her, in the back seat of Father's station wagon.

She remembered Father driving exceedingly slowly all the way back to the house, sometimes stopping for minutes at a time, then jerking forward again. She had had the feeling, she said, that something terrible, something truly evil, was taking place in that station wagon. And she strained her eyes in the dark for any sign of movement. But there was none. The car would stop, and then creep forward.

In the morning, we found him dead.

"How did they know?" she wailed. "How did they know?"

I shrugged helplessly, and burst into tears at the sight of Billy's body slumped over the rifle.

When we finally pulled into the drive of the Waring place, the boys leaped out and ran ahead, rested, excited to be out of the car, taking turns pretending to be accident victims needing an ambulance. We shook hands with Dedankalus and told him to give us a few hours to look around.

I went to switch on the lights and water and returned to find Darla gone, the boys shying rocks at the water just past the line of contorted cedars. When I was a boy, the place had seemed big enough to get lost in, much too big for us. Now it startled me how little had changed, with the smell of decay everywhere, the crumbling gatehouse, the dried up lawn and peeling paint and the ivy growing across the windows so that the rooms were suffused with a dim, green glow.

I thought, if there are ghosts, this is somehow what they must feel, as though they inhabited a reality more vivid, familiar and substantial than they themselves were.

I called Darla's name, and went hunting over the grounds, past the tennis courts and octagonal garage and through the greenhouses now open to the elements and littered with shattered glass. Old Dedankalus's cactus pots still crowded the wooden tables, but nothing grew in them. The earth was dessicated, cracked.

They had buried Billy in a regular graveyard, not on the grounds. We weren't allowed to attend the funeral. Darla stole a bottle of bourbon from Father's cabinet, and we drank it in her room till night came and we knew everything was finished.

"How did they know?" she asked again and again. Though I believe the truth had already begun to clarify itself like muddy water gradually becoming clear as the sediment settles.

I found Darla in the morgue, now used as a storeroom for years of accumulated summer furniture, boxes of Christmas ornaments abandoned when we no longer put up a tree, stacks of Father's business records in exploding file boxes, trunks bursting with childhood toys and old photographs — all the detritus of a family we no longer remembered, no longer felt part of. She was leafing through a photograph album which she held up as I walked in.

"Do you remember the puppy you had when you were three?"

I shook my head, feeling the weight of all the things I did not remember. She jabbed a finger at a snapshot of a smiling toddler struggling to hold a miniature dachshund in his pale arms. The dog has a sharp, wet nose and charming little eyes fixed knowingly on the boy's face.

"You only had him a couple of months. Daddy couldn't stand the noise and the mess."

"I don't remember," I said. "I look happy though."

"Mamma called him Romeo. But you couldn't say that. When you said it, it came out Vemeo." Her face had gone dead, expressionless, yet there was some steely desperation underneath, some determination to assert the truth at any cost.

I handed her back the album and began rummaging, finding a torn Bloomingdale's bag with our remaining croquet mallets and, at the bottom, the plaque that once held a chip of wood from the True Cross. Someone had sawn through the plastic to remove the relic. There was only an empty space where it had been.

"You must remember the night Romeo shit on your bed and Daddy kicked him around the room till he couldn't walk and then said he was taking him to the vet. It was after midnight. We never saw him again."

"I don't remember much," I said.

But I did remember the morning Billy Dedankalus died.

It was in this very room, the place of the dead, that we found him, purely by chance, since no one yet knew he was missing, and we only came here to hide out. It was our secret place, which, of course, Billy knew.

He had shot himself with the gardener's rifle, nesting the muzzle in the soft V of flesh just beneath his chin and firing up through the back of his mouth into the brain.

Blood had drained from his throat and mouth, soaking his T-shirt and jeans and pooling beneath the chair. But his face was unmarked and bore, partly because of the wide-open eyes, an expression of mild astonishment.

Darla dropped to her knees in the blood and gagged and tried to embrace him, and he fell over onto the floor, awkwardly, like a marionette. The impact of his fall compressed his chest, forcing air suddenly out his lungs, so that he sighed, or seemed to sigh.

Or maybe this was my imagination.

Darla's teeth began to chatter, an inhuman rattle. And I noticed that she was staring into the shadows beyond the X-ray frame.

There seemed to be something there, a shadow within a shadow, a trace of movement.

I don't know now what I saw. But everything had taken on an air of seeming, and what was real was Billy and the blood and the details of the hole in his throat which I have never forgotten — the jagged line of skin, yellow fat, darkening clots of blood, that awful exhalation of breath, as though he had been waiting for us.

I was only thirteen.

I went down beside Darla and tried to touch her, not to comfort her, but to try to stop that chattering, which I knew would drive me insane. She mistook my motive and grasped my hand and began to weep, smearing me with blood.

From where I knelt I could finally see what she saw, the gaunt face in the shadows, the pale dome of the woman's forehead above her charcoal eyebrows, her fevered eyes darting with anguish, tears glittering on her cheeks, her silent chest heaving.

As soon as I saw her, she began to fade, her eyes fixed on Billy. Love and pain fused in that look. I have never been able to separate them. There is no such thing as love without betrayal. You hold the thing that kills you as close as you can and watch it die, all the time whispering, *Love me, love me, don't go.*

Darla took my hand and pressed it.

But her voice was harsh, that tone of desperation. It rasped out the words.

I said nothing. I meant my silence as a confession. Her words were like a burst of light. I held the empty plaque in my hands. Her words went through me like blue fire. Choked with sadness, I remembered how she had looked with her smoldering hair and burned bedclothes.

But I quickly realized that whatever I had to confess was old news. Now she was going to die, and the story had taken on fresh meaning because, like Billy Dedankalus, her boys would always be alone.

We were in the morgue, and I suddenly felt like the only living creature in a room littered with corpses. I stumbled about among the corpses looking for signs of life.

I said nothing — more confession, it was pouring out of me, meaningless. I wanted to weep, but it came out a dry sob. For ages, I have been all dried up inside. I thought what I always think, How am I going to get through this? How am I going to endure such pain? It seems impossible that a human being could suffer this much and live. And just when you think you can't stand any more, it gets worse and you discover new possibilities of living.

This is the reason I have never owned a gun. There is only one person I would shoot and, like my father, I have always found it easy to kill.

Telling it, remembering the intensity, it seems impossible that we could get out of that room alive, that the ordinary world would let us back in. But Darla finally let go of my hand, and her voice began to return to normal. And the past receded until it was nothing but a presence and a dull ache, like a tumour.

I dropped the plaque to the floor. We had somehow agreed to take nothing, to leave everything for the next owner to deliver to the holocaust.

On the stairway, Darla paused. We were brother and sister again, leaving the intolerable splendor of the scene in the morgue for a lesser ecstasy.

She said, "I haven't seen them for years."

I nodded.

"But Lonny does. They're in his dreams."

I shuddered and glanced back, praying for a sight that would sear my eyelids shut forever, but the room was empty.

There was nothing there, nothing as terrible as the future.

ALBERTO, FATHER, AND BROTHER JOHNNIE / MANDEL PLATA, ARGENTINA / C. 1958

ALBERTO MANGUEL is a respected translator, novelist, literary critic and editor of a dozen widely acclaimed anthologies, including *Black Water: the Anthology of Fantastic Literature, Meanwhile in Another Part of the Forest,* and *The Gates of Paradise.*

You're Not Gay If You Can Whistle: A True Story

Alberto Manguel

"There's nothing wrong about a lie, because it leads to the truth."
Dostoyevsky, *Crime and Punishment*

Why am I writing this story?

I'm writing this story because, a few days ago, a certain editor asked me to read at a fund-raiser for his magazine.

That isn't exactly true.

I'm writing this story because after the editor asked me to read, I told my friend Stan Persky in Vancouver that I didn't think I had anything suitable and Stan, who is a careful listener, reminded me of something I had told him, something that had happened in my high school, in Buenos Aires, when I was fifteen or sixteen.

"There's your story," he said. "That is the story you can write."

That's not exactly true either.

I'm writing this story because what happened so many years ago, so far away, has time and again come back half-remembered, unclear and unsettling, and I am hoping that in writing it out something forgotten will be stirred to life, that it will rise to the surface like dead leaves at the bottom of a river and that I will be able to see *the event in itself* at long last.

That is true.

My high school stands in the political core of the city of Buenos Aires, and looks like a cross between a bank and a hospital. It has huge stairs that lead up to immense grilled gates and then, through a vast marble hall, into corridors of brown varnished doors. Memory, of course, makes the place look larger, but this is the stage of the first true transactions between myself and the world outside. Everything else before this time happened at home, *en famille*.

This is also true.

One of our subjects was philosophy, a sort of quick skimming of names from the pre-Socratics to the Existentialists, the History of Western Thought in two hours a week, for nine months of one year. Our grade eleven teacher is (I say "is" because now that I recall him he is present) a thin man with a small black moustache and a tweed suit. This week we are learning about Plato. We are asked to choose one of two texts: *The Symposium* or *The Republic*. It isn't an easy choice.

Sometime earlier this week a girl in the other grade eleven — her name has disappeared from memory; I can fill in the blank with any name; for reasons best kept to myself, I'll call her Sylvia — told her Spanish teacher something she had seen. This is what Sylvia told her: she had wanted to prepare some homework with a boy in my class — I'll call him Peter — and had gone to his house one afternoon. She had walked in, found no one, opened the bedroom door and seen Peter in bed with another, younger boy — I'll call this other boy James. What she had seen had shocked her.

The Spanish teacher summoned Peter and James to her office. (She was a stern, dumpy woman who wore a short fur coat in autumn and winter. She had married a man much older than herself, a friend of her father's, and her father still lived with them in a curious *ménage à trois*.) The teacher took the revelation very seriously. She told Peter that if he continued along this depraved path he would end up like most homosexuals, i.e., being murdered by sailors in the port of Buenos Aires. As far as

James was concerned, she said she pitied him deeply and hoped James's father would be able to straighten him out, seeing that James was still very young and therefore not entirely past redemption.

Peter's parents were notified and, on the teacher's advice, he was sent to a psychiatrist. James, as it happened, had a father who did not believe in straightening out. He pulled James out of our school and sent him to another one, never — as far as we knew — attempting to either blame Peter or change James's proclivities.

This is true.

I don't know whether, when we were asked to choose between *The Symposium* and *The Republic*, the philosophy teacher realized that he was asking us to choose between two much vaster worlds. He had summarized the plots for us. He told us that the *Republic* was a description of Plato's utopia; the *Symposium* was a discussion concerning male love or, in the teacher's words, ardent friendship. Choosing between the *Symposium* and the *Republic* became a choice between loyalty to Peter (and the consequent grave risk of being suspected as part of the dark underworld which ended, now we knew, in bloody corpses strewn along sailors' wharfs) and a safe, clean image of Sunday suits, Sunday sports, and hair lacquered back with Brillantine.

This is true, this is how we dressed, and the scent of Brillantine still brings back the barber's fingers, the sepia-coloured soft-porn magazine on his waiting table, my best friend seated in class, just in front of me, hair stiff as if he were wearing a helmet.

This isn't true.

Yes, it brings back those images, but above all the image it brings back is that of my father, naked, slowly combing back his Brillantined hair in the bathroom mirror, and I remember thinking at the time how much bigger his cock was than mine.

This is true.

The class divides. A few brave souls, more than one would have expected, choose the *Symposium*. I too: not through any brave gesture (I'm not attracted to any of the boys, I have no knowledge of being a dangerous and mysterious creature, I don't feel uneasy because I might be the victim of a misnomer, might be made to carry the wrong tag) but because my best friend chooses the *Symposium* and I know for certain that he can't be gay. We do things together, straight things: we play rugby, ask girls out to dance, discuss politics, read the newspaper. More powerful than all my literature, than all the subtle wisdoms taught by the books I've read at the age of fifteen — and they are many — is the common knowledge, the reality of clichés, of received ideas, of conditioned reactions. Later the definition will change: you're not gay if you are married, you're not gay if you don't get fucked, you're not gay if you can't name three Judy Garland films in chronological order, you're not gay if you can whistle.

After the division into *Symposium*-readers and *Republic*-readers nothing dramatic happens. Both groups are too confusing, too heterogeneous. The two texts are studied, a test is taken, Plato is disposed of, and we are on to the next chapter in our *History of Western Philosophy*.

Peter continues in our class until the end of high school (two more years) and then vanishes. Later I hear through a common friend that he married an older woman and moved to New York. In this age of sudden deaths, I don't know whether he is still alive. This is true.

I think back on Peter and imagine him in bed with James. I can hardly remember James (memory is such a fussy eater) but I can make out Peter's features quite clearly: pale skin, green eyes, freckles and black hair lacquered back. Now I imagine him naked on the bed, legs apart. I wonder now — I didn't wonder then this is true — what it would be like to be in bed with him. Someone I slept with long ago told me that he loved the head of my cock because it reminded him of his favourite part of a horse, the horse's muzzle. I know that in the summers Peter used to ride at his family's ranch; would he have drawn the same comparison?

In my thoughts I turn him round, his bare ass rising now towards me like a face seen in a dream. This isn't true: in my mind the cheeks of his ass become not the cheeks of a face but warm full breasts, his asshole like the deep dark wound in the middle of the chest of St. Teresa, pierced by Christ's arrow. The mound between his ass and his balls appears in my imagination hairless, impossibly white. I burrow into this conjured-up semi-mystical geography.

I wonder now — I didn't wonder then; this is true — why anyone would be concerned about the goings-on under someone else's covers, invisible, behind closed doors. I wonder why Sylvia cared, why the sententious teacher cared, why we in school cared about what Peter and James were doing, body against body, in their private afternoon. I drag out psychological reasons such as lust for the body that wasn't lusting for Sylvia's, envy of a youth that wasn't any longer the teacher's, fear of the temptation that might call upon us all — me, my friends, our fathers — and impair our maleness. I devise sociological explanations: norms established by a tribe, not followed; taboos broken, rituals changed, customs ignored. Nothing satisfies me: I'm still bewildered. It is the obviousness of the act that makes both its occurrence and its witnessing so difficult to comment on, except in poetical terms, removed through metaphors. It is its very naturalness that becomes the major obstacle to its being understood.

Subject for an essay: "In 100 words or less, explain why I feel that the fact of you not removing your hat at the door topples the entire structure of the world in which I know myself to be secure."

I come into Peter's arms (drifting back to more than twenty years ago, through jungles of experience and disappointment) as easily as if I were passing from one room of my house into another — I who can walk through this house in pitch darkness and not knock anything over.

This isn't true.

One moment at the heart of this story is lacking. Later that year (the year of the disclosure, the year of the *Symposium*, we met to try and organize a school magazine — I, my best friend, Peter and several others. Frustrated at some minor disagreement (so minor that my memory gropes for it in vain) I stood up and shouted: "I'm not going to work on a magazine with a *faggot*." I don't know where that shout came from, I can hear myself saying it even now, I can see the dining-room of the house in which I said it, our papers scattered across the table as if this had been a real working session for a real magazine in the grown-up world. I left the room, someone called me back, the discussion carried on as if nothing had happened. But something had. Peter never asked me why I had said what I said; I never apologized. Then, a couple of years later, high school came to an end and Peter vanished. This, yes, is now true.

This is also true: I don't know what caused my outburst, I don't know if somewhere inside my body I longed for his, and that longing turned to rage and a desire to do him harm. I don't know, and even if I did and if I had, it wouldn't change anything. Upbringing, fear, stifled lust, lack of knowledge or experience — none of these are good excuses. Across the years, I now offer him this text.

The other boy, James, finished his high school somewhere else in Buenos Aires. Several years later I saw him in Paris, working as a playwright for a theatre company that has since become famous. He had met another boy from my school (my mind goes back now picking through the classes, the boys whose lives seemed so different and turned out to be so similar, at least in the outcome of their physical desires, to mine) and together they had travelled to Europe. I don't know what happened to James after the playwriting, but I do know what happened to James's second boyfriend. He left James not long afterwards, and married Paloma Picasso.

This is true.

ELLIOTT HAYES was born into a theatrical family in Stratford, Ontario. From 1985 until his death, he was the literary manager of the Stratford Festival. His dramaturgical work included many stage adaptations, among them the play version of Robertson Davies's *World of Wonders*, mounted at the festival in 1991. He was the author of numerous short stories, novels, and plays, including the internationally acclaimed *Homeward Bound*. Elliott Hayes was killed in an automobile accident on February 28, 1994. He was thirty-seven.

Seven Poems

Elliott Hayes

one day it will be me whose ashes gleam,
whose name is etched, whose fear is gone.
one day it will be me mistakenly identified on the street,
my memory mulled over,
my dust swept up towards the sun
on a mystical sigh.
and then it will not matter that I have wept,
that I have come undone in public places,
that my face is drawn and my throat dry,
for as I ascend it will not be the end of me,
it will instead be you and I and everyone
I've ever mourned, entwined.

MOTHER AND CHILD

the moment of birth is a breath of grace
for mother and child.
yet that brief span endures and lasts
long past each successive inhalation,
for miracles are without time:
fast and fixed to a memorable hour,
they still move with us.

on humble days and in darkness
what was good then remains:
hope and fulfillment all at once,
as pole to axis, so life to life.

I won't watch sunsets
with those who cannot
spend money unwisely
or waste their want.
I am going where
anyone can dance undaunted,
and several hours
in steamy amber rooms
seem natural.

I will touch the dying,
kiss the cancer,
hike up your hospital white
and write on your thighs
with spit.
I will mangle perfect limbs
in awkward embraces
and sully small talk
in savage exchange.
I will boast scars and cures,
play Beethoven on a drum,
and bear your message
to the realm of kings.

FAITH

lacking formal worship,
I require seasons.

shaking
the stems of blackened basil
to harvest the humus laced
in their roots,
or looking over apples
on the ground
for one without worms,
I am entirely grateful.

It is the pervading scent
of fresh garlic,
saturating the soil
and permeating the calloused
skin of my palms:
epiphany
under the trees and over the leaves,
when frost has sharpened
then dulled the horizon,
and flocks of birds soar,
becoming black specks divorced
from the strange sound of their wings
beating in defiance
above us and between the branches;
as frogs, turtles and the small crustaceans

set themselves in mud
before the first ice forms
a mere pattern of scratches on the lake
and the dusk encroaches on noon,
sounding the angelus.

CASSANDRA

things are often left on the side of the road
at the site of a crash;
it may be a doll or only broken glass,
but the implication of all detritus
is someone else's concrete loss.

and when one person loves another
too much or not enough,
there is also simple evidence
to catch in time or only notice looking back,
and is as obscure as glass in gravel
or the speck of blood on a piece of stone
on a stretch of highway where few may pass.

still, some see and some do not
the abandoned wares of wreckless others
who have gladly won and somehow lost,
not feeling Cassandra's cautious breath
cooling coffee in the breakfast silence.

OBSEQUY

you were in mid-sentence when you answered the phone,
already offering to let me off by stating the homily first,
knowing the new volatility of blood drawn from a paper
   cut
and cold to the fact that all of us are asking each other
without asking you, if you have lost weight,
or will even talk about Christmas without him.
we have of course made plans
and know the current patter
offered during the wait for ashes,
seeing ourselves as ushers
leading the less modern and therefore more distraught
through the ritual which is now routine.

war was never this, or if it was it was suddenly over
in a way which this cannot and will never be.

you never warned anyone and were never warned
and singed your hand merely touching, merely caring,
merely breathing in the giddy extreme of being whole.

TALISMAN

I take your shirt in the morning
and leave you mine;
indifferent to the fact
at least until I smell you,
knowing it is you while others don't,
sensing the ordinary ecstasy of common ground.

and night when you are not there
it is the sight of your shoe,
a toy, or even the broken end
of a pencil you might have dropped
or drawn too hard with
that elicits only my joy.

BRIAN A. KILGORE

KATHERINE GOVIER was born in Edmonton, Alberta. She has lived in Washington, D.C., and London, England; she now lives in Toronto with her husband and two children. She has been a magazine writer and a teacher, and she is the author of four novels and three collections of short stories. *Hearts of Flame* won the 1992 City of Toronto Book Award. *The Immaculate Conception Photography Gallery*, published by Little Brown, Canada in the Fall of 1994, was nominated for the Trillium Award.

LISETTE MODEL, A LIFE IN PICTURES

KATHERINE GOVIER

Lisette Model, the Austrian émigrée to America who is best known for her photographs of the sun-sedated loungers of the Promenade des Anglais in Nice, used a Rolleiflex which had to be held in front of the solar plexus. Weegee, the American news photographer, recalled seeing her around New York in the forties. She stood square on to her subject, looking straight down into the camera, lens jutting from the front of her waist, one hand aloft with a flash device, a string bag of flashbulbs dangling from her wrist. The stance, combined with Model's refusal to photograph anything unless she was passionate about it, ensures that her most memorable dictum was "Shoot from the gut!"

Gutsy they are, but what attracted me more to Model's photographs is that they have characters and they tell stories. I first saw Model's photographs in the Jane Corkin Gallery in Toronto; later, in 1990, I saw the National Gallery of Canada's comprehensive show of her work. Her most famous images, "Running Legs," for instance, and "Coney Island Bather," had hovered on the edges of my consciousness for years. I wanted to know who made them, and why.

People have accused me of being obsessed with photography: the title story of my 1994 collection of short stories is *The Immaculate Conception Photography Gallery*, and the heroine of my novel in progress is a war photographer. If I am photo-obsessed it is because I think photography is the dominant art of the twentieth century. Today, photographic images on paper, on television and computer screens, and in film, constitute a language, in fact a culture, in themselves. But the photographer has always had to fight for credibility amongst artists. Mechanical, instantaneous, reproducible, mass-oriented, yet etched with the most basic component of vision, light, the photograph is a mysterious creation.

And Lisette Model's work is a mystery as well. Its literary quality first drew me in, the characters, the stories. But the stories, like the people portrayed, are mis-shapen. Something extreme is evident: the people are stretched, shrunk, squashed, projected onto glass, frozen in a grotesque gesture. They have been done violence to. And the story either has no ending or no beginning, no motive or no logic. People shout, but their words are ripped from their mouths. There is more than a hint of tragedy.

Model has been credited with opening the subject matter of photography to include the grotesque, the down-and-out, and with introducing emotion. As the teacher of Diane Arbus, we recognize Model's "school" as that which focussed on sights we might wish to pass over. The directness and energy of her best work finds no equal. But to stop there is to miss the point. Model's sense of story is contemporary, haunting, portentous.

Take that most recognizable image: "Running Legs, Fifth Avenue" (New York, 1940-41). Behind, a sidewalk, the back end of a Ford car complete with spare tire. In the foreground, a soft-focus leg and high-heeled foot of a hurrying woman, moving headlong out of the frame to the right. (Can a foot go headlong? This one does.) I respond with questions. What is the woman running to, or running from, in the hard light of day, her skirts and hose a haze, the hard dark square lines of the car a threat to the curve of her calf, to the sleek heel and eloquent, vulnerable instep?

Or, the less frequently seen "Man with White Sunshade, Menton" (1935); it begs questions in an atmosphere of stasis. A man sits on one end of the bench with his back to the sea, dressed completely in black with a white umbrella lowered so as to obscure his entire head. The stark white umbrella casts a bat-like black shadow beneath his seat. Between the two umbrellas, the one light and the other shade, he seems trapped, but not unwillingly, a long-legged mollusc, a bivalve between the two halves of his shell, patiently awaiting fate.

Any photograph by Model, a portrait of one of the strangers she felt akin to, a study of a store window, a celebrity photographed on assignment for a magazine, or — one of the rare later works — a captured stone cherub fallen among leaves (Fig. 3) will have this quality of interrupted narrative. It will be as bold as its subject, unshrinking yet withholding.

"We are the subject," said Lisette Model, "the object is the world around us."

Why then should I be surprised to discover that her biography took a similar shape to her photography? That she was a storyteller who could not finish the tale; a person whose backdrop was blown apart by war displaced to a new world in which she had to create herself; a woman who appeared to but did not escape the predicted life pattern for females in her time. One can assume that a sense of herself as a denied Jew, a transplanted European, and a woman in the predominantly male art world were clues to her work. But finally any study of Model's work must remain unfinished because her work was unfinished: after a sensational rise to fame in the forties, from the early fifties she produced almost nothing.

In October 1990, the National Gallery of Canada mounted a retrospective exhibition of Model's work. The curator of photography, Ann Thomas, researched and wrote a magnificent catalogue, "Lisette Model," National Gallery of Canada, 1990. The estate of Lisette Model decided, on the strength of that catalogue, to donate 200 prints and many negatives, as well as Model's teaching notebooks, diaries and other assorted papers to the National Gallery of Canada, where they could be consulted by students and critics.

The teaching notebooks, a series of small notepads and spiral stenographer's notebooks, were for me the source of Model's story, an autobiography, to the extent that one exists at all. They are decorated with spaceships or bound in neon pink covers, some are marked "twenty-nine cents." They contain her notes for the classes she gave and her theories about photography. The notebooks are also replete with the proverbial shopping lists; for instance (from Notebook 28):

```
soap
cookies
juice          BLOTTER
cheese         blouse              NEW SESSIONS: the Snapshot
soupe          shoes                            Sequences
                                        Abstract Surrealistic,
```

etc.

A lot of doodles, many empty pages, detailed lecture notes, and finally, a few out-bursts which speak volumes.

So, photo-curious and even more, photographer-curious, I have tried to compose a portrait of the woman behind the camera, the woman who shot from the gut. I read the notebooks, and I looked at the photographs and I have tried to find the way Model's work and her life meet.

BEGINNING: FACT OR FICTION?

Lisette Model had difficulty with fact. For her, photographs were not factual, or doc-umentary, but fiction. "Photographs are analogies, not replicas," she said. "This is not a dog, it is a picture of a dog." It is not Pearl Primus, or Dizzie Gillespie, but pictures of same. Insisting on this distinction was the equivalent, for Model, of insisting on her own powers. *She* made the picture; it was her response to the dog, or Pearl Primus, which was of interest.

About the facts of her own life she was most canny, as well. She would infuriate scholars by first agreeing to work on a biographical project and then refusing after the first difficult question was asked. She rarely divulged a truth regarding her past, and if she did, as writers like Philip Lopate were to find to their regret, she was cer-tain to retract it later. From time to time, she also falsified her age, exaggerated her family's wealth, invented formal schooling where there was none, and denied what were clearly her motives at an earlier time.

The bare bones of her life story are known.

Lisette Stern was born in Vienna in 1901, the second child and first daughter of Victor Stern, a Jewish doctor who was attached to the Imperial Army. As a property-owning Jew, her father lived amongst the upper middle class on Josefstrasse. In 1903 Victor changed the family surname to Seybert, in an attempt to avoid growing anti-Semitism. Lisette's mother, Felicie, had come to Vienna in the late 1890s from France, ostensibly to work at the court. Lisette and her younger sister Olga were kept at home with private tutors for most of their childhood, except for two years at an experimental gymnasium. Lisette's great passion was for music; she was a student of Arnold Schönberg, becoming friendly with his daughter Trudi.

In 1924 Victor Stern died of cancer; two years later Felicie Stern returned to France, settling in Nice. Lisette went off to Paris where, for eight years, she studied voice and underwent psychoanalysis. She later described this period of her life as her struggle to liberate herself from "the culture of the bourgeoisie." Then abruptly in 1933, at thirty-two years of age, she gave up music. She never gave a reason. But her decision was final. Various explanations have been suggested: that she had poor initial training; that she lacked ability; that she had a physiological problem affecting her voice in the middle ranges. Perhaps her renunciation sprang from her psychoanalysis: music was one more aspect of her childhood from which she had to escape.

For several more years she dallied, sitting in Left Bank cafés, first studying painting, but then, on the advice of a musician friend, Hanns Eisler, who had fled Hitler's Germany, taking up photography. She decided she needed marketable skills, a job, and something she could take away with her from a Europe which would soon be at war. As she wrote much later in her teaching notebooks,

"Maybe I should tell you how I became a photographer. I was trained as a musician from early childhood. I met a composer — He was horrified. Don't you realize war is coming and you have nothing in your hands to make a living? I bought a camera and an enlarger in order to develop prints. I took pictures having no idea whether they were good or bad."

I was struck by the tone of that passage. This account is not a natural explanation, one that might arise spontaneously in front of a class, but a scripted version, one which she must *prepare*. She was preparing a story to tell, beginning the myth of her own life.

According to her sister Olga, Lisette then walked the streets of Paris with a Rolleiflex and her friend Rogi André, herself a photographer and André Kertész's first wife. She modelled her style on one seen in the Communist periodical *Regards*. In the summer of 1934 she went to visit her mother in Nice. Although she would later deny ever having set out to be a photojournalist, having, in fact, savage words for that profession, Model's first photographs were published in *Regards* in 1935, under the title "Côte d'Azur," and later in *PM* magazine in the U.S.A. in 1941, titled "Why France Fell."

Already Model had begun to embroider the tale of her early life. She must have felt she had something to hide. Ann Thomas's careful scholarship has uncovered certain disturbing probabilities. Lisette's mother Felicie had in fact come to the Austrian court as a high-class prostitute. Furthermore, Model's physician father sexually molested his daughter during her childhood. Lisette's and Olga's isolation, and the fact that he had a habit of showing his collection of gynaecological drawings to Lisette and her friends, lend credence to this assertion by relatives and acquaintances. By 1934, the apprenticeship was over: the elements for the making of the photographer were all in place.

A PHOTOGRAPHER

In Nice, there on the Promenade des Anglais, sprawled in deck chairs under a pitiless sun, lay Model's first subjects. She approached them coldly, boldly, directly, with we know not what dialogue, and caught them as surely as if she had skewered them on a pin. These photographs, published between '32 and '37, made their creator famous. Even after her death they remain her most recognizable images.

I imagine that Model has approached with her camera. There was no telephoto lens to fit the Rolleiflex, so that she has come within three feet of her gambler on the beach. She asks him if she can take his photograph. Or does she not? I think probably not. Regardless, each one of her people is dressed, glittering with surface, *in character*. Perhaps they are secretly pleased to be caught in her lens. Is the closing of the shutter the conclusion of a negotiation, or the beginning of a nasty scene? Does it matter?

On the Promenade des Anglais, she was a detective who operated without secrecy, but who revealed secrets. As these early images became her most famous, Model often spoke about the morality of taking pictures of strangers. Her rationale for this method of portraiture was "I can because I am one of them."

Brilliant and fertile though these photographs are, they are not among my favourites of her work. The evil-eyed gamblers, the fat, cigar-smoking capitalists, the white, wrinkled women kissing their dogs, are like biological specimens, like T. S. Eliot's "patients etherized upon a table." Model's strong emotion was her hallmark, her ability to *know* the stranger. But at this point in her career the dominant response was not compassion but judgement and derision, even scorn. Her own words about liberation from "the culture of the bourgeoisie" come back to mind. Still, the energy of the confrontation will persist, even fifty years later.

As Model would later say, when she taught, the first thing that is there is the projection of the photographer. "Most people are terribly afraid to take pictures of people because they are 'invading their privacy.' Isn't it rather that when we see a drunk lying on the street, we feel that that is him but it can't happen to me? Or somebody who is a cripple — or somebody very poor or ugly or beautiful. Instead of feeling that the difference between one human being and the other is very small, and what happens in people's lives is approximately the same. Where is the great secret? What one is, everybody is . . . Because tomorrow morning I can be there — *which happened during the war all the time* — then one has to feel . . . as long as I have the feeling 'this is me,' I can do it."

Of her students, only Diane Arbus contradicted her, saying, "There is a difference between someone else's tragedy and your own."

NEW YORK

And Model *was* these displaced people. In October 1938, she and Evsa Model, the Russian Jew she had married in Paris a year earlier, emigrated to New York. They took an apartment on the twentieth floor of a building on Riverside Drive; from the windows they could see the Hudson. It was a new life, and a new view on a new world. Lisette could create a new story for herself. Her former music teacher, Arnold Schönberg, had warned another emigrant to the United States, "Don't say anything you don't have to say about your experiences . . . be very reserved and don't get mixed up in politics . . . " Lisette acted in kind.

Within a year, her mother and her brother in France were to feel the impact of the Nazi war machine. But Model had jumped into an intensely stimulating city. The myth is that she enjoyed immediate success in New York. The truth is that, as she said in an interview, "I didn't take a photograph for a year and a half. I was blind . . . "

No more could she walk the streets and see that essentially European phenomenon, the local population taking its leisure in public at eye level. Skyscrapers confused her sense of perspective, so she pointed the camera downward. Her breakthrough came when she began to photograph store windows, where reflections captured the life of the street as well as the glamorous images of New York, in an effort to show Fifth Avenue to her sister Olga in France.

Glamour, she concluded, was America's biggest export. "This will be my work," she declared. And it was. The bulk of Model's completed work is from the forties in New York. The "Reflections" (store window) series, "Running Legs," the images of denizens of haunts titled "Opera," "International Refugee Organization Auction," "Sammy's," "Gallagher's Steak House," "Lower East Side," "Lighthouse Blind Workshop," and of course, "Coney Island Bather"; these are her great photographs.

In "Reflections," manikins are admixed with the brooding shadows of passersby, dwarfed by leaning reflections of skyscrapers across the street, beautiful, ominous, surreal. To unravel the layers of reflection and counter-reflection is impossible; to discern which glass (lens? window? inside? outside?) we look through is the game; finally, judgement is suspended like the figures in the gleaming showcases. The photographer's own position is part of the puzzle: did she lie on the ground to get that shot? stand behind the glass? kneel? bend? She always shot from low down. Larger than life, darker than doom, male shadows are often cast on the "glamoured" female figures.

"I never liked an eye level camera," Model said in an interview. Her vantage point was always low. Her women, always above her, are huge. What size, I wonder, was her mother? Does what we see represent a child's view? The hugeness of adults, their great power, the oversize projection of their "life experience"? The people Model portrays are pointing, declaiming: there seem to be a lot of microphones, fingers raised in admonition, while the camera person is small before them. It is interesting that Lisette

Model was a tiny person. Critics have suggested that she could not have got her shots of strangers if she were larger; that male photographers, generally more threatening, could not work at this close range.

After "Reflections," Model had a foothold and could move into the real life of New York, often as a commissioned freelancer for *Harper's Bazaar* or another magazine. For these assignments she found her massive, expressive men and women. They weight the photographs, and bulge from the edges of the prints, unbudgeable, powerful. She chose subjects, she would write later, whose "life experience was not held back."

Late in the forties, Model zeroed in on performers. The dancer and performance artist Gert Valeska; the dancer Pearl Primus; the transvestite Albert/Alberta at Hubert's 42nd Street Flea Circus whom Arbus also photographed. She loved to photograph the sightless performers at the Lighthouse Blind Workshop, and Bud Powell, the jazz musician who was mad and only released from the asylum to play. They were all larger than life. Furthermore they *posed*. This was different than shooting strangers at the seaside in Nice; these subjects offered themselves. While grotesque in their way, they were treated with much more compassion than were the habitués of the Promenade des Anglais.

FIGURE 1: FRANK SINATRA, NEW YORK (C. 1939-1944)

Within several years, Model had achieved a phenomenal success in New York. The Museum of Modern Art bought her photographs; she published in *Harper's Bazaar*, *PM's Weekly*, *Look*, and *U.S. Camera*. She exhibited at the Musem of Modern Art and the Photo League. She became known in the community of photographers, people like Berenice Abbott, Ansel Adams, and Ralph Steiner undertaking to help her. The bulk of her energetic, original, lasting photographs were taken within this period. To see them is to see an exuberant, opinionated, and new kind of photography.

TEACHING

But after the fabulous forties, the fifties was a difficult decade. Her uncompromising vision led to a breaking of the relationship with *Harper's Bazaar* and other commercial outlets. Model seemed to lose her direction. Her work was no longer in demand. To make matters worse, she was investigated by the McCarthyites. The most difficult thing was to earn a living for two. Evsa's painting had never brought in much money, and now brought in less.

She began to teach, and she took fewer and fewer photographs. At the same time, Evsa became an invalid. Model began to spend more time seeing to the needs of her students, and her husband, and especially to the couple's own financial needs. This was a new theme: caring for others, nurturing.

Through teaching she gave prodigiously and earned minimally. At first she tried to give detailed technical advice. This was not her forte. Helen Gee, once a student, later a gallery owner, has said that the technical side was not strong, but that Model's great gift was to help students develop a belief in their own vision.

In 1957 Diane Arbus came to study with Model. Her most famous student, Arbus, quickly surpassed her teacher, then, in 1973, committed suicide. Model's reaction to Arbus's suicide was one of bewilderment. She once quizzed a writer about the source of Arbus's misery: after all, "she had a good husband, children who loved her, and she was famous." It was a most revealing remark. All those supports were absent from Model's life.

FIGURE 2: STUDIO OF ARMANDO REVERON, VENEZUELA (1954)

By now, Model was having difficulty producing work. She made excuses when asked for her portfolio. She did not develop her negatives. She denied this had to do with sacrifices made for Evsa, or with financial insecurity. But her life was being reduced and circumscribed to the small flat where they lived, and her classes with students.

It is in this period that the teaching notebooks become an indirect diary. It appears that Model began a new notebook each time she took on a new class, often by repeating notes she had written many times before. Later notebooks, while revisiting information contained in earlier notebooks, gave only a truncated version: by then she knew by heart what she was going to say.

One of her mantras had to do with Kodak, the inventor of the camera. She liked to point out that he was a suicide at seventy-seven, and to quote him as saying, "Why wait? My work is done." Teaching was a performance, and this was one of her best lines. Still, what did it mean?

I wonder, seeing this line repeated throughout the notebooks, about the resonance of suicide for Lisette Model. The idea that each of us has a specific task, and that life became meaningless once the task was completed, has a peculiar poignancy in her case. Fame came to her early, and easily, only afterward becoming elusive. Model's own productive career tailed off into years of strained finances, marital stress, and undeveloped negatives. "Why wait? My work is done." Did she think her work was "done," and that she was "waiting"? The quick solution to life would also have been an expression of her aesthetic: the art of the split second. If the essence can be frozen in a gesture, then further movement is superfluous.

But though her career as a photographer was over, her "work" was *not* done. She taught, and was able to put her working methods in writing. In the notebooks she left a primer of her method. "The world is our stage," Model was to begin teaching, "Almost anything can be photographed." Later she would add: "With all this freedom, there is one hitch. Not everything goes. There is the true and there is the false —"

"Working in photography means training your eye, nerves, body," she writes. She selects her subject matter, "by attraction — like a magnet, and then I don't question or hesitate." Known for severe cropping and manipulation of images, in the teaching notebooks Model says: "Composition is not shifting subject matter around to make it look more effective." She seems to insist on intuition. "We do not fabricate composition. Composition is what you feel and say about a subject . . . only what says more."

As she continued to teach, Model's ideas changed. In earlier notebooks she says not everyone can learn. "Only a few have god-given talent." Later, she amends this. Everyone has talent, but an artist also needs interest, love, work, perserverance, patience.

She also softened her attitude to press and documentary photography. In Notebook 3 she accused the news photographer of wanting only to get the picture first and print it first. It is not the picture which is important, but the event. The result, she concludes, is stereotype. Again in Notebook 5 she says the press photographer thinks in terms of a single picture and spot news: he does not express his personal emotions, only the emotions of the people he photographs. Yet later, in Notebook 18, she expressed admiration for "the sixth sense of the news photographer" — to know what was going to happen before it happens, to read into the faces of a crowd the shape of the next split second.

But the most interesting changes in later notebooks are the sombre notes which seem to refer to herself. "Fast success, fast results, money, glamour, stardom, leads to emotional disaster," she writes. "[Photography] becomes the battlefield between technique and expression."

I think of Model in the darkroom, cutting and shaping her images, burning out her negatives to get the effect she wanted, getting the photograph to include "only what says more." Doubt has crept in: the former assurance, the aggressively cropped photographs, the unerring instinct all waver. What could she not say? Or why could she no longer choose what to say? Satire was her strength, and satire, as Arthur Sisskind had pointed out, is difficult to achieve in photography, faced as we are with "the dumb stare of physical fact."

The notebooks continue their indirect narration of the story. As the years pass, Model's handwriting grew more spidery and difficult to read. One of the most poignant entries was, as dryly noted on the archival guide, the "signature of Lisette Model twenty-two times in pink marker." Again, I could see her, aging, teaching but not creating, a hostage to her own psychology, perfecting a pink signature, one which she could put on a photographic print were she to produce one. "Too much admiration of others," she writes, "leads to loss of confidence."

Teaching, of course, was a performance and an expression of herself. She had her small devoted following and her practised lines. "The world is our stage." "Photography is the art of the split second." "The camera has gone beyond seeing." Again and again she returns to Kodak, "My work is done—why wait?" And again she repeats: "The world is the stage. Almost everything can be photographed," but this time she adds, "subject matter has its fashion."

In her mature years, Model became more and more admired as a teacher. She took on the defence of the art of photography. In her notebooks, she quotes Sisskind, whose views about photography are heretical, presumably to refute in class. To Sisskind, photographs do nothing but imitate paintings. "They are reproductions of works that came into being through the collaboration of anonymous men and nature, *where neither they nor it were engaged in their more typical creations . . .* The assumption of intrinsic significance is a fallacy which the photograph shares with its twin the newspaper," said Sisskind. Her own judgements to the contrary she did not write down in the notebooks. Perhaps she felt the defence was too obvious to need recording.

THE PORTRAIT

Lisette Model wrote, in Notebook 17, "I have given many courses and workshops in the last twenty years, working with students, the immediate give and take . . . . When it comes to one's own photographs it is like looking at one's self optically only. To show and talk about my own photographs. I have refused, feeling that one sees less clearly one's own work — because [one] would have to see one's self from many angles and distances."

Portraiture was a special subject with her, as it would be, for the permanent stranger, the exile, who saw herself in any hapless individual who attracted her lens. "Is not the reason for millions of people to pick up the camera to find her or himself?" The only people Model refused to photograph were children: perhaps they were too painfully herself. She said children were "too sentimental," but they are also too vulnerable, too tragic, too helpless, too much in need. But she *did* in fact photograph children, or their replicas. There are the many broken dolls she found on a trip to Venezuela, and the fallen stone cherubs in Italy (Fig. 3).

FIGURE 3: ROME, (1953)

Again from the notebooks, "Thousands of times man makes an image of himself: in this image he came to believe . . . in this self-image he pointed out how to behave, how to move, how a prince, a general, a bourgeois should look. But when we observe these images we can see something strange, that there is a conflict or tension. Very rarely do human beings see this real face and there is a conflict between the individual and the general. Man has to hide not out of shame, but out of insecurity."

Again and again she returns to the subject of the individual and the photograph, repeating her original premise.

"Man wants to hide his face," writes Model, "[from] the instability [or] passing by of things. He seeks to retain what is stable or what remains. He becomes part of a religious community or a political community, in other words, the establishment. He seeks the accepted, the ethical, from the glaciers of solitude he runs into the warmth of family life . . . ."

In this explanation we can read everything that was denied Model, or that she denied herself: community, security, acknowledgement. Yet she would never have admitted to anything lacking, as her would-be biographer Philip Lopate discovered to his chagrin when he suggested that her spartan furnishings and dark rooms were a sign of hardship. She angrily denied it. They were only evidence, she claimed, of her "European sensibility."

But what of Model's family life in her time of need? In her fifties, her health gave her difficulty, first a back problem, then uterine cancer. The notebooks are not dated, only numbered, but I could feel as I read on that she was growing old, that a weight of regret was brought down with these few words on the lined paper.

On a sentimental trip to Italy, she took few photographs, mainly of the faces of buildings. The image of the stone cherub fallen into a bed of leaves entitled "Rome" was from this period (Fig. 3). There was precious little to visit. One of the privileges of exile is to invent a past. And Model had done so. Her family's middle-class status had grown in hindsight to become an aristocratic background; its holdings to a small fortune, mysteriously lost. Now she disposed of family property, but it amounted to very little.

Early in 1976, Evsa had a heart attack. In October he died.

In Notebook 23, Model writes somewhat dramatically about the "eternal discrimination" against photographers, "thanks as usual to painters." But the bitterness did not sound out clearly, and even then not directly, until Notebook 24 in this astonishing passage.

"My god. It is certainly a different decision after —— artist existence with these brilliant festivities, this kind of life offers daily in the highest point it is in possession of one's capacities to say: *this is the end,* and to retire into isolation and sudden non-existence with patience, to resign all glory, success and to postpone this love of taking leave until it is too late, and the cruel truth hammered into your ear: you are nothing anymore you aren't anything nobody wants you, you have failed to protect your once great name."

It is unclear whether these are her own words, or whether this is a passage copied into the notebooks from another source, possibly Marilyn Ferguson, "The American Conspiracy". I suppose it doesn't matter; it spoke strongly to her at the moment. I loop back to her words about Kodak, and the peculiar fascination they had for her once: "Why wait? My work is done." There shall be no ending, no explanation, no apology, only an exit without regret.

"And then my god" — the handwriting goes on — "looking back from the high point of old age, resignation and [unreadable] When one thinks it over what a tremendous price one had to pay for this glory and success. With incessant work restless giving ambition untold nervous stress and excitement over [unreadable] When every evening one had again to fight for fame, use one's elbows, defend oneself with one's teeth, never of course to rest — thus one can see, realize, understand how expensive this little fame is bought — which in no time is gone."

And is that the end of the story? In the last few notebooks, the rhythm of Model's mantras takes over. The period of time between repetitions has shortened, and the information itself is only alluded to: the mantras are simply named; like jokes with numbers, a shorthand version only is necessary to get the reaction.

"We realize the immensity of this medium."

"The camera deals with optics, physics, chemistry, mechanics."

"It took humanity thousands of years to discover and invent photography."

"The camera is an instrument of investigation, sometimes a weapon."

"It is very difficult to speak to photographs more so to one's own."

"Humans very rarely let their real face be seen."

Like her photographs, Model's story does not end. It reverberates. It is a dying fall. With her fascinating body of photographic work, Model gave an impulse and a spirit to her art form which broke the mould of what had gone before. Her teaching had immeasurable impact, but from the last fifteen years of her life she left no images. She retreated from "the silent art", "the fragments", to her chanted half-story. What she did create was a contrary, unforgettable persona in search of an ending. It was her final work of art.

This essay owes everything in the way of scholarship to Ann Thomas and the National Gallery of Canada, and everything in the way of opportunity to Karen Mulhallen, Descant *magazine, and the Ontario Arts Council.*

CHRIS GRIVAS

CHRISTINE SLATER is the author of a collection of short stories, *Stalking the Gilded Boneyard* (1993), and two novels, *The Small Matter of Getting There* (1994) and *Certain Dead Soldiers* (1995). She is currently at work on a third novel, from which the "Nightcap" excerpt was taken.

NIGHTCAP

CHRISTINE SLATER

My mother died drunk in her oxygen tent. Do you want to know where I was? I will tell you where I was. I was not there. In the room, I mean. Holding her hand. I was sneaking a smoke out on the stairway. Once upon a time she might have joined me. She called me her "co-conspirator," you know. I was not flattered. In her vocabulary, it simply meant toady. Yeah, I'd already brought in her flat little fifth of booze. Why, shouldn't I have? After all, she was conscious enough to ask for it. That, of course, was happening less and less . . . the consciousness, I mean. And the asking. In her last days, you know, she had finally become demure. But now, I mean right at that moment, it was my turn for a bad habit. My turn to be petulant. My turn to give in to it. My turn, period. But I will tell you about that later. There is so much to say, I may explode. Let me get organized. Let me shuffle the entrails before I read them. Let me tell you of the pure pleasure I got. I mean, from the smoking. From the rank sniff and sucking at the butt. The pleasure of being secretly disobedient. The pleasure of polluting the Toronto Western Hospital. My mother might have even appreciated it, but then, she always had to be the brat in the family.

First . . . I mean, I'll say this right off the top, it was very inconvenient her dying like that. Okay. Okay. I know that sounds crass. It was possibly unfortunate, but basically inconvenient. You'll see; it isn't just me, you know. And it took her forever, as if something physically resented the prospect that, at ninety-five, after a life so full it could be mistaken for swollen, it was simply time to go. I mean, the sheer nerve of it. She had always been so greedy. For life, I mean. I mean, she was greedy for life. And I was really trying, you know. I absolutely want to make that clear. Really, really trying. My sisters were useless. My mother's friends were either dead or distant. I put her in the hospital. Coaxed and cajoled and kitted her out. Thought to bring the flannel pyjamas in case her room was too cold. On the way, she fell asleep in the car. "Oh good," she murmured, groggy when we got there, "where's the goddamn bed?" Okay. So I made the arrangements for the house. I made the phone calls. I mean, and this should surely be apparent, I did *everything*. And it was just so inconvenient: the end-of-the-year-book blitz, the OPEL prize jury, reviews and interviews. I just had too much to do. Nobody ever gives me the credit for having just too much to do. I am a busy man. I can't help it if I've mastered the art of not looking like it. Busy, I mean. And because I was the one everybody at the hospital knew, I was the one who got the messages at the office, the pink slips of paper with only a doctor's name on it and the secretary looking unduly grave. I was the one who called in for the bulletins on the fluctuation of her condition, as if the whole freaking stock market depended on it. They never told me anything, anyway. We all knew the old girl would go when God stopped her bloody heart.

Of course, as soon as word got out of her hospitalization, everybody who knew or admired my mother had to get in touch with me. I mean everybody. I mean, absolutely *had to*. This was a woman who had never been sick a day in her life, who had never even been in a hospital, except to have her children and a broken foot set after a jeep knocked her over during the Spanish Civil War. Oh yeah, wait a minute. She had dysentery in Tangiers once, back when she was slumming it, chumming around, with the Bowleses. You know, Paul and Jane Bowles. Yeah, yeah, yeah. There was hardly any scene *anywhere* that did not merit a visit. She may not have stood front and centre, but she cast a long and curious shadow. Besides, she lied enough for long enough to have you to believe she'd actually had some great part to play in these amorphous self-propelled things when, really, by the time the war came and we kids kept her home, her currency was only interesting to those who thought to regard it as verging on the antique. It was a shame, too, because my mother, Marjorie Poole, was vital and interesting. Even I can admit *that*. She could have kicked William Burroughs's butt; in fact, she is said to have done so, but nobody wants to hear about that right now. Well, they put that stuff in the obituaries and everything, but, you know, she died out of fashion.

Okay. Anyway, I ended up speaking to everybody. I felt as if I spent weeks with the phone stapled to my head. The tyranny of the family name. The only son as only the son of. Yeah, well, I'd gotten used to that. Clambering without equipment up the slippery slopes of a parent's reputation. With your parent at the top ready with the hammer to hit you, should you make it within striking distance. Well, I never did make it to striking distance. So much the better, don't you think? I'm still here. In one piece. And I have a desk job.

Speaking of which. Speaking of the desk job, I mean . . . These calls . . . I couldn't possibly be busy now, could I? No, no, no. Who cared about the year end, the OPEL prize, the stockpiled reviews? I mean, there were occasions when *I* didn't care about it, but then, I always thought I had the right. Yes, I reserve the right to shoot myself in the foot. I reserve the right to imperil my career. Fuck, it's not a career, you know. I'm saying this in all confidence, you understand, but it's just a bloody job. Yeah, I know my place. My mother always taught us to know our place. But, really, I am just too accommodating. About the interruptions, I mean. Gregory's such a good guy, such a good son. Gregory would always have the time. *You want to see her? She'd love it, I'm sure. Don't mind the plastic, of course. Yes, yes, she does look a little freeze-dried. And if she grapples with consciousness long enough to say something about a drink, well, you know how it is . . . the mind, it's virtually gone, poor girl.* Ah, I did that well, didn't I? I had so much fucking practice. But how unseemly. How unseemly it was for her to die like this. Slowly. Old. Typically. I'd go in with the contraband and after her requisite sips and slurps, thinking of all the glasses she'd raised in her day, rinse her lips with a little water in the hopes of obliterating the smell. And the nurses would say from a distance, "Isn't Gregory such a good son?" But my mother never heard that. She didn't have to. She'd know I'd always ended up doing what she wanted.

She asked for her little cap from Tangiers, the red one with the gold embroidery she claimed to have gotten from Barbara Hutton. And I reached through the folds of the plastic and crowned her with it, you know? Long live . . . whatever. The plastic reflected green from the screens, the slight swing of the IV, the gold glimmering as it caught the shimmer of all those machines. You know about my mother, don't you? The Parisian adventures back in the twenties that seem so cruelly clichéd now; at the time, she hung out with the best of them. She slept with several of them too: Hemingway, for sure, but she always said that was an accident. That, I couldn't quite imagine, but she stuck to her story. Oh yeah, she had stories. She told 'em. She wrote 'em. And she made a great many of 'em up completely. She always said she was a journalist, but then, there was this pesky thing called fact.

She was never one for ties either. We kept her here a while — back when we were really little and our dad was still alive. It's not like she'd turned into the Great Domestic, but she curbed the urge to run away. Of course, by the time she did, she could honestly say she had done her duty, even if her maternal supervision had been limited to watching us warily through a fog of cigarettes and calling for our father, if something went awry. She was very hands-off. It made us self-sufficient, which I suppose was the point. But it also saved her manicure.

By the end of the fifties, she had left Toronto again. None of us was compelling enough to keep her here. And then there was that tiny issue of her career, her reputation treading water, and the adage that if you couldn't write something dramatic, then you should *do* something dramatic. So she went to Tangiers. Paris was passé; New York was getting full of those freaky boys and girls known as the Beats; yeah, well anyway, my mother had thrown her weight around those curbs often enough. You had to hand it to her: she was nothing if not inventive. And in some quarters, this passed for talent.

I could never understand how what was essentially running away could be construed as heroic, not after years of stories (hers and others) that so clearly admired courage and fortitude and facing the music. Switch around a few consonants and suddenly escapism became exile. And you didn't need to know how to spell to tell the difference. How very fucking romantic, I thought. I was young then; I was big into contempt. Yeah, but secretly I was probably just jealous. *She* initially ran away to avoid the work, or, more to the point — let me get right to the point — to avoid another cocktail party ambush inquiring about the status of the work. There was no work. She was not working. She stayed home enthralled by this thing called television. That's the truth. No really, that is the unvarnished truth. She had dried up completely, had become a fucking fossil, so maybe the desert was the best place for her. She ultimately wrote two more books there — a thin little novel best read in the state in which it was written: that is, stoned for much of the time. My mother supposedly ate *majoun* for dessert. Enough people did, though — read the book, I mean — because suddenly at sixty, she was hip. She so wanted to be hip. Not being hip was killing her. She was so afraid of becoming a relic when she preferred to be an icon. The second book was the anticipated memoir, one more pointless trip into the watery bowels of her cramped past. When life was tough, etc. Yeah, yeah, yeah. She grew up in bloody Rosedale, you know. Moved a few blocks down Sherbourne Street into a hotel, a tavern really, with rented rooms, and decided, albeit momentarily, that she was having a life-experience worth writing about. Three short stories worth, if memory serves. Then, in the late twenties, she went to New York, got a job writing for *Vogue*, met Conde Nast, says she slept with him, and went off to Paris with the magazine's money. "When I saw Scottie in Paris . . . " she'd say. I don't have to tell you how rehearsed it was, how superbly polished. She dined out on that brief chapter in her life for the next twenty-five years — those boring years when she'd married and became a mother, and Hitler was fucking up the world too much to really *go* anywhere. And all the best bars in Europe were closed. Success had made her full at the banquet of life. Oh yeah, she was full of it. "Did I ever tell you about the time I was with Hemingway in Havana . . . ?"

So anyway she dies. She dies at the worst possible time, the week between Christmas and New Year's. I have to have my sisters paged at Holt Renfrew. I mean, it was an amazingly bad time considering she was lingering and might have hung on a while. Yeah, well, she had this malicious streak. But one day, somebody comes in with her lunch and there it is. A body in its plastic shroud. She'd been complaining about the food since she got there. I got there while they were dismantling things; it looked as if they were taking down a Christmas tree. I didn't feel a thing. She just looked dead to me. Really, really dead. I remember thinking I ought to be thinking of something else.

So we had to have the funeral. My sisters went to town with that. They love to organize. They absolutely love to organize. They're twins, my sisters, Syrie and Cygnet, two years younger than me and much better preserved. They managed to get really fine flowers, considering the time of year. Syrie must have done that; she has such hostessing skills. She presided over the ceremony like a maître d', wearing her hat with the brim turned up so everyone could admire her new facelift. Cygnet did what she always did in a crisis; drink excessively. The woman is amazing. I myself have a big capacity for the bottle, but on a good night, Cygnet can outdrink me, without difficulty. I mean, she is *skilful*. Her eyes had started to look like the pimento in the olives that hung off her swizzle sticks. But she was a happy drunk, by and large, because she had no insight. She didn't know what exactly she had to drown. Personally, I could have come up with anything. You would have figured that already. I am not subtle. Not the least of it is being orphaned at fifty-six. This was utterly tragic. No, no, I mean that. I had no one left to blame but myself. I was no longer simply "the son of," not in a viable sense anyway. I mean, that had been my whole identity, hadn't it? Gregory Poole, son of the celebrated novelist, Marjorie Poole, journalist/adventurer/name dropper/bitch. Etc. Etc. There I've said it. Maybe I can grow up now. But I am not holding my breath. The night of the funeral, Cygnet and I went to the rooftop bar at the Park Plaza Hotel, walking along Bloor from the church just to get away from the grieving huddle. There was a CBC truck outside the vestry. The premier came. My mother would have loved that, the idea of a state funeral.

So Cygnet and I got to the bar, and we're frozen. It was the second day of the new year, and the cold glistened under a sky that shone like a black pearl. Upstairs, it was warm and quiet. It was always warm and quiet. Bars can be so comforting. Cygnet likes to start with two martinis: the first she drinks quickly, as if she's just finished a triathlon. She has the good manners to nurse the second. She absolutely savours it. I enjoy watching her drink. Her eyes assume that loaded, heavy-lidded look that women get when faking an orgasm. I should know, believe me. This, however, is the real thing: the pleasure is so pure, and drinking was so much less complicated. Poor Cygnet. Who could begrudge her? You know, when in doubt, swallow.

She sounded so sloshed all the time, what else could she do, but drink to explain it? At the age of seven, goaded by Syrie, whose malevolence has somewhat mellowed, she stuck her tongue to a fence on the coldest day of the year. They managed to extricate her; unfortunately, the same could not be said for part of her tongue. Cygnet had a little problem with her *R*s. With a few drinks in her, this passed for charming.

We were bred to be charming. None of us could possibly be talented. Oh, I can charm with the best of them. I am fucking Cary Grant. My mother didn't have to be, at least not in the same way, and certainly not in front of us. She had a skill. She called it the trade, making it sound posh and cliquey, and well beyond the bounds for the likes of us. It was as if her star had such a wavering light, she had to keep everything around her dark and subordinate in order to shine. We came at the worst time too; she had gotten good reason to doubt herself. She sat out the war; it was killing her.

I'm sure she married my father for lack of something to do. She was thirty-eight when she did it; he was eleven years younger. She thought he was gay. He adored her, which suited her perfectly. Massaged her feet with Shalimar, decorated her first house, *supervised* things. Was lavish with his attention and his praise. Of course, by the time we came along, which was quickly, he had very little to spare. In old photographs, he looks chipper, though quizzical, as if he hasn't quite figured out who the children belonged to. He was from New York, well, really, New Jersey, but no one wanted to admit to that. He said he wrote as well, but after a while, after too many massages and dinner parties and furniture purchases, he seemed not to want to admit to that too. Yeah, I must be one of the few men who ever breathed, for whom their father was so obviously and so immediately inconsequential. My mother made sure of that.

I remember her ordering him around, waving her ivory cigarette holder (a gift from somebody famous; I can't remember whom) like a sceptre. He took it too. He took it for eighteen years. Then one night he got drunk, got behind the wheel and flew to husband's heaven from the corner of Davenport and Avenue Road. The official story involved something about the brakes. Ah yes, a very bad break indeed. My mother just seemed relieved. Then she looked around the pew at the funeral, and remembered us.

She started to write again, after that. She wrote in the big room off the stairwell to the second floor. This was on Lytton Boulevard. We grew up on Lytton Boulevard. She asked a guy who'd done some carpentry work for my father to build us a treehouse at the back. Full of shaded sun and shadow. My sisters found it too high, but for me, it was as close to heaven as I've ever come. A few times up there, I thought of my dad, but memories burn up fast at that age. You are always making new ones. There had to have been more to him, I realize that. But all I remember, all I've remembered for years, is just a slow satellite around my mother. I fell out of that treehouse once and broke a wrist. I remember the housekeeper running out and cradling this crying boy on her knees in the yard, while my mother fetched the car with a hard-set look in her eye for having interrupted an afternoon's work. She was the first one to autograph my cast. So anyway, she would write in the big room off the stairwell to the second floor. Would write on her lap on the sofa there. We'd be told to go up quietly, not to look at her, as if the very swivelling of our eyes could distract her. There was always a bright light. I remember the patch of bright light on the carpet. It was like walking into an egg yolk. And I remember the carpet being dark and thick. I'd try to make my sisters giggle. Making faces. Making as if to tickle them, but my mother never seemed to notice. "She's so concentrated," my father used to marvel, the six syllables slowing his speech like a sprain. Yeah, I remember him saying that. My mother would always *look* concentrated, the reading glasses aggravated that, even if she was only working on the crossword puzzle in the *Globe and Mail*. She had her routine. The dutiful breakfast with the family. Toast and cereal and one black coffee. She watched her weight in perpetuity. Someone told me they recalled her having made fun of my father for his growing gut; she supposedly called it the continental shelf. Oh yeah, he had no choice but to go soft on her. Anyway, she'd pull in the paper from the porch, set the light upstairs blazing. She always sat on the same side of the sofa, the pad poised on her lap like a trampoline, to catch any tumbling idea. She had her routine all right. She had her ways. She had her sub-scriptions. Once, when I was about eleven, she gave me her copy of the *New Yorker:* "You seem like a reader to me," she'd said, and I was so proud she'd noticed. I read it all right. I could read all I wanted, and I did. The discards were bestowed upon me forthwith, at regular intervals, though it took me years to understand the cartoons. But I knew very early on that I was not supposed to write.

No, no, no, that's not right. I had to have inherited something. Just not the greatness. And ideally, not the spirit of adventure either. In the seventh grade, we were instructed to write a short story. I wrote one about two boys on a bender — pillow fights, *God's Little Acre*, smuggled cigarettes. My teacher gave me an A. I don't remember if I deserved it, but I think she had visions of my mother turning on her at the open house, thundering something about her son, and his story, and his bequeathed genius. But my mother would never say anything like that, in case it could be true. I carried the fucking family name like a birth defect; there were times when I think I would have preferred polio. Either way, I have been limping for years. When my mother read the story, ignoring the red-inked letter next to my name, she smiled, rolled it into something you'd smack the dog with, and said, "How could the parents not have known they were smoking, when you've established that the vents were open?"

Oh God, oh God, oh God, this is turning messy. This is strictly sick and bitter stuff. It wasn't all like that, you see. Do I have to put it in such a messy way? Clear and fair, clear and fair, clear and fair. Like a fucking weather report, right? Yeah. It wasn't her fault, you know. She actually did like us. I don't want you to think that she didn't like us. Only sometimes, she seemed surprised to see us. Like in her house. Needing things. You know, like a bath or something. It wasn't her fault. It wasn't her responsibility to give me a life. That's what I'm supposed to do, right? Take responsibility for my life, I mean. And this sounds so awful, so god-awful, so goddamn, fucking awful. No, no, no, no. It wasn't like that. It wasn't that messy. It was, you know. It just fucking *was*. Oh God, oh God, what have I been saying about myself? What have I been saying?

Okay, okay. I'll get another drink. I'll fix myself another drink. There's ice, you know. I think there's ice. A couple of whiskies, on ice, if I've got it. That'll do. I'm sure that will calm me down. Normally, I'm calm. No, really. Normally, I am really calm. I shouldn't do this, weak-kneed and woozy. I can't. I mustn't. A couple of whiskies should do it, don't you think? I have to keep things clear. I have to keep things clear and calm and accurate. Oh yeah, accurate. Let's not forget accurate. Let's not forget the truth. The Pooles often do, but no, this is not the time. The truth. The truth is in here somewhere. There is so much paper. Where is the truth? Where's the fucking ice?

I went to Queen's, you know. Did I mention that? Studied everything; mastered nothing. My mother came to my graduation wearing a carnation in her buttonhole. "That's Marjorie Poole," somebody said. I will always remember the accusatory swivel of that head as two and two fell into place and made four. "Hey, Greggie, is that actually your mum?" Yeah, I replied, glad to be getting out of there. Actually, she is. She signed autographs on the backs of people's diplomas.

When I got back to Toronto, I enrolled in grad school, mainly to delay thinking about my future. I wanted a million futures, a million faces, a million voices. I always did. It just all sounded so sour, once my voice had changed. No longer quite so typically adolescent, so delightful. I was a drifting, delinquent, graduated *man*. Men had to pretend to know what they were doing. A real man had a real presence, a real focus, a real voice. Oh yeah, I wanted a real voice all right, an artful, incisive, absolutely *delightful* voice. A voice people listened to without trying. But every time I opened my mouth, the voice I heard was my mother's — that lock-jawed *hauteur.* That summer I moved home with my mother and sister Syrie. A real man, all right. They let me mow the lawn. Cygnet had already gone to Hollywood then. She would soon marry her movie star. He bought her a car; she had to learn how to drive it, which I think, at the time, meant they were engaged. By August, I'd moved out. Found a place off Spadina. Two and a half rooms. Bad plumbing, the best view. Had my first girl in my first place. No, no, not that I was a virgin, or anything. Even in Kingston, there were *ways*. But I was rather a manly *poseur* at the time; played school sports, looked awfully average, found the odd girl in the odd dorm. But in Toronto, I could feel myself limbering up to live. Fucked a girl from my tutorial on the flat bed in one of my two and a half rooms. The first time I ever woke up with a woman was in one of those two and a half rooms. The thrill of seeing a bare breast spill over your sheets. The sheets you wished were cleaner. The thrill of that post-coital fumble for a smoke. The thrill of having a pretty girl from Oakville go down on you without asking. The extreme thrill of her bringing over a friend. Oh yeah. Yeah. Amazing. Christ, I was seeing double. I was delirious. And shortly thereafter, I woke up and decided that, as my behaviour seemed to suggest it, I would become a writer anyway.

So what does a writer write about? At twenty-five, nothing very interesting. I read too many novels by other people and pretended that was research. The search for my real voice continued, but I smoked too much and got hoarse. At the time, my mother was going through enough gyrations of her own: the world was not the safest place for middle-aged women and I think she felt real fear for her future. She was mere steps, mere minutes, away from leaving for Tangiers. And I know her departure is what gave me the courage to write. Oh yes, I am wise now. Her literary legacy and its bloated shadow followed me like a cloud threatening rain. And I was so grateful to be rid of it. Didn't understand, because I was not wise then, that I was just glad to be rid of *her.* I did not understand that, in truth, everything stayed behind.

But I had inherited more than just the name and the old girl's ego and the first hundred grand. I got the long, rakish face, the fleshy hands, the smoky, congested laugh. I hung on to it all, name included. Well, okay, the money didn't last that long, but I kept what I could and never regretted it. Really, I never have. No, no, no, *really.* I want to have a smidgen of courage at the end of it all to say I stood up to what made me. That I stood up to what terrorized me. That I stood up. That I fucking well stood. A month after the first postcard from Tangiers, I started my first novel. Took me fourteen years to write it.

Oh yeah, the day jobs. Okay. Okay. I'll admit to them all. I'll admit I had no patience either. For the most part they were all a blur. I hosted an arts program on CBC Radio. Yeah, after all this time and practice, there were people who actually liked the sound of my voice. That was okay. The job, I mean. I mean, I stayed with it a while. I quit one day when the coffee was particularly bad. Any old port in the storm, y'see. And, by this time, I was soaked to the skin and the load I carried, well, it did not double as a life preserver. Quite the contrary. Yeah okay, and if I sound as if I'm whining, stay with me, all right? You'd understand if I went into it all, but I do not want to go into it all now. And all that time, too many people came up to me to say how much they loved my mother. All my life too many people came up to tell me how much they loved my mother.

This was always curious. It still is curious. That people would presume that they knew someone through something so off-the-scent as a book. All writers lie. They steal too. My mother told me that much. And people have always said, "How wise!" "How funny!" "How accurate!" I never saw my mother as essentially any of those things. I was too vain. She still had the ability to surprise me, but I had lost the ability to enjoy it. In my old age, you'd think I might have learned to enjoy it. But I was too busy being bugged and bothered. I was too busy being tired. It is not good to be so tired.

Is fifty-six old? Too old to be set adrift by a death? I feel old, I feel old. I shall wear the bottoms of my trousers rolled . . . I have no one. When a parent dies, you see the measure of your utter finitude. The ties you've made and loosened. The ties you've let go altogether. The ties you've ripped off impetuously, when you have felt nothing but slow strangulation. The ties that passed for commitment. Bugger it, you know? I wasn't so different. But, bearing the old girl's ego, I should not have thought it could happen to me. This whole human frailty thing. She had done a good job of convincing me she was immortal. I certainly believed that. She was just too fucking stubborn to die. When it did happen, I had become an old man myself: an old man alone. Oh, I have heard those mermaids singing, but I *knew* they were not singing for me.

I married Lily Bragg when I was twenty-eight years old. I cast off those twenty-eight years of bachelorhood, cast off carelessly, unanchored, into the seas of marital bliss and blunder. Oh, the ugliness and cheer of it. Sixteen years of uncharted waters. I am bloody fucking grateful neither one of us drowned, though the skies did threaten. I hated the fact that we were typical. She was eight years older, and I was her second rotten husband.

Lily. Oh, Lily. When we met . . . I remember the arch of your back as you walked. That incredible patrician posture. Your beautiful fingernails. Your sensible jewellery. The way you fucked me on our first date. How I lay my head on the rug between your legs. How your cunt smelled like a cannery. How I loved it. Loved it. Loved you.

We met at somebody's party. Somebody's best friend — mine or yours — I can't remember. And you wore a blue sweater. I admired something: your watch, your wit, your face. Something. We played charades. I was always very fine at it when I was drunk. I had drunk a lot that night, but not enough to forget you. We played games. Stupid things like the names of movies or Broadway musicals. *Fiddler on the Roof*, *Zorba the Greek*, *Dr. Strangelove*, or *How I Stopped Worrying and Learned to Love the Bomb*. Yeah, I never stopped worrying, did I? But I did learn to love, I suppose. I have you to remind me that once I learned to love.

I asked you your number. I asked you out. Drinks, it was. Something safe. We met at the Park Plaza Hotel. It was winter and I waited a while. The place was empty when I got there. But when you arrived, wearing pants and high-heeled boots, the room got warmer. And my face flushed from the very sight of you. I drank vodka martinis. You ate an entire bowl of almonds by yourself. You lived nearby. You invited me back. Or did I invite myself? No, no, no. I'm only joking. You did the asking. I ached for you to ask me. You mentioned that the bed was new.

Before Lily, I had just dated girls. Not one worth remembering. I think they all looked like Sandra Dee. Lily was a woman. Just like a woman, so went the song: *with her fog, her amphetamine and her pearls.* No, no, no, that's not right. I bought Lily her first real pearls. She was never, ever foggy. And as for the amphetamine, well, everyone was on diet pills in those days. *Nobody feels any pain* (boom, boom), *tonight as I stand inside the rain.* I never did find the proper shelter. Didn't realize I lugged it with me. Yeah, this fucking portage through life. She was a publicist. Did I mention that?

Okay. Okay. Here's what I should mention. My mother felt far behind me. And I think I was happy. Happy to have her close from a distance. She wrote us all letters. The weather. The endless stream of visitors name-dropped on the page like ink blots. She still used an old Cross fountain pen. Somebody famous gave it to her, only I can't remember whom. Only Cygnet saw her in Tangiers, accompanied by her wastrel actor husband who spent the trip refining his tan on our mother's terrace. Good old Cygnet, you know? She'd do anything once; and often twice, just to be sure. The best trip, the best time, I ever had with her, my mother, I mean, was meeting her in France and spending three weeks in a rented car, driving from Marseilles to Malaga in our own sweet time. I was separated from Lily then. I think I would have gone anywhere with anyone. But this trip was special. For the first time, we got drunk as equals. She said, one noisy night somewhere, that she was sorry about the marriage not working out, even though she barely knew Lily, and I remember hugging her on that short stagger back to the hotel, wishing we had always done this, wishing we were really friends, wishing she were Lily. The wind blew fiercely, forewarning a storm. I kept my big arm around her broad, bony shoulders — to steady the both of us, I think. My mother felt warm and real beside me. The black sky cracked in thin, thunder-stroked splinters. But still, it would not rain. We made it in time. I got to my room shivering. I was shivering though the night was mild and the lightning threw daggers against the stuccoed walls and the arch to the toilet looked sinister suddenly. And I was still shivering. I thought of Lily. I thought of every Sandra Dee I'd ever dated. I thought of Lily. I thought of charades. I thought of the dog she had bought me for Christmas years before, that had been killed that spring. I thought of the way her gold bracelet fell gently against her wristbone as it bent to hold a glass. I thought and I thought and I thought and forgot. I saw pictures patterned on the whitewashed ceiling, and I got into bed for warmth and a better glimpse, feeling safe because my mother was nearby, all the while music from the bar below was slinking up the stairs like a whore. Oh yeah, *"It was raining at first, and I was dying of thirst, so I came in here . . . But what's worse is the pain in here. I can't stay in here . . ."* But I fell asleep, in what had become the usual stupor, before I could roll off the bed to go anywhere. I fell asleep comforted by the soft snores of my mother through impossibly thick walls. Yeah well, you know . . . Or so I'd like to think.

Okay, okay. What next? What happens next?

So after she dies, this is not chronological, after my mother dies, it's the new year. And I am still ragingly busy. I mean absolutely ragingly busy. I told Syrie she had to write all those thank-you cards because she had the best penmanship, and, dare I add, under my bad breath, the most time. Cygnet was busy getting drunk and running back to California where her twenty-year-old son was soon to elope with the twenty-six-year-old star of a teen TV show. A twenty-six-year-old starlet with a bad temper and a reputation for not showing up where she should and frequently where she shouldn't. I mean, this brat marries my nephew and it makes the cover of the *National Enquirer!* It was grotesque. Cygnet was invited to the wedding at the last minute and was told to pick up a cake on her way. She went to Ralph's, for God's sake. A supermarket. Bought two vanilla birthday cakes and a sleeve of plastic wineglasses with stunted stems, and smacked the cakes together using the glasses as support. She did this in the *parking lot.* Wearing her mother-of-the-groom dress, a maroon velvet number she'd once worn to the Emmys. The boy wore running shoes. The bride wore a see-through nightgown and a floral lei. It was a BYOB reception and I think they sent out for pizza, but Cygnet said everybody loved the cake.

Anyway, now that I'm back to work, everything is supposed to be back to normal. Like I know what that means. I'm killing myself. I'm killing myself to get all these books out — everything that didn't make the Christmas lit. supplement — and there are these losers, they're too stupid to call bastards, because that would imply cunning, who won't review a book unless they can drool over it, just in case the author is ever in a position to assign them funding. I have several people who think they have made this pact with me, but, listen, I just send them the books I know they'll like anyway. I just send them the shit. The politically correct stuff. The books with the really ugly covers. There are a few honest reviewers out there. And I value all three of them. They only get $150 for their opinions; it ain't big money, you know. Not worth lying over. There's nobody in this country worth being afraid of, but, of course, no one's asked me to review anything since I took some studiously self-conscious piece of crap and said that if the writer wasn't a Native Canadian and a recipient of a scholarship from McGill, the book would have never been published. Well, after that, I became a kind of blowhard, you know. That Greggie Poole, he just doesn't know how to keep his mouth shut . . . You can always count on Greggie to speak his mind . . . So like his mother, too bad he doesn't have the tal . . . Oh well, Greggie's always been too honest for his own good, hasn't he? Such a shame they've stuffed him behind a desk. Poor Greggie, I hear he's not writing much any more. Yeah, yeah, yeah. *I've* heard it all before. I've heard it all in my own hot head. Goddamnit, I *am* an honest sonofabitch. And I have no company.

Ah, but Lily . . . dearest Lily. There were times you never liked me much. You would tug my arm or roll your eyes vigorously at me after I'd bellied up to the bar in one of my loud shirts and louder ties and then turned to loudly lord it over the surrounding multitude. We knew all of the same people. This wasn't such an advantage, was it? For better. For worse. And worse and worse and worse. You thought I was a real asshole, didn't you? "Pontificating," you said. You said I was pontificating. You said I didn't know when to shut up. You said. . .Well, I said I spent the first eighteen years of my life sitting at somebody else's graven feet; it was bloody well my turn. Then you said I was immature. You said something stinging about at least my mother having sort of earned it. Then I said you were too fucking soft on all these people. Then you said all these people *paid* you in one way or another; I didn't have to go around *alienating* them. I said you could only alienate people you like and respect; alienating people you didn't like and respect is called relief. Yeah, I knew you thought they were a bunch of jerks. But you could only show your contempt for one person at a time; and at the time, it was clear who that one person was. That was when you started rolling away from me in the bed, rolling past the dip in the middle, your legs artfully scrambling to the other side, your long, bony back facing me like a fortress. Once you had liked my big mouth and all that it could do to you. But, by then, it had just become bigger and louder and thoroughly annoying. Yeah, yeah, yeah. I may talk too much, Lily dear, and you may think, because of it, I don't listen any more, but it hasn't stopped me from *seeing*. And I hear more than you think.

Okay, so after the funeral, there were the three days of obligatory bereavement leave. Paid, of course; otherwise, I wouldn't have considered it. So I loaded up at the LCBO and rented videos; watched two John Grisham thrillers in a row and passed out. I grieved. Oh yes, I grieved. Tried to write something appropriately elegiac. Couldn't finish it. Tried the *Globe* crossword puzzle. Couldn't finish that either.

Back at work, my best excuses abandoned me. There were no more pink slips awaiting me, the misspelled medical bulletins lodged under the blotter. Fewer forgiving looks from the staff. No more pointless "sorrys." Instead, the usual demands to be cogent, smart-mouthed and clever. To be diligent. To do my bloody job. So I start spinning the Rolodex, just to get the books off my desk. I mean, there are a hundred fucking books sitting there. Thank Christ, I don't have to actually *read* them. But many, of course, I do. I live alone now, you see. And the dog's dead.

So I digress . . . I have this habit of digressing. Have you noticed that I have been in the habit of digressing? Anyway, the books are off, and the desk starts to breathe again. And this god-awful ugly press kit from the OPEL foundation sits in the centre of it. I am chairperson of the jury this year. The sheer honour of it. I feel myself inflate at the very thought . . . I feel dizzy with the potential of my own corruptibility. Yeah well, I got roped into this, the way I get roped into everything; the call comes when I'm too drunk, too harassed, or just too tired to bother saying no. That's one whole syllable, you know? Yes indeed, that is one whole syllable.

So I was asked to get involved, against my better judgement, by Judith Falkender. Judith Falkender heads the Arts Council. That's so much water under the proverbial bridge that I feel my socks dampen as I sit here. Have I told you yet that I was once involved with Judith Falkender?

She was older than me, well, about sixty, *at least* about sixty, and did well to hide it. First of all, she went to a better plastic surgeon than Syrie whose mouth was so shellacked into place she was starting to look as if she'd had a stroke. Judith never looked less than lovely. I mean, classically lovely. Just so; nothing obvious. Just the Ferragamo loafers and the plain wool skirts at the knee and the brooches pinned to the blazers. The only thing remotely cheap about her was the affair we'd had — sometime between her second and third husbands. Or was it the third and fourth? Needless to say, I was merely diverting. I was most distinctly not her type. I was too individual, too noisy, too lazy, too poor. Her husbands had two things in common: they liked being Judith's lap dogs and, if they were not actually rich, they were at least well connected. One of them was a count, I think. You know, one of those phoney Ruritanian shticks. But I always knew she genuinely liked me. Sent flowers to *me* when my mother died. Totally classic. We weren't that close really, and it was better that way. When she was with me, she always went to bed with her makeup on. It was better that way, too.

Anyway, Judith played with the system like the ties of her suitors. As opposed to my approach which was to jerk chains until somebody gagged. Yeah, yeah, yeah: I have no finesse. Not for that, at least. It was always the same suck-hole, you know? Filled with people you couldn't possibly want to *owe*. If I had a buck for every invitation I've ignored in my life, ignored, I've been told, *at my peril*, well, you can guess the rest of it. I'd be in Fiji right now with my bottomed-out butt in a grass skirt and beautiful brown girls to look after me, bringing me fruit and drink with their little tits swinging en route. I would deflower every one of them. I would be kind. And they would all love me.

It's just a daisy-chain. Let me come right out and say that. Everybody's lips on everybody else's ass, all pining and primping for the same siphoned-off taxes. When I did show up for one of these things, with the cash bar that gouges you shamelessly if your alcoholic palate has a set of standards that doesn't include domestic beer, and the piddly plates of boring cheese — two kinds of Cheddar and a hunk of solidified Brie — for the amusement of watching these really famous writers, I mean, totally rich and successful, amble towards the buffet with all the esprit of a feed steer, as if they were poor or something. As if this was somehow compensating for the years of struggle: expensive drinks and damp crackers. As if they didn't have infinitely better cheese at home. I mean, it would be funny if it weren't so repulsive, so absurd, so typical. And whoever it was who was launching their book would be bombed and either overly modest or hysterically arrogant, their eyes, nonetheless, wide with the terror of impending glory or ruin, and their agents and publicists attached to either arm, the way convicts are escorted to the chair. Can't tell you how many times I've seen the poor bugger who's guest of honour vomiting into a urinal. Or how many times after one of these things, I've wanted to. And, of course, the young kids, the wannabees hanging off every unoriginal word of the never-been-theres, these losers who go to three parties a week, minimum . . . I mean, if they were genuine writers, wouldn't they be at home doing it instead? I ought to know. I always said I was busy whenever I declined, hinting mysteriously at something deeply brilliant awaiting me at home. Then it became bitterly ironic: what the hell was so deeply brilliant after all? My deeply brilliant grocery list? The pad with my deeply brilliant "Jeopardy" scores? Other people's bad, brave writing? It's a sham, I tell you. I tell everybody. Nobody listens. And I still get the fucking invitations. People think I must have some influence, or something. But there aren't many people left in the world who have that when you think of it. And I *know* I'm not one of them. But for all my attempts to the contrary, I know 'em all. I've seen 'em all. God love 'em, the poor fucking idiots.

As for the OPEL prize, well, it's relatively new because some behemoths decided we had to have another jerk-off literary award, or we just would not be civilized. Simply not civilized. It doesn't mean much, this prize, not that any of them do. It's dutifully covered by the media for the minute or two it takes to announce the name of the winner, but it actually doesn't sell the book. God forbid it should sell the book. I remember walking past the Edwards' store at Yonge and Eglinton and seeing one of the books shortlisted for the OPEL on the remainder table outside the front door. This was before the actual prize giving, so I went back after I knew it had won, and the same three tatty copies were still sitting in the shadows of a faint winter sun. No signs, you know. No stickers. No nothing. Just $20,000 to the winner and something to italicize in the next book jacket biography. People aren't impressed by awards here, unless a Canadian gets one from the States. Then it has to matter; they're so much smarter down there.

I get $2,000 for chairing this jury. Two thousand dollars for the time it takes me to read three shortlisted books. Works out to about $250 an hour, which is easy money. Flagrantly easy. Like any good whore, I can work on my back. In bed. Drink handy. And my bed has been bereft of any real activity for some time. Oh, oh, I was telling you about Judith, wasn't I?

So Judith and I have an affair. A way of sealing the friendship. You have to do that sometimes. We were good together in a perverse sort of way; rather, I mean we actually looked good together. In a perverse sort of way. She was so slender and gleaming, her voice as finished as a fine piece of wood. I was so dog-eared and loud and so doggone lovable. Her hand would disappear into the crook of my arm as we walked into a room. Her hand reminded me of the bones of a quail: so small, so articulated, so perfectly breakable. And she weighed it down with an enormous emerald.

One night, back in the fall . . . This is to get back to the point of all this . . . She and I met for drinks at the Delisle. She gave me the pitch about the prize. Same old redundant stuff. Attempted to flatter me by saying if I'd picked up the writing again, who knows what would happen. As if I could expect a call from the Nobel committee. As if she'd actually *read* me. Blah. Blah. Blah. I let her talk. I let myself listen. She said I would make the perfect jury chair: I was so respected. If not respectable, I added silently, wondering if I had the qualities to make the perfect jury table. This was all such bullshit. I said okay.

This was before I learned who my fellow jurists were, and by this time, it was too late to do anything but act judicial. I'd had affairs with two of them too. And so goes this story. But later. Later. I have a few things to dispense with first. Just a few. I promise. Please, please God, don't think of this as some long thing about my long, lost love life. It isn't even interesting to myself any more.

Still, I should get back to Lily for a minute. There is little in the way of real remnants and reminders. So like a real divorce. As opposed to those shrines and keepsakes we make of our dead. Lily is very much alive to me. Oh yes, all the more so. We can talk about anything now, just like we did when we were dating. Funny, isn't it? How you make the commitment, only to seal it with silence. Now, there's none of the tension. None of that "If I say this now, will she reward me later?" Or "Does she really want me to be honest?" Ah well, I'm honest in everything, that's my downfall. Now and then Lily just gives me a call. Did I mention she is a publicist? She is always on the phone. And she calls to check up on me, but not in an ex-wifely way, if you know what I mean. I've always had this horrible nightmare that I'll be dead for days before anyone remembers they haven't seen me lately. I see myself lying stiff in a chair with the TV on and Regis Philbin reflecting off my glassy, opened eyes. But that will never happen, as long as Lily's there. There's someone out there who's thinking of me, who isn't *me*. Lily comes over when I'm sick. This is hardly ever, but it's a nice thought. Brings ginger ale, for God's sake, and knows I'll never drink it. Walked the dog when I had one. Buys me *People* magazine. And when my mother lay dead and unretouched in the basement of the funeral home, Lily bought me dinner, and drove me home. Came to the funeral and sat near the back. I remember Cygnet waving to her as we walked up the aisle. I would have liked to wave, too. But I was too tired to salute a thing.

Yeah, all this and we broke up despite it. Lots of years. Lots of stagnant water under that rickety bridge. We had to move three times to accommodate just the books. Never occurred to us to throw anything away except, when the time came, the rings. When I left, hauling all my worldly goods to the non-existent curb to await my ride . . . well, when I left, that was the most deadening feeling in the world. Shuffling the gravel in the unearthly morning quiet, the sun squeezing out from the darkness of dawn, it was so still I was afraid to swallow the lump in my throat. It was so quiet, I swear I could hear Lily part the shutters above me. But, although I could not pack it, I knew I was taking my imagination with me. Lily was never one to look back. Nor, for that matter, was I. Once that had made us well suited, all this fucking forward thinking. But that early morning, by myself on Balmoral Avenue, I only saw what was the smallest wedge of my future, and in it, I stood absolutely alone.

Ah, this is sentimental shit. Bloody sentimental effing shit. Sorry about that. Nothing worse than self-pity. Nothing easier, either. You know that's not the point of this. You should know, that's not the point. This isn't what I'm here for, you know. I'm not taking any pleasure out of this. I'm only rambling. Preambling, really. This is my preamble. My prologue. I'm going to get on with it, I promise. Yeah, really. I have always promised that. Besides, this is all about the OPEL jury. It isn't about me. Yeah, okay, so it's about me. But not in the way you probably think. Really. I'm not here to make you feel sorry for me. The point is, I want you to know the point I was at when this OPEL business began. I was floundering, see? Treading water with the sharks. That's what it's all about. Hang on. Hang on. It'll get clearer. I should have organized myself better. I am spitting out the truth through the hole in my life raft. Hang in there, okay? Pay attention. Are you still paying attention? Well then, I have to tell you a little more about my sisters.

My sisters are important, okay? I've got to get my family off my back, before I can straighten up and get into the rest of it. The daughters of Marjorie Poole. What about them? You've seen enough of the son for a while; let me take you into the sisterly shade.

So Syrie became a woman at about fourteen. I don't mean she began menstruating or having sex or anything like that. She just stopped being a girl. Stood suddenly straighter. Wore gloves. Knew already that boys were mostly dumb, and, at best, a necessary burden. Knew already that most men weren't as interesting as they thought. She had our father to thank for that. True to form, she married the best possible bore.

Now, not everybody thought Frank Kemp was boring. This is a purely personal opinion. But I really do think he fooled people. Had the very finest blood. Couldn't get a Rhodes scholarship, so his parents pulled some favours and got him into Oxford anyway. He wasn't too bright, you see, but he faked it. Smiled easily and well. Aimed to please. He had good hair and a dimple. Made a lifetime career of disarming people. Ended up as minister of revenue for a while. Spent the rest of his time as a tax lawyer on Bay Street. Bought Syrie an excellent address. Fathered photogenic children. He blended well, if you know what I mean. Toyed with running for the Liberals after Trudeau, but tested the waters in private and found them thoroughly chilled. Went back to Forest Hill and the tennis court and the plush office with the tinted window overlooking city hall, which I will swear on a stack of relics he never once glanced out of, not that he was too busy or anything. Old Frank was totally dense. But, man, it kept him safe. He was one of those men with his hands endlessly on his hips. He was, my mother once said, "totally fumigated of original thought."

But Syrie was made for this sort of life, even if she was not born to it. Marjorie Poole's daughters ought to have married academics or journalists: intelligent guys with scatter rugs in smoky rooms, and more influence than money. Men like our mother, if you get my drift. But both of them, both Syrie and Cygnet, wouldn't do it on a dare. I'm not certain why, really, except they saw enough of what passed for our parents' marriage and probably thought there *had* to be another way. Funny too, but they both married, you know, *real men*. No, no, no, no. Don't get this wrong. What I mean is both of them married *guys* . . . My God, our father might have been a lot of things, but a guy . . . Oh no, he was not one of them. So Syrie humiliated our mother entirely and became, you know, the deferential consort. Ran the effortlessly impressive household. Went to Liberal fundraisers as if she actually *enjoyed* them. They had two kids. Mattie, the eldest, who married equally well, had twins and retired at twenty-eight to go to the mall in her Volvo, while her tennis jock husband went to work for his father. Two of a kind, they were, she and Syrie. Mattie married at Timothy Eaton Memorial Church in an $8,000 wedding dress from New York, orchestrated up the aisle by Syrie in a Valentino, and borrowed children, barely old enough to walk.

The son, Syrie and Frank's son, is another story. I will spare you most of it. He chose to find himself, because he had nothing better to do, and his parents were always paying. He never had the wit to realize that the effort's mostly pointless; we are all the same meat and matter, full of the same array of godly gifts and tired shit. We may come in exotically different packages, but it's all the same for most of us. Otherwise, we'd be special. Nobody I know is that special. So Marlon, this is Frank and Syrie's son, goes to grad school for theology, law school for whatever, and up to the Arctic to rehabilitate a group of native alcoholics; hell, he could have just tried his hand with Auntie Cygnet. He wrote a screenplay and asked for my feedback and for once in my life, I was avuncular and laconic, which passed for encouraging. Marlon now stays home and keeps Syrie company while working part-time as a phys. ed. instructor. His parents are actually quite proud of him: he didn't cause fatal car accidents, OD on cocaine, rape a Havergal girl, or enjoy a brief career in petty theft, like the children of some of their friends. Marlon was one of those kids who was almost so smart he was actually stupid. Stupid, as in the ways of the world, you know? I can't stand people like that. The very opposite of his father who was so innately out of it, he was taken for clever. I can't stand people like that, either. I can't stand the fucking con.

And as for Syrie, she wintered in Arizona until the first facelift; now she and Frank go golfing in Bermuda every spring, where Frank adds to her jewellery collection as he gets ruddier and more handsome. The sun's baked in the trenches around his eyes, and his teeth gleam as grandly as his hair. Syrie is content enough, though she is wound so tight it's hard to tell if she's happy. I suspect she isn't, but she's got more of what she wanted out of life than most. She's very well known in the circles in which she moves. Had a whole chapter written about her in a tell-all about the Toronto social scene. She professed to be appalled and litigious, but I'm sure she was secretly pleased. After too many years of being "daughter of" and "sister of" and "wife of" and thank God, seldom "mother of," she finally got a chapter of her own, even if it was in a bad book about a layer of local society few knew about, but those who did pretended it was important so Toronto could seem even more like New York. No, no, no. Toronto will never be New York. And we prove it by not being grown up enough to admit it. Syrie and I, we're not that close. No, I wouldn't say we were close. We are friendly and ambivalent. One Christmas, I stared at her over the turkey carcass and realized I hardly knew her at all. God bless us, everyone.

Now Cygnet's a different story, but let me get a drink before I go on. I found the ice, you know. I found the ice, and I made some more, and the bottle's still full enough not to panic and I know the stretch will do me good. Yeah, a stretch. The bottle's in the kitchen, I think. The hall beckons with its escorting light. Is it just me, or does the light seem awfully bright? I'm going to bring the bottle back with me. Oh yeah. One stretch is quite enough.

Okay, Cygnet. She was delicate. And like my mother, she needed the strokes. She had to be told how wonderful she was. She had to be told this on a frequent basis. Syrie and I, we were the hardy ones. I don't know if Cygnet ever heard it often enough, and well enough, or at least enough to keep her peaceful and happy. I do not know that at all. I do know now, however, that Cygnet seems to find what passes for comfort at the bottom of a once-brimming glass. She likes TV, too.

When her first serious boyfriend dumped her, when she was about nineteen, I guess, she scratched herself a couple of times with a razor blade she used for shaving her legs. The cuts were so shallow, she only needed Band-Aids. My mother told her not to be so stupid and melodramatic. Told her there wasn't a man on the planet worth drawing blood for. All these years, you know . . . all these years, I had thought she had been so callous, when now I see she had been only right. Cygnet sought refuge in movie magazines, where all men seemed handsome and harmless.

Eventually, she got out of bed long enough to go somewhere. She went to Hollywood where, in 1962, she met Hollis Dawes.

Hollis Dawes was born in Yorkshire to a family that ran a county paper. Now this was interesting. I always found this interesting. But Hollis did not think so. He went to London, lost his imagination, his accent and any innate originality, and became an actor, did all right in the fifties — bit parts in good movies, better parts in bad — and parlayed his inoffensive good looks and basic Britishness into a pretty lucrative American career. He already had his first TV show by the time Cygnet met him. Was one of those gadabouts who owned more than one tuxedo. Considered an all-purpose escort, quick with the compliments and the monogrammed lighter, he romanced several actresses whose names I fear I cannot mention here. And on December 5, 1963, he married Cygnet at the Beverly Wilshire Hotel with George Maharis as best man.

Now Cygnet just loved this life. Absolutely loved it, until she realized that the dips and furrows in Hollie's fortunes were innately, nay intimately, tied to her own. Then she got drunk enough not to mind the invitations to all the second-rate parties.

Things were more or less over for Hollie by the early seventies. He wasn't big enough to withstand not being hip. I mean, he wasn't fucking Frank Sinatra or anything. He didn't work for years, told everyone he was "taking the year off," and Cygnet said that too, but, really, he just sat around the house in Santa Monica watching television, and one year grew into several. They had the one son named Van, the good-looking idiot — he had that ridiculous wedding, Cygnet and her lop-sided cakes — who hung out at the mall, I guess, waiting for someone to make him an offer. So like his dad. Poor, poor Cygnet. Men seemed so weak around her, as if they thought her fortitude was innate rather than ingested.

Hollie braved on, though, and for this, I quite admired him. I really quite admired him. I knew my mother couldn't have done it, this exile to one's own living room. Hollie went to Broadway, to replace the lead in a semi-successful play, went on the road with it, and then returned to the coast for a slew of TV appearances in shows like "Columbo" and "The Love Boat." Hung around the old haunts with new people. Died in 1986, supposedly after having sex with a twenty-year-old who gave

177

him one too many poppers. Died in the saddle, they said. Poor, poor Cygnet. She was almost sober at the funeral.

Cygnet liked Los Angeles, which worried me: how far had all this drinking taken her? So she stayed there a while in the big beach house, living with Van and her vodka, until he found that better offer. He was actually on "A Current Affair." Ah, culture. She exchanged the house for an apartment in Westwood, and a better car; then got a place on the waterfront in Toronto with a nice view of the Gardiner Expressway: "city views," they say. Yeah yeah, yeah: that is, if you can see it. At night it was glittery enough, but Cygnet's eyes were too blurry by then.

So, my family . . . This is my family. Lily. Cygnet. Syrie. Frank. Old Hollie. Van. Marlon, such dazed and drifting boys. Mattie . . . My father. The rotting fruit of the womb. The offspring of the icon. She knew Faulkner, you know. She visited Paul Bowles in Tangiers. She knew 'em all. And she would most certainly tell you about it. She died a while ago. I mentioned that, didn't I? She got old. She got sick. She died. My mother died drunk in her oxygen tent. And I was not there. Oh, where are the cigarettes? The coat, the coat . . . I think they're in the coat. My coat hangs like a carcass in the hall. I can barely see it. But the light there's so bright. I think the cigarettes are in the coat in the hall. In the pocket, I think. If I remembered to bring them. Oh God, a prayer . . . a prayer to let them be there. In the hall where the coat is. In the pocket. I can't remember which one.

It's late and I'm tired. I talk all fucking day. Now, I come home to talk to myself. I miss Lily. I miss the dog. I miss my mother in ways I would have once thought were impossible. I miss having her as my best and finest excuse. I miss the confidence that came from settling so long in her shade. Where am I now, you know? Except in an old man's apartment, in the dark, in trouble. Oh yeah, I am asking for trouble. I've thought of it all day: I am the elder now. And I do not like it. I have no laurels on which to sit my aging ass. I do not even have my anonymity. I am famous for my failures, my inability to live up to . . . *what?* No, no, really, my inability to be the son my mother could be proud of. And yet I know if I threatened to equal her, she would have hated me absolutely. I kept myself small for her. In the hopes that she would love me unreservedly. In the hopes she would think me respectful.

III
ON THE VERGE OF BECOMING

ANNE CARSON was born in Canada and is currently a professor of Classics at McGill University, Montreal. She is the author of *Eros the Bittersweet: An Essay* (Princeton, 1986) and *Short Talks* (Brick Books, 1992), as well as *Plainwater*, a collection of essays and verse forthcoming from Knopf (1995), and *Glass, Irony and God*, a collection of essays and verse forthcoming from New Directions (1995). She has recently written and co-hosted a PBS TV documentary series called "The Nobel Legacy," which aired in April 1995. In her off hours she paints volcanoes and bats.

The Fall of Rome: A Traveller's Guide

Anne Carson

I

By this time tomorrow I will be a man of Rome.

II

I
am

going

to
visit
Anna Xenia.

III

Long cold fingers
dipped in blue roses

pry open the red world.

A motionless aeroplane
goes shrieking over
the oceans of Europe.

IV

The captain has turned on the FASTEN SEATBELT sign.

V

Anna Xenia will be waking now.

VI

We fall helplessly into Rome.

VII

Who I am doesn't matter.
As you see me

fighting to survive,

fighting to be esteemed and honoured
(so that my past vanishes),
you will dismiss me as nothing terrific.

Fair enough,
but there is one thing about me:
I can take you to Anna Xenia.

VIII

She is a citizen of the ancient republic,
historian of its wars

and ravishing

in
her
armour.

IX

Now although I hate to travel
I go a lot of places

and have noted

certain recurrent phenomena.
A journey, for example,
begins with a voice

calling your name out
behind you.
This seems a convenient arrangement.

How else would you know it's time to go?
On the other hand,
who is it?

and what do they want?
So too a friendship
begins before the first meeting,

an empire
before the first conquest.
Anna Xenia has studied at Oxford.

Maybe
she can explain
some of this to me.

X

First meeting.
Pacing the sidewalk in front of my hotel

in a sweat, will she look different? do I look

different? what if I don't recognize — perhaps
she is here already! — I wheel:
there.

She is. Smiling hard.
Holding five gigantic red flowers
upside down (Roman custom?) at which

I clutch,
all language vanished from my mind.
We knock each other over

in a violent embrace
and hurtle off
to find Rome.

XI

What is the holiness of the citizen?
It is to open

a day

to a stranger,
who has no day
of his own.

XII

There is a wonderful lot of talk in Rome.
I walk about in it

moving zigzag,

parting it like a comb,
hearing it coil
together

behind me.
Entrata.
Uscita.

XIII

A stranger makes no fissure.

XIV

Second meeting.
When I think I have walked enough

I go to Anna Xenia's.

She is as beautiful as an island.
She looms on tiny hooves
and makes Nescafé.

There is a wonderful lot of talk in Anna Xenia.
She cocks her head like Cicero
and pretends

I am someone talking back.
Good afternoon.
I'm well thanks how are you?

XV

From deep within
my traveller's clothes

I watch these conversations take place.

Italian is a beautiful language,
also very difficult.
So long.

XVI

Then I return to my hotel.
Take off the big coat.

Hang up

the enormous trousers.
Sit down to wait
for the nightmare.

XVII

As the master of the day is Anna Xenia,
the master

of the night

is dread.
I position myself.

It fills up the room.

XVIII

It seeps beneath doors,
beneath sleep,

it fills up the bed,

the corridor,
it rises to cover *Entrata*
and *Uscita*,

no way out,
no way in,
a stranger

sleeps
in a solution of dread.
Romans hate a stranger.

XIX

Why have you
come here?

You

have
broken in,
why?

XX

I think I will call my nightmare The Fall of Rome.

XXI

Alaric invaded Rome in 410 A.D.
The nightmare

was waiting for him.

He stayed three days.
Entrata
Uscita.

XXII

What was the holiness
of Alaric?

It was to run

and keep
running.
Out the dawn side.

XXIII

A stranger is someone who runs by night
down streets where Alaric ran,

falling in a nightmare of God.

Excuse me please tell me, which way to the exit? *Entrata.*
Entrata.
Entrata.

Sores breaking out.
What is the holiness of the stranger?
He has none.

XXIV

A stranger is poor, voracious and turbulent.
He comes

from nowhere in particular

and pushes prices up.
His method of knowing something
is to eat it.

XXV

Yes, Romans hate a stranger.
Swaying miraculously on their stilts

Romans stand for a state of civilization.

With the names of the cities
and rivers
and principal provinces

clearly marked.
With the seats of disease
identified.

With the holy days
lit in a row.
No

grinning.
No
nakedness.

XXVI

How do Romans know
who is the stranger?

Pronto.

Evil picks him out.
Anna Xenia explained this to me.
"Every stranger is a villain in the true sense."

XXVII

You think I am talking about jet lag,
a touch of insomnia,

a little traveller's ennui.

No.
I hate to bother you,

but I am talking about evil.

It blooms.
It eats.
It grins.

It has 28 eyes.
You can see it racing down the centuries of all the strangers
who have come here —

since Aeneas,
for all I know,
wings outspread.

A stranger is evil.
The sores may be so thick-matted
you can hardly see

his ears and tail,
but no Roman
is fooled by that.

If he weren't evil he wouldn't be
a stranger,
would he?

XXVIII

Now,

I have a tendency to dread.
I have to watch it.

XXIX

I grin.
I eat.

Thousand of cuts morning and night,

practising fierce techniques of horrible war! useless.
Dread masters me.
I do not master dread.

XXX

A stranger is master of nothing.

Who in a nightmare
can help himself?

XXXI

On the other hand,
it gives me a pretext

for travel (travel

justifies dread:
other places really are
terrible).

XXXII

And besides, in this case
there is no mistake.

Romans do hate (as I say)

a stranger. And
their reasoning
is empirically

sound.
What is the holiness of empire?
It is to know collapse.

Everything can collapse.
Houses, bodies
and enemies

collapse
when their rhythm becomes
deranged.

XXXIII

Rome collapsed when Alaric ran out the dawn side.

XXXIV

A stranger is someone who comes on the wrong day.

XXXV

Forgets to telephone.

XXXVI

And interrupts the Roman at his work.

XXXVII

You are asking for trouble
if you surprise a Roman

on a day

when he thinks he is free
of public
performance.

XXXVIII

He will come to the door of his cage
as cold and furious

as that beast whose tawny skull

he loves to smash
on other days of the week
in the name of the *Pax Romana*.

XXXIX

A stranger is someone who stands in the doorway,
drenched in confusion,

and permits the dog to escape.

Anna Xenia chases the dog
down five flights.
She comes back

to find me still in the doorway.
It is a difficult moment.
Third meeting.

XL

Excuse me, may I come in, nonetheless?
Shall I sit down, all the same?

A stranger is someone desperate for conversation.

Then why is it I never have anything to say?
We perch in our armour
at the kitchen table.

Lunch has been cleared away
and she has got her smile up
as far as the mouth.

Please speak more slowly.
It is my first visit
to Rome.

XLI

Faced with a villain
a Roman knows what to do.

Rant.

Papal history. The
persecution of Tasso.
The pomposity

of Seneca.
The insincerity of the Communist Party Secretary of Rome
(whose wife collects topaz).

The landlady.
The doorlocks.
The plumbing —

XLII

it is noble.

Like Cicero addressing the Senate,
Anna Xenia grows as she talks —

XLIII

she pauses mid-tide ("Shall I

make us some Nescafé?") just as

the waterpipes gasp and go dry.

XLIV

A stranger is someone
who sits

very still at the kitchen table,

looks down at his knuckles,
thinks some day we will laugh about this,
doesn't believe it.

XLV

"Uccidi! flagella! brucia!"
I beg you.

"This Roman water!"

What is the problem?
"Shuts itself off whenever it likes!"
What is the reason?

"There is no reason!"
Shall we notify someone?
"There is no one to notify!"

What can we do?
"There is nothing we can do!"
I have brought with me to Rome

(as you advised)
Helpful Phrases for Travellers
in the pocket Italian

edition.
Helpful phrases come to mind.
Please show me to the lifeboat.

XLVI

A stranger is someone
who knows little of plumbing.

If water stops

he goes to another city,
washes his face
in *acqua minerale,*

or begins a novena.
And helpful phrases
lie close at hand.

I see we have a breakdown.
May I speak to the manager?
Where does one get the train for Milan?

XLVII

But in a Roman life
are only impossibilities.

Che posso farci?

Nothing you can do.
It is simply a bad, implacable Roman fact
like the way they drive.

XLVIII

Nevertheless, I feel I should say something.

XLIX

I lunge for words.
She knocks them away.

At one point (how stupid

can a stranger be?)
I even ask her about God!
This is terrible. This is

broad daylight and the nightmare
is filling up the room.
Senza uscita.

L

You don't remember me at all, do you?

LI

A stranger is someone who walks in
and for an instant
I don't know it is you —

an instant
almost as troubling as death,
or so

some believe,
for example
Proust:

"*. . . c'est admettre que ce qui était ici,*
l'être qu'on se rappelle n'est plus,
et que ce qui y est,

c'est un être qu'on on ne connaissait pas;
c'est avoir à penser un mystère
presque aussi troublant

que celui de la mort dont il est,
du reste,
comme la préface et l'annonciateur."

Now Proust
spent no time in Rome.
And he has a complex way

of understanding what a stranger is
(he gets it inside out)
which would not stand

Roman scrutiny.
Nonetheless,
his piercing eyes

open wide
on what the real trouble is.
It is that voice behind you.

LII

For, if you think about it,
all first hatred of strangers

contains this idea of death,

of your death which will one day walk up to you
in just such a fashion.
Buon giorno, death will say.

LIII

What is the holiness of conversation?

It is
to master death.

LIV

You think I am being melodramatic.
One awful conversation about waterpipes

isn't the end of a friendship.

Well, a stranger is someone
who takes dread a little too seriously.
Out

on the street again at sunset,
sores open,
moving blindly.

There is a loneliness that fills the plain.
Total.
Lunar.

Who in a nightmare can help himself?
Good morning.
Excuse me.

Good night.
Yes this is my (our) first trip to Rome.
I am (we are) having a topnotch time.

May I introduce you to my (our) wife (husband,
son, daughter, mother, father, masculine friend,
feminine friend)?

You are welcome.
You are very welcome.
It is two

in the morning.
I would like to speak to the chief of police.
There is a black planet speeding towards us.

LV

Fifth meeting.
When she smiles like that

she is as beautiful as all my secrets.

Anna Xenia has decided
we must visit Orvieto.
A thing like this can save a stranger's life.

LVI

For Anna Xenia,
as for most Romans,

driving is war.

Perhaps, on the way to Orvieto,
she will explain to me
why this is so?

Yes (slams horn) *naturalmente!*
Her explanation is lengthy.
Well exampled (horn).

Solidly convincing.
At the end she pauses.
Short silence.

Suddenly
a whoop of laughter

and she slaps the steering wheel.
"You're right,
there's no reason at all!"
It delights her all the way to Orvieto.

LVII

Now,
Orvieto.

The city is of Etruscan origin,

once a papal stronghold.
On top
arises

a pedestal of volcanic rock.
On top of the rock is a word.
In the years from 1290 to 1600,

there were 33 architects,
152 sculptors,
68 painters

and 90 mosaicists
at work shaping the word
into a cathedral.

They covered the outside
with jewels and stones and gold.
They filled the inside

with 17 perfect horizontal stripes,

in alternating courses of black and white stone,
60 metres long.

They inflected the word
into one clear command.
Think of it.

Think what it means
to be a stranger
and to walk into the word "Live!"

LVIII

For the first time since I came to Rome
I am thinking beyond death.

I laugh.

She looks.
She laughs.
It is sunset

and we are driving home.
Masters
of *entrata* and *uscita*.

LIX

What is the holiness of mastery?

Let us help ourselves
to a theory of the martial arts.

LX

It is to cut your opponent
just at the moment he cuts you.

This is the ultimate timing.

It is lack of anger.
It means to treat your enemy
as an honoured guest.

LXI

Besides the cathedral,
at Orvieto there is

a second tourist attraction.

It is a well.
The *Pozzo di San Patrizio*
was built by Pope Clement VII

to supply the town with water
in case of a siege.
It is over 62 metres deep.

There are 248 comfortable steps
from the top to the bottom of the well: 248 spiral back up.
They are not the same steps.

LXII

Designed concentrically
the two staircases fit

one within the other

like a jacknife blade
within a jacknife,
so that two people

one coming up,
the other going down,
can never meet.

LXIII

Meanwhile I know you will be pleased
if I leave with you

to chew over in your own time,

a small question of interpretation
which arose out of my visit to Orvieto.
The cathedral contains a chapel,

now known as the Signorelli Chapel,
decorated in 1499 with monumental frescoes,
painted pilasters, panels of grotesques

and false windows
by the famed Luca Signorelli,

for a fee of 180 ducats paid pro rata.

Around the lower walls of the chapel
Signorelli has added
a series of grisaille medallions

illustrating scenes from Dante's *Commedia.*
They are monochrome,
eerie in appearance

and iconologically
controversial.
For example,

one medallion depicts the scene from *Purgatorio III*
where Dante is accosted by a mob of souls.
They are demanding an answer.

E urgente.
Permesso?
They point.

Dante's text makes clear
that it is Dante's shadow
which has mastered the attention of the whimpering shades,

for throughout the *Purgatorio* (you well know)
only Dante,
as a living man,

casts a shadow.
Dante makes no mistake
about what the laws of optics require here.

Shadow is a matter of interception of light.
The dead intercept nothing. *Capisco.*
Much less clear

is Signorelli's rendering of the scene.
He had given everyone a shadow.
Why?

The standard guidebook explanation
fails to nourish me:
" . . . Signorelli has assigned shadows

to all figures,
unable to suppress
his naturalistic training

even at the expense of poetic veracity."
Non capisco.
I point. _____

_____

LXIV

There are three ways to master death.
Here is the third one (the one

Anna Xenia told me

on the way home from Orvieto).
Signorelli is painting late in his studio
when they carry in his son,

killed in a riot.
He sits up all night with the body,

making sketch after sketch

and throwing them into a pile.
From that time
all his angels

have the one
same
face.

_____

LXV

Sixth meeting.
Three years ago today

Anna Xenia's son died

on a night of heavy rain and bad traffic.
He was broken but lucid.
"What time is it?"

he kept asking.
It is two in the morning.
"No!

Impossible!
Look at the light pouring there!"
He points.

_____

LXVI

Her marble tears run down her marble face.

A stranger is someone who has no handkerchief.

Who has no words to say.

Whose shadow mind is burning
as he sits watching her hands
and thinks how rare!

to see a Roman
talk
with no gestures at all.

_____

_____

LXVII

There are divers things you can learn
from a guidebook.

The Hachette Guide to France for example,

provides four pages of maps showing
distribution of roof styles,
while Osamu Dazai's

Travels of a Purple Tramp
mainly relates the regrets
of this sad and stumbling person,

and how much he drank,
on the way to visit his hometown of Tsugaru.
From Marco Polo you find out

exactly how to get to China.
From Herodotos,

a theory of why
Egyptian women urinate standing up
(because the men do it sitting down).
A traveller can warn you

of climate
of prices
or other people's etiquette

and make himself useful
in fond and sharpening ways.
But no.

LXVIII

Instead,
I pour over you

this bath of dread.

Why is a nightmare
drawing a circle
around us?

LXIX

Last meeting.
Anna Xenia is at my hotel very early,

dressed in red.

It is important to strike a positive note,

towards the end.
I (we) have had a topnotch time.
Italian has proven a beautiful language,
also very difficult.
On this,

my first visit to Rome,
I have mastered a few words
(entrata, uscita)

and suppressed others
(villano, morte).
You have been most kind,

in speaking slowly
and inviting me in for Nescafé.
Although tongue-tied myself,

your conversation has led me to uncover
certain false answers
to life's basic questions.

(That stranger was myself! etc.)
Once or twice we spoke our hearts:
"cet immense désir de connaître la vie"

as Proust so simply calls it.
Please summon a porter.
It is time to go.

LXX

We kiss in slow motion.

She turns and heads off
in her small red soldier's coat.

Off, and stepping cleanly
towards the first day of school.
Off and down the ramp,

almost deaf in the glare of the white sand ahead,
the tiny gladiator,
stuffing her shadow into her mouth as she goes.

Until
we meet again.
So long.
_____

ROBERT GIARD

STAN PERSKY teaches philosophy at Capilano College in North Vancouver, B.C., and is the author of *Buddy's: Meditations on Desire* (New Star, 1991) and *Then We Take Berlin* (Knopf Canada, 1995).

THE TRANSLATORS' TALE

STAN PERSKY

It had been reported in the press that the two men, translators in Tirana, Albania, had shared "a tiny, Spartan office" in the state publishing house for most of the previous twenty-two years. For some reason, that touching detail particularly fascinated me. "Behind battered typewriters," the article said, perhaps a bit melodramatically, "they have battled to keep fragments of literature alive in the darkness of Stalinist orthodoxy."*

The story had been published a few months before, in April 1991. Reading the brief account of the two now middle-aged men, one wondered the simplest things. How had they spent their time? What did they talk about? Keep necessarily silent about? What loyalties had caused them to persevere? How had they maintained their sanity? — for it seemed an ultimate test of sanity. It was something like those stories one occasionally

---

* Paul Koring, "Awakening from the Nightmare," *The Globe and Mail* (Toronto), April 10, 1991.

ran into ages ago, in which a pair of Japanese soldiers emerged from a jungle in
Burma or Java twenty years after the war, never having heard that it had ended.

In the case of Mr. Simoni and Mr. Qesku — those were their names — the
endurance had been similar, but the cause was rather more recognizable to us. The
convulsions that swept away régimes across Europe, from Warsaw to Bucharest, in
the late 1980s, had at last, in the early nineties, reached the hills of what was once
ancient Illyria. And blinking into the uncertain sunlight — for it was hardly clear
that our vaunted free markets would provide a panacea for their woes — there
appeared the translators of Tirana, having, you could say, kept the faith. It was a faith
that transcended the generations-long remoteness which shrouded their land.
Albania was not a Burmese jungle nor an island in the Indies, but a southern
European nation wedged between Greece and what was then Yugoslavia, a mere
eighty kilometres across the Adriatic from Bari or Brindisi in Italy; yet for all that, it
might have been as distant as the moon, so successfully and for so long had its
Glorious Leader sealed it off as the last and purest bastion of Communism.

That spring and summer, I was in Berlin, thinking about the fall of Communism (it
was more than a year since the opening of the Berlin Wall), reading a little philosophy (that's the subject I teach at a college in Vancouver), and pursuing the amorous
adventures that leisurely evenings in bars and cafés sometimes yielded.

I was often to be found at a table in the Café Einstein in the late afternoons at
the beginning of summer, like many of the other patrons, engrossed in a book or
newspaper. Though it was something of a reading-list staple when I went to school,
somehow I had never gotten around to Joseph Conrad's *Heart of Darkness* until then.
Or perhaps I had, and had merely read it carelessly as a student — since, upon taking it up now, it seemed both fresh and yet strangely familiar to me.

As I began (or began again) the tale of a journey to what had once seemed like the
ends of the earth, it called up the ideas I had about Albania, a preoccupation that had
been inspired by the brief newspaper article about the translators I'd read earlier that
spring. (In fact, I'd clipped the story and tucked it into the back of my notebook.)

I never really admitted to my friends in Berlin that I intended to go to Albania. At
most, I'd say something casual and indirect like, "I wonder if it's possible to fly to Tirana
from here?" Perhaps I didn't even want to admit it to myself, fearing that a glimpse of
its foolishness might put me off. Nonetheless, however desultorily, I made the necessary

phone calls, inquired at a travel agency, checked the airline office. One day, I got my friend Manuel (he was also my current amorous adventure) to accompany me to the Albanian consulate in east Berlin, only to find the dilapidated building locked and to be informed by a caretaker that I needed to contact the office in Bonn.

My *method* — to use a word that appears prominently in Conrad's tale — was circuitous at best. Indeed, it was a sort of game that I called "following the story," in which one set certain events in motion, or created the possibility of setting them in motion, by some ordinary but deliberate act — reading a book, walking a certain route, going to a particular place (say, the bar where I met Manuel). And if something happened as a consequence, the challenge then — the whole point of the game, really — was to attend to the ensuing possibilities in such a way that the pattern of meanings we call a story resulted.

Reading the opening pages of Conrad's story, I found it easy to identify with its narrator, Marlow, the veteran sailor who was making his way about Brussels to secure a posting on a Congo riverboat of the Belgian trading company that, for all practical purposes, ruled that distant African land. I too had been to sea. As I read — while at the same time arranging my own curious journey — Albania seemed as distant as Marlow's destination, and Comrade Enver Hoxha, who had ruled it, was a figure as forbidding as Kurtz, the god-man who dominates the Polish writer's tale.

Of course, I was aware of the cliché of reading Conrad in that way. The "heart of darkness" was everybody's metaphor; whoever travelled to what might be regarded as an obscure corner of the earth invoked it. But there was nothing I could do about it. If you're a reader, sooner or later you read Conrad, and by happenstance, I was reading *Heart of Darkness* at exactly that moment.

In the end (the end of the beginning, that is), I found myself filling out a visa application form while seated at a table in the Café Einstein. I was in the high-ceilinged room of the villa that overlooked the café garden, which was more than half empty that particular afternoon, leaving to the tame sparrows in the garden who hopped up onto the tables almost no one from whom they might filch a stray crumb of *Apfelkuchen*. Wettest, coldest June in memory, the German tabloids blared, along with requisite references to "global warming" and other climatic disturbances. And still chilly, even into July. The black-jacketed waiters moved among the bundled-up patrons at a glacial pace, carrying hot drinks on sterling trays.

When I asked my friends, in that studiedly casual voice I'd adopted for the purpose,

"I wonder if it's possible to fly to Tirana from here?" they invariably replied, with barely restrained politeness, "But why would you want to go there?" Or else they would fail to hear me correctly, and make me repeat the name of the Albanian capital, and then they, who had been almost everywhere, would quizzically repeat it themselves — "Tirana?" — in the slightly astonished tones reserved for impossibly distant places or vanished cities of the past.

Sometimes they would attempt to dissuade me by pointing out the difficulties of acquiring a visa. "I phoned," I'd report. "To Bonn, of course," one of them assumed. "To Tirana," I said. "You can phone Tirana?" they warily asked. "Easier than East Berlin," I replied, drawing a wan smile from my friends for all the times we'd tried to make an appointment across the once-divided city.

The attaché in Bonn suggested I needed an invitation from someone in Tirana in order to complete my visa application. When I asked him if he happened to have the number of the state publishing house in Tirana, he supplied it, and soon after I attempted to phone Simoni, one of the men mentioned in the newspaper story. Astonishly enough, after bursts of static on the line and a babble of languages (Albanian, English, German, Italian), then a long pause (he had been walking down a flight of stairs), I was speaking with Simoni himself. He promised to send a note of invitation. And thus, I "followed the story," even as I was following other stories (the blond-haired Manuel, for example, with whom I was in the midst, or perhaps at the end, of something, had abruptly — but only temporarily, I hoped — decamped). Well, if the invitation from Tirana arrives, if mail service from Tirana even exists, I told myself, then I guess I'll get some snapshots from the machine at the train station to stick onto the application form. And indeed, one by one, each of the items appeared, until at last I signed my name in the Café Einstein and sent the papers off.

A few nights later, a Saturday evening, while I was in the bath at the place I was staying, the phone rang. Annoyed, and dripping down the hallway, I picked up the phone to be told by the Albanian attaché in Bonn — unusual that he should be working on a Saturday night, I marvelled — that my visa had been approved.

In the post, along with the papers, he sent me a picture postcard, signed with his best wishes. I didn't know what to make of such an unbureaucratic gesture. It was a picture of an ancient boy's head, marble, from Apollonia, one of the places down the Adriatic coast that the Greeks had set up in the fifth century or so B.C. "Best wishes," the picture postcard said.

***

I was on the Berlin–Zurich–Tirana flight, with a date to meet the two translators at seven p.m. at the base of the Skanderbeg statue in the town square. I hastily acquired the necessary background from *Eastern Europe on a Shoestring*. Skanderbeg, the potted history tersely informed me: fifteenth-century warlord; castle in the hills at a place called Kruje, a bit north of Tirana; fought the Turks twenty times, never beaten. National hero. Of course, once Skanderbeg was out of the way, it was the Ottoman Turks for the next five hundred years. Succeeded by King Zog, then the Fascists, and finally by the Glorious Leader, Comrade Hoxha.

I don't know what I was after. Oh, to find Simoni and Qesku, certainly. And to find out how a country in the middle of Europe could more or less disappear from the face of the earth for half a century. But I think I also wanted to know what was there. As if to make up for an oversight on our part. Sure, Albania had been sealed off for god knows how long, but was that sufficient excuse for our failure to consider it? Of course if we had, would anyone have bothered to pay attention? Marlow's celebrated utterance (I'd tossed my copy of *Heart of Darkness* into my bag) echoed in my mind, "And this, also, has been one of the dark places of the earth."

So I had a rendezvous. But first there were the "pilgrims," to use Conrad's term for them. I mean, if I could think of it, then surely the business pilgrims would already be figuring out how to turn a dollar. He was a Swiss engineer, named Weber. Boarded at Zurich. The Texans were seated in front of us. As soon as we were up, the engineer had a powerful thirst. Scotch doubles, and beer to wash them down. By the descent, he had persuaded the flight attendant to sell him some cans of beer in a paper bag. But he knew the country, I had to give him that.

When Weber wasn't courting the woman in the window seat, I asked him the usual traveller's questions. I'd heard of the Hotel Tirana. No, the Dajti, he firmly recommended. Reservations? No problem, he'd fix it up if it came to that. And was there a bus into town from the airport? *Kein Problem*, I could ride in with him. Hail fellow, well-met. Well-lubricated, too, by the time we were on the ground.

The airport was a patch of cement in the countryside. Thirty degrees on the ground at four p.m. By the time I was walking down the double row of palm trees into the terminal, I was poached in my own juices. Lads in green with machine guns. The usual madhouse — babies, relatives, heaps of baggage. "Fixers" everywhere. I'd heard the term back home during the Gulf War six months earlier, at the beginning of 1991.

Weber had several thousand dollars in trading goods, by my estimate. Cigarette lighters, Swiss Army knives, textiles, camcorders, the whole store; vast amounts of personal belongings, bottles of Johnnie Walker, cigars, suitcases for an expedition. We showed our papers, then lugged the whole caboodle past the boys with guns, and we were in the courtyard of the terminal. I'd barely a moment to get my bearings. Sheer confusion, it was. Crush of relatives, officials, much weeping and kissing on the cheek, the yard crammed with cabs, children begging for coins, the swelter. A whole family to greet the engineer, with hugs, kisses on both cheeks, bouquets of flowers already wilted in the heat; of course, I must be introduced, our party divided into two cabs, the engineer's trading goods stuffed in the trunk — he's already passing out cigarette lighters. And then we're off.

It was the moment of pure exultation in a strange place, whether there's anything to be had or not. Soon enough there would be the practicalities, interviews, putting together bits and pieces of history. But for now, we were barrelling down a country road, honking at peasants on horsecarts, bicycles, sheep in the road, shirtless men, in a field, squinting through the sun at us — just an instant to glimpse their bodies.

The countryside was dotted with concrete mushroom caps, overgrown now — apparently defence outposts, gun emplacements, and the like. The Glorious Leader was ready to fight the Turks, the imperialists, Titoists, Russian revisionists, the Chinese renegades after Mao — everyone he'd broken with in the name of Marxism-Leninism, in the name of Comrade Stalin, of the truth. I had the unnerving sense — for the briefest moment — of peering into Hoxha's besieged mind.

At the fork halfway between Durres on the Adriatic and the capital inland, we took the turn for Tirana. And all the time, the engineer, sitting in back between a pale girl, in a white blouse, and her father, lectured the lot of us. I missed most of it, I confess. Words lost in the wind, while the driver was running peasants on bicycles off the road with his terrible honking. Of course, the pilgrim had a plan to set the country right, something about playing Beethoven on the radio, and the phrase, "They're really children, you know" — how often had I heard that one before?

Finally, we came upon the city. All the main roads of Tirana converged on Skanderbeg Square. It was a huge open space. I marked the equestrian statue as we passed; that's where my rendezvous was. Around the edges of the big traffic circle in the square, various official buildings, "people's palaces," windows bashed in and boarded up after the recent rioting. I was informed right off that the towering statue of the Glorious Leader, set in the middle of the traffic circle, had been pulled down by the people three months ago.

We dropped off the girl and her father, and some of the engineer's booty. He genially ordered them about, drank his beer, handed out gifts; he was a lean, nervous pilgrim, but no fool. Then back to the square, this time south, past yellow and red stucco buildings — government ministries, Weber said — and down the Martyrs Boulevard a block or so to the Dajti. A four-storey job done by the Italians before the Second World War, big Mediterranean pines all around shading it, and facing a spacious public park. Crowds of fixers, drivers, cadging children, and arriving pilgrims in the driveway. Naturally, no available rooms. But the engineer was jovial, extra bed in his suite, no problem for the night, fix you up in the morning, he'd enjoy a bit of company — more like an audience for his unpacking. I barely had time to splash a few drops of water on the dusty wraith I'd become, and the engineer was off, for business in Durres, I think it was.

An hour later, at the onset of dusk, I made my way over to the square. I sat beneath the fearsome Skanderbeg, perched on his mount. Presently, two men arrived, as ordained. The younger one, Pavli Qesku, struck me as rather elegant — mid-forties, lean, prematurely grey hair, tinted glasses. The other, older, one good ear so he had to position himself on your left to catch the conversation. That was Zef Simoni.

I'd brought books for them — I suppose it could be said that I was a pilgrim in my way, too — but rather than examine them at once, they suggested we take a stroll down the Martyrs Boulevard. They pointed out where the statues of Lenin and Stalin had flanked the thoroughfare; now only pediments remained. Everything had come down in the last six months, more than a year after the wave that swept the rest of Central Europe, more than five years after Hoxha's death. The party had attempted to make the transition; had assumed that everything would continue forever — simply parade the image of the old Glorious Leader, gradually add that of the new one, a man named Ramiz Alia. They figured they would carry on into eternity. But now everything was breaking up. Statues toppled, street names altered.

I'd noticed on a map that the continuation of the boulevard north of Skanderbeg Square had been named for Stalin. I wondered if it still was.

"Oh, we never called it that, anyway," Zef said, dismissing the issue in an understated, slightly ironic way I would quickly get used to.

"But this is still the Boulevard of National Martyrs?" I inquired, just to check.

"Well, after all, this is true," Pavli said. "We are still a nation and, indeed, there have been martyrs."

"So there is no need to change it," Zef added. They had been in each other's company for so many years that they had acquired the habit of completing each other's sentences, as old couples do.

I was impatient to get to the heart of it, to the only question I really had for them, namely, how had they survived? As we passed the Hotel Dajti on the left, and the twilight came down on the big park facing it, they represented themselves as timid men, unheroic, cautious creatures, never members of the party though they had worked in the state publishing house translating the Glorious Leader's works and speeches all those years, Zef into German, Pavli into English. Another translator, Jussef Vrioni, had put Hoxha into French. I'd seen Vrioni's name — about a month before in an article in an American magazine, where he'd been cited as the French translator of the great Albanian novelist Ismail Kadare, who was now living in Paris. I'd even glanced at *The General of the Dead Army*, one of Kadare's novels.

But the immediate answer to my question was relatively simple. They had translated literature — Dickens, Conrad, Lawrence, Orwell even — I knew that already from the newspaper piece. But there was a new bit. They made dictionaries. It was an obvious thing for translators to do, now that they mentioned it, but it hadn't occurred to me. "So," I said, "in a sense, words saved you."

We crossed a little trickle of water just beyond the hotel, the Lana River. It flowed in a ditch below us, beneath the boulevard overpass — grass slopes, a bit of paving-stone embankment; to the right, from the west, the last of the light hit it.

"Working with words saved us from the situation in which we lived, sort of," Pavli replied. Then he added, almost more to himself than me, "Yes, to a certain extent, it is true."

"A justification," Zef explained. "In our work as translators, we used words to express other people's thoughts — and we were not in agreement with those thoughts. So we wanted to use the same words to express, not *our* thoughts, but something neutral at least." It was put with perfect modesty. My curiosity was at once satisfied. Strange, how quickly it went. Now, we were simply evening strollers, casually conversing.

The boulevard, a broad four-lane thoroughfare, ended abruptly at the university, which was set at the base of a hill. The students had demonstrated here the previous December, and then again in February. That, apparently, was what had started it. We took the footpath that wound around and up the wooded rise. St. Procopius hill, Zef informed me.

Somehow, we got onto the subject of China. I don't remember what led to it. Perhaps something about Zef's bad ear. He had been to China during Hoxha's alliance with Mao, and the Chinese had restored some of his hearing. Even now, he had only one good ear, supplemented with a bit of lip-reading. Anyway, it got me thinking about my time in China, in '77, just after Mao's death, around the time of the breakup of Albania's "firm and eternal friendship," as the formula went, with Beijing. I found myself recounting an odd little conversation I'd had with my minder. We were speaking of sexual practices, and I'd asked, a bit mischievously, if there was homosexuality in China. My guide affected to be shocked. No, none at all, he firmly assured me. None whatsoever. So I asked him if the Chinese masturbated. Oh no, he said, and then, curiosity getting the better of him, he asked me, And you, in the West, do you masturbate? Why, yes, I replied, all the time.

Zef and Pavli burst into laughter, got it right away. "So, there was even a correct line on sex," Pavli chuckled. I was about to rattle on when Zef interrupted to point out some buildings to our right. "The barracks of the National Guard," he said, making it clear by his tone that the institution wasn't exactly loved. The path switched back up St. Procopius, but an unpaved road forked off towards the barracks. It was dark now, and all you could see were some lighted windows and boys in uniforms inside.

At the top of the hill we came out of the pines onto an outdoor café, which was our destination. It was well-attended, mostly couples and some guardsmen in pairs. A table was found for us, and the waiter brought us drinks.

"Raki," Pavli said, naming the alcohol. "Perhaps you won't like it."

It was acrid stuff, perfectly drinkable, of course. And there was bread, soup and some roasted chicken. My hosts half apologized for the poor quality of everything, but in fact it was fine. A perfectly delightful café on a summer evening, and a bit cooler up here on the hill. After the food, more raki, and we smoked cigarettes.

One of the young guardsmen broke away from his friend and came over to our table to ask for a light. I held the flame to his hand-rolled smoke.

"You've just lit the cigarette of a National Guard," Zef said.

"Of a boy," I insisted.

"Who might masturbate in the barracks," Zef quickly added, accepting my distinction. We all laughed at that.

Oddly enough, we didn't talk about politics at all that evening. Zef mentioned that he had learned to read Greek, and had read Plato's *Phaedo* in the original. It was a work I was familiar with; I often taught it at school. Indeed, I had opinions about the death of Socrates.

I confess I did most of the talking. As I said, I had views. The part about Socrates's last day in jail, his weeping friends, the hemlock he drank, all that was true in my opinion. But the part about the immortality of the soul, I insisted to Zef and Pavli, that was added by Plato himself. I don't think Socrates believed any of that. Socrates simply thought you died and consciousness ceased or — well, it doesn't matter about my views. But it was all so wonderfully odd. I'd come all this way, to the moon, to the last outpost, to enquire about the fall of Communism, and instead, we were talking about Plato, just as civilized people anywhere might have done. Of course, I had to acknowledge that the places where civilized people could talk of such things were much diminished in our time, even in my own part of the world.

It had grown late, the café had emptied, the guardsmen were back in their barracks. They walked me down the hill, back into the heat of the town, now in darkness. Behind the hotel there was a sleek building which bore the only electric sign I'd seen. It alternately flashed the temperature and the time, lighting up the night. The Institute of Strategic Studies, Pavli informed me. They came into the Dajti with me for a minute so I could give them the box of books I'd brought, and arrangements were made to collect me in the morning.

The engineer soon returned from Durres. He produced a bottle of Johnnie Walker and we sat on the balcony outside the room, overlooking the Martyrs' Boulevard — little traffic at that hour, only the gear-grinding of the occasional truck, a late-night bus.

In the morning, the engineer and I took breakfast together. The other pilgrims were there, impatient with the service, anxious to get on with business, to make the world go. Weber was soon off, the brooding Swiss of last night — he too read some philosophy — giving way to the nervous energy of deal-making that characterized the busy pilgrims.

Across the corridor from the breakfast room was the bar, where the engineer left me with one of the fixers he knew, in case I needed anything. I escaped onto the cement front veranda of the Dajti. Even though the flashing digital sign — forever reminding us of time and heat — reported nearly thirty degrees before nine o'clock, a nice breeze came in from the park across the boulevard. Below me, in the drive-way, the taxi operators were taking the pilgrims off. There were all sorts of kids hang-ing around. Small ones, and teenage boys, too.

One boy in particular attracted me. He was in his mid to late teens, blue-eyed, with pale sandy hair and a quick smile. He was with a couple of his friends, and at first all I noticed was the boys' friendliness among themselves, the way they leaned against each other, casually draping an arm over the other's shoulders. Then the blue-eyed boy and I exchanged glances and there was a brief, wordless encounter, the sort of meeting I might have forgotten if nothing else had happened. Our eyes met again, he offered a smile. It was nothing, really. But as he passed behind me on the veran-da, he touched me. He ran a feathery hand across my shoulders, just as he did with the other boys he was with. And as quickly as he'd appeared, he was gone.

Just then, Zef and Pavli turned up to show me around. I tried to make apologies for my chattering on about the *Phaedo*.

"No doubt, you like the part about the soul," I said to Zef. He had told me he was a Catholic. But apparently there was no harm done.

"It was very good conversation," Zef assured me.

"Yes, nice to talk," Pavli seconded.

We crossed the square — already you could feel the morning heat — and were soon in a maze of side streets and then back lanes. There were some market stalls set up on the walks. Little potatoes, green onions, dark fresh figs, all in small quantities. The women spent hours gathering the day's provisions.

"Looking for things that don't exist," Pavli said.

"Or hunting for things," Zef amended, "this is called shopping."

We came to a five-storey building, made of bricks, oddly spaced, a hand-done job it seemed. "Zef's flat is on the top. He built it himself," Pavli told me. Looking up, you could see from the fresher colour of the brick that the top floor had been added recently. One could imagine the difficulties of a man in his fifties hauling the bricks up those stairs, mixing the cement, mortaring them in himself.

By the time we climbed to the top, my shirt was soaked through. Zef's wife met us, and while we settled in, she brought us bottled water, raki, some Turkish Delight, and then coffee. I reminded myself that I was in one of those southern European cultures where they give you everything they have, however little it may be.

There were shelves of books along the back wall. With a very slight ceremonial gesture, Zef presented me with a copy of the German-Albanian dictionary he had compiled and which had been published the year before. He quoted Milton on justifying God's ways to man. "I had to justify myself to myself," he said, by way of explanation. "To do something useful."

About noon, we went down, and made the short walk over to the publishing house where they worked. First there had to be a formal meeting with the director in his suite of offices. Pavli translated. I had been through this sort of thing before. Formalities to be observed, cups of bitter coffee served. I intimated that I had some access to paper supplies, something the director — who, of course, was a party member — could note in his report if necessary. Even though it was all breaking up, the party in the midst of a chameleon-like effort to appear in more acceptable colours, much of the organizational infrastructure was still in place. And all the old habits. Although the director was the only party member I would actually meet, I was little inclined to question him about his view of the recent political changes. I knew I'd only get the current official line, and in any case the shade of "the last Communist," Hoxha himself, still lurked everywhere. On the stairway, going up to their office, Zef said, "Very good," appraising my performance, and the three of us laughed about it.

Then we were in the "tiny, Spartan office" that I'd read about in the newspaper piece. Well, a small professional quibble here, a detail. It was Spartan in the sense of equipment, absence of books, of course. But not tiny. Larger than the cubbyholes most journalists or instructors had in the newsrooms and college offices I was familiar with back home. Spacious enough for facing desks, walls a bright, pale green, and there was a big window, with a breeze coming in, and a view from the second floor looking west to the hills, in the direction of Durres on the coast.

We talked about making dictionaries. There was a large, old one on a revolving stand on Pavli's desk. I'd never thought about them before, not in this way.

"Where do you start?" I wanted to know.

"You begin from anything you like," Pavli said. "Just collecting words, finding phrases, putting them on cards, keeping files. But that is only preparatory work. The real work begins when you touch a typewriter and put a white sheet in, and write *A*. What shall we write about *A*?" he asked.

I'd wanted to know how they had survived all those years, and here was a clue under my nose. You know how you're so familiar with an object that you barely notice it? You're looking for a big answer — something about the spirit or history — but the answer is right in front of you in a simple, material thing. In the German-Albanian dictionary Zef had given me, in the old dictionaries in their Spartan, but not tiny, office. It's a matter of seeing it, of resisting your own familiarity.

Zef had said, "We wanted to use the same words to express, not our thoughts, but something neutral at least." Harmless things. Words. And in the pages of his dictionary were thousands of words — *tree, sky, beach, sea* — each one an expression of thought uncontaminated by the régime.

"Something neutral," Pavli repeated, adding, "despite the fact that, sometimes, other people, outside us, put in words that expressed the reality that existed at that time. Like they did with Zef's dictionary. They put in expressions like 'the dictatorship of the proletariat,' and 'scientific socialism,' and so on."

"Not very 'scientific,' " Zef commented wryly.

"But also the definitions," Pavli said. "Here, look." He came to the word *liberal*. " 'One who makes concessions towards shortcomings and mistakes,' " Pavli read, " 'who is not exacting towards others; who allows irregularities which harm the work of society.' This dictionary is full of such stupidities."

Over the years, they slowly compiled words at night, while at work they duly translated documents, position papers, the works of Comrade Hoxha. On the far wall facing the open window that looked out towards Durres, there was a bookcase containing the books of the Glorious Leader. Zef went to it, pulling out a couple of paperback volumes to give me. He made a show of banging them against the side of the case to shake the dust from these translated, but never-read, memoirs. On the cover of one called *With Stalin* was a photograph of the two men, shot from below, standing on a rampart. Later, in the hotel, I skimmed its hagiographic, childishly humble accounts of Hoxha's reception in Moscow by "Comrade Stalin."

Pavli walked me back through the mid-afternoon heat to the Dajti. We arranged to meet again in the evening. The desk clerk had a room for me. Weber, the engineer, was still out when I moved my things to the new room. It was small but sufficient

— a bed, a writing table, lace curtains, shower, a little balcony, and a roll-down metal shade to keep out the heat. The room faced east, looking directly onto the blinking electric sign with the time and temperature. By the time I came up from the bar, bringing back a litre of mineral water, I was soaked from my exertions. I showered, made my notes, replenished myself with liquids, read a page or two of Conrad and then napped.

Pavli came to get me in the early evening and took me to his apartment where Zef was already waiting for us. Pavli's wife brought us raki and then went into the kitchen while we watched television. There was an interview with a visiting Albanian political leader from Kosovo — the southernmost, so-called autonomous, province of Yugoslavia, but actually under the thumb of the Serbians. Two million Albanians lived there, and now, with the disturbances in Yugoslavia, the old dream of Greater Albania was in the air again. I happened to learn a little about it only subsequently when I read a translation of a novella by Kadare, set in Pristina — the Kosovan capital — about a failed uprising a decade or more ago. Zef and Pavli watched the interview intently; such discussion was still something of a novelty on Albanian television.

Then Pavli's wife brought in food and they switched channels to an Italian game show. It was announced as a "light supper," but in fact it was a full plate, carefully laid out. Mussels, olives, tomatoes, onions, hard-boiled eggs, and a fruit compote for dessert. All the time we were watching the politician from Kosovo, Pavli's wife had been working in the kitchen. The women evidently did all the domestic work; the arrangements were quite traditional, as we say (giving much more dignity to the word "traditional" than it deserves). I thought of a feminist friend of mine back home, and knew exactly what she would make of it.

After Mrs. Qesku cleared the table, I turned on the tape recorder for our formal interview. Now I was at work, as I had been a hundred times before, in many places. And later, in some other place, no doubt far away from where this encounter had occurred, I might hear those voices again, or they would be transcribed into a sheaf of notes, which would find a place in a manila folder or in the depths of the maroon-coloured gym bag I lugged around with me, a familiar object I sometimes described in jest as "my office."

Zef Simoni was born in 1933 in the northern town of Shkoder to a well-to-do Catholic family. As in neighbouring Yugoslavia and Greece, the ending of the

Second World War inaugurated civil war in Albania. While Greece was allotted to the Allies, in both Yugoslavia and Albania the partisan triumph was not impeded.

"Immediately when the partisans came into Shkoder," Zef recalled, "they started shooting people in batches. Behind the town graveyard. And after having a batch of people shot, they put up a proclamation with the names and the crimes they were supposed to have committed." Zef was eleven.

"So they came in 1944?" I calculated.

"Yes. And they were my first exercises in literacy." I was momentarily puzzled.

"To read the names," Pavli supplied.

"It was just reading matter for me," Zef said. I had a glimpse, no more, of a boy peering up at a freshly pasted sheet on a brick wall, absorbing the litany of the newly dead with a chilling innocence that separated the act of reading from the acts to which the proclamation referred. Outside, in the night, we could hear the shouts of children at play.

Pavli's wife offered us brandy. "It is a very fine brandy made at home," Pavli recommended. "Wild cherry." We each accepted a small glass.

"They were people of a conservative mind," Zef said, recalling his family. "Right wing, I would say now. My father was first an import-export merchant, then he had a printing shop, then a magazine, and he made some translations. He was the first Esperantist in Albania."

"He has translated the *Pinocchio*," Pavli added.

"Into Esperanto?" I wondered, slightly amused at the mention of the strange dream of creating a mutually understandable artificial language. But no, he had put the famed children's tale into Albanian.

"He has translated the biography of Skanderbeg into Esperanto," Zef said.

"So, you're a second-generation translator," I observed.

"Second generation," Zef nodded, laughing.

Once again, it was a matter of words. Words for civilization, words in self-defence. But wasn't the party's concern also the use of language?

"Propaganda is made of words, of course," Pavli agreed.

"But everything is distorted," Zef pointed out. "You are told you have freedom, which others, you are told, have not. And you have not freedom. You are told you have free speech — it is written in the constitution — and you land in jail for saying the wrong things. You are told you are free to move about, and you must have documents to move from one city to another. Everything is told it exists, and it doesn't exist, or exists its counterpart." Zef spoke rapidly, forgoing the niceties of English grammar in his excitement.

"My own family," Pavli said, "was a little more exposed to such propaganda. My father was a partisan, then a Communist, and fought in the brigades of the national liberation army. After the war, he began to realize that there was something amiss. But he couldn't grasp what it was. He was a tailor. In a small town in central Albania. Slowly but surely he began to realize that the cause of the situation was the party itself, and he began to dislike it, until, in 1949, after five years in the party, he refused to be a member." Pavli had been five then. "But in my family there are still some people who believe that the party is good, just that something went wrong somewhere. There are some people who are still Utopians, who have the hope that socialism is something good for humankind."

I was curious to know how they had become friends. "We worked together," Pavli said. "They just put us in the same room," Zef added, "and they just said, work together." The two of them laughed at the simple absurdity of it.

"And this has gone on for over twenty years," I said, laughing also.

"Yes, twenty-two years," Pavli confirmed, "except for a period of three years when I was in Peshpatia, a small town in the mountains."

They had escaped the terror of executions and jailings, but not entirely. They had spent the years together carefully. "Very careful," Pavli reiterated. "What we said in the streets, what we said in the café."

"We expressed our more delicate thoughts in English, just in case," said Zef. "We were very careful about where we talked, how we talked."

"Or we had code names for things."

The way their voices alternated reminded me of the strophe and antistrophe of a Greek chorus. "Code names?" I repeated.

"For the government, the party, the leaders, our party secretary." Like a children's game, I suggested. "It was very childish," Zef said, "and very horrible."

"But it was not Newspeak," Pavli added.

Yet their caution did not protect them completely. Pavli was shipped off for three years in 1975 to a sort of internal exile.

"The reason they gave Pavli for sending him to Peshpatia," Zef began, "well, the true reason was that he didn't accept to become a member of the party — the specious reason they gave him was that you keep too much Zef's company. They kept me in Tirana."

"But Zef was frightened then."

"In their sick mind, I was infected, hopelessly. There was some hope for saving Pavli."

So Pavli was shipped off to work as a schoolteacher in a mountain village. "Did you think that you would ever return?" I asked.

"It was a closed chapter," Pavli replied. "I just took my bag, my typewriter, and my books."

"Were you married?" I asked.

"Yes, but happily we had no children then. My wife could go on working here. Fortunately, the government needed her work because she was chief engineer of the porcelain factory. She kept working in Tirana, and I went to Peshpatia."

"Chinese style," Zef said.

Pavli's wife was sitting in an armchair, away from the table the three of us were gathered around. For all her fulfilment of the traditional duties, she was an educated woman, skilled, and able to follow our conversation in English, occasionally supplying a correction to their account. I saw her then as if for the first time. I had only a moment to imagine their three years of separation, caused by an ideological whim, which they treated, in retrospect, as a minor inconvenience. Compared to so many others, I suppose it was.

Pavli had gone on, speaking of Peshpatia. "The headmaster of the school was a very nice chap, very understanding. He gave me a whole room to myself, a bare room of course, but it was a room. There was a round stove which the schoolboys were careful to supply with firewood. It is fifteen or twenty degrees below zero in winter there. I was all by myself. The dictionaries were there, and whenever those people, security, came from time to time, unannounced, to search my room, they saw that they were harmless books. I never gave them cause to suspect."

"And in the place of Pavli," Zef said, picking up the other end of the story, "into the office stepped in a chap who had been Pavli's schoolmate. He had some connections with the Minister of Internal Affairs, and I am sure he informed on me, but he informed only on the good side." Zef laughed at the small irony of informing "on the good side," then added, "I was very careful of course."

"My former schoolmate didn't do anything while he was there," Pavli noted. "He was supposed to be a translator, but he couldn't do the job. When Zef was away, he just sat there doing nothing." The pride in their ability to do good work, regardless of its futility, gave an edge to the tone of contempt with which Pavli referred to the plant from Internal Affairs.

Sitting there, comforted by cherry brandy, I had to remind myself that I was listening to an account of political terror. Not executions, torture, jailings — though there was that, of course — but quiet terror, everyday terror.

"When we translated that book which I gave you, *With Stalin*," Zef began again, "we worked night and day."

"Three months of hard work in the midst of summer," Pavli said.

"Then they gave us four or five days to recover," Zef continued. "On one of these days, the chief of the enterprise came to me and said, 'You are invited to the Tirana branch of the Ministry of Internal Affairs. I don't know what they want from you, but you must go.' I went there. Certainly, I was very afraid. But I tried to keep control of myself. I told myself, maybe they had some translations for me to do. I was ushered into a room and there were two armchairs, and they smelled of sweat, a heavy stink of sweat. Because the people who went there sweated profusely under interrogation."

They asked Zef about various people he knew. Zef offered bland replies. The fencing went on for some time. Then the interrogators asked about a certain person. "I said yes, I know him. I couldn't say I didn't. And what are his opinions? they asked. I said the generally current opinions. And what are his literary tastes? I mentioned the most conventional tastes I knew of. Then they told me, he has been slandering the party, and you must know. I know nothing, I have not seen him for six months. After that, they gave me a cigarette. They did not make direct threats to me. They told me, look, we are going to arrest this man. If you warn him, first, it will be useless, and second, you will be arrested too. So, I went home. On my way home, I wanted to have a double portion of cognac just to steady my spirits." He laughed in recollection of his fear. "Then I thought that I might be followed. If they saw me drinking, they might think I had something to fear. So instead, I went straight home, and lay in my bed for about half an hour. Only then did I come out and go to the café, where I had my double portion of cognac. In about six months' time, Pavli, who knew nothing about these things — "

"Zef didn't whisper a word," Pavli interjected.

"Had I told Pavli, he would think, first, that I was a hero, and second, that I must have blurted out something. So I said nothing. And six months later, it was Pavli who mentioned to me that so-and-so had been arrested. And still I said nothing."

"You didn't tell Pavli about the interrogation?" I asked Zef.

"I learned of it only last year," Pavli said.

"When did this incident happen?" I asked.

"In 1980," Zef said.

"You only told him ten years later?" I said in astonishment.

"Ten years," Zef said, and we all broke out laughing, but perhaps for different reasons. They laughed simply at the mixture of absurdity and horror, and because now it was possible to laugh at it, and because it was a small thing compared to what others had endured. And I laughed nervously, almost embarrassed to be made a party to this terrible intimacy.

"After six months, Pavli told me, you know this chap so-and-so has been arrested," Zef repeated. I turned off the recorder, stuffed the tapes into my gym bag.

It was a story no different from those we had heard countless times in recent years. But that was the point of it. There was nothing "Albanian" about the anecdote. The insidious method was ubiquitous: anyone, even the most intimate of one's friends, might inform. A remark you'd made, in the sanctity of your home, thoughtlessly parroted by your child at school, might bring the authorities to your door. No letters unread by the censors, no movement without approved documents, and of course, no passports. Your fate decided in rooms, committees, none of which you had access to, but in whose anterooms you waited. And though the digital clock recorded the minutes, the Glorious Leader had made time stand still.

Yet from the outside, to a visitor, the place must appear but a small, dusty, inconsequential town of barely a quarter-million inhabitants, baking in the sun — poor, but with people going about their business. There was little visible sign of the oppression, or the methods that made it possible. It was as if I had travelled the length of a river — like the river in Conrad's story — to reach, as Marlow did, the kingdom of a madman.

The parallels were eerie. Like Kurtz, Hoxha had not always been mad. He had begun with the intention of improving the lot of humankind, the great dream of our time. And those of us on the left had even grudgingly admired him, as the ruler of a tiny, mostly agricultural country who had rather heroically broken with first the

Soviets, for deviating from Stalinism, and then even the Chinese, for abandoning Maoism. But in his obsessive effort to perfect human beings, to create, like a god, "the new man, the new woman," he had gradually turned the inhabitants into slaves.

"You translated Conrad," I said to Zef.

"And perhaps you think you are a bit like Marlow?" Zef joked, intuiting my pretension.

But there was no Kurtz at the heart of this darkness, no self-critical last cry of horror to ponder. All that remained was the rubble of Hoxha's rule. And the inhabitants, of course. We had thought of them almost as savages, just as Conrad had recorded that men of the imperium thought of distant peoples of a different colour a century ago. Yet I had discovered, as had Conrad, that they were the same as us.

I didn't think all that at the moment; only later, when the voices recorded in my little machine had become words on pages. But there was something more, something that did occur to me as we spoke, though I didn't mention it to Zef and Pavli. I had yet to free myself from the human dream that had given way to the dictator's inhuman methods. Does Marlow murmur, quoting a forgotten poet, "Spirit of the night, teach us to bear despair"?

It had gotten well on into the evening. There was more to ask, of course, but they had arranged for me to do interviews with some other people beginning early the next morning, a Saturday, and the following day we would hire a driver and go to Durres, so there would be time to talk then. However, I couldn't resist asking about the present, now that the nightmare was over, or almost over.

"The change can be seen if you follow a couple of people walking in the streets," Pavli said. "They have stopped turning their heads back to see if we're following them. We no longer turn our heads back."

Zef walked me back to the Dajti through the silent streets of Tirana. From the balcony of my room, I faced the electric sign flashing in the night. It was almost midnight. Just under thirty degrees. The sign blinked on and off, flooding my room with pale light, and then plunging it into darkness. In bed, I turned away from the wall where light flared every few seconds.

Six hours later, I woke up. Beyond the Institute for Strategic Studies, beyond where the town ended, there were pale brown mountains, with Mt. Dajti to the east. A haze lay between it and the edge of town. I stood on the balcony drinking coffee.

Directly below me, three floors down, was the raggedy, semi-abandoned garden of the hotel. Palm trees, an empty fountain, untended bushes. A skinny yellow cat prowled through the brush.

The opposition Democratic Party was headquartered in a sort of villa, set back from a busy street, with a wide gate at the front to admit vehicles. Inside, even at eight a.m., clusters of men were gathered in the driveway-courtyard, petitioners perhaps, or local functionaries. An outside staircase led up to a warren of offices. We were ushered into a large room with a long rectangular table. At the head of it, talking on the telephone, was a stocky young man in his late twenties, with unkempt curly black hair. There was a window behind him, covered with shutters through which slivers of sunshine filtered, playing upon the gauze curtains that hung before it.

When he put the phone down, we were introduced. His name was Azem Haidari, he was a graduate student at the university who had come from a small mountain village, Treppoja, in the north; married, two children.

"If you want," Haidari said, via Zef's translation, "I will tell you about the democratic movement in Albania, the Democratic party, the political life, and the Parliament." As a result of the elections in the spring, he now sat as a member of that body. We had about an hour's interview, variously interrupted by the urgency of the telephone and by people poking their heads through the double doors with brief messages for the young politician. It was a standard interview, he spoke as a man with responsibilities. But I saw that both Zef and Pavli rather admired him. They liked his vigour and, apparently, the colourful mountain villager's way of speaking — he didn't mince words. When he was on the phone, I could get a hint of a more animated indigenous style that no doubt had popular appeal. But with me he was diplomatic, without irony.

As much as anyone, here was the person who had loosened the grip of Hoxha's successors. "The dictatorship was so savage there was no possibility of even thinking of establishing another form of government, because the mere thought of it put your life in jeopardy," Haidari said. But the explosions in Eastern Europe had had their echoes even in Albania. "Mr. Alia, recalling the fate of Ceausescu," he went on, "saw that he had to do something for democratization."

"So Alia was watching television," I remarked, recalling the footage of the execution of the former Romanian dictator and his wife which we saw the Christmas after the opening of the Wall.

"But his speeches, his manoeuvres, were only intended for export," Haidari said dismissively. "They were intended to give the impression that something was being done, whereas nothing was being done." It was that impasse that led Haidari to take political action, organizing the students. The way he put it was very innocent — it was the language of the nineteenth century's "springtime of nations" — and yet it had the self-deprecating awareness of a man standing before a mirror, giving an account that would later be read as history. "When I was a student, I always recalled President Kennedy's words, 'Ask not what your country can do for you, ask what you can do for your country.' So I decided to give my all to Albania, even my life. At first, the possibility of emerging alive from the first demonstrations after forty years of communist rule was very slim indeed. Nevertheless, against all these odds, we succeeded in carrying out our peaceful demonstrations. The moment came to do something for Albania and I am very happy this offer of sacrifice was accepted." That was all it took, if not to topple the régime, at least to shake its foundations.

Later, towards the end of the hour, the mountain man declared, "I love life, but I have the opinion that life should be loved only for as long as it lasts, and we should not think to prolong it more than its course. You can't escape your fate." It was not the first time I'd heard young men fearlessly proclaim such things, and I've seldom doubted them. Yet it was always eerie to hear someone say it. I couldn't imagine dying for my country.

Just at that moment, the phone rang. Haidari picked up the receiver and soon was speaking most animatedly. I saw alarm in Zef's and Pavli's eyes.

"There's been a shoot-out," Pavli said, following the progress of the conversation. "One of his cousins, a young cousin of his, has been shot."

"Where?" I asked.

"In Treppoja."

"How did it happen?"

"The situation is stable," Pavli said, ignoring my question.

"But who was shooting?" I wondered. Haidari's voice subsided.

"He made a speech in parliament about Kosovo," Pavli explained. I put it together in bits and pieces — the arrival of the visiting politician from Pristina we'd seen on television had heated the political atmosphere — then there was Haidari's speech on the suppression of the Kosovan Albanians by the Serbs — no mincing of words, apparently — and somehow the news of the speech — was it heard as a call to arms? — was connected to the flare-up in his home village, not far from the border.

On the outside staircase going down, Zef said, "In six months, he could be dead." Meaning young Haidari, courting fate as he was. Then we were back in the streets, in the unforgiving heat. Mid-thirty degrees before noon. As we walked, Pavli recalled that the former student leader had accurately predicted that the newly elected government would be forced to form a coalition with the opposition "by the time the cherries were ripe."

"And when do they ripen?" I asked.

"In May and June," Pavli said. "And it happened. Now he says the present government will fall by the time the watermelons are ripe at the end of the summer. By the time the watermelons ripen." Pavli seemed taken with Haidari's agricultural turn of phrase.

Our next interview was with a writer named Trebeshina. It was held at the apartment of a young friend of his, also a writer. Trebeshina was in his mid-sixties, but you could see he had been badly used. He spoke in a hoarse whisper through yellowed and broken teeth. His was a tale of jailings and neglect. He had been imprisoned twice by the Fascists, against whom he had fought in the Second World War, and three times by the Communists. The first time, in the fifties, was a literary jailing. "I was always against the socialist realism," he said. "I was of the opinion that if there is realism, there is no need for socialist — or Fascist — or so on." He wrote an open letter to Hoxha and got three years for it.

I didn't quite catch the reason for the next incarceration, but the third one, in 1980, came about when he publicly declared his refusal to vote. For that, he got a long stretch. He'd only been released in 1988. And though he'd written much after the open letter, none of it had been published. He had been ignored, neglected, always at odds with the Writers' League. He didn't share the conventional estimate of the great Kadare. "A collaborator," Trebeshina rasped. When I asked him about hearing of Hoxha's death while he was in prison, he replied, "He's not dead." At the end of his fragmented recital, Trebeshina said, "I always wanted to ring the bell for the others, but I did not. During all my life, I was a Don Quixote."

Pavli walked me back to the hotel. We went along the Lana River, where a peasant sat on the grassy embankment, tethered to a couple of grazing sheep. The electric sign now registered thirty-six degrees. Pavli left me in the driveway of the Dajti. He and Zef had arranged a meeting with Kadare's translator, Vrioni, for the evening.

I had worn my lightest short-sleeved shirt, but I was soaked through, and slightly dazed, grateful to get to the shade of my little room, clutching the bottles of water I'd acquired in the bar on the way up. Before I showered and napped, I made my notes, the paper practically melting under my hand. It was as if all substance had dissolved into a primordial ooze — the water I drank greedily, the perspiration pouring out of me, smearing the ink, dampening the pages. The interviews with Haidari and Trebeshina had been ordinary enough, the sort of tales of courage and suffering in a heretofore almost unknown place, which are then inadequately condensed into the columns of the dailies. But this time I had been affected. I could feel the ends of my nerves. Perhaps I, too, like Trebeshina, was a Don Quixote. It seemed to me that your entire life as a writer leads to the one street you are walking down, to the miserable little pile of dark figs you are looking at, to the rasping, bitter voice you are listening to. Everything has led to this moment. And yet, you do not know the story, except as it unfolds before you. You do not know the story, I repeated to myself.

I went down to the veranda of the hotel early. The boy was there, the one I had seen before. Perhaps I'd gone down early because I'd gathered from Zef's tone that our anticipated meeting with Vrioni was a rare prize and I didn't wish to be late. Or perhaps because I hoped to see that boy again. I had thought about him, several times in fact. He had made an impression.

We greeted each other like old friends. We shook hands, and he touched me on the shoulder. Blue eyes, nut-brown tanned skin, radiant smile. His name was Ilir. Ilir as in ancient Illyria. It was impossible not to think of the head of the boy in the postcard that the consul in Bonn had sent me, to see something in it more than mere well-wishing.

Ilir was with a friend his own age, to whom he introduced me. They both had a little English, though I had some difficulty following the anecdote they were trying to tell me. His friend was a music student, as was Ilir, or perhaps a dancer, I couldn't quite get it.

They knew all about current music. "Michael Jackson," Ilir said, naming the pop star, "he is a great man. And M. C. Hammer, very beautiful." I was rather amazed by their knowledge, though also appalled that, of all things, this was what had penetrated the ideological defences of their shrouded land. "But how do you know all this?" I asked Ilir. They had seen it on television from Belgrade, which apparently transmitted the European version of the American music channel, MTV. So, score one for the Global Village. I was too charmed by Ilir to be contemptuous of the pap the world wanted to feed him. Indeed, it seemed to me remarkable that in this remoteness he was nonetheless a thorough contemporary of lads his age anywhere in the world. If I had to choose between Hoxha and MTV, well, why not?

There was a complicated story about a man named Hussein — "not Saddam Hussein of Iraq," Ilir laughed, referring to the Gulf War at the beginning of the year. This Hussein had promised them some papers, but I couldn't make it out. For what purpose? "Rap," Ilir said, "for the rap." There was something about videotapes, but I got it mixed up.

Then Zef and Pavli turned up for the evening at Vrioni's. I shook hands with Ilir's friend, but the farewell with the boy was more elaborate, kisses on both cheeks, hand-holding, assurances that we must get together again. I was quite dazzled, infatuated of course. I don't think it was entirely sexual . . . well, but who knows? Or, if I did know the extent of my desire, I preferred to keep my understanding of it inarticulate even to myself. It was just that it was so astonishing to come upon someone like him, here, in this place.

Walking to Vrioni's, I must have babbled, telling Zef and Pavli about the boy. They seemed amused I was so taken, the way you are when a visitor comes to your hometown and enthuses about something there that you've never thought of, but that nonetheless leaves you pleased for both your visitor and yourself.

On the way, they reminded me that Vrioni had also for a time worked in the publishing house as a translator. In fact, at the time of Pavli's exile, Vrioni's name had also appeared on the list of those to be sent off to get "closer to the people."

"He was sent too?" I asked.

"He was meant to be sent," Pavli said, "but on special instructions from His Highness — "

"Who knew some French," Zef interjected,

"Who read His own books in French," Pavli continued, "and liked the way they had been rendered in French — "

"Because Vrioni had translated His own works," Zef put in.

"There was no one who could translate His works as well as Vrioni did," Pavli added.

"So He was not going to saw off the branch He was sitting on," Zef concluded.

Vrioni lived in a detached two-storey house with a small front garden. His wife greeted us at the door. We were led into the living room where Vrioni was waiting for us. He was a tall, elegant man. I was told later that he was seventy-eight years old, but I never would have guessed it from his looks or his manner. He was the son of a wealthy landowner, and had been raised and educated in France before the war. When he returned to Albania after the partisan triumph, Hoxha had him jailed for thirteen years. Then he became a translator, of Hoxha's books as well as those of Kadare.

His wife brought in a bottle of Johnnie Walker, with glasses on a tray, and, after placing them on the low glass-topped table before us, retired upstairs, explaining that she was feeling poorly. Our conversation was in French. Vrioni could speak English, but he made it clear that to discuss certain concepts only French was adequate. Zef and Pavli filled in for my deficiencies.

We hit it off right away. I mentioned that I liked jazz, and uttered the name of the legendary French jazz guitarist, Django Reinhardt. Immediately, Vrioni lit up. He rummaged about beneath the sound equipment at the side of the room until he produced a cassette. The room filled with the instantly recognizable arpeggios of the three-fingered jazz guitarist, joined by a violinist. It was Reinhardt's version of the "Marseillaise," accompanied by Stéphane Grappelli, recorded just after the Allied victory in 1945, Vrioni told us. For a few minutes we simply listened with pleasure and sipped our whisky.

Vrioni was most dubious about Albanian prospects. He began to tick off on his aristocratic fingers the reasons for his doubts in that precise manner of French intellectuals. First, the level of Albanian culture was abysmally backward. I interjected that I had met a sixteen- or seventeen-year-old boy in Tirana who was marvellously well-versed in contemporary music, having watched television from Yugoslavia. My host was unimpressed. He continued his dissection of the country's gloomy future.

I mentioned that I had seen his name in the American magazine article about Kadare. It was clear that he had more than a proprietary interest in the Albanian writer. His translations into French had made Kadare's reputation. Without the translations, which had so pleased the French public, the great novelist might be unknown today. There was a hint even that something more than translation was involved. It was almost as if he regarded himself as Kadare's co-author. And he had also translated the Glorious Leader. Vrioni went to the bookshelves on the far wall, and returned with a couple of volumes, opening one to the title page. On it was Hoxha's inscription, in his own hand, to his "Comrade" for his "tireless work" in rendering the leader's writings into "perfect" French. Vrioni translated Hoxha's praise of himself with considerable drollery, assuming our appreciation of the implicit ironies.

I noticed that, on the low table before us, there was also a copy of the French translation of Milan Kundera's latest novel, which I had recently read myself. That led to Vrioni's enquiring about a Mexican novelist he had only heard of on his last trip to Paris. Did I know of Carlos Fuentes? I remarked to him that this conversation might take place in any capital of Europe. Yes, people were always surprised to encounter a cultivated Albanian, Vrioni said. "Of course, you know Montesquieu's *Persian Letters?*" he asked.

In that eighteenth-century work, the imaginary Persian, through whom Montesquieu provides his portrait of the ills of France, appears in a Paris salon and is asked, with near-disbelief, How is it possible for a Persian to be in Paris?

"I, too," Vrioni said, "have also been at a salon in Paris, and upon identifying myself as an Albanian, I was asked, by a man who knew his Montesquieu, But how is it possible for an Albanian to be in Paris?"

For all his civility, even the charm of his vanity, there was something unsettling about Vrioni. I remembered the rasping voice of the broken Trebeshina, the Don Quixote; at the name of Kadare he had spat the words "A collaborator." To be able to write, and to use his fame as a platform from which to criticize the régime, however indirectly, had he not also lent that renown to a justification of the régime? Had Kadare not faced the moral dilemma of the person who sustains the culture, which he imagines as belonging to posterity, but only at the cost of semi-collaboration with the totalitarian power, which he must persuade himself is merely temporary? Was that not also true, albeit to a lesser degree, in the case of Vrioni? Here we were in this comfortable home, with whisky on the table, the latest novels, a modern sound system, and amid all these elements necessary to the maintenance of a civilization was the very hand of the Glorious Leader, the madman, thanking his "tireless Comrade." I could, if I wished, reach out and touch the signature of the dictator.

Vrioni's ailing wife appeared at our departure. It was already night as Zef and Pavli walked me back towards the hotel. The Martyrs' Boulevard was jammed with people on Saturday night, walking in family groups, sitting on the low wall along the park, milling about in conversation in the hot darkness. I was overwhelmed by the sheer physicality. When the ideological shroud is pulled away, what you're left with is warm, human sweat.

We wanted to arrange for a car for the following day. Ilir was with some friends in the congested driveway beneath the veranda of the Dajti. He dashed off into the shadows to secure a driver, soon reappearing with a man who appeared trustworthy enough. We agreed to meet in the morning, and Zef and Pavli melted into the throng of strollers on the boulevard.

I told Ilir that we were going to Durres the next day. "I also," he said. "For the swimming." But perhaps we could meet later in the afternoon for a soft drink. "Yes, yes," he said enthusiastically. His voice was like the chirring of birds. We would meet at five. The boy had a way of being almost constantly in physical touch, with hand-holdings, an arm wrapped around you, a caress. Upon parting, an embrace, a kiss on both cheeks, the smoothness of his skin.

In my room, I admitted that I had been conquered — I had let something into my heart. But what was the nature of such feelings? And what was the relation between them, and the more casual feelings I had for the blond boy in Berlin? I recalled in Plato's works a conversation about profane and exalted loves. There were things I almost didn't want to know, moments when my desire seemed an abyss of the self. Yet desire too, I knew, belonged to the story.

In the morning, as the sun came in through the chinks of the half-pulled metal shade, I could hear the birds below in the otherwise empty garden. The driver proved to be quite reliable, and we were promptly on the road for our little holiday. As we passed buses jammed with like-minded weekenders heading for the sea, I found myself involuntarily glancing up at the windows of the packed vehicles on the unlikely chance that I might catch a glimpse of the boy on his way to the beach.

At Durres we inspected the ancient Roman amphitheatre, first century I think it was. It had been but semi-excavated, located right in the middle of a residential neighbourhood. The heat was stunning. It was a relief to duck into the shaded galleries and interior stairways. A Byzantine church had been installed into its midst in the Middle Ages; the whole place was a rockpile jumble of two millenia. At last we emerged into a portal overlooking the whole of the site. I can't recall if they had dug all the way down to the great half-circle stage of the theatre, but it was easy enough to imagine. When we at last clambered off the heap, I was grateful to our thoughtful driver, who had found a water tap which he ran for his parched inspectors of antiquities.

Then there was the local museum to see. It was across the street from a narrow beach at the sea's edge. I only had half an eye for the ancient statuary, for now I was longing for the Adriatic, which I could smell from there. "Where I come from," I said to Zef and Pavli, "it's considered good luck to dip your hand in the sea, if you're a visitor." I've no idea if that's true (although it was the case that I lived within sight of an inlet of the Pacific), but my hosts apparently felt we had fulfilled our duties as tourists, and obligingly led me across the road. It was a scruffy beach, pebbles and shells mostly, but the Adriatic stretched out before us in a long, low succession of thin layers of wave. I reached into it and wet my hand, scooping up some water to my face, while the sea ran over my foot.

I displayed sufficient enthusiasm for this natural wonder that Zef and Pavli decided to show me the beaches at the south end of town. It was a five-minute drive. Down the wide stretch of sand was an area of resorts and hotels, where the workers and their families went for holidays and where the country's few tourists had been permitted during the old régime, to provide a source of foreign exchange. We stopped at one of the hotels to get a cool drink. We sat in a large, cavernous hall that gave out onto the crowded beach below and the Adriatic rolling in, and sipped an orange-flavoured concoction. Afterwards the three of us strolled through the mob of bathers, families, groups of boys playing football in the sand, bodies everywhere. Absurdly, I hoped to spy Ilir in this multitude, though I knew I wouldn't. But what struck me was that when the ideological fog lifted, what you had were the people — not the abstracted version, as in "the people," but the physical fact of them — and these people, the Albanians, were not so different from the rest of humanity, not dissimilar to the Italians or Greeks, who were on their own beaches that Sunday afternoon.

In the car again — now we were travelling inland and north, to Kruje — the image of that human flesh shimmering in the sun remained with me for some while. I turned to Zef and Pavli, sitting in back.

"Communism never talked about the body," I declared.

"It never talked about the spirit either," Zef countered.

"But it had an equivalent to the spirit," I replied. "It had the notion of revolutionary consciousness. At least, that was a mental thing. But they claimed to be materialists, and yet they didn't speak — except mechanically — about the body." To be fair, in the world I came from the body was relentlessly displayed, but for all its commodification it was rendered almost equally meaningless.

Of course, the return of the body is not the same thing as the birth of a citizenry, I admitted. The madman had broken many bodies here, but when the kingdom fell apart — for a variety of reasons, including the simple fact that it didn't work — the body of, say, old Trebeshina was, in a sense, replaced by that of the boy I was enamoured of.

Yet bodies, left to themselves, form only the relationships of a society — at best, the wisdom of the elders, at worst, the gangs of the cities. Whereas the dictionaries Zef and Pavli made belonged to culture, even a universal culture, out of which citizens might emerge. I had no more idea of how it might turn out here than anyone else. But wasn't that true of so much else of that new entity that we referred to by the old name of Europe? For the moment, it was simply bodies that impressed themselves upon me. Bodies that, as Pavli had said, no longer had to turn their heads to see if someone was following. Perhaps I had a touch of sun, I don't know.

At Kruje, in the mountains, there was a reconstruction of Skanderbeg's castle and a sweeping view of the valley below. We dutifully toured the site of the warlord's redoubt. Nearby there was a little outdoor restaurant, and we sat in the walled garden by a fountain, and feasted. Below us, at a table placed near the edge of a precipice, commanding a view of the valley, was a party of Italians. They were very jolly, yodelling out into the mountains, hoping to produce an echo. The waiter told us, however, that far from being the frivolous tourists we might imagine, they had taken in some Albanian young men who had fled to Brindisi — I remembered the footage of overloaded boats I'd seen on TV the previous spring — and now they had come to visit the parents, to bring them news of their sons.

Sheep wandered about the garden, eating bread from our hands, nudging up against our knees, while we dug our fingers into their white, oily curls. But even as we feasted, dipping our bread into the dish of oil in which the olives soaked — Zef said, matter-of-factly, "I haven't tasted olive oil in two years" — and as the Italians hullaed and yodelled, our talk strayed from the bucolic surroundings.

"What did you think the day Hoxha died?" I asked rather suddenly.

"It isn't very Christian," Zef answered, "but it was perhaps the finest day of my life."

"How did you hear about it?"

"We were not together at the time," Pavli said.

"First, there was only classical music on the radio," Zef remembered. "And we thought something had happened. And of course the only thing that could have happened was that He died. So we waited for the official announcement, which was on the twelve o'clock news."

"I was travelling that day, to my hometown," Pavli recalled. "I took my little daughter with me. I went to see my father, who was sick. On my way to the train station, I met an old journalist. He approached me with sort of — I can't explain what his face was like when he saw me — but he desperately wanted to tell me something. He approached me with half a smile and said, 'He is dead and gone.' I got it immediately. When I reached home, I told my father, I gave him the news. He just rejoiced. 'I saw him go before me. I don't mind if I die now.' Those were his words."

Pavli fell silent. We listened to the water falling in the fountain.

Zef said, "We hoped that his death would be the end, but the régime lingered on for another six years."

"The true end of the dictator," Pavli continued, "was on that famous day when his ten-metre-high statue was brought down. My wife was walking with her bicycle in the square and she saw people gathering, rushing about, and the police throwing tear-gas bombs. Nobody cared about their lives, they just rushed towards the statue, and managed to bring it down. Afterwards, a tractor pulled it to the campus, where the students were on a hunger strike. They cut off his head, which was sent to the students. And then the body — "

"It was dragged along," Zef interjected, "like a dead crocodile."

"Without its head," Pavli added.

In the mid-afternoon we came down from Kruje, back towards Tirana. I would be leaving the next day, so, though there would be a farewell, this was in a sense the last of our conversation. And at the end, as we had begun, we spoke of dictionaries. It was as if they hadn't made themselves clear enough, hadn't got it right, and it was somehow important to them that I understand.

"If we had been hot-headed, and just burst in a fit of passion and told them everything we had in our minds, we would have been content for a while, but our work would not have been done," Pavli said. "Dictionaries are not *our* work. It is something which belongs to the whole people, and people who make dictionaries are only a few idiotic, I would say, hard-working asses who take upon themselves the work of a lifetime."

"Eccentrics," Zef said, chuckling. "But it was some sort of justification."

"Or a revenge on our own selves," Pavli offered, alternatively. "After having humiliated ourselves, serving Him so devotedly, we wanted to do something to atone for what we had done."

Zef disagreed. "I, for my part, didn't think of it as atonement. I considered it only as a reply to people who, after liberation — I was always hoping for liberation — to people who would ask me, and during these years, what have you done? It was meant as a reply."

"So that you could say?"

"I did something useful," Zef concluded. The car pulled into the driveway of the Dajti.

I went down to the hotel veranda at five. Ilir was there, in a white T-shirt and jeans. When we went into the bar to get mineral water and soft drinks, he wouldn't let me pay; instead, he made some arrangement so that I was his guest. Upstairs, in my room, we sat on the little balcony facing the electric sign. I coaxed him into shedding his T-shirt, what with the heat. A fresh, glowing patina of tan that had been acquired on the beach at Durres that day burnished his torso.

He was a dancer. His father wanted him to study law, I think it was, but he wanted to dance. There was some difficulty with language; we used Zef's dictionary to get through the rough spots — I would think of a word we needed in English and translate it into German, and look it up and show Ilir the corresponding word in Albanian, and then say the English for it. Cumbersome, but a bit like a game. He was in one of those folk dance ensembles approved by the régime.

But the boy's passion was for ballet. Classical and modern ballet, although he called the latter "abstract." "Ballet abstract," he said. He told me the story of a ballet he was in at school — *The Silver Birds* — written by his teacher, his "choreograph." And then I finally got it about "the rap." What he was interested in was "rap dancing." He'd seen this fellow, Hammer, an American, who was a performer of rap dancing, on Yugoslavian television. And the famous Michael Jackson, of course. I hadn't paid much attention to any of that, but one absorbs it, since it's in the air, so I knew what he was talking about. The sound of rap was like the staccato of a firing squad, I'd thought. But Ilir's idea was this. He too wanted to be a choreographer. And the ballet he wanted to create would be a combination of classical ballet and rap dancing. Well, why not?

We sat on the balcony and chatted away for a couple of hours in the late afternoon.

There were other stories. Something about his sister, or sister-in-law, wanting to flee Albania for the Italian refugee camps, how he'd pleaded with her not to go. And once he'd been to Turkey for two or three weeks — I didn't quite get why — he'd stayed with a family, and they'd been very nice to him, but he'd gotten homesick.

It was all quite marvellous. I'd gone all the way to this benighted place, and I'd found what I'd been seeking, I suppose, in more ways than I'd expected. Ilir was outgoing, unselfconscious, his voice was a little breathless. Perhaps all the pidgin English, pidgin Albanian, made it seem much simpler than it was. I didn't think he represented the "spirit of Albania" or some such nonsense. There was a temptation to make that of him, of course, he was so full of his own light. But that's a dangerous sentimentality, too. He was simply himself. But he was of the place also, he would have to live here when Vrioni and Don Quixote and the translators had gone on. He might even make a ballet, if the place wasn't overtaken by chaos, if it didn't revert to hill banditry and blood feuds, if, against the odds, the musical body of this boy and the "deliberate belief" (as Conrad calls it) of the dictionary-makers could forge a citizenry. Ilir wanted to see me again the next day, before I left. He would bring me a *regalo*, a gift. He'd come at nine the next morning.

That evening I took dinner in the hotel, a large hall at the end of the long corridor, beyond the bar and breakfast room which flanked its length. Through the dining-room windows you could see the boulevard, filled with people, passing up and down in the middle of the huge avenue. The pilgrims, myself included, were at their cutlets. The Texans were at a table on one side of me; I gathered they were off to Cairo the next day. Apparently they'd done a deal for oil rights down at Flora — to the south, below Apollonia, the old Greek town — in return for which they would provide computer equipment (probably obsolete) from head office in Houston or Dallas. And at the table on my other side there was another businessman, with a woman, earnestly lecturing a local fellow, who seemed quite deferential before the pilgrim's sermon on efficiency and whatnot.

I took the air for a bit, among the strolling crowds, before retiring to my room. Before I nodded off, I saw the end of it, of the story I was following here. When you're vouchsafed — in advance — a glimpse of the tale in its entirety, you simply shudder with gratefulness to the god for whom the Greeks named that town of Apollonia.

Ilir arrived promptly at nine. The haze was just lifting from Mt. Dajti. He had a plastic sack filled with *regalos:* a bottle of Albanian raki, another of wine, some candies, and a collection of video and cassette tapes — Beethoven, and a local singer, and M. C. Hammer, which he'd taken off the radio, TV footage of the visit of the American secretary of state to Tirana — even a snapshot of himself. He emptied his treasury upon me. Would I send him a video of Hammer or Michael Jackson? "Yes, of course," I promised, "but there's one more *regalo* I'd like." He was puzzled. What more could there be?

"I'd like to see you dance," I said.

"But where?" he asked.

"Here," I said. At first, he made the faintest show of resistance, but he was an artist, and accustomed to performing. Beethoven is not really for dancing, he pointed out, even as he snapped the tape into my little interview recorder with the familiar dexterity of teenagers everywhere.

He placed himself in front of the gauze curtain before the window. It was embroidered with birds, and the faintest breeze moved the cloth. I pressed the button and symphonic strains emerged. At first, I didn't think it would come off. There was barely sufficient room to move between the bed and the doorway to the bathroom, three or four paces at most. I don't know what I expected — that it would be quite provincial, or crudely amateurish, perhaps.

I needn't have worried. He struck a pose, this boy in T-shirt, jeans, and sneakers, and quickly found space to soar and plunge and turn. I don't know how to describe it. You could say, I suppose, that his terrible innocence took wing — if it was innocence, if it was terrible. What does Rilke say? "Every angel is terrifying"?

When the Beethoven ran out, he immediately found the woman pop singer on the tape, and danced a mixture of Turkish and folkloric movements. For the finale there was a performance of rap dancing to Hammer chanting the refrain, "Can't touch this," repeated again and again. It was one of those boasting songs from the American ghetto, full of aggressive sexual double entendres and self-acclaim for the performer's artistry. Although I'd only paid annoyed attention to it when I'd seen it in passing on television, it now struck me as quite beautiful. I saw the art of it. Ilir simply viewed it as another form of modern dancing. For him, the elements of the culture had no gaping spaces. For his needs, Beethoven and Hammer were contemporaries. And the tiny room was as adequate as the stage in the amphitheatre at Durres.

At the end, he collapsed into the chair at my desk, heaving for breath. He was covered in a light sweat — it gathered in the trough above his lip, and in the hollow at the base of his throat. I could smell him, breathe him in. He glowed. I offered him a can of cola. It was soon time for him to go; he had a test at school that day. An embrace, kisses, a hug in which for a moment I held that dancing body against my own. "Can't touch this," I said. "Can't touch this," he repeated with a grin.

The rubber tires of the plane squeaked down onto the tarmac at Tegel airport in Berlin as I turned the last pages of Conrad's story. I was left at the end with Marlow, Conrad's yarn-spinner, his interminable voice having ceased, his face as impassive as that of a meditating Buddha.

I got up, reaching into the overhead baggage rack for my maroon-coloured gym bag. Coincidentally enough — and this was one of those thousand things you couldn't possibly make up — my seat companion was a riverboat captain, just returning from some place in Africa where he worked for a German resource company. We wished each other well at the end of our respective journeys.

That evening I had a drink at the Café Einstein, and when I said to a friend I'd run into there that I was just back from Tirana, he made me repeat the name and then tried it out himself, as if uttering the name of some place on the moon. I extracted Zef's dictionary from my bag as evidence that I wasn't making it up. "But why did you want to go there?" he asked, tolerantly amused.

I soon took my leave, making my way in the cool, damp night across Nollendorfplatz, beneath the soot-stained nude statues embedded in the upper facade of the Metropol Theatre, into the web of narrow streets to the west, where the bar I frequented was located. It was late, and the blond boy wasn't there.

In his place was a rangy young man in his early twenties, tall, rather dark, athletic, not exactly my type. How quickly the sublime was replaced by the vulgar, I thought, slightly bemused, yet noticing that I wasn't tempted to exalt the former at the expense of the latter.

We struck up a conversation in broken German, the one language we had in common. He was from Zagreb, in Croatia, an economics student; his family had sent him off to Berlin for safety in the midst of the Yugoslavian shooting. By chance, one of them, his mother, or perhaps a grandparent, was Albanian, and he seized with delight upon Zef's dictionary, which I had placed upon the bar between our elbows. When we encountered a word in German that was outside his vocabulary, we repaired to Zef's translation of it into Albanian, just as I had done with Ilir. I was a bit frightened of him, but in the cab he took my hand in his much larger one, reassuring and exciting me by circling his finger in my palm. At home, I satisfied him as best I could.

LESLIE HALL PINDER has written short fiction, non-fiction and two widely acclaimed novels. *Under the House* (1986) was published in Canada, the U.K. and the U.S. *On Double Tracks* (1990) was published in Canada and the U.K., and was short-listed for the Governor-General's award for literature. She has practised law in the area of native land claims since 1978.

A Deeper Theft

Leslie Hall Pinder

I am a novelist and a lawyer. Three years ago I was commissioned to work with a composer in developing an opera inspired by the life of Canadian anthropologist Wilson Duff.

In 1957 Duff took an expedition into the Queen Charlotte Islands to salvage the totem poles of Haida Gwaii. Some of the most beautiful poles were at Ninstints. Bill Reid, not then the great carver he has since become, was on the crew. They cut down the poles, crated them, and brought them out. I thought the opera was about these poles. But I also learned that many years after this trip, Duff assembled an exhibition of stone artifacts; the heart of the exhibit was twin masks. Until he brought them back together, they had been kept in museums in different countries for over 100 years.

Duff committed suicide a year after the exhibition of the masks. The extent to which all these events are related is what I tried to discover in researching and writing the story of the opera and in creating the libretto. The work on the opera became so interesting, complex and ultimately difficult that I started to keep a detailed journal of what I was going through.

On September 18, 1992, ninety minutes of the opera-in-progress was performed for an invited audience at the Museum of Anthropology in Vancouver. The audience sat amidst the poles removed from Haida Gwaii by Duff and the others. Bill Reid, now in his seventies, was in the audience, watching the young baritone George Roberts playing his character in the opera. Members of Wilson Duff's family were there. The museum is also the location of Duff's suicide.

The role of The Lover was sung by Candice Burrows. In the opera she ultimately transforms into Raven.

Since that night of September 18, 1992, I have not worked on the opera's libretto. Instead, I light another fire in a different wild. This piece is now part of a novel-in-progress. I am creating a story out of what happened, and the bounds of fiction and non-fiction, the sacred and profane, and the poetic, start to blur. Imaginatively, I am trying to follow where Wilson Duff went, and it seems to be a treacherous journey.

In what follows, the lines of the libretto are interspersed between my journal entries. It was after the visit to the Museum of Civilization in Ottawa that I wrote the last two sections for Duff.

THE WORLD IS AS SHARP AS A KNIFE

(An Opera)

Character List (partial) (draft)

Wilson Duff	Anthropologist
Bill Reid	CBC newsman and later Haida artist
Miriam	Duff's wife
Daughter	Miriam and Wilson Duff's child, age 4
The Calculators	Those who organized the expedition to Haida Gwaii

The Lover	The woman loved by Duff and Reid
Native Chorus	The chorus that represents the people of Haida Gwaii
Duff's Chorus	A chorus of men and women of many different racial backgrounds
Eesalatsil	Fictional name for Charles Edenshaw, master Haida carver

In some of the stories, the beginning is Raven who needs to be born, and so he creates his mother. In some of the stories, there is heat melting ice into a drop of liquid which becomes a monster who is hungry, needing a cow to eat. Always there is a fall: through a hole in the sky, out of the garden, into the water. But the scientists say that in the first three minutes the content of the universe was mostly light.

I am writing about the beginning, but I don't know anything yet. I am writing ideas for the opera. I am trying to find some lines about the beginning of the world for the mezzo-soprano to sing.

[*Lecture theatre. Wilson Duff is at the podium. Behind him is his chorus.*]

DUFF'S CHORUS:
Nothing had to happen forever
in order for this something to start
and then —
it took only three minutes.

WILSON DUFF:
Earth was not found yet
nor heaven.

DUFF'S CHORUS:
To the north and south of nothing

were regions
of ice and fire.
And at the end of the first three minutes,
the universe
was mostly light.

WILSON DUFF:
This is Raven's story
It is the only one to tell
It goes like this:

Raven
being born
needs a mother
to be born
needs to love
being born
makes the light.

[*There is a brilliance, like the light inside a window getting
    brighter. It fills the theatre.*]

Then Raven steals what he has made —
like that — snatched.

[*Darkness*]
[*The Calculators' voices boom out*]

THE CALCULATORS:
Come come now.
Antecedents

Consequences —
Wilson, deal with cause and effect.

WILSON DUFF:
I shall
All at once.

THE CALCULATORS:
Where is the beginning?

WILSON DUFF:
Begin with yourself —
Or with this.

[*Wilson Duff points to a stone mask.*]

There are in fact two masks made of stone. They are
   twins.
One is sighted and one is blind.

The masks are Tsimshian. The unsighted mask was collected in 1879 by I. W. Powell, deputy commissioner of Indian Affairs for British Columbia. It is being held at the Museum of Civilization in Ottawa. The sighted mask is kept in Paris. It was obtained by Alphonse Pinart, an explorer, in 1872. I do not know how it ended up in Paris. The opera will be about Wilson Duff, who brought them together for a brief time in 1975.

THE CALCULATORS:
If you came upon the masks separately
you would want to collect them;
you would ask the price;
you would check your wallet

WILSON DUFF:
But when you know there are two,

when you know them together
you do not ask the price —
because you could not pay.

THE LOVER:
I am unnerved by them.
It is too much for us to withstand
seeing them side by side
in our present state:
Our hearts weak from not caring
Our spirits tired from not engaging
Will they sear us
like too much beauty seen?

I sit in the reception area of the museum, waiting to be taken inside to the blind mask which is kept here in Ottawa. All the doors leading out of this area are locked. This place seems designed to be what it is not, but I don't know yet what it is.

WILSON DUFF:
This stone is not rock.
A genius has entered here.
This rock is a bird in my hands, is flight.
Such a transformation does not come for the asking —
it does not come without exacting a price that must be
    paid.

Sandra comes to get me. She unlocks the first door and takes me down the hall to her office. The mess of her room seems almost unsavoury, there are so many piles of paper everywhere. And she is harried, dishevelled, absorbed in things beyond this realm: she knows the divinity of a basket, the holiness of a fish hook, and when she talks I understand the sacredness of these objects, but she hasn't attended to herself. The last time I saw her, she spoke the way people do when they are afraid no one wants to listen: she covered her mouth so that I had to lean forward in order to hear her words.

We go to have coffee at the far end of the building. I am only interested in seeing the mask, but I am patient, polite. The restaurant has vast windows overlooking the river and the bridge. I see that in order to get to the heart of the city I would have to cross the bridge. The streets there are like those in other cities: Cuzco, Lima, Vancouver. And I know them because at the centre of those cities is London, and London is the city in our night-dreams. That is what is across the river. But here inside the museum is a different space: protected, hypocritical, manipulative, explosive.

Directly in front of the restaurant windows is a long stretch of tended lawn and on it are three Plains Indian tepees. The skins look vulnerable in this wide expanse of green, in this manicured availability. I wonder if they would look less so in a dry and rough terrain.

It seems we are looking into something which has passed. The sky is lowering, weighted, accumulating, as though informing me that any sense of comfort is false. And suddenly a great snake of lightning cuts through this heavy sky as if the sky were its own hair or thoughts, and it touches the top of the tepees. Thunder bowls through. We are all shocked, motionless, afraid.

The sound pegs into me, grounding me with knowing: here I am — in this place close to the mask. Only thin, scraped skins keep us from these loud gods. We are nervous and excited, anticipating, fearing and desiring another shock. It is difficult for Sandra and me to shake ourselves free but we leave and go further into the building.

From the outside the museum looked very beautiful as I drove towards it: flowing lines, a place a civilization might inhabit. But in here, in these hallways, the smell of hospital death starts immediately and intensifies as we enter the interior corridors and move to the centre of the building.

Sandra places the palm of her hand to the wall and the door opens. Door after door after door. Every step we take is towards a bend in the road, always a bend in the road, never emerging, rounding the corner. Cluttering the halls are the huge garbage bags filled with plastic wrap needed for moving the artifacts from city to city, from one country to another.

We reach a door that is thick metal and she can't open it. To the right there is a doorbell.

A young woman comes. She is smiling, welcoming: pert, pretty, cute — all the old words from team sports, from cheering something on that is muscular, grunting, certain.

Behind this young woman is a warehouse. The ceiling is forty feet high; the room is filled with shelves. The young woman is wearing a white coat and clear plastic gloves over her hands. The place is antiseptic, like a medical laboratory. There is no dust. The light burns from high unreachable bulbs. Sandra and I seem ancient and ugly, from another time, haggard. She says something to the woman. We move into the warehouse.

> [*Both masks are together on a table in the museum gallery.*
> *There are totem poles in the background. At first the scene*
> *is filled with a kind of levity.*]

REID:
[*Referring to the bringing together of the masks*]
Like the first three minutes of anything
this could never be done again. The universe begins.
[*Turning to The Lover*]
But after all our needs are met,
after all our loves,
where do we go
for redemption?

On the shelves are hats, wooden masks, boxes, bowls, cedar cloaks, baskets — the things the natives had used in their daily lives. They had been borrowed or stolen, purchased, given away or collected and brought here. It is so strange that they are here.

THE CALCULATOR:
[*To Duff*]
You seem upset —
But the natives who "cared" for these artifacts before
you
still sold them for a price —
And anyway you know about things that are taken
and never returned. The Ninstints poles.

And what about the Raven's rattle, Wilson.
What about the thefts which were all your own.

DUFF:
You butcher the living
and try to revive the dead.

There are other young women in the warehouse, all wearing plastic gloves over their hands. They are the caretakers — nice, friendly, soft, as though they might love their work and the things they almost touch. All these aboriginal things suspended in time.

The hats created by the master carver, Charles Edenshaw, are sitting on milliners' stands, looking for all the world like a display in a shop window, ready to be chosen, removed and worn out into the street.

But the wooden masks on the shelves upset me.

It is not that they are dormant or asleep, but rather they look stunned — as though petrified and still paralysed where they sit looking out from these shelves. They are not looking at me but into a horrified beyond — that is what has been captured here: the moment of being taken alive, the moment of seeing the invader's face or feeling his hand or simply knowing that all the locks have failed and the murderer is in the house. A malformed presence has overtaken them.

We move through the warehouse with its white, chalk-white, dead-white walls. And the lovely young women, whom Sandra calls the conservators, follow.

I realize — as I look closer at the cedar bark hats and ask Sandra if I can touch one of them and she says yes and I do — I realize that my physical intimacy with these objects is much less reserved than hers. I want to put on the hat.

I stop; the others go ahead of me.

These are real things you would need during real days, every day. A bowl for soup; a cane for walking — now kept in scientifically controlled conditions, the way that you would keep a specimen of something, especially if you did not really know what it was but thought it must be an important clue. At the scene of a crime everything is taken for evidence: all the dishes, cutlery, knives — the food on the table, the dust on the floor. It is bagged and brought here. These things are kept because they hold secrets we eventually will be able to uncode. Right now we do not know.

The circular distributed by the Smithsonian Institution in 1880 emphasized the need to acquire a "full series" of native American skulls "to be procured without offence to the living." But, other than that, no object was singled out. "Almost everything has its value in giving completeness to a collection." There was some urgency because "many articles are perishable and the tribes, themselves, are passing away or exchanging their own manufacturers for those of the white race." Franz Boas, anthropologist, collector, watched a potlatch feast at Fort Rupert in 1930. While the meat was being distributed, the host chief made a speech. He said to his guests, "This bowl in the shape of a bear is for you and you." The speech was the same one Boas had first heard 40 years earlier. The only difference now was that the carved bowls were not, in fact, in their midst. They were in museums in New York. The Chief said "this bowl" to the empty space where the bowl should have been.

NATIVE CHORUS:
We trade;
we get what we want,
and you do too.
You buy. There is plenty.
Then you want more.

EESALATSIL:
I go to my house.
The storage is empty.
I take my bent box;
I give it away.

NATIVE CHORUS:
There is a touch of the conqueror
on your face.
And when you are talking
you are glancing over my shoulder;
You are looking at my land.

RAVEN:
[*To the Traders and Settlers*]
Be still, be guests for once.

NATIVE CHORUS:
They break into the houses of our dead.
They rake through our lives.
They take our bones.
They sell these stolen things
like owners
like conquerors
like kings.
The price goes up.
They sell these holy things,
like scavengers,
like jackals
like greedy men.
The price goes up.
To Chicago
New York
Ottawa
Paris
Brussels —
our treasures vanish.

EESALATSIL:
And we start to carve for you
pipes that don't smoke
to use with coal that won't burn.
You buy.

NATIVE CHORUS:
What has happened to our love —
florescence —

our mutual song?
What has happened to the news
that came across the waves
on feathers we set down
for your bow to spread
to lay aside, to open.
You came towards us
like an echo
answering our very own song.
Now your echo contains a blast.
What have you done?

In a glass box on a shelf as high as the top reach of my hands I can see the stone mask. It is not so much a mask but the visible part of a body in repose. It is surrounded by these other shocked and frightened wooden faces. That is the value — perhaps even the purpose — of stone, then. The wood continues to carry the horror, but not this stone; this sleeping head dreams, unconfused, uninvolved in the nightmare that has been absorbed by the other members of the family.

I look for a long time, looking through the glass at this mask. Finally, I notice that there is another box beside this one, exactly the same size as the glass box, but it is a wooden box, painted blue.

The conservator then tells us there are two unsighted masks here, one is the original and the other is a copy. She doesn't know which box — glass or wood — contains which. She goes to check her records.

What is this other mask? Where did it come from?

What would Wilson Duff think of this? What do I know . . . that the duality of the mask is not, in fact, a question of there being two, but rather there is a doubleness in its soul that is always maintained. It is maintained here, even in the absence of the sighted mask. The twinness in front of me is represented by the authentic and the inauthentic. But now I am suddenly unsure if we have even identified the correct qualities in the mask. I had thought they were blindness and vision, even Oedipal blindness: self-inflicted, tragic, bringing insight. Until this other double appears.

My mind is baffled. And yet I know now that the mask within the blue box is unsighted because I cannot see it. The other mask is there behind the glass; I can see it. The sightedness has to do, then, with me. And so the logic of the case is that the authentic unsighted mask is the one hidden in the blue box, kept in darkness, where I am blind now. I am behind the mask.

The conservator returns to tell us that the records say the real one is in the blue box.

> [*Duff is in the museum storage area. His wife and daughter*
> *have come to take him home. He puts his arm around*
> *Miriam, and holds the child's hand.*]

DUFF:
An ache has started in my throat.
I thirst —
I long for more.
I want to lay bare the very thing
this art is made to disguise —
where everything's wrapped in light.
I am excited,
yet my moods disperse and gather.
They make this different light.
[*He lets go of his daughter's hand and turns around slightly*
to indicate the totem poles. He sees The Lover standing
there. She moves forward.]

THE LOVER:
Wilson Duff.

DUFF:
[*Thinking that she is a visitor who has wandered off limits*]
Yes.
You shouldn't be back here.

THE LOVER:
[*Her anger controlled*]
I wanted to visit Ninstints
sometime in my life.

DUFF:
[*Not understanding*]
Yes.

THE LOVER:
It's now too late.

MIRIAM:
You are angry.

THE LOVER:
[*To Duff*]
I was angry before I saw you —
I came to say you should have left the poles.

DUFF:
They should not have been salvaged?

THE LOVER:
Salvation does not have such a stunting purpose.
They should never have been taken.

DUFF:
[*Looks at her with growing annoyance*]
Collected.

THE LOVER:
Stolen.

DUFF:
[*He removes his arm from Miriam's shoulders*]
Saved.

THE LOVER:
[*Focussed anger*]
Chopped down. Axed.
The place will shake from the blast
that severed all those limbs.

MIRIAM:
You seem to make your inquiries with a blade
as well.

DUFF:
We did the right thing.

THE LOVER:
[*Speaking very directly and intently to Duff*]
The poles don't belong in stairwells;
The poles don't belong with floodlights
in offices
as ornaments
as curios.
You've cut them down
and now they are yours.
You arrested what belongs to that place;
the consequences fall.

DUFF:
[*Undefensive*]
I am ready.
Something is luring me —

MIRIAM:
[*Suspicious at this charged atmosphere which has quickly
    developed between The Lover and Duff*]
— on a path with a slipping descent.

THE LOVER:
You expected tasks requiring all your strength and
skill —
But the world has gone from flat to round.
These tasks are a different kind.
They require your soul.

[*Duff looks at The Lover with amazement and intense
    curiosity that she should be saying these things.*]

MIRIAM:
We must leave now, Wilson.

[*Wilson nods in agreement, but it is to what The Lover has
    said, not to Miriam. Miriam sees that Duff is caught. The
    exchange has attracted Reid's attention; he turns and looks
    at what is going on.*]

MIRIAM:
Ask her to go, Wilson.
[*Aside*]
He is pushing back the dark —
And then she comes near,
pulling night-time in her wake.
It's not a jealousy I feel,
but curiosity about this dance.
She reminds me of him.

DUFF:
There is some power I almost apprehend —

MIRIAM:
[*She continues to move stage right, almost backing away.*]
Why is she here, Wilson?

DUFF:
[*To The Lover*]
I am trailing a god
who is looking for me.

MIRIAM:
Wilson, be careful.

DUFF:
[*Turning to her, suddenly annoyed and rough*]
Careful of what?

[*Miriam is angry and humiliated by his remark. She picks
up her daughter and leaves. Duff is ashamed of himself.*]

We are going to take down the mask. Sandra asks the conservator to call an assistant. I stand, attending, sensing the gathering of a strange ritual: simple, completely foreign, entrancing — as the assistant brings over a special ladder which she places beside the shelves.

In the beginning was the word. In the beginning was Raven. The first bird to be sent from the ark was the Raven, not the dove. The Raven didn't return. It is the beginning of the world, or the beginning of a deeper theft.

At Sandra's direction they move the box out of the dusk of the shelf and over to a small white table, like an operating table. In this light I can see the deep, kingdom blue of the box. As they place it on the table, Sandra says, "We'll need a small screwdriver." And yet she knew that a screwdriver was not needed. I know she remembers that in 1975 when Wilson Duff brought the sighted mask back from Paris, there was a gathering at his house. They had to use a small screwdriver to open the four corners of the box.

> [*Duff hands The Lover the tool to open the box. His colleagues at the university are surprised he would give her such an honour because they do not know of their relationship. But with the intimacy of this sudden honour they know. The Lover takes the screwdriver. Everyone is intensely conscious of the task, of each corner, the significance of four —*]

But on this blue box there are latches like keys that have to be turned. Sandra points to them, indicating that I should open the latches. I do, solemnly, yet I want to hold on to this moment just before, this not knowing — to go back again in the story, circle around, not have this, yet, be the beginning — perhaps there is no foothold, landfall, place to be. What now? But my movements are too slow and the ceremony is blocked. Sandra looks at me, confused, and so I proceed. When the last key is turned, I indicate to her that she should take the next step. As she starts to lift the lid I notice that there is a handwritten tag on the side that says "travelling box."

Sandra lifts out the block of white Styrofoam and places it on the table. She looks at me again and then removes the top part. She reaches both hands inside and pulls out the mask, holding it like a precious thing. She places it on the table. It rocks slightly. It has a bowl's centre of gravity.

I am inadequate to the task. My conscious mind is not fast enough to relay all the impressions that come. I want to be left alone, and I am being watched. And yet I need to be watched in the presence of such significance — not to protect the mask but to protect me. Still I long to be alone. My senses make lists, but there is too much information for a list or a chronology or anything in a row. Something in me almost starts to shut down. It is everything I can do to keep looking, not to avert my eyes; and one thing I am certain of: all the representations of this mask — all the photographs, descriptions, articles — have not revealed the most essential thing. This is a transformation mask — a human being is becoming amphibious, living in two elements, becoming frog. Or the frog has become human. In that thin membrane which borders two dimensions, between the human and the animal, between the air and the water, between spirit and material — the places of ambivalence, the raw space, the space that gives no comfort — that is where this one lives. And so I understand why the lips are thick. I understand the eyebrows, the cheeks, the shape of the face. They are all in motion, becoming another; it is the shock of evolution. Not development, not the slow, gradual, comfortable ordering of things, the hierarchy, moving into the place of the father, cared for by the mother; but the almost horror, the almost shock, the almost death of this place between worlds, without precedent, unaccounted for and unexpected. Unwanted.

A green colour had either been massaged into the stone or induced out from the stone. It was not shown in any of the photographs, nor ever described.

Red ochre is around the ears, as though the ears are sore.

This mask is not blind. This mask has closed eyes. If I touch them, they would feel the way eyelids feel, the round orbs of the eyes beneath the lids.

It is unsighted, not looking out, blind in that way.

I reach over and lift the mask up. The mask is so balanced, so strong, I need to hold it in two hands.

They are standing right beside me; they don't want me to touch the thing, as though I might taste it, eat it, consume it now, right here, on the spot.

And then I say to Sandra, "May I put it on?" But she doesn't know. She shrugs. She does not know what to do. And I raise the mask to my face.

So dark. It is not the darkness of the world into which we are born; it is the darkness of the unborn world. How comfortable I was calling out the beginning of the world, the first three minutes, pretending I stood next to a fatherly god. This darkness is terrible. I am going to be sick. And then I can hear the sound of the river contained within this stone, the river that comes from the stone. There is an ocean. This rock was the ocean's bed. I have been inside this darkness. I can hear the earth. The faces of all the people who have worn this mask touch my own.

> DUFF AND THE LOVER:
> Between God and the world
> is creation.
> Between God and humanity
> is revelation.

Between you and me
is redemption.
Is creation.
Is revelation.

THE LOVER:
You must put it on . . .

WILSON DUFF:
Shall I?

THE LOVER:
Yes.

[*Duff puts on the mask. Blackout. Then lights up gradually
  as Duff removes the mask slowly from his face.*]

WILSON DUFF:
I know this darkness
I have been inside this mouth.
I know its smell.
It is a Ninstints night.
I am laid open by this shape.
It disguises me.

I peel the mask away from my face. Sandra says, "The masks are about Raven stealing the light." "Oh," I say. I look at the mask. I am sighted again, its twin.

WILSON DUFF:
[*To The Lover*]
There is a secret. One we did not know.
[*He holds the unsighted mask. He looks at the sighted one.*]
They've never been seen like this, ever.
Only one or the other has been seen before.

THE LOVER:
Yes.

WILSON DUFF:
It is not just that they are twins.

THE LOVER:
No.

WILSON DUFF:
They do not belong simply together.

THE LOVER:
No.

WILSON DUFF:
They belong inside one another.

THE LOVER:
Yes.

WILSON DUFF:
They belong like this.
[*With his back to The Lover he puts on both masks and then
turns: is unsighted; turns, is sighted. The mask comes
alive. He does this again and again. As he approaches her,
closed eyes, open eyes, a screen shows the mask getting larger.
When he is very close to her, The Lover puts her hands up
and takes the masks from his face.*]

WILSON DUFF:
[*Examining the sighted mask and absorbed in its effect on
him*]

Traces of red paint on the inside, here —
or blood from the dancer's mouth
as he clenched the loop of willow between his teeth.
The transformation exacts its toll.
I am ready.
This stone is awake into its own death.
I can have it both ways
I am ready.

Sandra puts the mask back in the box and slowly covers it. This strange, undiluted thing. I feel as if I am allowed infrequent and supervised visits with my only intimate; the visit is almost too painful. She is the woman we are keeping locked in a room.

We call a conservator. The youngest comes. She is putting on plastic gloves — I don't know why she had taken off the other pair. She lifts the box. Now the gloves look different; for all the world they look like the gloves of a surgeon.

THE LOVER:
[*To The Calculators*]
Let us keep them for one more day —
We will treat them as you do:
artifacts, relics, curiosities.
Their provenance will be told.
We will pretend they are only stone.

Everything we have done, everything I have written, is only approximate. We have only been close to the target. The target has to hit us.

I who have come here catch the plane home, from Ottawa to Vancouver.

WILSON DUFF:
[*To The Lover, full of innocence and hope*]
An invitation is here.
If we could only accept it this time,
then we could flourish again
with someone to catch us if we fall —

with someone to catch our wide
overbounding zeal:
our love, florescence,
our mutual song.
There is news of a new human race
that comes across the waves
on feathers they set down
for our bow to spread
to lay aside, to open.
This stone is not rock.
A genius has entered here.

[*Holds both masks*]

In my hands I bridge a gap:
hold all darkness as I began
and light, too light for my eyes —
If I do not resist
I will not burn.
This stone, this tension in me,
I love.
It does not break me up
I can hold it
I can master it,
I am it.
This is redemption
I will not die.
If once we convince the spirit to come
it could never leave again —
It needs me to pick it up,
and hold it between my teeth.
A stone has opened its eyes.
God cannot do without me.
He needs to be contained

in me.
My sail unfurls
The wind snaps it out.
Bend the wind
Bend my box.
Bend.
I am finally ready.

MARK FRUTKIN has published four novels and three books of poetry, including *Atmospheres Apollinaire*, a finalist in fiction for the 1988 Governor-General's Awards. His most recent novel, *In the Time of the Angry Queen*, was published by Random House in 1993. He lives in Ottawa with his wife Faith, and his son Elliot.

The Lion of Venice

Mark Frutkin

In Venice on Ascension Thursday in the year 1254 of Christ's Incarnation, her look penetrates his metals as easily as light passes through water . . .

His nostrils tremble with moisture and flare open as the winged statue of the Lion of Venice sniffs the air from atop his high column carved of violet Troas granite.

From his pose of extravagant stillness, he readies himself to pounce. Again he sniffs. An uncanny impossible scent has quickened him into life — the smell of crushed almonds with flashes of honeysuckle, lemon, gardenia, cinnamon, clove, as well as the fresh clean odour of damp earth and starched cotton, stitched by an intriguing thread of seaweed. He instantly recognizes it as the smell of desire. The eyes of the Lion of Venice, all white and seemingly empty, gaze down towards the source of the rising scent.

The towering doors of the Church of San Marco ease open on a flood of morning light and Maria stands on the threshold looking out into the blinding square. In that moment, everything changes, and though Maria senses something different in the air, she would never entirely understand what it was.

The others sense it too — her family, the milling holy-day crowd, the soldiers and the monks — each in their own way, sense a change, deep, utterly irretrievable, profoundly subtle. A fillip of light, a wind curling in from the sea, an impossible distant chime — each hears it and defines it in their own way. For the pious it is an angel coursing overhead or an imperceptible whisper from God. The less religious among them glance instinctively at the lagoon where gondolas shimmer like black moths, glance east where the sun continues to mount in the distant sea-borne sky, and in silence, they wonder. And then it passes, the quizzical ripple of light that comes when Time has ripened, when the planets and stars have aligned themselves, when each character in the city has shifted into place, when all the words in silence are prepared. And in that fraction of an instant, everything awakes and changes, even the statues high and low awake for a moment to ponder their reflections in the canals, and, as soon, fall back asleep into their strong silent dreams.

Maria follows her parents out the wide doors of San Marco, floating from the cool dark into the brilliant sunshine illuminating the piazza. A stiff wind whips blue and gold pennants at the square's edge. The sea breeze flows over the water, holding off, for a while, the rising heat of a Venetian morning.

The impossible magic of the Mass, of transubstantiation, still worries Maria's head. How is it that things can change into other things? How is it bread and wine can be transformed into the Body and Blood of Christ? Shading her soft dark eyes, she steps into the light and looks up.

When his gaze meets Maria's, across an impossible distance, the Lion of Venice shudders. Her look has pierced his metals as easily as light passes through water. It lasts a moment only, but it brings life flooding into his hollow form. The girl of sixteen, strangely excited for she thinks she has seen the wings of the statue quiver, turns and hurries off to catch up to her parents, already working their way to the middle of the square where they greet another prosperous merchant family, the Polos, parents of her betrothed.

For three days the winged Lion raged, struggling with the inner storms that tore at him, dragging him off in two directions at once, ripping him in half. To the casual observer, the great statue and symbol of Venice appeared as it normally did, that is to say, unmoving, mounted still at the top of its column; but the mind of the Lion had been set to spinning, in confusion, in desire, in frustrated longing.

The fresh morning weather of Ascension Thursday had passed and Venice was becalmed in the hottest month of May anyone could remember. Heat drained from every pore in every stone in the city. The sun was barely visible through the mucilaginous haze muffling the lagoons. And yet the sun seemed everywhere at once: bouncing off the viscous stinking water of the canals, flowing out of every crack and crevice in the dankest alleys, igniting the sweaty gold florins falling on a barrel in Maria's father's waterfront warehouse. Grackles on roof peaks stood silenced, their beaks spread wide, mouths open. Caught fish hit the air and went slack with the heat, their eyes clouding into white. The night held no relief. The stored heat of day radiated from the stone walls of palaces and cathedrals. The streets were crowded all night with men, half-dead, unable to sleep, dragging themselves through claustrophobic alleys and *cortes* like sluggish ghosts.

The canals offered no respite. The water was the temperature of an unctuous bath, and reeked like the pus of swamps.

After two desperate nights of twisting and turning in bed, Maria, on the third night, falls into a deep and dreamless sleep. Her cotton sheet, glowing in the darkness, slips off and slides like a cataract of white onto the floor.

The Lion, who stands still as the vaporous night in the doorway leading from the balcony to her room, turns his intimate gaze upon the girl. Her white nightdress, with lace at the throat, has gathered round her waist. She lies on her stomach, left leg raised, exposing the milk-white of her nudity. Ringlets of black hair on her forehead are soaked blacker by her sweat. The Lion waits a long time and watches.

A short while earlier he had stood rooted to his column on the Molo overlooking the lagoon, his inner storms echoed by pulsations of heat lightning on the horizon to the east, shudderings of distant thunder from the dead-still sea. Suddenly from the enormous darkness a tongue of lightning shocked the Lion out of his metallic paralysis . . . and he leapt! . . . off the column onto the nearby doge's palace roof and thus to the cobbles of the piazza. In an instant he was following the scent of the girl, the scent that had never left his nostrils for a moment since first igniting him three days before. He hurried, his strange proud demonic head sniffing the marble paths, tail and tips of wings twitching, hurried knowing this was his one chance, in all eternity, his only chance.

Hunched over, nose to the ground, the Lion scurried on, ignited by the wisps and gusts of her scent flashing in his nostrils. He scrabbled along the complex map of her trail as it wound through alleys, along canals, across squares. It ended at a house not far from his original starting point on the piazza. Leaping across a narrow canal to a shallow second-storey balcony, he entered through the door, left open in the hope of admitting air but allowing entry instead to this vortex of desire.

The overpowering scent of the girl in her room strikes his nostrils like a thick charged wind, like a seaweed- and anise-laden fog rolling in off the sea. It cuts his breath short and sets his ears to ringing.

In the half-dark, when he hunches down, what meets his eye is a beast like himself. The hazy metallic mirror strikes him dumb with the odd image it throws back.

I am a bizarre and freakish animal, half-lion, half-mythical beast of unknown origin. My mouth frozen open, a cat's ears and a cat's nose but nothing like a lion's head. There is too an air of the amphibian about me, as befits a beast of Venice. I am ugly, thoroughly grotesque, and yet I emit a kind of demonic intelligence. It must be my eyes of faceted chalcedony, of alpha quartz. Wound with veins they look everywhere at once. And these wings, these unreal towering wings — what am I to make of them? The curls of my mane suggest more sheepdog than lion. How could human woman ever come to love this, this beast of odd proportions, this rude demiurge, this congeries of metals fused around a hollow core, this bound fury, this monster split between its animal form and its empty human heart?

The Lion fills the room entirely with its fourteen foot length, the walls pressing in, its long tail curling up against a corner of the ceiling like an eel caught in a fisherman's pot. Each shift in the beast's weight elicits creaks from the floor of the room, but the Lion hardly moves in the cramped space.

Still he stands watching her, his every fibre taut with electric tension, his soft pads tingling, his wide flat nose moist and pulsating. He watches her breathe and pegs his breath to hers, his chest rising and falling in unison with the sleeping girl. Desire is not centred in any particular part of his body, but shoots through his stomach and throat and out his limbs, shivering along the ragged edges of his wings. At one and the same time he feels weak and strong; his legs shake, the blood pounds in his head. He fails to stifle a groan, a cat's purr of rough tenderness, that escapes his throat. The girl stirs and seems to reply from her sleep with a soft groan that also holds a rough edge and yet is infinitely more tender than his. He stands in utter stillness, contemplating her face and form, stunned by the depth of her fierce beauty, the buttery glow of her skin, the black shine of her hair, the curves and declivities of her limbs. His great head shifts and he runs his slab of sandpaper tongue along the thigh of her upraised leg. Her skin tastes sweet and salty, the aroma rising from hidden corners and crevices of her flesh making his head spin. He watches her breathe. She has not moved. He knows he will have to take her with an impossible tenderness, to avoid waking her and ruining his one chance. He knows he will have to summon all the strength of the ages that has accumulated in his metallic bones in order to take her gently enough.

Breathing with her, his wings erect and fluttering like pennants in a distant harmattan, he steels himself and mounts.

Of course, they blamed the Polo boy, once Maria had begun to show and it was no longer possible to hide the swelling mound of her belly. They didn't know when or how it had happened, but surmised that the deed must have been accomplished during the hot spell after Ascension Thursday, on one of those unbearable nights when the men had taken to the streets to seek relief from the heat. The boy must have climbed in an open window when Maria's father was out, dragging himself through the sweltering alleys. Maria denied every accusation as, of course, she would. The Polo boy too insisted on his innocence. The families consulted a priest who explained that it often happens that a henchman of the devil, some slathering incubus or other, will penetrate a young girl while she sleeps without her knowing it. The issue of this union might be the devil's own, though, in many cases, it happens that the child is normal. "Not to worry," said the priest, waving his right hand in the air while slipping the proffered coins into the pocket of his cassock with the other, "it happens, no one knows why, the influence of the planets likely, or some evil done long ago. In such a world as this, where it is said hyenas can change their sex at will and weasels conceive by the ear and deliver by the mouth, anything is possible. Call me again when the child is born and I will determine its state at that time. *Buon giorno.*"

The two families, being merchants with a supremely practical bent, decided that marriage was the most efficacious cure for the affliction at hand and so Niccolo and Maria, not unwillingly, for they harboured a deep affection for each other, were summarily wed. In due time, the child was born, without cloven hooves, and was pronounced thoroughly human by the priest who slipped several more glittering coins into his pockets for his trouble. The boy was given the name of Marco, an appellation befitting a long-enduring Venetian family, for St. Mark the Apostle was the city's patron saint and his remains had long before been translated into the Church of San Marco at the head of the city's most illustrious piazza. And indeed the name was doubly fitting, for St. Mark's symbol was a lion.

* * *

Many years later, Marco Polo, after his travels to the East, finds himself sharing a prison cell in Genoa with Rustichello, a Pisan with a bad smell and a peasant's voice.

Marco had his face turned to the wall and stared at a shadow there, a faint stain. It reminds him of something. His eyes were open but perhaps he dreamt. The chirping birds were just beginning to tear away the shreds of night with their beaks, to carry the dark shreds disappearing into the brilliance of sky.

This fading shadow reminds me of . . . something distant and almost lost in the light of day. I am in my mother's womb, floating upside-down. I am floating in a canal inside her. I am also outside her, high up in the room looking down at her lying in the bed with her knees raised. She faces the window. In the distance, across the two cities of Venice, one in air and one reflected in water, the statue of the lion on its column. The light everywhere brilliant. Light passes through her, through the throat of the sand-glass at the juncture of her thighs. On the wall of my cell of flesh an image appears — the lion, upside-down, like me, both of us upside-down, on the wrong side of the world, on the wrong side of time.

Marco awoke. Rolled over. There, staring at him, sat Rustichello.

"Dream?"

Rustichello, his cell-mate, was a Pisan scribe and poet who had garnered a smattering of fame for his romances. This specialist in chivalry and its lore shared a prison cell with Marco in Genoa, salt mist drifting through their perfect square window. Marco sniffed the air — the smell of freedom, the open sea. Captured in a battle with the Genoese fleet, Marco supposed he was lucky to be alive. He had been a gentleman-commander of a galley with a hundred oars and a crew of 250 men, part of a Venetian fleet of sixty vessels that engaged the Genoese in the Greek sea. To the sound of kettledrums and horns, the Venetians had sailed straight into battle and prompt defeat. Seven thousand of his countrymen were captured, their ships towed backwards to port, their bright banners, their proud lions, dragging in the waves. Marco remembered watching, amazed, as they landed and the commander of the Venetian fleet leapt onto the quay and beat his brains out in despair against a stone bench.

Already it seemed to Marco he had spent a lifetime staring at the four walls, a lifetime caught in a stone crypt with the disputatious Pisan. All I want is to be left alone, he mused.

Look at him, he thought, glancing at Rustichello who had occupied the cell several weeks longer than Marco. He has perhaps fifty years, lank dirty hair of an unseemly length, fat as a friar with thick soft hands to match, his nails yellow, half his teeth broken or missing, long ears with fleshy lobes, tufts of hair growing from his nostrils. An obsessive mind, too, with penetrating eyes round and small as peas. And a sour smell, as of grain fermenting. I suppose I too will smell the same soon enough. Something about his voice, though, always a question in it, a certain wonderment, a touch of the musical, in a peasant way, the voice of a peasant singing in the fields.

Rustichello continued his argument. "The hour is late. I smell the sea, its salt, its damp. One word at a time — you see, it comes one word at a time. The book already exists, Marco, it already exists, we can only hope to reveal it a word, a phrase, a sentence at a time; we bring it down out of eternity, where it already exists, into time, where men, all men, can see it, taste it, smell it."

From his straw-stuffed mattress, Marco said, "All men? Even the great Khan, from his gold-lined tomb? Pshah! If he taught me anything, he taught me this: the uselessness of letters."

"Lord God of Angels, let me write the book, Marco. A description of the world. Tell me . . . look, here, I have paper, quill, ink. I am ready. I am listening."

Marco gazed into the blackness, gazed hard into the flat black glyph of the small window: "Descriptions of the world . . . so many . . . words. Tell me, Rustichello, about Pisa; how is it there?"

"Much like anywhere else. Like Genoa. Like Venezia. The time passes there as it passes anywhere. Why do you ask?"

"What does the air smell like?"

"The air? The air of Pisa? Like a swamp on a hot afternoon. But, you avoid me." He tapped the dry quill on the blank sheet. "Let me write the book. Now. I and all the angels in heaven are listening."

Marco, silent, continued to gaze into the dark.

* * *

The tale begins, indescribable and strange, only to come to an abrupt halt.

Rustichello places the bottle of ink before him on the upper left-hand corner of the slab of wood, removes his hand, pauses, his gaze held by the bottle, then shifts it a half-inch further to the left of the parchment. The thick glass inkpot is stoppered with a cork, its bottom singed. He removes the cork and places it on the slab before leaning forward to stab the ink with his quill.

"No, no, no — it wasn't like that at all, not at all." Marco sits on his mat, forearms on knees. "It was a journey of revelations, a journey in which the names of those cities and lands — Soncara, Timochain, Vokhan, Kain-du, Zai-tun — rang on my ears with an indescribable strangeness, as if the voices that spoke them were long thin reeds of glass through which the wind sighed. We never knew what would come at us next — a pack of goiter-ridden merchants, a band of brigands a hundred horses strong, a trackless desert we thought might never end. We had no maps. Do you know what that means? We lived on the edge of the unknown — and I, starting out as a young man, grew into that unknown. How can I hope to relocate that tale? All would be lost in the telling because I know, I know what comes next . . . and that's not how it was."

Rustichello stops writing and looks up. "Yes?"

"The book must repeat that journey in its essence and the essence of that journey was the unknown. Impossible. I tell you, it is impossible. The book must be something new — not a remembered map, a retracing of steps, a kind of stupidity embellished with lies and exaggerations . . . impossible . . . impossible!"

His voice rises at the end as his shoulders arch forward, his head drooping. Leaping to his feet, Marco snatches the paper Rustichello holds in front of him, tears it to shreds and shoves the pieces into Rustichello's mouth. Rustichello lets him do this, watching in resigned silence and only turning his head in slight resistance when the Venetian grabs his chin with one hand and forces the bits of paper between his lips. When Marco is finished, Rustichello looks away and spits the glob out onto the floor. He reaches down, stands and, with quiet care, places the quill and jar of ink on a high shelf above his mat.

(an excerpt from the novel *The Lion of Venice*)

IV
UNIVERSALS AND PARTICULARS

ERIC MCCORMACK was born in Scotland and came to Canada in 1966. He teaches at St. Jerome's College, Waterloo. His three books are *Inspecting the Vaults* (1987), *The Paradise Motel* (1989), and *The Mysterium* (1992).

THE THIRD MIRACLE

ERIC MCCORMACK

"As saith the ever subtil Duns Scotus: three
species of miracles there be of which we
may observe but two: miracles
in natura, among things inanimate and
the beestes; miracles *apud homines*,
among common humanity; of that third, most
remarkable, miracles *in obscuritate*,
nothinge is revealed."
— Robert Burton, *The Anatomy of Melancholy* (1621)

A rare natural phenomenon was reported in the Lowlands of Scotland in 1858. On
the seventeenth of November, a bitter wind shunted a wedge of black clouds from
over the North Sea onto the land. The underbelly of this cloud mass was so shiny, it

acted like a huge obsidian mirror, reflecting all the countryside it passed over. Inverted forests, lochs, rivers, thatched roofs, churches with their spires, were visible up there. Some people with acute eyesight said they could see horses, cows, and scatterings of sheep. They said they could even see their own reflections looking back down at them.

They didn't enjoy the sight for long. After a few minutes, that nebulous world melted and crashed down on their upturned faces in the form of black hailstones. We wouldn't know the event ever happened, but for the many eyewitness reports.

In that same year, Robert Owen died in poverty near his birthplace in Wales at the age of eighty-seven. Owen was a baron of industry who did an about-face to become one of the great social reformers of the nineteenth century. He's almost forgotten now except by scholars. The books he wrote, the journals he founded, rot silently in the recesses of library basements. Even the solid stone memorials to Owen — the buildings in which his disciples tried briefly to live by his co-operative theories — have been demolished.

One of his communes was established in 1825 on the banks of the River Clyde, twenty miles east of Glasgow. It was called Orbiston, after the property it sat on. The core of the commune, an ugly four-storey building, became home to 250 men, women and children, some of them refugees from the obscene slums of Glasgow. The communards ate and slept in that main building. In various outbuildings, they practised their trades: printing, silvering mirrors, turning lint wheels, making musical snuffboxes and window blinds; their iron-foundry produced brass bearings, screw-presses and ornamental gates. The commune had its own school where children and adults could together learn to read and write.

The Orbiston experiment lasted three years and ended, as all Owen's communes did, in failure: some of the members didn't really like working; the others didn't really like having to support them. A familiar story. Within a short time, the land was sold off, the buildings were razed, the communards went back to where they came from. Those who'd escaped from Glasgow had nowhere else to go but the city. The labyrinthine slum at the East End — the infamous Gallowgate district — devoured most of them.

I'm one of those who hasn't forgotten Robert Owen or Orbiston. It happens that I was born and brought up within sight of where the commune stood. Even today, you can decipher the sunken outlines of the main building's foundations; the mossy ruins of the outbuildings are now a favourite spot for lovers; and the site of the communal vegetable gardens is the ninth fairway of a golf course.

A few hundred yards away, a warren of grey, post-war public housing projects begins, and sprawls for mile after mile westward. That was where I grew up. Part of it is still called Orbiston, and some McCormacks live there right now. This new Orbiston has rates of unemployment and crime as high as any in Britain. You could ask around the streets all day, and you'd be lucky if you met anyone — aside from those McCormacks, of course — who knew much about Owen's commune.

In 1960, when I was an undergraduate at Glasgow University, I set out to write a paper on Orbiston. In the course of my research, I came across a few issues of Owen's personal magazine — it had a fairly grandiose title — *Weekly Letters to the Human Race*. In an editorial, Owen said something that caught my attention: that one of Orbiston's former inmates, a man named Cameron Ross, was a poet. When Orbiston collapsed, he had to return to where he came from — the Gallowgate. He died not long after.

A poet from the Gallowgate in the early nineteenth century? I never would have believed such a thing.

Glasgow at that time was an awful place to be poor in, darker and more satanic than any of those mills the Industrial Revolution spawned. No part of the city was worse than the Gallowgate (the public gallows stood at the east gate of the city). Row upon row of narrow three-storey tenements hunched together in a successful conspiracy to keep out the light of day. Labyrinthine wynds and muddy closes served as public latrines. Brothels and shebeens punctuated the rows of tenements like rotten teeth in rotten gums. Each piece of spare ground stank of garbage. In all of Europe, Glasgow was at the forefront in its rates of unemployment, starvation, suicide, infant mortality, alcoholism, insanity, prostitution and violent crime. Tuberculosis, cholera, typhus, pneumonia, syphilis and gonorrhea were as common as head-colds. No fish of any sort swam in the lower reaches of the Clyde, the most polluted river in the Western world.

In the Gallowgate, no policemen patrolled the streets, for this slum was already a prison. There were no churches in the Gallowgate. Its inhabitants were already in hell.

Which brings me back to Cameron Ross. How could someone become a poet in such a place? Perhaps that was why Owen remembered him. I made up my mind to try and find out more about Ross. There were no other references to him in Owen's writings, or in any histories of the communes. I searched the libraries, without any luck at all. But I didn't give up — I had one secret resource: an uncle of mine, Jack Muir, eighty years old, then living in a retirement home for railway workers. Of all my living relatives of that older generation, I was fondest of him. He was one of those self-taught working men, cautious with his learning, aware of how easily he might be judged to be pretentious among those with few pretensions.

It was because of him I wanted to write about Orbiston in the first place. He was a direct link. When he was young, Jack Muir had actually known old people who'd been part of the original commune.

The past isn't nearly as distant as we sometimes think.

I went to see him during Sunday afternoon visiting time at the home. He was a frail, small man, his hair thick and grey. His face was withered now, with lines like railway junctions at the corner of blue eyes that were still a young man's eyes. I told him about the progress of my work on Orbiston. Then I asked him if he knew anything about this Cameron Ross.

"Oh yes," he said. "The poet. I heard all the stories about his death."

I asked him to tell me more.

"I don't know much. He was married. He wasn't a tradesman; he was just a general labourer at the commune. After it folded, he and his wife had to go back and live in the Gallowgate."

He talked on, and I let him. Jack Muir had been a ticket clerk in a small country station for forty-five years, and he'd spent most of his time reading — and talking. He was a good talker.

What follows isn't, of course, in his exact words. But I do know it's the *way* he told it. Sometimes, that's all it takes for people long dead, people you loved, to come back to life for a while, even after more than thirty years. And sometimes, you get goose bumps. Occasional words, occasional phrases are so right, you know those must be the very words they used, and that their voices are now your voice.

Jack Muir's Story

When Cameron Ross and his wife went back to the Gallowgate, he was around thirty years old. They had no children. They lived on the third floor of a tenement right by the Cross. He took any jobs he could find, heaving coal, or stoking the furnaces at Dixon's Blazes across the river. She did laundry and housework in the big houses at the West End.

In winter, the days were short. The few hours of daylight were choked with fogs. On one of those dreary mornings Ross's wife woke up to get ready for work. They slept, like everybody else, on a straw mattress on the floor. She knew as soon as she woke that something was wrong: the blankets were very damp. She felt around in the dark, and discovered that at Ross's side of the bed, they weren't just damp — they were wet and sticky. She got out of bed and lit the oil lamp by the stove. Blood. There was blood on her hands and her arms and all over her nightgown. She went over to the bed. It was soaked in blood, especially where Ross was lying. Blood was still seeping through the blankets, oozing down, turning hard on the cold planks of the floor. Streaks of wet blood ran down the wall beside him. Ross was just lying there, wide awake, saying nothing, his face all pale and sweaty.

She sent for the doctor. The nearest one lived two miles away in Charlotte Square, so it was more than an hour before he arrived. He could smell that awful blood smell even when he got to the landing outside their door. Inside, he couldn't believe the amount of blood on the floor, and on the bed. He examined Ross's body, back and front, but there was no sign of a wound, no sign of where the blood came from. Ross said he was feeling a bit weak, but all right. He had no idea what had happened.

The doctor was suspicious. He knew as well as anybody about the violence in these slums. He didn't ask any questions. He left a bottle of cordial for Ross, and went home to his big house and his respectable patients.

For the next few days, Cameron Ross was too weak to go to work, so he just sat at home, bundled up in his coat to keep warm, and he did a lot of writing in his notebooks.

Now these slums were like villages, rumours spread so easily. If Ross had looked out of his window, he'd have seen more than the usual number of people from all along the Gallowgate. They were strolling slowly past, looking up at his third-floor window, hoping for a glimpse of him through the sooty panes.

Just when he'd almost recovered, it happened again, seven days after the first one, just before dawn. As though it was some kind of pattern. This time, when Ross felt it coming he woke his wife. She lit the lamp and brought it over to the bed, and so she saw it happening. The blankets at his chest turned dark and blood began to glisten on them. She pulled them away. The top of his nightgown was soaked with blood. She unbuttoned it all the way down and couldn't believe what she was seeing.

The tip of something sharp, like a knitting needle, seemed to be poking through from *inside* of him.

Ross had raised his head slightly and was watching it too. The thing was moving slowly, drawing a red line down the centre of his body, slitting the flesh neatly like a melon, from his neck to his groin. His wife tried to staunch the blood, but it was hopeless. No amount of towels or rags helped.

"Cammy, Cammy," she kept saying.

Cameron Ross was lying back now, looking up at her as though she wasn't there. She ran outside and stopped a group of men on their way to work. She asked one of them to please go for the doctor.

When the doctor came into the apartment this time and saw the blood, he wondered how such a thin man could have lost so much and still be alive. Ross's wife told him about the wound, and how it seemed her husband had been cut open from inside. The doctor examined the body, but again he couldn't see any sign of a cut, or any trace of a scar. He checked every orifice. Nothing. As he sponged away the blood he marvelled at Ross's skin: he'd never seen skin so smooth in all the time he'd practised in the slums: Ross didn't have a boil, or a carbuncle, or a rash, or a pimple. In fact, it was the purest skin he'd ever seen. Ross couldn't speak, but his wife kept telling the doctor what she'd seen with her own eyes.

"A sharp thing," she said. "Inside Cammy. Maybe the point of a knitting needle. Maybe the nib of a pen."

The doctor said he'd need to see the thing for himself. She must send for him right away if it happened again.

When Ross was able to get out of bed this time, all he wanted to do was write. In between complaining about the cold, he wrote in his notebooks for hours on end.

His wife couldn't read, but she liked to sit watching him at his writing. By now, everyone from that part of the Gallowgate had heard about the blood. It was the talk of the wash-houses and the pubs. Hundreds of gawkers came and stood outside the tenement, looking up at that third-floor window. It rained a lot, a cold rain in from the Firth. One day there was even snow, grey snow that disappeared on the grey streets of the Gallowgate.

The third occurrence was exactly seven days later, at dawn. When Ross's wife heard him groaning, she got up and ran to the apartment across the landing. One of her neighbours went for the doctor.

He arrived less than an hour later, but even that was too late. Ross was dead. His dead eyes were staring up at blotches of rot in the ceiling. His wife was sobbing.

"That awful thing cut Cammy in two from the inside," she said.

But, again, there was no sign of a wound. The doctor couldn't see much blood this time, either. Even though he'd only been dead ten minutes, Ross's body was so cold, the sheen of blood on it was brittle. He looked as though he'd been coated in thin red wax. His wife said he'd been complaining about feeling cold all week.

"Poor Cammy was so cold. He said he was too cold even to write."

The doctor consoled her, but he was glad the case was over. He didn't know what to make of her account of the thing inside her husband. The case made him very uncomfortable. He was a decent man, the only doctor in Glasgow who would make a house call in the Gallowgate. What was there to do but go home and try to put the whole matter out of his mind.

Now the people of the Gallowgate wanted to see Ross's body. They queued by the hundreds, from morning till night, up the three winding stories of the tenement staircase and along the close, out into the street and down to the Cross. And on the day of the burial, a big crowd went to see the coffin lowered into the earth at the pauper's end of the Necropolis. It was a cold, wet day.

Afterwards, some of them wanted relics. They kept at Ross's wife about it. She was a simple woman and didn't think there would be any harm in it. At first she gave them loose pieces of paper with Ross's handwriting on it. Then she tore pages out of his notebooks and handed them to people who couldn't read. She tore out page after page till they were all gone. Someone asked for a piece of his shirt, so she tore that up. She tore up the rest of his clothes into patches, and gave them away till there was none left. The first time someone asked her outright for a piece of the blood-soaked nightgown, or anything with blood on it, she was surprised, for she was a simple woman. But she did what she was asked. After a while, the only thing that remained of Cameron Ross in that apartment was her memory of him.

"Good," she thought. "Now, Cammy, we'll have peace and quiet at last."

But it didn't take long for rumours to spread, who knows why. Maybe envy that one person's life or death in those slums should be more remarkable than anybody else's; that one person might be remembered while the rest of them were condemned to be forgotten. Who knows. But rumours began to spread that the whole story about the blood was a lie, a trick. Some said there was nothing strange about the blood, that Ross had tuberculosis, and his blood was no different from all the others who hawked up blood on every street corner of the Gallowgate, coughing themselves to an early grave. Some said the blood was nothing but the cows' blood that swelled the gutters in the mornings outside the slaughterhouse at the Saltmarket. Others said the blood was the blood of dozens of Gallowgate children who'd been murdered over the past few years — yes, they said, Ross was probably a maniac; maybe he even sucked the blood of their murdered children.

That was bad enough.

But the most deadly rumour of all was this: that the blood was Ross's wife's blood. That the "relics" they'd begged for were her menstrual rags.

She came home from work one night to find her apartment had been visited. The stink from the brown smears on the walls told everything. She left and never went back. That set off the rumours again: she'd been drowned in the Clyde; she'd gone to work in a brothel in the Gorbals; she'd emigrated to Canada. Some, even among those who'd seen Ross's corpse in its coffin, said he wasn't dead at all — they'd heard that Cameron Ross and his wife had been spotted walking together, laughing, on a street in London.

That was Jack Muir's story of the death of Cameron Ross. He lay back in his bed now, dead tired. But he had the contented look of a man who'd told a good story — a comforting feeling before sleeping. Or dying, for that matter.

I asked him about Ross's poems — did any of them survive? did any of them get published?

"I don't know," he said.

Before I left, I had one last question.

"Was Ross a religious man?"

He shook his head.

"No. The old people told me he said awful things. He even said the existence of the Gallowgate proved there was no God."

I left Jack Muir to his rest, and I didn't see him again till a month later. That was the day I saw him in his coffin. His story-telling days were over. And he never did see my paper on Orbiston.

The reason I'd wondered if Ross was religious was this: I'd been reading about the phenomenon of the stigmata. How certain people, holy or unholy, can be afflicted with bleeding wounds, like the wounds of Jesus. Psychiatrists have dismissed the whole thing as a form of female hysteria, even though many of the sufferers have been men. You still hear about it today, but mostly it happened in the sixteenth and seventeenth centuries. A long time ago.

Miracles. They always seem to have taken place a long time ago. Nowadays we use the word very loosely. We might say Orbiston was "a social miracle" in its day; or that Robert Owen's conversion to socialism was "miraculous" considering he was a nineteenth-century capitalist. As for Cameron Ross, I wouldn't quite know which word to use. In some ways, he's even more ephemeral than an obsidian cloud. He's a composite of a single reference in a magazine no one reads any more; an old railwayman's memory of what he heard from people long dead; and my memory of a conversation more than a quarter of a century ago. Yet there's a kind of substantiality about him that hinges, in some odd way, on knowing so little about the human being, Cameron Ross. Who was, apparently, a poet. Who died in the slums of Glasgow, in the early part of the nineteenth century.

Which is not so long ago.

CYNTHIA FLOOD's two collections of short fiction arc *The Animals in Their Elements* and *My Father Took a Cake to France* (Talonbooks, 1987 and 1992). A linked sequence titled *A Civil Plantation* is in progress. Cynthia Flood won the 1990 Journey Prize and the 1993 Western Magazine Award for Fiction.

A CIVIL PLANTATION

CYNTHIA FLOOD

I am the only man in this English school, the only one, and I am here because I can-not teach.

Why did I give the child that mark for her picture? What have I done, oh what have I done? What would my mother say? And the fragrant lady, and Fitzgerald?

The child Amanda had drawn the English settlers planted up to their waists, their necks, in the black earth of Munster. They were in tidy rows. Their mouths were open with screams. Crumbled earth crusted their red faces. Eyes bulging, they tried to push themselves from the soil. A woman held her dirty baby up above her own half-buried head. Where did Amanda find such images?

Where shall I go tonight? I could stay here, lie in this bed and bite my nails, my nail-beds, till morning. I hold no key to any other door.

One reason why the English failed to create in Ireland the plantations they had envisaged was that they could not control the people whom they planted. Relatively powerless though the tenants were, and though many did take root and so displace the native vegetation, as a crop they were not what the London corporations and the ex-army officers and the minor nobility had had in mind.

Some tenants married Irishwomen. Many complained about the quality of the land assigned them. Others were unsuitably lethargic about the practice of their religion, or adopted reprehensible Irish agricultural practices such as tail-ploughing and creaghting. *Hibernia hibernescit. Caoruigheachta*: the creaghts, herds and their human attendants, moved about frivolously from pastureland to pastureland. Some tenants even solidarized with the uprooted Irish (but not so far as to vacate their land). Ungrateful and quarrelsome, homesick but land-hungry, insistent on leaving or refusing to leave, tenants caused endless problems for the planters. Contradictions such as these persisted even unto the sixth, eighth, eleventh, fifteenth generations of plantation in Ireland.

Where shall I go?

Every night, quite late, I leave the grounds of St. Mildred's School — or St. Stephen's or Miss Rammell's as the case may be, or The Gates or Fairways or Hillscott House — to breathe a somewhat greater air, move in a wider world. I am, after all, Mr. Greene: Foreign Affairs.

When I return to St. Mildred's, perhaps an hour later, all the windows are muffled. Who sleeps where? The tall paired windows at the southwest corner of St. Gabriel's House belong to the headmistress, I know, and matron holds a room near the San, but I do not know where lies loud-voiced Miss Trout History, snobbish Miss Lincoln Geography, lovely Miss Flower Religious Knowledge, widowed Mrs. Wilmer Maths. . . . Where lies that fragrance? A few vertical slits of light shine, tonight, illuminating slivers of rain.

Earlier today I spent my hour with the Third Form. I was Mr. Greene: Specialist in History. I returned their work. Amanda received from me her picture and her paragraph and her mark. It seemed the only possible mark. I could bear no other. Many severe and justified criticisms of her work could be made. She did not draw what was intended, expected. Her picture was not confined to the left page of her notebook but overflowed the margin of the right, reserved for her paragraph. It must be said, however, that exception could not be taken to that paragraph, an almost verbatim version of the notes I had dictated. Amanda's drawing, also, admittedly, indeed undeniably, demonstrated a certain vitality.

Contemporary critics of the plantation schemes — *contemporary* covers a parade of centuries — also refer, often, to the poor quality of the English and, later, Scots who were taken, or sent, to Ireland to be planted. Not all analysts were as damning as Fynes Morrison, who exclaimed that the English settlers "were generally observed to have been eyther papists, men of disordered life, banckrots, or very poore . . . by which course Ireland as the heele of the body was made the sincke of England, the stench whereof had almost annoyed very Cheapside the hart of the body" (Canny, 21). A later and more laconic commentator described Ulster as settled by "the scum of both nations" (22). Many undertenants were in fact unemployed, or had been discharged from the army, or were destitute, or had no experience of farming, or knew no trade whatsoever, and were, in short, plainly desperate.

Mr. Greene's mother's ancestors may have been in this last category. Certainly Mr. Greene's mother was scornful of any connection with earth. In her small shop, she sold tobacco, sweets, newspapers, ice cream, and postcards for trippers. Hating Ireland and the Irish, she was pure English.

In the light, the daygirls of St. Mildred's come and go along the drive. Mistresses leave for errands in the town. Vans bring laundry and bread. The post arrives. Fitzgerald, the school's factotum, rides his bicycle to fetch white paint for the ruled lines and boundaries of the playing-field. Occasional taxicabs bear parents, anxious or angry. . . . But at night? Until three nights ago I believed that no one but I broke the order of School to move about alone in darkness.

Until the gravel of the courtyard gives way to the damp hard-packed earth of the drive, my shoes crunch. Does a curtain move? Does some woman envy my masculine nocturnal solitude? In the dark, there is no need to hide my bitten nails. On either side of the drive rears up a twelve-foot rampart of hollies and rhododendrons, the foliage sometimes freaked with moonlight, now slippery with rain. I smell wet earth. I feel damp on my scalp, under its scurf of faded red. To imagine hiders in that glittering dark green is not difficult. Scrambles, chirrings are audible. Rats? Snakes? Larger beings? I walk on the crown of the roadway. *Kern in the woods?* At the drive's mid-point, a walker, such as myself, now, is invisible both from the school and from the road. I stop — foolish. I am not large or strong; Fitzgerald is the black Irish, a coarse lantern-jawed face, but I am the slight red kind. I sense no leaf-crackle, footfall, hot breath.

In Amanda's picture of the Elizabethan plantation, hands protruded from earth, thick tongues from mouths. Never have I seen such a thing. None of this did I have in mind. In picturing the second Munster plantation, no other girl drew anything similar. Amanda — misunderstood. Of an adult we would say, "He has distorted," or "has falsified." Where did her vision come from? She is Canadian. She is a child. Perhaps she simply does not know where power lies. My first decision was therefore to give her three out of ten. She may not know, but she must learn.

Blaming the planters themselves is much less common. Who writes history, after all? However, the literature does uneasily show that many planters resembled real estate developers, flipping, scamming, hightailing it back to London to spend the profits. Some neither ploughed nor sowed nor reaped, but logged off all their trees, bought more land, logged off . . . (43). More than one English planter vomited his way across the Irish Sea to inspect his new property and, like Snailholm in 1610, took a single disgusted look at the rooty fibrous soil and left (Perceval-Maxwell, 120). (On his seasonal visits to his mother in the 1920s and 1930s and 1940s and now in the 1950s, Mr. Greene was invariably seasick, in both directions but with different causes, on the Swansea–Cork ferry.)

Of those who did stay in Ireland, many failed to build the required (and extensive) bawms and outbuildings. Many failed to plant the right numbers of single males of the right ages who represented the right numbers of families. These procrastinating undertakers faced threats from their English masters of forfeiture of their lands, which further shrank their motivation to plant and build, which intensified the threats. . . . Locked in this dialectic, thousands of fertile Irish acres (which the official English surveyors had finally grasped were *not* the same size as those on the big island) lay fallow first, then neglected, then in wild ruin.

Turning south at the gates of St. Mildred's school, I begin my nightly circumscription of the grounds. A rather broad pathway, well kept and smoothed by Fitzgerald, hugs the great rectangle of wall. Heading east next, then north, west, and south once more will bring me back. On Sundays, girls and mistresses follow this same pathway, clockwise before matins, counter after evensong. The girls are exhorted to walk lightly, like ladies. Soundlessness is the ideal. And so they walk — home, temporary home. Such is St. Mildred's to me, also, for a week in each of the year's three terms, yet I do not join the sacred crocodile. I am the only man in the school; with whom would I walk? Difficulty charges any answer. It is better that the question not be posed.

Foreign Affairs: in the life of the school, I am not only the only man, but Mr. Greene: Foreign Affairs, or Mr. Greene: Current Events, or Mr. Greene: Specialist in History. I give guest lectures. Why does Mr. Gaitskell think we must tighten wage and price controls? I can explain his ideas to the Third Form. To the Lower Fifth, I show the meaning of the first-quarter drop in net gold and dollar earnings of the sterling area. I help the Sixth to see why we must be firm with Iran about the Anglo-Iran Oil Company and very firm with the Soviet Union about the peace treaty with Japan and especially firm with Egypt about Suez.

When I perform thus, a mistress stands by me. In the Third Form, Miss Trout does so. She stands too close, her rumpled full-breasted solidity by my rather thin neatness. Giggles among the girls. I clasp my hands so the bitten nails curl under. My topic was England. Led by the great Renaissance explorers and soldiers, she transformed the mapped world. Miss Trout struck Ireland with her pointer. Indeed, I do like to tell the story of Munster, naturally not of the lamentable first plantation nor of the shocking Desmond years, but of the second, begun in 1584 and a favourite project of Elizabeth's, and of its healing effects upon the Irish landscape. As usual, Miss Trout concluded my talk with "Now girls, questions?" Blank silence is customary. Amanda broke it. "Mr. Greene, did Queen Elizabeth ask those Irish people if they minded? If it was all right to come and live on their land?"

Robert Blair in 1623 spoke of the need of the rightly faithful, i.e., Protestants, "to *plant* religion [emphasis added]" in Ireland (Perceval-Maxwell, 270).

More than a century later, when a Methodist preacher "first *invaded* the county of Monaghan [,] an attempt was made on his life by a man who had screened himself among the bushes [emphasis added]" (Phillips, 33), while a co-religionist of the 1750s described himself as "almost continually in danger of having [his] brains beat out" (34).

Here, beating the stone bounds of this school, I am inland, covert Irish at England's centre. Westward over the Irish Sea is my mother, also inland, covert, Methodist in the Republic. No one here knows she is there. No one here knows I am from there. When the mistresses and I walk and talk on the Great Lawn, rolled in green rules by Fitzgerald, the conversation is of Attlee, Bevan, Bevin, Churchill, George. Once, Miss Gregson Science mentioned Walton's shared Nobel. Miss Lincoln Geography wondered at De Valera's Spanish name. I did not speak. My habit of saying little, unless lecturing, hardened long ago.

I have heard the child Amanda call plimsolls *running shoes* and say *ranch* so it rhymed not with *staunch* but with *stanch*. I have heard the scornful laughter. One word can be fatal. I have frequently heard it so. Vowels often inform. A wrongly emphasized syllable may also tell a tale; one or two of the mistresses at St. Mildred's are rather suspect, I think. Miss Pringle Headmistress and Miss Hodgson Assistant are irreproachably Home Counties, but Miss Lincoln's speech is carefully not northern, while Miss Flower's gentle tone may overlie an origin involving coins and counter and till.

Amanda's accent is certainly better than it was last term — her first here, I believe — and she smiles, but is not talkative. Miss Flower informs me that Amanda takes her studies in Religious Knowledge rather seriously. Her form has engaged with the Thirty-nine Articles; Amanda has asked, quaintly, about Article X, on Free Will. *The Canadian girl,* the others call her, or *Our.* And yet, until her drawing lay before me, I had supposed her content.

When I was shipped to my English school, ridicule met me too. I too took up the shield of silence, but turned out to be that oddity in England, *good at languages.* A flawless English accent. *Irish as Paddy's pig,* I cracked the code. Crude: Amanda's drawing was crude. Of her form's nineteen pictures of Munster, only hers merited more than one look. She had used rather, in fact very, strong colours. I believe Amanda had not even tried to stay within that red rule. Surely, disobedience merits punishment. Ignorance of the law excuses no man.

Wild Ireland: through centuries of plantation, the Irish resisted, yet another reason why those imperial fantasies (colonists on plump smiling farmlands near prosperous snug smug villages) solidified into such tortured fact. Pickled Irish heads were shipped to Whitehall packed in salt. English settlers, men and women both, ran naked under scourges to the gates of Cork. Munster's lush grasslands dried out with fire and famine.

Resistance: the *Shorter OED* shows *kern* as deriving from the Old Irish *ceitern*, a band of foot-soldiers, a light-armed Irish foot-soldier; one of the poorer class among the "wild Irish," it says. And quotes Shakespeare (who else?), whose Richard II in 1394 shouts jovially to his men,

> Now for our Irish Wars:
> We must supplant those rough rug-headed kerns,
> Which live like venom where no venom else,
> But only they have privilege to live (II:1, 155-58).

The royal pronominals *our* and *we*, the verb *supplant*, the adjectives *rough* and *rug-headed*, the nouns *venom* and *privilege* are voluble of hierarchy. *Privilege* is surely ironic?

When I tell the Lower Fourth or Upper Fifth about yet another resignation from the cabinet (I am inclined to doubt that Labour will survive October 25), or M. de Gaulle's gains in the recent French elections, or the honourably heavy British participation (second only to that of the Americans) in the UN contingent in Korea — when I tell thus and so, a mistress stays with me in the form-room. I am not left alone with the girls. This is because — I have noted this previously — *Mr. Greene cannot keep order*. I cannot *teach* a class. The fact is widely known.

Another option was to reward Amanda's daring. (Did she even see what she drew as daring?) Her picture sprang from the page. I gasped. Such a reward would be unprecedented, but Mr. Greene: Specialist in History, Visiting Guest Lecturer, could confer such an honour. Eight out of ten, even nine, I could allot, for her powerful colours and lines. Trouble might ensue. Some little girls, who had received sixes and sevens and fives for their limp full-skirted ladies smiling beside pallid fields, might object. They might cry. They might lodge official complaints.

In my long-ago youth, even though I never once felt confident in the presence of other pupils, I dreamed of standing before rows of worn neat desks, faced by small attentive countenances. Each child in my dream had pen in hand. Each wrote down, carefully, tongue sticking out at the corner, my words. Together we turned clean pages. Together, my pupils and I memorized imports, exports, the changing names of political parties. We located battlefields and capitals, charted royal genealogies, weighed the terms of treaties. We drew beautiful maps. Our voices in recitation were low, our handwriting neat on the blackboard. I was the only man.

Never in my life have I seen such a classroom. Where do these ideas come from?

My Anglophile mother shipped me from Ireland to England, not long after a neighbour in our small town said to her, of me, approvingly, that I would *make a fine young Kerryman soon*. Perhaps, by telling my mother what she wanted to hear — I am a good teacher — I came to believe I could make it real, later, elsewhere, in other buildings or with different people. I also believed that when I was ten, or fifteen, or twenty-one, or thirty, I would stop biting my nails. All girls giggle. Even the child Amanda did, when Miss Trout's "Questions, girls?" cut off my peroration on the new Great Powers Partnership of Britain and America. Amanda asked, "Mr. Greene, why don't you ever say anything about Canada?" The giggles turned towards her on my immediate reply: "Canada, Amanda, is not an important country."

The sad sequence of my non-roaring twenties, in which I lost two teaching posts and left two others, led to my less sad but still-depressed thirties, in which I discovered my true gifts, such as they are. To wit: I tutor rather well if permitted to work with one pupil at a time (a child alone does not laugh at bitten nails or balding head), and I give a rather good lecture if someone else will keep order while I deliver it. Thus I earn my living. The old Irish hedge-schoolmasters, those peripatetics with books on their backs — I am reincarnation, or simulacrum, or perhaps travesty. For my mother in Ireland I embellish somewhat the social standing of my English pupils and of the girls' schools I visit each term. In describing to her the conversations on St. Mildred's beautiful Great Lawn, I substitute sherry for tea. I suggest that Fitzgerald came to St. Mildred's from a great house in Wiltshire and that Miss Flower is a Roedean girl.

She is gentle of demeanour, neat, soft-voiced. Miss Flower is not slight, however; she eats her pudding with enthusiasm. Solid roundnesses lift her twinset. I intuit that, like me, she would want to give Amanda's picture a high mark. Like me, she would gasp fearfully at the sight of it. Miss Trout, I am sure, would understand absolutely none of the subtleties of my dilemma.

Yet how dare I speak of these women thus contemptuously, name them as timid or coarse, when one or the other has crossed so terrific a margin? A schoolmistress has left her room at night to move by silent stairs and passages, on grass and path and gravel, herself hooded, half-naked, to a sexual target within the walls of School. Never have I dreamed of daring such a thing.

Even to such a man as myself, these feminine communities bring occasional invitations. They are coded, yet clear, for although I am not a master and have no residence and cannot teach and am in appearance not imposing, I am a man. Sometimes I have gone so far as to show understanding of the tongue being spoken, but I have never responded. I have taken no initiative.

As for my early forties, they were The War (Second World). I worked on codes, not at a high level nor yet at the lowest, and received my mother's weekly fusillades about the Republic's neutrality. Everyone fought his own War.

Sometimes the term used is *wood-kern*; the modern *guerilla* seems approximate. The *New History of Ireland* says that the Londonderry colonist "with the sword in one hand and the axe in the other" was a universal image, and quotes a seventeenth-century Fermanagh undertaker as complaining that "although there be no apparent enemy, nor any visible main force, yet the wood-kern and many other (who have now put on the smiling face of contentment) do threaten every house, if opportunity of time and place doth serve" (Vol. III, 205).

Uprooted, displaced, pushed ever westward (duplicates of the indigenous peoples of North America then simultaneously being pushed), kerns and many others (Irishwomen certainly among them) fought to regain what had been theirs. The flight of the earls: great sad corrupt defeated kerns.

Nightly, in rain or moon, I flee for an hour from St. Mildred's, to walk this rectangular external pathway. I am not frightened, for no shrubs conceal the high walls of School. On the path's other side lie either flat market-gardens or the lamplit fringes of the city . . . pubs, canal, railway, the length of road where the country buses stand all night. From my many previous visits to St. Mildred's, I know that solitary women stand at the canal's edge, by the notice-board displaying the bus timetable. In similar locations not far from Miss Rammell's, The Gates, Fairways, women wait. My occasional activity with them does not take long. Money, not very much, is the key. To these women, my inability to exercise authority is unimportant, as is my provenance. They open to my insinuation. Relieved, I resume my circumscription of the grounds.

Water-needles fall athwart the rows of kale. Decomposing vegetable matter is in the air. The odour is not unpleasant, not unlike that of mown grass after rainfall. In this mild October, red-faced Fitzgerald continues to mow the Great Lawn into wonderful stripes, dull green and shining. He mows and rolls, rolls and mows. Carrying a short spear, he patrols St. Mildred's, stabbing sweet wrappers, newspaper, bits of prep. Sometimes, meeting him, I point out a missed paper target. He nods, I nod. The girls call him *The Oirishman*, and laugh at his brogue.

Standards are essential. Amanda's picture did not meet my standards, was outrageous, ludicrous. Never have I seen such a thing. Historians write admiringly, and I spoke so, of the planned abundance created in Munster, of bog drainage, wall-building, renovation of the peel-towers: English order from Irish anarchy. A failing mark for Amanda would have been entirely justified. Oh that I had given her three out of ten! Even four — a reprimand she could not misconstrue. She would have felt humbled. She would have felt her inferiority. She would have felt who was stronger.

The literature on the English and Scottish plantations in Ireland also unravels the knotted feelings of the undertakers, servitors, tenants, and undertenants towards the Irish. Emotions identified include *gratitude* for the natives' skilled tutoring in their land and climate; *scorn* for their religious beliefs, hygiene, architecture, bards and rhymers, diet, dress, hairstyles (the *glib*, or long forelock worn by men, was outlawed because it concealed facial expressions), language, methods of farming; fear of their rage; *bewilderment* at their kindly humour; and *anger* at their higgledy-piggledy furtive bloody erratic ineffectual yet unceasing resistance. Just so were the feelings of the early Europeans in America towards the persons whom they met there and towards the persons whom they imported from Africa.

Returning to St. Mildred's, I crunch wetly past the sainted dormitory houses, St. Anne's, St. Hilda's, and downhill to the main school. The path is plain earth. Three nights ago, my steps were silent in the rain.

This building during the day holds geometry, needlework, Greek, chemistry, domestic science, girls and mistresses, Miss Flower, Miss Trout, Miss Lincoln, Amanda with her unblinking eyes. At night it houses only me, the only man. From one side of the old mansion protrudes a small two-storey addition, originally perhaps for a gardener or chauffeur. Now the daygirls keep their bicycles in an open-fronted space below. Above is my brief residence, my booley. An overhang above the outer door shields me from rain as I insinuate my key; an inner door concludes the steep dark stair.

Three nights ago, as always, I locked both behind me. My tiny domain was dark, warm, smelling of burned wood. The fire was out. I hung up my damp coat. At the window to draw the curtains, I saw a hooded cloaked someone who stood below, hand raised at my door. My return had been watched for.

Ports: in Ulster, Coleraine was chief. Cork. Queenstown. Lough Swilly. Through such orifices of the Irish body politic moved the colonists, heading inland along few roads, many rivers.

Modern historians distinguish three patterns of expanding settlement in Ireland: direct plantation, internal migration, and colonial spread. Were these behaviours experienced differently by the Irish? The question is unasked. (The Irish ways of moving about the land — creaghting, and transhumance or booleying — were contemned, the latter "on the ground that it provided hiding-places for outlaws and malcontents . . . and as conducive to laziness and licentiousness" (Butlin, 152-53). Nor do many historians show interest in the tenants' feelings about being English or Scottish in the new land. That Sir Thomas Smith in 1573 forbade his tenants and soldiers to take Gaelic wives suggests that many wanted to marry the country (Canny, 24). Many did, in spite of such prohibitions.

And yet — in the twentieth-century Republic, a widow whose forbears had come there almost two centuries earlier, as undertenants (her mother's side) and Methodist evangelists (her father's), insisted that she and her son were *English*. This woman frugally contrived to send her only child away from her, *home* (her term), to school in England. Before he left, the barber clipped his red curls close, close; he maintained the style for the rest of his life. On his visits to Ireland, his mother complained that her son was not as nice looking as in boyhood. In fact, Mr. Greene never lost the boyish look of a colonized child.

I had been watched for. Who stood outside my temporary door? In darkness I made my way down the stairs.

Opening to the wet night, I met at once a sweet sharp lavender scent, a rough hood, a damp smooth cheek. A pulling hand placed mine on a plump warm naked breast, its nipple stiff to my palm. My other hand met nakedness to the waist under thick tweed. Her perspiration smelled of lavender. Dark water dripped from the overhang. Awkwardly her head turned, the hood flopped over her face, my nose was in her warm hair, I breathed lavender rain till the pit of her mouth opened under me. Her fingers searched for purchase in my short hair.

In the *rising* or *rebellion* or *revolt* (the term chosen depends on the historian's politics) of 1641, the Old English — women and men descended from the Anglo-Norman invaders of centuries earlier — allied themselves with the Irish on a two-fold basis of unity: Catholicism and nationalism. Events in 1642 England doomed those Old English. Repudiated by what Clarke terms "their mother country," they tumbled down the social scale until they were "*submerged* in the eighteenth century peasantry and became *indistinguishable* from the native Irish [emphasis added]" (45).

For centuries, the Old English had been born and raised in Ireland. How much more native can you get?

After two long kisses, my visitor startled, though I had heard seen felt only her. She left, her cloak swaying down the path into the dark rain. Lavender lingered on my jacket.

The next day, at luncheon, I surveyed the mistresses. I breathed searchingly. Might there be a fragrance, a blush?

How does such an identification with one country — *there* — develop in a person born and raised *here*, whose parents and grandparents were born and raised *here*?

At the school which the pupil Amanda attended, the mistresses had untrammelled access to all ports of entry: eyes, ears, mouths. The girls sat in ready rows, up to the neck in their uniforms.

Next day, walking up to the dining hall, I saw Amanda emerging alone and late — the dinner-gong's echoes had ceased — from a belt of pines west of the playing field. A number of such plantations occur in the school grounds. Though none is large enough quite to conceal a person, they do, in daylight at least, afford some privacy. A desire for solitude is less characteristic of junior girls than of seniors, who are perhaps moving towards being mistresses. The child must have felt explanation necessary, for she said, "Those trees smell kind of like the ones at home. And the dead needles too." *Kind of*— one would not hear that from an English girl. She ran away from me.

Dining hall: mutton fat, perspiration, bitter Brussels sprouts, Bisto. A roar of eating girls. Clack of cutlery on plates, splash of water-pitchers. The Irish linen cloth at high table had been darned, *passim*. Being a Guest Lecturer, I sat between Miss Pringle and Miss Hodgson. The headmistress and her assistant smelled of soap. Their bosoms drooped into their belts. Their heads bore dry knots, not clouds of living hair. My scalp tingled. High-breasted Miss Lincoln Geography? But high colour lay on her cheeks — I had smelled no cosmetics the previous night. Widowed Mrs. Wilmer Maths was surely faithful to memory. In any case her blouse lay flat. Miss Flower's did not. Nor did Miss Trout's. Had Religion or History sought me out?

Eyes, ears, mouths. Other bodily orifices of the young females were also crucially involved in their indoctrination. The passages of waste and blood outward, of anything whatsoever inward, were stringently rule-bound by a revulsion charged with passionate right and wrong. Surveillance of the lockless lavatories, baths, and dormitories was constant. Any stain on sheets or petticoat or knickers magnetized clusters of interrogating mistresses.

The second time, two nights ago, I was already in my solitary bed, having examined the tortured faces and bodies in Amanda's picture.

With my nostrils full of woodsmoke and old wool blanket, I settled my body on the lumpy mattress. A knock. Disbelieving, I looked out. Another knock, soft but purposeful. Oh who is she? Surely not my fishy protector in the Third Form, not that screeching common laugh? O sweet Miss Flower, gentle, holy...yet both mistresses were the right shape.

People also speak of ideas being *in the air*.

A Scottish writer of the late fifteenth century described a local crime involving mutilation of animals as so awful that even "wyld Irisch and savadge people" (Perceval-Maxwell, 15) would not have committed it.

The Irish were, according to a seventeenth-century English historian, "more uncivill, more uncleanly, more barbarous, and more brutish in their customes and demeanures, then in any other part of the world that is knowne" (15). By this period, many similar descriptions of savages in the new-found lands were sailing back across the Atlantic.

That second night, my visitor stayed long enough to untie the cord of my olive Paisley dressing-gown. My two hands held her breasts. She touched my key. There was no rain, no wind, but again she fled. Again I did not hear or see whatever made her leave me, though it was a long time till I slept.

To exert wholehearted dominion in Ireland, the planters and undertakers defined themselves in polar opposition to the native population. Their aim was money, either directly, as rents, or mediated, as grains, wool, beef, lace, timber, barrelstaves, linen, butter. Their methods included abolishing the system of land tenure formed by Brehon law and erecting primogeniture on the crushed bones of the clans. Their means was force. (The state is a body of armed men.) And yet "the Crown had never sent a force to Ireland which was not eventually reduced 50% or more by desertion, defection, and an erosion of patriotism" (Berleth, 22). *Hibernia hibernescit.*

Regularly, luncheons at high table began with a rather lengthy report from Miss Pringle on King George VI's rapidly deteriorating health. Next, in rotation, the mistresses introduced a topic intended for general discussion and edification. Today, Miss Maywood Classics gave us *The Value of the Greek Myths in Modern Life.* Her bosom, I observed, would have overflowed my palm. Miss Berridge Music and Miss Barnes Games were too tall. Miss Michaelson Art had deeply pitted facial skin. Science's Miss Gregson was thin as a lath. Miss Maywood spoke at some length.

Out the dining-hall window, I watched Fitzgerald pushing the roller slowly across the Great Lawn. His wet face reddened with effort. "Irreplaceable Fitzgerald!" Miss Pringle admired, interrupting Miss Maywood. "Indispensable," said Miss Hodgson.

I am not the only man. This man of my age and country rolled English grass on which I walked with the mistresses.

Distant Amanda gazed at air. She had not yet received from me her picture and her paragraph and her mark.

Between forkfuls of mutton, the Classics mistress spoke of Cadmus, oracle, dragon. I breathed attentively, hoping for lavender. *Sotto voce*, Miss Hodgson asked if I had a cold.

For prep, the Third Form were to draw for me a picture of the brave colonists sent by the *first* Queen Elizabeth — on 23 September our George had had a lung resection, and although his progress was said, by his Queen no less, to be good, we must not underestimate the seriousness of the situation, nor must we delay prayers for the young woman who would soon be another Queen Elizabeth — a picture of those brave colonists sent by Gloriana to Munster after the Desmond Rebellion. They were also to write a paragraph about her excellent plantation scheme.

Having reached Cadmus's decision to throw the stone, Miss Maywood speculated: Did he fear that the creatures sprouted from the terrible seeds would see the sower as their enemy? Or did he simply throw because he felt like it? Miss Trout enlarged the discussion by deploring the tendency of various modern European countries towards civil war. With regret, Miss Hodgson mentioned the Balkans prior to 1914. Miss Lincoln unsuccessfully attempted a further enlargement by referring to the Mau Mau.

I did not speak of Ireland. Its current relative quiescence makes such a reference gratefully unnecessary. The island is, in any case, although not uninteresting, of no importance.

This afternoon, when I returned the Third Form's work, Miss Trout asked if I might "look ahead" a little in the history of England's colonizing efforts, subsequent to the Tudor conquest. Before I could begin, Amanda burst out, "Why don't you talk about Ireland *now*? All this stuff is hundreds of years ago." This breach of classroom manners drew mistress and pupil out into the passage for an angrily low-voiced exchange.

After Fitzmaurice retook the town of Kilmallock for the Irish, it was sacked, burned, and razed. Wolves then lived there. In Munster, the land was so badly damaged as to be unable to support an invading army (Berleth, 60).

Miss Flower and I walked side by side out of the dining-hall. Lavender: I believed the fragrance was in my nostrils. She spoke gently of the differences between the Greek mind and ours, and with courteous regret of my impending departure. She spoke with concern of the little Canadian girl, who, she said, had been most distressed at the story of Cadmus and the men born of the dragon's teeth, as told to her Latin class by Miss Maywood. Miss Flower had found Amanda crying in the lavatory. "They all killed each other. They didn't know why, what made them do it," she had, apparently, said. I said nothing.

Tea that afternoon was in Miss Pringle's sitting-room. The October chill was decisive. Rolling of lawns would cease. Lavender was in the air. Offering bread-and-butter so that I might circulate, I sniffed. The fragrance was infuriatingly traceable not only to Miss Flower but also to Miss Barnes, Miss Trout, and Miss Gregson. Cadmus reappeared in the conversation. In my anger I told the company of Amanda's tears in the lavatory. I may perhaps have rather embellished the tale. Miss Maywood and Miss Trout led the laughter. Miss Flower looked at me, not, I thought, with dislike, not with aversion to my forcefulness.

Last night was the third visitation. Waiting by the door, I opened before she could tap and pulled her in. One gasp is much like another. Who was she? I was naked under my Paisley, she half so under her hooded tweed. My fingers tugged at metal and cloth while my tongue found hers. My key was up and hard. We would ascend into my temporary domain, mix woodsmoke and lavender. I held her decisively, not bewilderedly. I used strength. It was my penultimate night at St. Mildred's. As the teeth of her zip-fastener opened to me, a torch flared light on my face.

Elizabeth's plantation of Munster began in 1584. Fourteen years later, the numbers of English settled there may have been three or twelve thousand, depending upon whether single males or families are tallied.

Flaccid again, I stood talking to Fitzgerald after she fled.

He apologized. On his midnight patrol, he had seen a cloaked figure approach my door and, as he thought, force entry. The Irishman was doing his duty for the English girls and mistresses, for the visiting speaker.

During the planting seasons in Ireland over the centuries, a common expectation was that for every Irish farmer evicted, an English colonist would be killed. Their deaths for their country (which?) were not sweet and meet. Favoured Irish weapons were the battle-axe, broad-bladed sword, crossbow, and spear. In turn, hangings of Irish rebel leaders, at least of those not dismembered at home, were a regular feature at Tyburn. There also hung the English captain Thomas Lee, who turned Irish and outlaw after years of service. He identified himself finally as a "bog soldier" (Berleth, 21-22).

Long past Elizabeth's time, Ireland remained imperfectly surveyed. Better maps were available of the eastern seaboard of North America than of Kerry or Donegal or even of Ulster.

That Fitzgerald might be among those at large in the darkness at St. Mildred's had not occurred to me. I had not understood the nature of his work.

Large and solid in his bulky mackintosh, wielding his torch as we talked outside my door, Fitzgerald seemed strong. I myself felt unusually so. A woman had been seen to seek me out; this man had seen her. Respect had sounded in Fitzgerald's tone to me. He did not speak as factotum to Foreign Affairs. Now, however, he was about to resume his dark passage through the woods and shrubberies, while I was to go back inside.

The 1598 insurrection in Munster did lead English and Irish to kill each other in large numbers. However, the Irish knew why they killed. They were clear. They killed to regain their land, animals, homes, and rivers.

Marks have meanings. Five out of ten means *barely passable*. Seven means *on the way to better quality;* even six and a half suggests a curving up from *ordinary*. I did not give her such a mark. I did not give the three or four that would have said *dreadful, disgraceful,* that her work had horrified me. No. I did none of these. In the end, with my red pen I inscribed, at the bottom right-hand corner of her picture, the numeral 6: the mark of mediocrity.

In analysing the Virginia plantation, Nicholas Canny hypothesizes that because those "who arrived with Daniel Gookin from Ireland in 1621 did not bear Irish surnames . . . these were in fact English*men* [*sic*] whom Gookin had, some years previously, brought as tenants to his estate in Munster and then *transferred* to his newly acquired property in Virginia [emphasis added]" (25).

While the other girls, giggling, compared their marks, Amanda stared at her earth bound human rows. Miss Trout reminded the Third Form of their good fortune in receiving a visit from a Specialist in History. Most girls clapped. Amanda raised hate-filled eyes. Averting mine, I addressed Miss Trout in a manner open to a flirtatious interpretation. Her breasts shook.

A kind of human creaghting may thus be seen in Ireland and in Virginia and in Mr. Greene's story: transhumance.

At that final tea this afternoon, I sat, Mr. Greene: Foreign Affairs, among the mistresses. I held all my knowledge tightly in my head: my origins, my languages, the visitations, Amanda's picture, her questions, her mark, her look of hate, my own hate, my recognition of Fitzgerald . . . all was safe. Then my slipping tongue gave me away, gave all away, all. My tongue rhymed my *a* with *mathematics* as I said, "*Rather!*"

The chatter of the English ladies ceased. Their eyes observed me as their ears decoded. A familiar silence filled Miss Pringle's sitting-room. Years ago, before I understood that I must meet pupils individually or have protectors standing by me before the rows of desks, I heard such silence often. Laughter follows. I left Miss Pringle's study. No, I fled.

The rain had stopped, the clouds blown off. The wind said *Autumn*. Litter blew about the playing field; the tuck shop was nearby, and the girls had scattered brightly printed cellophane. With his spear, Fitzgerald was at work. He had missed a scrap of white. I called, pointed. He picked the paper off his spear-tip and his bony jaw split in a smile. I looked. The genitals of the tiny Biro-blue figures, his and hers, swollen and joined, were clear, though not artistic. We laughed, hard and long.

Now I must return to my tiny domain that is not mine.

The wood fire will be out entirely. There will be no smell of lavender and no more visitations. Trout will not swim nor flower blossom, for no English mistress will lie with the Irishman who cannot teach, who has no residence, whose red hair barely coats his head, who dares not venture out but skulks in his room. Oh that I had given Amanda ten out of ten!

Tomorrow will be a cool grey October morning, begun by porridge, tea, and toast at the high table. Any lavender in the air will not signify. The mistresses will be polite, as to a person incurably afflicted. Miss Pringle will speak of the Confirmation class, Miss Hodgson of parental delinquency with fees. Packing my cases, once again, will be next, and then the perusal of the railway timetables, the booking of a seat, the purchase of newspapers for the journey so that on arrival at St. Stephen's or Miss Rammell's I may be truly *au courant*, Mr. Greene: Current Events, Foreign Affairs.

No. The trees and shrubberies of St. Mildred's shall house me for tonight, shield me from the rain whose sound in turn shall be my shield. I shall practise my wood-craft, trailing Fitzgerald as he does his midnight and small hour rounds, and watching my back lest Amanda should be on the loose with her stabbing lines and sharp colours. Whatever other wanderers, rule-breakers, foreigners there may be in the grounds at night, I shall meet. I may learn where the other man sleeps his few short hours. Shall I even see a visitor approach Fitzgerald's secret door? I shall cry no alarm. There is no pretence in him. Later, I shall make my way down the drive, not on the road but within the rampart of shining foliage, there learning another kind of silence and another way to hide. Whom shall I see? Who else goes forth at night, in search? Whoever passes will not know at first that it is I who make the hollies crackle and the pebbles jump. She will peer from side to side but not knowingly at me. Shall I let her find my body among the leaves? Shall I beckon, draw her to me, find her breasts, touch her tongue, insinuate my key? Finally, I shall move beyond the school grounds, out to the dying vegetable fields and over the low walls hedging the suburban houses of the city. No one will expect me there. The dawn will find me awake and alert as I have been all night, by a bare espaliered peach or in a greenhouse. Food and drink I shall take from a sill, a doorstep, an unharvested kitchen garden.

In appearance I am not distinctive. My shoes are stout, my jacket warm. No citizen will think, *That man does not belong here*. My failure to appear at Miss Rammell's will be a cause of only temporary, mild concern. In the life of a school, lectures on Foreign Affairs and Current Events, given by a quiet nail-biting middle-aged visiting hedge-teacher with little hair, are easily substituted. Also, should telephonic enquiry be made by Miss Rammell to Miss Pringle, the inevitable revelation of *Irish* will explain all. *Irresponsible, unreliable, I always thought, so did I, rather. . . .*

Where shall I go? I know exactly: west. All England has been mapped, in detail. Yes, I shall move cunningly, kernishly, night by night from school to school and shire to shire, from wooded grounds to shrubberies to pine plantations and empty bicycle sheds. Against all dangers, my weapons shall be my wits and my knowledge of the English tongue. So armed, I shall reach the coast of the Irish Sea. . . .

The overhang shelters me as I open the door. In the morning, I must remember to return to Miss Pringle her key.

BIBLIOGRAPHY

Andrews, K. R., N. P. Canny, and P. E. H. Hair, eds. *The Westward Enterprise: English Activities in Ireland, the Atlantic, and America 1480-1650*. Liverpool: Liverpool University Press, 1978.

Berleth, Richard. *The Twilight Lords*. New York: Knopf, 1978.

Butlin, R. A. "Land and People, c. 1600." In Moody, *New History of Ireland*, Vol. III.

Canny, N. P. "The Permissive Frontier: Social Control in English Settlements in Ireland and Virginia, 1550-1650." In Andrews, 17-44.

Clarke, Aidan. "Genesis of the Ulster Rising of 1641." In Roebuck, 29-45.

Moody, T. W. *The Londonderry Plantation 1609-41*. Belfast, 1939.

————, F. X. Martin, and F. J. Byrne, eds. *A New History of Ireland*, Vol. III, *Early Modern Ireland 1534-1691*. Oxford: Oxford University Press, 1976.

Perceval-Maxwell, M. *The Scottish Migration to Ulster in the Reign of James I*. London: Routledge & Kegan Paul, 1973.

Phillips, Rev. Randall G. *Irish Methodism*. London: Charles H. Kelly, 1897.

Robinson, Philip. *The Plantation of Ulster*. Dublin: Gill and Macmillan, 1984.

Roebuck, P., ed. *Plantation to Partition*. Belfast: Blackstaff Press, 1981.

JOSEF ŠKVORECKÝ, born in 1924, came to Canada after the Soviet ambush of Czechoslovakia. He became Professor of English at the University of Toronto. He is the author of some ten novels, including *The Cowards*, *The Engineer of Human Souls*, and *The Bass Saxophone*, and many other books. In 1984 he received the Governor-General's Award, and in 1992 he was appointed Member of the Order of Canada.

TITLE-PAGE MISSING

JOSEF ŠKVORECKÝ

I recall a moment in my youth, an epiphany, alas more than half a century ago, when Dvořák's music first touched me, inseparably linked to a visual sensation. During a rehearsal in the darkened auditorium of the *fin-de-siècle* theatre in my native town of Náchod, I heard the haunting melody of the "Wedding Song" from *Rusalka*, and I saw, in a spotlight, the face of one of the singers. In those remote days, when I was a teenager, I loved the singer with all the intensity of youth. The beautiful melody and the lovely face merged into what Henry James, I suppose, would have called a "germ"; a bud which remained in my memory for many, many years, like a seed preserved in the darkness of a cellar. When I eventually began writing the novel *Dvořák in Love*, in the unformed chaos of the initial idea, these two beautiful elements — the sound and the face — stood out. They became the keynote of my composition. I visualized the lovelorn youth and his lovely sentimental melodies, and the intended recipient of those musical messages, the lovely

323

Josephine who rejected him. I plotted the novel around those two centres of loveliness: the melodies of the songs, and the face preserved in an old photograph.

I had been warned, before I commenced the work on my book, that there was very little to write about — except, of course, Dvořák's music. But otherwise? A life of work, later of international success, no marital infidelities, no scandals, just the uneventful life of a touring maestro consisting of events in concert halls, not in life.

Well, there were other aspects, too, and I tried at least to touch upon them.

In the course of my work, however, I realized that it was not only the configuration of aural and visual beauty that lured me to the Master. I noticed something else, and it linked me directly to him.

I have always stood in awe of writers who seem to have known exactly the worth of what they were doing, and knowing that, they saved their energies for the Work, with an uppercase *W*. James Joyce, I guess, would be the archetype of writers who never invested much effort into making a living but relied, instead, on their Creator — or on the Creator's secular substitutes — to provide. These writers kept rejecting offers to write reviews, articles, the various literary ephemera that most of us do, hating the loss of time, but helpless and torn between the urge to write and financial necessity. These rejectors of ephemera were — and are — *real* writers: not generous with their time, but generous with the gift of their art which is here for us to enjoy. Or, perhaps, just to admire.

I never belonged to their select company.

And as I was doing research for my novel, I came across the reminiscences of one of Dvořák's friends. Acording to this person, Dvořák, towards the end of his life, experienced what today we would call composer's block, and he confided in that friend self-reproachfully: "I've enjoyed everything I have done. That may be the root of it. I always wrote a polka, or any silly trifle at all, with the same zest, the same delight, as I wrote an oratorio."

When I read this sad remark, I experienced my second Dvořákian epiphany. Because that was my case.

Dvořák was a firm Catholic, a true believer. Some musicologists who read my novel felt that I had an unjustifiably low opinion of Dvořák's purely intellectual qualities. But for me his "theoretical approach" to music and his "method" — if it can be called that — he himself described best, in another remark, to a friend: "Music is a great gift. I have had that gift, to the full. But the giver may decide that one is no longer worthy of such a gift. He can take it back."

This was the very man who passionately studied the works of his musical idols, and it would be preposterous to doubt his deep knowledge of musical theory and technique, even though he did not acquire it at a conservatory, but largely through self-study, self-education. And yet next to the miracle of creation, he felt himself to be only a humble user of the mysterious gift.

As a boy, I almost died of pneumonia which, in those days, was a life-threatening illness: antibiotics had not been discovered yet. The long recuperation excluded me from the activities of my peers who were mostly engaged in sports, in physical competition. The theory then was that young survivors of the killer-disease had turned into fragile flowers that must be kept in greenhouses. So I turned inward, and soon discovered the joy and torture of putting dreams on paper. At that very early age — I was about nine — I decided I would become a writer. I even wrote my first "novel" when I was about ten: an imitation of the romantic frontier writings of James Oliver Curwood, set in the — to me completely unknown — Canadian wilderness.

In those remote days nobody had heard of literary theory and training, certainly not in the backwoods where I was growing up. There were no creative writing courses, no manuals on the art of fiction, and moreover the Nazis had closed Czech universities. I was left to myself, to the trial-and-error method, to the encouragement of a few intimate friends, and to God.

Like Dvořák, I was a firm believer. I prayed to God daily, sometimes several times a day, to make me a writer.

Well, He did. I wrote my first novel, *The Cowards*, after passionately reading and rereading Hemingway's *A Farewell to Arms*, not after having received instruction in prose techniques from professors at the university. In those days, anyway, shortly after the war, the teaching and study of literature consisted mostly in memorizing dates and titles of books, certainly not in analysing narrative modes, or the proper use of symbols, nor of deconstructing beautifully crafted works of art to the point of dismantling them into ruins. I read, and perhaps I may say, I studied Hemingway by myself just as Dvořák had studied Beethoven, Mozart, Brahms, and other great composers. In my case it was Hemingway, and later Faulkner, and before that Sinclair Lewis, now practically forgotten in his native land.

While writing *The Cowards*, I prayed. Sometime during the Second World War, I had read an essay by the Czech poet Josef Hora in which he coined the term "magic realism" — long before Gabriel Garcia Marquez, and in another sense. Hora wanted prose fiction to shine with the same kind of magic that great lyrical poetry exudes, and urged fiction writers to give as much care to every single word as lyrical poets do. My magical text, which I did not quite understand but which, in my mind, I repeated again and again as an incantation, while drilling holes in aircraft parts in the Messerschmitt factory, where I involuntarily worked, was Eliot's "Ash Wednesday":

> *Because I do not hope to turn again*
> *Because I do not hope*
> *Because I do not hope to turn . . .*

I wanted my creation *The Coward* at the end of the Second World War to possess something of that Eliot sort of magic, and I prayed. My head was empty of theory, but full of Hemingway's prose, and of the dramatic and emotionally charged events of the Götterdämmerung in Kostelec. After I'd finished the novel, I had no idea how it had come about. Did I really write it? No, it was a gift, a gift that could be taken back . . . And so, with every new book I have ever started, I have felt the gnawing uncertainty, would the gift still be mine, or had it only been franchised for the previous effort? And again I have prayed, like that great man, Dvořák, who also had been so uncertain about the gift.

Dvořák was not above writing "silly trifles"; he was not stingy with his energies, and did not reserve them for the Works with the uppercase *W*. They might be trifles, yet to me they are also little things of beauty which — as the decades that have followed Dvořák's departure from the Vale of Tears have proved — are a joy forever.

In the course of my research for *Dvořák in Love*, I learned about one such trifle: Dvořák's arrangement of Stephen Collins Foster's song "Old Folks at Home." Dvořák wrote the arrangement for the school orchestra of the National Conservatory of Music in New York where he was then director, and for the coloured mixed choir of St. Phillip's Church. The score, after the concert on January 23, 1894, in Madison Square Garden, was lost. Mrs. Josephine Harreld Love of Detroit who, in her youth, was a friend of Dvořák's admirer, the singer Harry T.

Burleigh, located it for me. Our company, the Sixty-Eight Publishers of Toronto, brought out the score in facsimile, and had the song, in the Master's arrangement, recorded in English in Detroit, and in Prague with Czech lyrics. Surely it's only a musical trifle, a mere arrangement, a bagatelle. But to me the sound of enjoyment, the Master's zest, is present in the simple score.

The much loved Czech writer Karel Čapek wrote a book of essays, *Marsyas, Or, On the Edge of Literature*, on what, nowadays, would be called popular literature: romantic novels, crime stories, pop songs. He did this long before trifling works of marginal muses were to become the subject of serious academic study in North America. Čapek, too, in many ways, was like Dvořák: he did not save his energy for the upper-register Work — although he did write quite a number of pretty important books. He, too, produced marginalia and ephemera with the same zest as his epoch-making play about the robot *R.U.R.*, or *The Makropulos Secret*, immortalized by Leoš Janáček. In *Marsyas* he explains his ideal of a writer's work: "Every copy of [his book] would travel from hand to hand, from hands marked by pinpricks and corrosive laundry detergents, reddish with kitchen cleansing powder, soiled by inkspots, into hands bruised by some other kind of hard life, until finally the title-page of all copies would be lost, and nobody would know any more who the author was. And it would be unnecessary to know because everybody would find himself in the book."

I have thought of this statement when I have been listening to the many and various jazzed-up renditions of Dvořák's *Humoresque:* Emilio Caceres's lively duet of violin and bass saxophone, John Kirby's gentle big band sound, or Oscar Peterson's inspired jazz-piano virtuosity. Apart from my belief that Dvořák, who loved the sounds of America, would not consider such impieties an insult to his art, but rather as homage to his art's perennial life, it seems to me that Čapek's ideal of the book with the title-page missing was — in an unexpected way — realized in a democratic land, where Dvořák felt so good, where, however, only the very few musically educated would be able to name the original author of the lively *Humoresque* tune as it reappeared in the perennial jam session of the jazz greats.

There are traces of America, of its music and rhythms, not only in Dvořák's celebrated Symphony number 9 in E Minor *The New World*, or in his "American" String Quartet in F Major, but also in works considered negligible such as his

"American Suite," opus 98B. In them, I again hear the same joy, the same zest, the same touch of the divine gift, as in the masterpieces. This is not to say that, in comparison to the celebrated masterworks, these minor works are just as excellent. I am not speaking about originality and depth, about miracles of orchestration, but simply about Dvořák's own feeling: "I've enjoyed everything I've done."

Musicologists tell me, and I think I can hear it myself, that there are definite traces of America, of its folk music idioms, in his little-known "American Suite." True, to quote Dvořák himself, "When all is said and done, it is just more Czech music." Yet, as he also said: "If it hadn't been for America, I never would have written it." There is something deeply touching about this Czech-American mixture — and also something essentially North American. In North America — in the United States, just as in Canada — unlike in countries of the Old World, one can become a Canadian or an American without ceasing to be a Czech, a Bohemian. In Germany or in Switzerland, one must prove one's *Einbürgerung*, or adaptation with the aim of merging into the German *Bürgertum*. In North America, people ask you with genuine interest: "Hey, what's your accent?" When you tell them that you are Bohemian, they may think you are a Gypsy, but they don't mind. These are countries where racism is moribund, and equality is changing from an ideal into reality.

I hear a premonition of this beneficial development in Dvořák. He absorbed whatever existed in his day of American music, certainly the Negro spirituals; he turned them into Czech sounds, and created — in their spirit — the "Largo" from the *New World Symphony*. His countrymen, in their turn, turned the haunting melody into a church song "Veliký Bože nás" ("Though Great God"), and in America, that same *New World* melody became a pop song, "Going Home."

The title-pages of Dvořák's compositions have gone missing; the works belong to everyone.

The great second movement of Dvořák's *New World* magnum opus did not become just a pop song. If the Dutch musicologist Visman is not entirely off-target, Dvořák's greatest work resounds in the music of Duke Ellington, a master who was very much removed — by origin, by career, by race — from the Czech maestro, although he learned orchestration from one of Dvořák's own black students, Will Marion Cook.

Listening again and again to the "Come Sunday" section of Ellington's *Black, Brown and Beige Suite*, I became convinced that Visman's hypothesis is not pure fantasy. There seems to be something similar about the progression of instrumental voices in the lovely piece, harmonic rhythm, perhaps, the breathtakingly beautiful alto sax solo by Johnny Hodges which, like the sound of the English horn, echoes the vast distances of America. The missing title-page, the mysterious, uncharted ways of cultural cross-fertilization, the gift given to the Master, now bequeathed to the great black musician, Duke Ellington,

I wonder.

When I think of the oeuvre of Antonín Dvořák, not just of its highlights, but its entirety, I feel again a closeness to him. If he wrote every silly little trifle with delight, I listen to those tasty crumbs from the rich table with equal zest. I have done the same in my work which, in no other way, I want to compare with that of the Czech genius. Still, I have enjoyed every silly review, every insignificant translator's footnote I have written, just as I have enjoyed writing my novels. All I can hope is that some of my pieces will share the fate of Dvořák's minor compositions: that in some of my books, too, the title-pages will be lost, but it will not matter because everybody will find himself in those books.

DISCOGRAPHY

Stephen Collins Foster: "Old Folks at Home"/Ten, jehož dům tu stál/
Arr. Antonín Dvořák. Bambini di Praga and Pavel Kühn Male Choir with the Prague
Philharmonic Players. Soloists Milada Čejková and Vladimír Doležal. Choirmistress
Dr. Blanka Kulínská. Choirmaster Pavel Kühn. Conductor Bohumil Kulínský.
Published in Canada by Sixty-Eight Publishers, Corp. 1992

Emilio Caceres: Humoresque in Swing Time
"Stuff" Smith and His Onyx Club Boys. Arhoolie Productions, 1979
Emilio Caceres /violin/, Ernie Caceres /clt. and bass sax/, Johnny Gomez /g/
Recorded in 1937

Humoresque. John Kirby Version
Leader: Billy May, Trumpet: Pete Candolik, Clarinet: Abe Most, Alto Sax: Justin
Gordon, Piano: Ray Sherman, Bass: Morty Corb, Drums: Nick Fatool. TIME-LIFE
Records, 1971. Originally recorded in 1939, Vocalion. Arr. Evan L. Young,
Trumpet: Charlie Shavers, Clarinet: Buster Bailey, Sax: Russell Procope, Piano: Billy
Kyle, Bass: John Kirby, Drums: O'Neill Spencer

Humoresque. Oscar Peterson
Oscar Peterson Quartet. Oscar Peterson /piano/, Armand Samson /g/, Bert Brown
/b/, Roland Verdon /dm/. Recorded August 17, 1945. RCA Masters

Antonín Dvořák: "American" Suite, Op. 98B.
Berlin Radio Symphony Orchestra. Conductor Michael Tilson Thomas. 1976,
Columbia Records CBS Inc. 1977

Duke Ellington: "Come Sunday" from Black, Brown and Beige Suite
Rec. 1944. RCA Black and White Series. The Works of Duke, Complete Edition, Vol. 19. Shelton Hemphill, James "Taft" Jordan, William "Cat" Anderson /tp./, Ray Nance /tp.v./, Joe "Tricky Sam" Nanton, Claude Jones, Lawrence Brown /tb/, Johnny Hodges, Otto Hardwicke /as/, Al Sears /ts/ Jimmy Hamilton /ts, cl/, Harry Carney /bs/, Edward "Duke" Ellington /p/, Fred Guy /g/, Alvin "Junior" Ragwin /b/, William "Sonny" Greer /dm/

CATHERINE BUSH is the author of the novel *Minus Time*, which was short-listed for the SmithBooks/ Books in Canada First Novel Award and a City of Toronto Book Award, and has been published in Canada, the U.S. and the U.K. She is currently completing work on a second novel entitled *Radar Angels*.

Radar Angels

Catherine Bush

No one ever guesses what I do.

What I love is the expression on people's faces when I tell them, that instant of vulnerability and revelation, before they compose themselves again. Sometimes the shift is as small as a quiver of the mouth, the flicker of an eyelid, but it's there nevertheless: a transformation.

"What do you do?" people ask. At dinner parties or in pubs, the friends, or friends of friends, or strangers. Some of them are doctors, an epidemiologist, a psychiatrist, a man who mends musical instruments, a woman who choreographs the artificial stars at the planetarium, a journalist.

I am in a small, high-ceilinged room, crowded with people, holding a glass of aqua libra, wearing a long skirt made of some silky fabric, slim over the hips and skittery above the ankles of my black lace-up boots. When I talk, I'll touch distractedly the combs that hold back my hair, a sort of nervous, talismanic gesture. Touch the tortoiseshell rim amid the thick strands. Or else, in the midst of a thought, I'll take a comb out and catch back the loose and wispy pieces as if reeling in the end of a sentence. I wear lipstick, dark red, plum brown, and hate to go out without it. There are no rings on my fingers.

"And what do you do?"

My accent turns corners in the course of sentences, wavery, mutable, revealing that I come from somewhere else. Not England. Not London.

I study war. Not Defence Studies or Conflict Studies or Peace and Conflict Studies but War Studies. That's what I have a degree in. I'm an explorer, on a research mission, really. I work for an organization called The Centre for Contemporary War Studies. This isn't something I would ever have predicted.

You should see the pulse of muscle, the tiny constellation of fear and dismay or intrigue and surprise in people's eyes when I tell them.

The phone began to ring as I hurried down the outside stairs — that two-note English ring, not the single North American ring that I grew up with but the one that, after ten years, I've grown accustomed to. My flat is the basement flat, the garden flat, and there is indeed a garden behind it, though a small one.

It was my telephone, no mistaking, close and insistent through the glass of my front window. There was no particular call that I was expecting. It could have been anyone in the wide, wide world.

High on a platform of metal scaffolding across the street, a workman sang Beethoven's "Ode to Joy" at the top of his lungs while down below, another stirred a vat of boiling tar, sending the nostril-pinching scent of it to drift along the street. The "Ode to Joy." What, I wondered, compelled him to sing that? I longed for an explanation. A train clattered beyond the ridge of the rooftops, hurtling north out of Euston Station. It was late May. In the tiny front garden, the first rosebuds pushed forth like lips.

I unlocked the two locks, top and bottom, swung open the door and pushed it shut behind me. In a small flat it does not take very long to reach the telephone. "Hello," I said breathlessly, breaking into the line in the suspended instant before my own automated voice picked up. "I'm here. Wait a moment."

"Hey, Cay," sang out the voice of my younger sister, Lux. "How are you?" There was a garble of other voices in the air beyond her, as in a train station or an airport.

Or, for that matter, in the music TV station where Lux works in Toronto. She could have been ten minutes away, at the Camden tube stop, or half the world away, or anywhere in the world. You never knew with Lux. She had a habit of unexpected annunciation. Hearing her voice without warning springing out of the phone, I would imagine her floating up above the globe, or, like a satellite feed, materializing as a shimmery form in several noisy cities at once.

"All right," I said. "Where are you? Or do you want me to guess?"

"Want to guess?"

It was just after six in the evening by the little black alarm clock on my desk.

"Dar es Salaam," I said. Where it would be eight o'clock.

"Nope," Lux said.

"Sydney."

"I don't know if you're getting warmer, Cay." I stared at the map of the world tacked to my wall. In Sydney, it would be four in the morning.

I pulled out my desk chair and sat down. "You're in Toronto but you'll be in London tomorrow."

"Oh, well almost bingo," Lux said delightedly. "Day after tomorrow."

"Do you need somewhere to stay?"

"No, it's business," Lux said. "They're putting me up. But I'll come and visit. Do I need to make plans now or can I call you when I get there?"

"How long will you be here?"

"Three days," Lux said.

"Then just ring when you get here."

"Ring," Lux said. "I'll ring."

Lux has the kind of voice that it is very difficult to get annoyed at. A voice that people confide in and trust. There must be some vibration in her throat that people respond to, a specific microtone or timbre. Her voice is seductive without being overtly sexual, without making you feel that seduction is exactly what is at stake. It can go low and throaty but then opens up, lighter, like a road spilling, widening into a clearing or a field. A voice made for radio, I suppose, and this is where Lux started, before she moved to TV, to host a show called "Mondo," which these days I can even watch in England, if sleepless I go channel-scrambling in the far hours of the night.

Our father is the one responsible for our names. Arcadia. Lux. What kind of man would give his daughters names like these? An idealist. A nuclear engineer. He is. He was. He is. Two years ago, he disappeared, slipped his set of keys back through the letterbox in the house in Toronto where I grew up. He has not been seen or heard from since. There are holes in the world through which people can fall. At every step lurks the possibility of disappearance.

When I was born, he had just finished graduate school and begun working for Nuclear Energy of Canada. He lived with my mother in a small apartment in Ottawa, not far from the canal. He believed that the names you gave to children were of the utmost importance and that these should not be ordinary names. His own name was — is — Benedict Hearne. He would come bursting in the door of their apartment, snow in his dark hair, a briefcase under his arm, salt flecks nestled in the tweed of his jacket, and call out possible names to my mother Ann. Atom, if it was a boy. Adam Bliss. Names that meant something, heralded something. He was not, as far as I know, superstitious but he believed that names should have a certain resonance. And he convinced my mother, despite her reservations, despite her fear that we would be teased in the school yard and bear the two of them grudges, because of our names. And we were teased in the school yard. Bemused teachers often asked us to spell our names out loud, which made my face turn red in embarrassment.

The light in his face convinced her, the wings of passion stretched tight beneath his skin, his brightness, his enthusiasm, as he crouched beside her rocking chair or leaned beside her at the kitchen counter. A young man, at thirty a year younger than I am now. What exactly did he believe in? Fission. Fusion. Energy. Heat. Light.

He came bursting through the apartment door and saw a young woman in a butter-yellow cardigan, whose fingers and ankles had swollen in the late stages of pregnancy. A barrette held back the near black, growing-out bob of her hair. A blue fluorescent light burned above her head. A north wind hissed through the pine tree outside the window. Love. The future. *If it's a girl we'll call her Arcadia.*

What kind of landscape did he think he was promising me?

Whenever Lux visits, I dream. It's as if she's a comet trailing shreds of Toronto like an aureole that I breathe in or ingest somehow.

I am sitting at a café table opposite a young man named Evan. A bouquet of white flowers spills from a vase between us and he has tugged loose one flower, twisting it between his small, precise fingers, distractedly pulling off one white petal after another. He looks the same as he did when I last saw him, no older, or if he doesn't look the same, it doesn't matter, because he conjures up the same fierce sense of familiarity in me. We lean forward, an awkward dance, like birds with broken necks, straining for some sharp, unescapable intimacy. So much still remains to be said.

Then I am fleeing through a subway train, clambering through the windows between cars because the doors won't open. I clutch my bag and an extra pair of shoes. Passengers watch me, slumped on the vinyl-covered benches. When the train pulls into a subway station, an above-ground one like Davisville or Rosedale, I burst through the rattling doors, into the cool night air. A dark emptiness rises above the broken slope of the station roof, and there is Neil, on the platform. He sits on a bench with his hands in the pockets of his overcoat so that his shoulders are hunched, arms pushed tight against his chest. Dark hair falls across his forehead. At the sight of him, my throat releases in elation and relief. He gives a quick coy smile, still hugging the overcoat to himself. A breeze gusts between us. As long as he does not open his coat, then everything will be all right. As long as he does not open it, because then I do not know what I will see, or at least I know what I do not want to see. Blood on the ground, on the slats of the bench, blood seeping through his jeans and the cotton folds of his shirt.

I woke in the still dark of my bedroom. This was the landscape that surrounded me: the white walls slate grey in the darkness; the window that opened towards the garden; the room so small that the bed itself engulfed it and the bed was not that large, only a double bed. I pushed back the duvet and slipped out, shivering, bare feet on the worn carpet, snatched the old silk robe hanging over the door of the closet and pulled it around my shoulders. The little turquoise numbers on the digital clock glowed like eyes. It was 5:06.

I righted myself in the landscape of the familiar, pulling doorknobs and corners out of the shadows, reclaiming them as points on the map, making them once more familiar. The rooms slumbered, suspended. Through the kitchen window, the corkscrew torques of the little apple tree were visible and the bushy mass of the rosemary tree, gnarled and old, perhaps as old as me. I poured myself a glass of water. Put a sprig of rosemary under your pillow to remember your dreams: someone once told me this, but I've never needed to.

In Toronto it was just after midnight, and perhaps Lux was packing in preparation for flying out the next evening or taking last-minute notes or making love with her girlfriend Haydee in the muss and abandon of their shared bed.

In the study, I knelt in front of the gas fire and lit the invisible swish of gas with a match. Flames leapt into life. It was a fire that looked almost real, filled not with fake lumps of coal but little moulded logs, while the flames leapt and dazzled among them. There was no smell, though, just the warmth and hypnotizing flurry of orange and blue. Even though it was late May, the weather had, for the last week, been gusty and cool. Outside, the light was slowly growing. I pushed one of the small armchairs to face the fire and sat, knees scrunched to my chest.

Lux was coming and they surged up again, as always. Evan and Neil. My radar angels: that was how I thought of them. Like ghost images that appear on an airplane radar screen to befuddle the pilot. There and not there.

Here, in this room, it was clear to me how much I was not who I had been in the days when I had known Evan and Neil. On the bookshelves that rose on either side of the fireplace were rows of books, books with titles like *How to Make War*, or *A History of War*, or *Civil War*. On the white wall opposite me stretched a map of the world dotted with coloured tacks, marking regional hot spots, like needles pricked into skin. There was safety in this room, though, a cool solidity, an assurance of purpose. There were days when I worked so hard I barely left this room and the walls seemed calming and clarifying, like a white cocoon.

In some fashion they were always there, Evan and Neil, a neurochemical presence, in combinations of proteins and neuropeptides, synaptic receptors, encoded within, carried with me. And certain things were very difficult to forget.

Once, in late May, in the spring of our final year in high school, I pulled open my locker and a little folded piece of birch bark fell out. I knew who must have slipped it there. I set down my armful of Duotangs and unfolded the delicate square. "Meet me at five by the bridge," Evan had written. That was all, but I knew which bridge he meant.

At four forty-five, I walked north from the subway, with the piece of birch bark in my pocket. A line of apartment towers rose at my back. The sidewalks were awash in little green flowers tumbling from the trees. Past a row of old brick houses, a cement bridge spanned a sea of green, the tops of the trees rising to meet it like great heads. Far below, in the hollow of ravine ran a ribbon of road down which cars sped.

From this bridge, Evan had told me, he and a childhood friend named Pete had once thrown long tubes of burned-out fluorescent lights, stolen from an apartment building dumpster. The tubes had spun through the air and smashed in white clouds of dust onto the road. Had they thrown them at the cars? No, Evan said, of course not. But to be in a car and see a white missile hurtling towards you. Did they think of that? This was what I thought of.

Evan was not there when I arrived and so I waited, pressing a finger to the pale dust of pollen that lay upon the cement arm of the bridge. We had been going out for almost a year. Tree flowers drifted and caught in my hair. Either he would come or he wouldn't come and then this, in itself, would be the message. I waited for him, as always, in a hum of unsettled expectation. And then, there he was, running down the slope of the street towards me. Jogging shorts flipped at the edges of his bare, muscled legs. His worn red T-shirt billowed, a knapsack jostling on his back. He'd told me he was training for a marathon. He knew more of the etymologies of words than anyone I had ever met. He came to a breathless stop, a diamond of sweat clinging to the chest of his T-shirt. He was only a little taller than me, small and compact. When I kissed his lips, I tasted salt. Around my neck I wore a tiny necklace of silver links that he had given me. To love him, I sometimes thought, was like walking over a bridge, along the edge of a cliff, along the rim of the unknown, with a delicate tracery of fear, like a tiny silver necklace, around my neck.

"Come on," Evan said, gesturing, and I followed him. At the end of the bridge, he headed off the sidewalk, into the trees.

"Ev, where are we going?"

He didn't answer but loped ahead down the slope, along a sliver of path that led under the bridge. Our shoes kicked through the damp rot of last year's leaves. A roar of cars raced past below. Evan dropped his knapsack. He tugged off his red T-shirt, and I thought for a moment that he wanted us both to strip down and make love on the cement slabs of the bridge's underside, in the cool pool of stagnant air, surrounded by ragged bits of old graffiti that read *Sarah loves Henry* and *KALI* — but I wasn't sure I could have done that.

Out of the pocket of his knapsack, he pulled a knife: small, sharp, blue-handled. Flicked free the blade. I stood very still, listening to the swift thumping of my heart. I thought, it's too small a knife to kill me. Anything seemed possible. The sky quivered, yawned wide with amazing possibility.

"Do you love me?" Evan asked. His eyes were narrowed, in determination and tenderness. He held the blade of the knife down, not pointed at me. The skin beneath his collarbone was flushed from exertion, the hair at his temples darkened to the colour of dark sand, the rest of it swept back like winter field grass.

"Yes," I said. And if I'd said anything else? He moved very quickly, too fast to stop him. With one hand, he pressed flat the skin on one side of his chest, cutting deftly into the skin with the knife, which he held in his other hand. At first only the pink sear through the flesh was visible; then an outline of blood bubbled up. A letter *A*. On the other side of his chest, he carved a circle. An *O*. Silently he folded up the knife.

"Evan." I pulled old Kleenexes out of my pockets, the only thing I had to stanch the blood. Anything seemed possible: he would hand me the knife, ask me to pull off my jacket and shirt.

He threw his arms around me, binding us, pressed the chest of my jacket to his bare chest. "Alpha and Omega," he whispered, his lips to my ear. "From the beginning to the ending. Because I'll love you forever, Arcadia."

JAMES MILLER is Faculty of Arts Professor at the University of Western Ontario. In 1988 he organized Canada's first interdisciplinary conference on AIDS and the arts ("Representing AIDS: Crisis and Criticism") and curated "Visual AIDS," a travelling exhibition of AIDS posters from around the world. His anthology *Fluid Exchanges: Artists and Critics in the AIDS Crisis* was published by University of Toronto Press in 1992. He currently teaches an undergraduate course on post-Stonewall gay history and culture.

My Night at Valdek

James Miller

"What you've got to realize about this place," advised my friend Mark, as he led me up a winding staircase into his favourite gay bar in Prague, the Kavárna Valdek, "is that nobody knows which clock to trust any more. Imagine — a city full of clock towers and not one of them reliable! There's no Big Ben here, no Greenwich, no Standard Time. Schedules are a nightmare. Valdek's supposed to stay open until three a.m., but you never know whether that means six in the morning or three in the bloody afternoon. It all depends on whose watch the manager looks at, and whether he's sober when it feels like closing time. We all feel the times are changing here, and changing fast, but nobody's quite sure which time is changing at what rate or for whom. Everyone's racing against different clocks. On the surface life goes on with the usual bumbling energy, but underneath it all we're knackered to the point of nervous collapse."

I had to admit that since my arrival on Mark's doorstep six days earlier, on the first of September 1992, my naively romantic impression of Prague as a vortex of newly liberated artistic and erotic energies had been somewhat shaken by the economic frenzy in Wenceslas Square. Everyone there seemed to be running around with a Happy Face, greeting a bright future of Big Macs on tiny incomes.

"Bohemia's always been bonkers, of course," Mark continued, "but it's worse now because of the national crack-up. You'd be cracking up too if you were experiencing free market capitalism, the revival of democracy, the sexual revolution, the women's movement, gay liberation, and the AIDS crisis ALL AT ONCE."

I tried to imagine it. It was hard without several large glasses of *pivo*, the sacramental beer of the Valdek faithful, into whose all-night services Mark had initiated me a few evenings ago. My mission that evening (aside from the usual rites one performs in such places) was to deliver a brief talk on AIDS prevention with an urgent invitation to all the flock to attend the opening later that week of an exhibition of safer sex posters Mark and I had put together in a gutted 1920s movie house in the Old Town. My theme, I had decided, would be the joyful mysteries of latex.

"Go easy on them tonight," Mark went on in the dingy landing, handing our jackets in at the coat-check to a Kafkaesque night-creature who sat beetle-browed and bug-eyed beneath a sagging clothesline hung with ancient issues of *Blueboy* and *Honcho*. "Remember: no political sermons. What the boys of Valdek desperately need is a friendly little chat about HIV transmission and how to prevent it."

I trusted his judgement. This was only my first trip to Prague, while Mark, a British "ex-pat" in his early twenties, had been laying tracks down (and tracking down lays) on the Valdek dance floor for over a year now. "My year of living dangerously — with safes, of course," he assured me.

I knew he had suffered for his safety standards. The godless Slovaks he loved to cruise at Valdek were usually bewildered, and always put off, by his quoting chapter and verse to them on the AIDS Apocalypse.

We entered the smoky nimbus of the bar and sat down at a table facing the dance floor at the intersection of Valdek's two main chambers. Mark explained that Valdek had once been a rather seedy but popular Hungarian restaurant frequented by gypsies. I could imagine their unholy curses when the joint was taken over and hallowed by gays.

Even in its present "tastefully appointed guise" — as Mark commended it with gleeful irony, in the style of Charlotte Bartlet's Baedeker — the shrine of St. Valdek (whose historical identity no one seemed to know a thing about) retained something of its original heathen ambience. It was an oddly ecclesiastical space, long and nave-like at first, then veering off into an L-shaped ambulatory, full of gay brothers in pre-clone disco habits reminiscent of the early seventies. Somewhere off in the mystic darkness, through a little doorway, was a sanctuary with another bar in it for erotic prayers and meditations.

Pivo flowed like prevenient grace.

Our beers were not long in coming. Mark downed his in a gulp and was off to find one of his few safer sex converts, a wraith named Tomáš who knew a bit of English and had promised to act as my interpreter. My talk was supposed to happen in an hour — "around midnight," Mark whispered with a parting smile, knowing that I knew that meant anytime the spirit moved Tomáš. Time was a fluidly erotic dimension in Valdek.

Space was a bit easier to pin down. "The manager thinks you should speak right out there on the dance floor," Mark advised me when he returned to our table after a dance or two with Tomáš. The Dance Floor of Desire seemed like an appropriate spot for a "friendly little chat" about Sex and Death, though I could hardly imagine the dancers stepping back with much alacrity to hear a reluctant Canadian academic bringing the Good News about fisting with calving gloves and other safer sex tips. If they erected a statue of me on the Charles Bridge to commemorate my unusual proselytizing mission, it would have to be called "Father James Preaches to the Doubtful Slavs."

Vanity of vanities, saith the Preacher.

In pivo vanitas, rejoineth the Sod.

For a boozy hour I reflected on the difficulties of preaching to the perverted. In my first conversation with Mark I had been amused to learn that the slang word for "gay" in the Prague dialect of Czech was "*teplej*," which literally means "warm." An unbearable lightness overcame me, I recall, at the thought of what a really bad Czech drag queen could do with a lip-sync rendition of the Beach Boys' classic paean to heterosexual bliss. Just how did those northern girls keep their boyfriends "warm" at night?

My levity was short-lived. A dire philosophical thought struck me. What if the gay usage of "*teplej*" dated from the thirties when psychologists with a taste for fascist eugenics had promulgated the pseudo-scientific theory that homosexuals (imagined as always in heat) had higher body temperatures than heterosexuals? A quick glance at a thermometer was all it would have taken to determine someone's sexuality. I tried to suppress the chilling vision of Nazi doctors shipping hundreds of "warm brothers" out of Prague to the pink-triangled ignominy of the death camps. Surely some progress had been made since then.[1]

No doubt the rapid changes in the political climate of the Eastern Bloc since the fall of Brezhnevite Communism have quickened gay community development in the Czech capital. After decades of official hostility to all things homo except homophobia, gay life is really looking up these days — as I was repeatedly told. It's now possible for two men to dance together at a club without fearing psychiatric detention or arrest for espionage. It's now possible to buy good-as-new issues of jerk-off magazines ("look here — only a few pages stuck together!") under the counter at tourist newsstands.

It's even possible to find a club other than Valdek to go to now on a Saturday night: well-heeled opera queens will find it within walking distance of the National Opera, on the Castle side of the river, a few blocks over on Zborovská Street. "America" it's called. Just opened. As its alluring name suggests, it's for American tourists looking for a hologram of gay life back home, complete with pix of Jeff Stryker, ACT UP stickers, old Marilyn Monroe movie posters, Calvins till you drop, and dense clouds of duty-free Eternity.

That's progress in Prague. On the epidemiological front, progress is statistically measured in the country's ludicrously optimistic prognosis for "containing" the spread of AIDS (which is still commonly perceived as a gay plague existing only in the Decadent West) to the usual stigmatized risk groups. After years of officially denying the crisis, the Czech government now "admits" to the WHO record keepers that 25 "abnormal" people have contracted AIDS since cases were first counted in the country: that's a mere increase of 23 cases since 1986. Hardly anything to get heated up about. Only a few warm brothers out in the cold.

According to Jiří Presl, a beleaguered doctor of Mark's acquaintance who had helped to place the AIDS poster exhibition in the Old Town, the Ministry of Health was blithely unconcerned about the transmission of HIV to drug addicts through the sharing of dirty needles. Jiří had recently tried to start a needle-exchange program in

---

[1] In "Warm Brothers," the incendiary sixth chapter of *Strange Loves: A Study in Sexual Abnormalities* (New York: Dodsley, 1933), p. 97, the ultra-homophobic American clinician La Forrest Potter ironically traced the body temperature theory of homo–hetero differentiation to the great German sexologist and gay rights pioneer Magnus Hirschfeld.

the city, but to no avail. The government was now threatening to take him to court for promoting the drug trade.

Despite the cold comfort afforded by the low WHO statistics, the action at the "warm" bars of Prague, I can tell you, was decidedly hot. Whether the Kundera-like zest of the Czech gays I observed at Valdek was mainly due to a sudden release of pent-up erotic energy after the fall of a puritanical communist régime, or to slow demographic pressures heating up the scene in a city with over two million people but only two gay bars, was hard for an outsider to tell.

One thing was clear, though, even to Father James. In the bleakly ironic bugger-all spirit of Kafka's Bohemia, gay capitalist enterprise here was hard at work creating the perfect free market conditions for the rapid transmission of HIV. Teenage hustlers in flashy silk shirts and very tight white jeans were thick on the ground at Valdek, and could be picked up at the Central Train Station nearby, I was told by a comparison-shopper, for the low low price of one hundred crowns for a whole night. Condoms were not a regular part of their wardrobe. So attention gay-mart shoppers: you'd better get in on the action now before the price for sexual tourism steeply rises to Western heights, as it inevitably will.

Welcome to Bangkok on the Moldau.

Mark waved to me from the DJ's booth. It was showtime. Suddenly I was struck by how varied my Bohemian "congregation" was: besides the white-jeaned hustlers there were older professional-looking men in neatly pressed suits; loads of lean mean cologne queens who'd switched allegiance from America; several Market Square pseudo-gypsies with coloured threads plaited in their long greasy hair; here and there a leatherman wiping the *pivo* drops off his vest; a chorus of ruby-lipped teenage girls rumoured to be hustlers' chicks and not lesbians; a couple of Mark's elusive Slovaks; some German tourists; and an assortment of Valdek's more eccentric habitués.

Among these was "the Secretary." That was Mark's affectionate name for a tall spinsterish woman of a certain age, in a wool suit, white blouse, and pearls, who was reputed to haunt Valdek for the sole purpose of luring lost gay lambs back into the straight fold. No one was quite sure whether she was in earnest or in drag.

Catching my name (and nothing else) in an announcement from the DJ's booth, I made my way to the disco pulpit. Madonna had just finished an anthem urging us all to keep keepin' together, keep keepin' together, for ever and ever. Amen, thought I. *Ora pro nobis, o semper virago.*

On cue the perspiring crowd, perhaps grateful for a short breather in the relentless rites, cleared a generous space for me on the dance floor with the irrepressible zeal of ballroom extras in a zany 1930s production number. Tomáš, a dorky smile on his vaguely apostolic face, handed me a mike and stood on the right side of the Father ready to translate my homily on Condom and Gomorrah into the Czech equivalent of gayspeak. Mark hushed the crowd from the sidelines, and I began.

"*Dobrý večer . . .* good evening, ladies and gentlemen! Um, that's about all I can say in Czech, I'm afraid, so bear with me as my friend Tomáš here . . ."

I nervously pointed the mike at him. Scattered applause. He looked doubtful. Doubting Tomáš.

". . . helps me out. Okay, ready? I, um, bring you all greetings from the University of Western Ontario, and um, the HALO Club."

It seemed an absurdly formal introduction under the circumstances. I'm sure I sounded like a befuddled papal legate whom some malicious queen in the Vatican had sent to the wrong address with the wrong inspirational speech. Never before have the coupling of Western and the HALO Club in the same breath produced more puzzled looks in a mature audience.

"That's H-A-L-O: the Homophile Association of London Ontario," I desperately explained, "where I'm occasionally to be found on a Saturday night. HALO's kind of like Valdek . . ." (Only cleaner, I caught myself thinking in a spasm of anal-retentive waspiness.)

"Only closer to Toronto," I loosened up. "And with weaker beer."

No response to my *captatio benevolentiae*, save for a few coughs and bewildered grimaces. The flock was being polite. Grabbing the mike before I could go any further, Tomáš proceeded to rattle off a much longer and more entertaining introduction than my own — which could only have gained in translation. Everyone chuckled at his stiff imitation of my clerical formality and broke into a laugh when he blanked out on the Czech for "halo" and had to resort to pantomimic gestures: fingers circling over his head followed by angelic winging of his arms. Who could blame the Valdek faithful for concluding that I belonged to some charismatic sect of holy fools crying in the desert of Western Decadence?

With the Iron Curtain down, it was time to put up the Latex Sheath. Forever and ever, world without AIDS, amen. So the Gay Spirit moved me to proclaim, but something told me that I might as well have been selling the Iron Condom here for all my words were worth. Clearly it was going to be difficult pitching Western AIDS Awareness across the language barriers of Eastern Europe: the confusion of tongues had buggered all.

Sensing my crisis of faith, Mark tossed me a condom as a visual aid. It was like one of those miraculous communion wafers in the Golden Legend that could clear the mind and harden the . . . whatever. Somehow it got me (and Tomáš) through the basic facts of HIV transmission as well as some of the finer points of safer sexegesis. We were an unlikely hit as a team: me, the straight man (for a change); him, the gay wisecracker. Short of thrilling the multitude with a live demonstration of advanced rubber foreplay in the highly evolved Deutsche AIDS-Hilfe style, our improvised teamwork succeeded pretty well in getting the main message across to the doubters and dancers: that condoms were something every cool "*teplej*" should warm to.

On that hopeful note I should have ended my homo homily, announced the dates of my poster display, and quit the Faereopagus. But something possessed me — the radical demon of the ACT UP Reformation, I guess — to go on with the show, to drag my poor interpreter into the martyr's arena of cultural activism. Ignoring Mark's sage advice about restraining my activist zeal, I launched into a reckless jeremiad on the politics of representation.

"In the Gloom-and-Doom campaigns of totalitarian government health agencies, as I'm sure you're well aware, condoms are either censored off the agenda or represented as the Devil's latest fashion crime. No sex is the only safe sex in their books. Punitive chastity is the order of the day. Don't believe the pharisees who preach Family Values. Don't, whatever you do, repent your gayness: that won't save you from the World, the Flesh, or the Virus."

I was on a roll. Tomáš looked bewildered. There was no way he could keep up with me, and no familiar Czech for what I was saying.

"So much for the Right. Now for the Centre: what do so-called liberal democrats preach in their AIDS advertisements? Self-survivalism, defence of the bourgeois good life, protection of the general public from viral attack. That means fortifying all straight white middle-class taxpayers with the consoling idea that AIDS somehow 'belongs' out there, beyond the pale, with the 'risk-groups' maliciously identified with the Virus. And that's why liberal public health officials represent condoms as shields for their precious dicks, or as coats of mail for their entire bodies, or even as long cylindrical bombs to be lobbed at their sexually anarchic enemies. That's us. They might as well be stoning us for adultery and promiscuity outside the City of Man."

"Bolshy!" someone yelled.

I heard "*Bolshoi*" — which I knew meant "great" in Russian. Was this some balletomaniacal way of shouting "Amen, Brother"?

Bewildered looks all round: confusion of tongues.

Zeal spurred me on.

"Now, in the agitprop produced by radical activist groups like ACT UP in New York City and OUT-Rage in London England, the lowly condom takes on a very different set of meanings. It becomes a symbol of gay liberation from the shackles of sanctified monogamy; a badge of defiant allegiance to the erotic counterculture of the prelapsarian seventies; a magic talisman to enhance the sovereign joys of promiscuity; a tiny banner of protest raised against the massive indifference of the establishment and the huge profits of the drug czars . . ."

"Bolshy!" rang out again.

Was Father James being heckled?

"Bolshy, bolshy rubbish!"

I peered at the Doubtful Slavs. Half the flock were idly flicking cigarette ashes onto the floor. The smoke and confusion slowly settling in Valdek seemed a world away from the shadows and fog of Dvořák's Romantic Prague.

"Cut the Bolshy crap!"

Some unromantic soul among them, some true believer in the Free Market credo, was none too pleased with my act-uppity left-wing heresies — which must have sounded hopelessly retro to anyone who had lived through the past few decades of Czech history.

Earlier that week, strolling through the maze of the Josefov, I had come across an old clock on the Jewish Town Hall with gilded hands that ran anti-clockwise: a weird Kafkaesque sight if ever there was one. I thought of it now, reminding myself that a retrograde dial wouldn't look so weird to someone used to reading Hebrew from right to left. The radicals of the AIDS activist movement, it struck me, also read time on a kind of retrograde dial through eyes painfully sharpened by Jewish memory. Drawing relentlessly retrospective parallels between the epidemic and the Holocaust, they resist the appalling silence that equals death in defiant protestations of the need

Clock Tower of the Jewish Town Hall: Židovská radnice, Prague

for counterdiscursive militancy. How unlike the resignation to silence and death preached every hour on the hour by the great Catholic clock in Prague's Old Town Square! Christians gazing at its apocalyptic mechanism would see time running out in an hourglass turned by Death, and recall that the end was drawing nigh when the whole chiming World would be silent.

Which clock was timing my night at Valdek? Like the silence-breaking gay militants of ACT UP, I had dutifully washed my soul in the blood of Foucault; yet, in all the confusion at Valdek, at the vanishing point on the Eastern European horizon of AIDS Awareness, I couldn't help wondering whether the Read-My-Lips missionaries were not dwelling somewhere over the rainbow in Cloud-Foucault-Land. Were we ready to make the Great Break with the past merely because we considered ourselves saved from the ideological corruptions of the present? Was our political future actually running counterclockwise to the revolutionary changes in the New Europe? Could AIDS activism ever work HERE in a million years?

I was due back on earth. Mark was waving at me and pointing at his watch, which was evidently running clockwise. I thanked Tomáš, plugged my exhibition, bowed to uncertain applause from the flock, and faded back to my table for a contemplative immersion in *pivo*.

"Look out," warned Mark. "Your heckler's still on the warpath."

"Who is he?" I gulped, observing the ominous approach of a fat bearded bear with a gold neckchain.

"He's one of the pimps who works out of Valdek," Mark explained in a whisper, "a total sleaze-bag, of course, always snogging with his boys in the back room. But an interesting social type. Czech by birth, I'm told, but he got out in '69. Went to Australia to do God knows what, and now he's back in Prague living it up on the wages of sin."

He did not introduce himself — or the punky kid he was tugging with him under one arm — when he confronted us at our table near the sanctuary door. Facing reality, I knew I was not in for a Platonic dialogue.

"Dickhead," he growled, "Wot's the bloody idea pitchin' safes to the Cheskies?"

Aussie accents, like the devilish dialects in Dante's *Inferno*, were divinely ordained for debunking. They have always daunted me, and the pimp's patois (which sounded like Melbourne Underworld with a dash of Peter Lorre) did little to put me at ease. He went on with his catechism, expecting no response from me.

"Who do you think can afford condoms here even if they wanted to save their skins? Who the hell gave you the right to tell us what to do?"

"The Management," interjected Mark. "They want to keep their customers alive. It's good for business."

"You make me laugh, mate." Which he proceeded to do, in a chundering sort of way.

"Bugger off," said Mark.

"Not till I've told yer Bolshy friend here a thing or two. Ha! Does he think condoms would improve business down at the train station? Ask any of my boys — ask Lukáš here."

Lukáš sheepishly looked up. He didn't understand a word.

"Ha! Germans, Austrians, Hungarians, Poles, Americans — they all come here on business, want a good fuck, cheap. Nobody wants to suck rubber. Not even Lukáš's girlfriend! Eh, Lukáš?"

The Doubtful Slav said nothing.

"What you gotta realize about the Cheskies, mate," insisted Lukáš's capitalist mentor, oddly echoing Mark's earlier animadversions to me on the threshold of Valdek, "is that they're all livin' in dreamtime, as the Abos would say. Especially the homos here."

"Why's that?'" I asked defensively, half inclined to drain my glass of Pilsner Urquell and flee. Sinister troglodytes have this effect on me — especially when they're about to launch into a beery harangue after midnight in a gay bar in a galaxy far, far away.

"You'd be stunned yerself," he was quick to rejoin, "like everyone here, if yer country was splitting up for nothing."

"It probably is. Have you heard of Quebec?"

"Poor sods," he went on, ignoring my vague historical analogy. "They don't know what's hit 'em. First, it was bloody Perestroika . . ." which he pronounced "Perry Stryker" as if Gorbachev had sprung one of Jeff's lesser known porn brothers on the Boys of the Eastern Bloc.

I never found out what calamitous events succeeded the advent of Perry Stryker, for just at that moment our dialogue was cut off by a booming announcement in Czech from the DJ. For a few minutes I couldn't make out what was happening from my side of the language barrier. It was my turn to be confused. The dance floor was being cleared again, I noticed, and the flock was reconvening around its perimeter with a magnetic enthusiasm that drew the pimp and his stud-puppet into the thick of the dreamtimers.

* * *

"You've got to see this," Mark advised, ever the Virgil to my reluctant Dante.

We made our way into the crowd and were soon jammed up against the strata of sweaty bodies before us by the pressure of smoky bodies behind pouring out of the sanctuary. Directly in front of me was the puzzling shade of the Secretary, an incongruous silhouette against the disco glow of the club; for a moment I was tempted to grope her and lay to rest the secret of her identity. But some things, like the Trinity, are better left as mysteries.

A reverent silence fell upon us as the grinding rock anthems ceased and the garish red and green of the disco lights faded to a warm wash of lavender across the floor. Absurdly, as if a pastoral idyll were about to begin, the music started up again — only now it was a soft crescendo of flutes and violins accompanied (I could hardly believe my ears) by recorded birdsong. Surely the Second Coming was at hand, or at least the Golden Age when Jeff and Perry Stryker would return as lusty goatherds innocent of HIV.

I wasn't half wrong. Into the melodious clearing stepped a shirtless and beltless youth, all dimples and perky pecs, his feet unshod, a Chesky Corydon. Slowly he unrolled a little green mat he was carrying and lay down upon it, face to the floor, exposing a strategic rip in the seat of his jeans. (They were hustler-white, of course. Ripping them, given the price of jeans in Prague, must have been a painful sacrifice to his professional gods.) A few moments later he was joined on the floor by a somewhat older swain, similarly dressed, and then, much to my surprise, by a woman, destined to play the nymph in this idyll of desire. She looked like a blonde version of Paulina Porizkova minus the Revlon lipstick and the Vogue wardrobe. In fact, minus any wardrobe. The invisible birds twittered on. The flutes and violins sounded like early Dvořák.

I don't know whether it was a hot flash of insight or a cool shower of irony that came over me at this point, but something sudden, certain, and direly needed, like an apocalyptic shock treatment, brought me to my senses and revealed to me my ludicrous position in the Valdek Universe. In preaching to the perverted, Father James had verily (if unwittingly) served as the opening act for a live sex show.

How would I ever put this on my CV?

Damn the managers of the bar, I laughed to myself, for not letting me in on the demonic joke until it was too late to escape its implications. Multiple ironies crowded in on my soul like the multiple bodies pressing me forward orgiastically to get a better glimpse of the show. Though the two male performers occasionally fondled each other's arms or thighs, their erotic attention was resolutely focused on the Bohemian nymph writhing langorously between them.

Why, in heaven's name, were they performing a STRAIGHT sex act in a gay cruising bar? Had some malicious queen given them the wrong address too? If such a scene had been enacted at the HALO club back home or at any gay bar in North America, it would certainly have required a running commentary in Old High Camp by a bitchy drag queen, and would probably have elicited satiric hoots and catcalls from the audience along the lines of "So, that's how it's done!" and "Show us how babies are made, Mummie and Daddie!"

But the Valdek faithful looked on in reverent silence, transfixed by the mystic horror of Heterosexual Intercourse, as if it were the Primal Scene. Not the Primal Scene of Freudian Family Romance, mind you, but its piously homophobic counterpart in the Bible of Family Values. Played out before their eyes was a blatantly capitalist reinvention of the Myth of the Fortunate Fall: it only took one daughter of Eve (for a price) to "convert" two sons of Adam from guilty gays into innocent straights. Here, ironically, was the Secretary's poor benighted dream come true.

Directly in front of me stood two West German leathermen who, alone in the crowd, were shaking their heads and muttering disparaging remarks under their breath. "*Scheise*," one of them snorted back in my direction, "Look at that, Herr Professor Kondom! After your talk, they don't even practise zafer zex. In Hamburg they'd be laughed out of the bar — or thrown out on their asses — for this. Why don't you throw them a preservative?"

I felt my hip-pocket for one, but realized, with a sinking feeling, that I had left that demo safe of Mark's — along with my naive faith in the righteousness and efficacy of AIDS activism — back at my table near the sanctuary.

The day after my night at Valdek I found myself face to face with the Archbishop of Canterbury. No kidding. Providence must have brought us together as fellow missionaries to the Slavs.

One of the unexpected yet surely providential delights of coming out as a "warm brother" is that you're endlessly treated to (and never shocked by) the strangest juxtapositions of social experiences, particularly when the fluid little strata of the gay underground heave up suddenly against the great tectonic plates of the Straight

World. Institutional Christianity being one of the cooler and less flexible of these plates, I'm rarely surprised by all the seismic activity — the sexual shocks and theological aftershocks, the political tremors, legal crackdowns, psychological crack-ups, and ecclesiastical schisms — recorded daily all along the well-charted fault lines between Homosexuality and the Church Militant Here on Earth.

It just so happened that the Most Reverend George Carey, former Bishop of Bath and Wells, now Primate of All England, was attending a meeting of the Council of European Churches in Prague that week, and at the request of the chaplain to the city's small but loyal British congregation, had agreed to preside at Sunday Evensong in their prettily restored medieval chapel near Náměstí Republiky.

Now Mark often went to services there, being an ardent Anglican for all his wayward ways. Or maybe it was because of them. In any event, he was on such familiar terms with Father Hilary, the chaplain, that no one thought it at all queer for Hilary to make an announcement about our AIDS exhibition at the end of the service that Sunday. When Mark woke me up in the early afternoon with a call to devotions after the depravities of Valdek, how could I refuse? Though "lapsed" hardly begins to describe my remote historical relationship with the Church of England, I was once confirmed in its "faith and fear," and can never resist a celebrity communicant.

At least not for long: I did groggily complain that a Valdek hangover was not the best mental preparation for an audience with the Archibishop of Canterbury. Though a media profile of Carey I once read described him in oddly idyllic terms as "broad-shouldered, rosy-cheeked, and usually genial, if not downright jolly, in manner," I knew his gritty political reputation as a very low-church evangelical who was dead set against the ordination of uncelibate gay men. In short, no friend of Father James. Why should I get out of bed to meet my avowed doctrinal adversary, the Fount of Theological Wisdom from which had flowed the foully homophobic arguments against the ordination of gays in the trial of Reverend Jim Ferry?[2]

---

[2]In February 1992 the Reverend Jim Ferry, of Unionville, Ontario, went on trial before an Anglican ecclesiastical tribunal known as "Bishop's Court." After a small group of disgruntled parishioners outed him as a "practising homosexual," he was charged with wilful disobedience and disrespectful conduct towards his bishop. In March 1992 he was found guilty, and Terence Finlay, the Bishop of Toronto, removed him from his pastoral charge and revoked his licence to preach. For a full account of his mistreatment, which reads like a Kafkaesque rewrite of a Trollope novel, see James Ferry, *In the Courts of the Lord* (Toronto: Key Porter Books, 1993).

"There'll be a slew of cute Czech pastors concelebrating with Carey," Mark predicted, "and a high tea at the chaplaincy afterwards."

I put my theological doubts aside.

Whether it was the spirit of ecumenical brotherhood or mere curiosity that possessed me to take the Body and Blood of our Dear Lord Jesus Christ from the Archbishop's own hands that afternoon I'll never know, but the upshot of it was an unexpected opportunity to compare our rather different proselytizing missions and the impact of our respective sermons on those who had ears to hear.

As I was recovering from the shock of taking Communion after years of resolute apostasy, a mauve-haired lady sitting in the pew in front of me turned round and whispered enthusiastically: "Did you know that the Archbishop is a charismatic, my dear? They tell me he's been known to speak in tongues!"

I never speak in tongues, though tonguing in another sense has always had a charismatic effect on me. Jesu, Joy of Man's Desiring. "Maybe he'll give us a demonstration," I ventured.

"I hope so," she confided. "I've come all the way from Vienna just to see it happen!"

"More exciting than watching the Infant of Prague model his new fall wardrobe," Mark observed. "I hear it's royal blue satin with silver accessories. I prefer the Archbishop's purple myself."

"Indeed," the lady said, somewhat bewildered.

Unfortunately the Archbishop did not favour us with a refreshing hour of pentecostal tonguing after Communion, preferring to exercise that particular gift of the Spirit (I gathered) on more private occasions. He did deliver a brief sermon, however, so the lady didn't return to Vienna totally disappointed.

"My text today," Carey began in an excellent deep voice, surprisingly graced with traces of a Cockney accent, "is taken from Paul's valedictory address to the elders of Ephesus before his departure to Jerusalem. Acts, chapter 20, verse 28: 'Take heed therefore unto yourselves, and to all the flock.'" He said the verse very slowly, placing particular emphasis on the words "heed" and "all."

Though his mission was clearly to encourage a revival of evangelical Christianity in Eastern Europe after the fall of the godless Communist Empire, his encouragements had to be couched in cautious terms in view of the social and political instability of the newly independent Slavic states. Hence the proselytizing argument of his sermon (Win Back the Doubtful Slavs to Christ) recalled the homilies of the empire-rebuilding bishops during the conversion of the Barbarian Kingdoms in the Dark Ages: prophetic messages of renewal flowed from clever typological misreadings of the Acts of the Apostles. Carey's typological explication of Paul's warning to the Ephesians related directly to the perilous position of the Church in contemporary Czech society. Ephesus signified Prague; the Ephesian flock, the tiny isolated British congregation; the Ephesian elders, Father Hilary and his fellow clerics; and the outbound Paul, the Archbishop himself, who was leaving next morning for the Holy City of Canterbury.

Though there wasn't much room in this neat series of parallels for the likes of me or the mauve-haired lady from Vienna — we weren't exactly members of the flock and certainly didn't qualify as elders — the thrust of the sermon was generously diplomatic and inclusionary. The Anglican elders were to take heed for themselves not only by shepherding British ex-pats towards the comforts of Tory Heaven but also by nurturing the tender plants of Democracy and Christianity on Czech soil. Urging us to pray for the politically martyred and now physically ruined Dubček, whose spine had been broken a few days earlier in a terrible car accident, Carey contrasted the hopelessness and disillusionment of the Czechs after the Prague Spring (subliminally symbolized by their former leader's paralysed body) with the buoyantly dynamic mood of the people now. Though it was September outside the chapel, inside the congregation was basking in what was beginning to feel like the Canterbury Spring. The Old Czechoslovak Socialist Republic had been Gehenna itself, a land of forgetfulness, a wintry desert. Now, praise God, the emergent Czech Republic was feeling the warm light of the West.

The thought of "warm" light took me back to the Valdek dance floor with its flaming ironies. I had certainly taken heed of myself last night, but had Mark and I really taken heed of our flock? What would become of Tomáš, and Lukáš, and the Secretary, and all the others?

At the tea following the service, I watched the Archbishop working the crowds in his usually genial, if not downright jolly, manner. When he reached me, I introduced myself as the curator of that Canadian AIDS exhibition that Father Hilary in a racy tone had advertised at the end of the service as "sure to be interesting since no one under age fifteen would be allowed in!"

One of his daughters, he told me, was taking a specialist course in HIV education and prevention, and by the way, did I happen to know his wife's sister who lived in Kitchener, Ontario?

No, I hadn't had the pleasure. His next question, which didn't really come out of the blue, floored me nevertheless with its perfect aim:

"And what are YOUR views on homosexuality?"

Fairly pronounced, I admitted, suspecting that his were too. Father James could not resist the temptation of intellectual intercourse with so eminent an authority on the woes of Sodom: so I promptly "outed" myself and popped a tiny spinach quiche into my mouth to prove my identity beyond a shadow of a doubt.

To my surprise, his views on homosexuality were not as rigid as I would have expected from an evangelist for the Enemy Establishment. Before coming to Prague, he explained, he had had to chair an acrimonious meeting between conservative and radical clergy on the perennially controversial issue of gay ordination.

"Frankly, I'm bewildered!" he blurted out, scrunching up his broad shoulders and scratching one of his rosy cheeks. I almost invited him to Valdek that evening to meet some other bewildered souls. Catching my eye, and realizing the enormous implications of his potentially schismatic confession for those poor sods who worry about the eschatology of the closet, he swiftly "inned" himself with the inevitable media-weary demand: "But don't quote me on that!"

I wouldn't dream of it, I assured him.

V

THE BODY OF DESIRE

Susan Swan is an internationally acclaimed author whose fiction has been published in Canada, the U.S., the U.K., Germany, Italy, and Holland. *The Wives of Bath*, a gothic tale about a murder in a girls' boarding school, was a finalist for Ontario's Trillium prize and the U.K.'s Guardian Fiction Award. She is a professor of Humanities at York University and a regular contributor to TVO's book show, "Imprint."

A Poem to My Body in Five Instalments

Susan Swan

I. Graven Image

my eyes are in love
with my face
they seek
its image in every surface
and are wise to the possibilities
of aluminum alloys and plastic

face-face is seen in the mirror first
and tells the body
we're home

once trapped my face
in a chrome napkin
holder and couldn't
leave it

glamorous face
the place I
know best

stalked by
my eyes
all across town

II. Ye Olde Beane

my skull & its
flycatcher hair
a yellow motel
advertising asylum
at half-price

New Ideas Welcome!
at Ye Olde Beane

head-top, airport for mosquitos
& other aliens who drill
my crown, dead-centre
in the looking glass
you are a figment
for sore eyes

III. True Confessions of the Female Organs

my lips the little labial liars
blow down wet kisses
before they mouth
TRUE CONFESSIONS OF THE FEMALE ORGANS
Forgive Me for being your Cunt:
A Torso in Turmoil!

O bebop body — my split-level sweetheart!
How can I make IT beautiful?
How can I romance the most important
hole in my life?
THE CAVITY THAT MAKES ME LOVEABLE

Is it a case
of functionalism
versus aesthetics?

his cock
is his secret heartthrob
but is my puss
pretty?

IV. MORE IDOL TALK

This is so much idol talk
The Real Snow White Killer
my face is tops
and keeps
the body down
her domestic grind
has made her blind
but she still dreams of clouds
and screams for air
doesn't anybody
know she's there

if my face
lived
between my legs
so I wore my genitals
on my head
I could make
my lips croon a honeymoon
tune a torch song
for the vulva

now the face tells me
my tree frog toes
have run off to the circus
my backside wanders
without the barest mention

& why do my legs dash
up and down
like a goon squad a pair
of civic giants
with twin moronic
faces

I know my sad-sack thighs
too well to flatter their
sick vision

breasts like children
who didn't meet parental
expectations — who else
can dilly-dally with the belly
where air is an uphill skier
cutting crisp herringbone tracks
or a whooosh of lake waves
rattling grains of skin
into fabulous wrinkles

neck & arms
cast-offs
from my torso
the face plays any game
it wants but says it's
bottom's up
for the rest of you

the upper me
has the lower

half
by the tail

even my stomach maintaining
a firm pressure against my belt
envies the face polished twice
a day because it's the body's
graven image

V. Dear Body

you with a life of your own
trailing your silky water weight
across the universe
without my orders

you & I, my dear, are stuck —
in a certain generation
those who come after
when they look back
from inside their nifty
mutated forms
morphed to please
every owner

these happy freaks
will pity us

and so dear body — until the future washes us
smooth and pure the way
the sea washes danger
out of glass, I
enclose here
heaps of topsy-turvy love
& salute you
in all your fractured
loveliness

Descant *was the first literary publisher to take an interest in my fiction. It published an excerpt from my first novel,* The Biggest Modern Woman of the World, *and many of my early performance pieces and stories. Its support came at a crucial time.* A Poem to My Body *was composed several years ago, after I spent the night in a Toronto dance studio. I set the evening up as an assignment — a date with my body. The studio had mirrors on its four walls. The performance and poem are my entry into the traditional debate on the mind-body split.*

W. P. KINSELLA is the author of several short story collections, including *The Fencepost Chronicles*, *The Miss Hobbema Pageant*, *Brother Frank's Gospel Hour* and *The Dixon Cornbelt League*. His novels include *The Winter Helen Dropped By*, *Box Socials*, *The Iowa Baseball Confederacy* and *Shoeless Joe*, which won the prestigious Houghton Mifflin Literary Fellowship Award, the Books in Canada First Novel Award and was made into the movie "Field of Dreams". Kinsella was born in Edmonton, Alberta and makes his home in Western Canada and California.

MURDEROUS WAYS

W. P. KINSELLA

"I got one shot off at the target, then Rand called my name, loud and urgent. 'Mariel,' he called. I whirled around and the gun went off. He had been right behind me. There he was falling back, his chest opening before my eyes.

"What did he want? I guess I'll never know. I couldn't find anything amiss, but I knew Rand well enough, long enough, to recognize in his voice, not terror but genuine alarm."

That's what I'll tell them, the police. Oh, they'll give me a hard time. They'll be suspicious, but sympathetic, at first. There's no phone at the shooting range. I'll have to drive Rand's truck out three miles to a gas station and phone 9-1-1. Hard time won't be the words for it, once they snoop around and find out about our relationship, once they know who Rand is.

But no matter what they think, what they suspect, they'll have to have evidence, witnesses. There will be no witnesses, only Rand and I know what went on between us. It was an accident. I killed my lover. The police may even choose to keep our relationship quiet after they recognize Rand. I'll just be a young divorcée who Rand, in all his kindness and public spirit, was teaching to shoot because I needed protection.

My ex had threatened my life, had stalked me for years, left obscene notes in my mailbox, threatening messages on my answering machine. This is true. I have the tapes, the notes, a restraining order.

Why would I want to do harm to someone I love. Even if our love was illicit. What a strange, archaic word. Like mistress. No one is a mistress any more. Though I considered myself Rand's mistress. I used the word in front of him all the time.

Three weeks ago I woke with a shudder in the middle of the night, moonlight blue across my lonely bed, one of those three a.m., end of the world, blood-surging wake-ups.

I'm going to kill my lover, I thought. At the same instant I knew how and where I was going to do it. The shooting range. My red-bearded lover. I thrill at burying my face in his beard, I love it when my own scent is there, his beard damp from our lovemaking. Rand is six foot four inches. I'm five-foot-nothing. He jokes he could carry me in his pocket. My hair is crow-wing black; I can tuck the ends of it in the back pockets of my jeans. I know how sexy I look in tight jeans. I know how sexy Rand thinks I look in tight jeans. Sometimes when we're alone, at the shooting range or in the woods, I'll kneel on the damp grass and love him with my mouth. Afterward, he likes to stare at the stains on my jeans. "They are reminders," he says.

Other times, after we've been shooting, we make love in Rand's truck, the heater on, the windows fogged, the leather seat cold on my back — the smell of grease, gasoline. Rand's belt buckle clanging against something.

I'm going to kill Rand.

I've had one of those revelations that anyone who wasn't blinded by love, by lust, by eternal hope, would have recognized years ago. The revelation is so trite I hesitate to repeat it. Rand, though he may love me — he has to love me, I couldn't have given him five years of my life if I didn't think he loved me — is never going to leave his family.

I wouldn't be planning to live on, if I didn't think he loved me. If I didn't think he loved me, I'd be careless. I'd pick up his gun, the .44, from the shelf at the firing range. I'd fire it into his chest, watch the surprise in his dying eyes, then place the cold barrel against the centre of my own chest, against my heart.

Rand is famous. Though people here in Wyoming either don't know about his fame, or don't care. Rand Sutherland is an outsider here in Wyoming. His ranch is between Glenrock and Douglas, off the beaten track, the house with the blue-tiled roof not visible from the highway. His land is fenced with tightly strung rows of barbed wire, or "bob wire" as the locals call it. The gate to his ranch is electrically controlled, the cattle guard rumbles omniously whenever a vehicle crosses it. I've only been to Rand's ranch twice, both times when his family was away, once to Disneyland, another time when his wife's father died in Pennsylvania. My whole little basement-less house, on one of the back streets of Glenrock, would fit in Rand's bedroom. We made love in his bedroom all afternoon — I couldn't stay overnight because the ranch foreman and his family live only a few hundred yards away.

Rand engages in the most unlikely of occupations. My huge, red-bearded lover, who prefers riding a horse to driving, who loves guns, stringing fence wire, branding cattle, writes a syndicated column on food and wine, which appears weekly in about seventy newspapers all across North America. The column appears under the byline Sebastian T. Rand.

"Sebastian sounds all English, uppercrust and snooty. I was still Randy Sutherland when I sent out samples of my column. I'm completely self-taught. My degree is in political science from Rutgers. I'm an Easterner, through and through. One of the things I ask my editor at the syndicate is to read each column to be certain I haven't let any Wyoming creep into my language."

I met Rand six years ago. My ex contracted to do the haying on Rand's ranch. I fed the men, kept them supplied with water, occasionally drove the truck hauling bales. Rand hopped in the cab with me one afternoon.

"I need a little of that air-conditioning," he said. He was bare to the waist. There were clover seeds in his chest hair. Each of his hands would make three of mine. I inhaled involuntarily. The odours of sweat, leather, clover were overpowering. My impulse was to stop the truck and throw myself into his arms.

"Actually, I don't care diddly about the air-conditioning," he said, picking up one of the water bottles from the floor of the cab and taking a long drink. "I don't think I've ever seen a woman with such beautiful hair. I wanted to see you close up."

"Are you impressed?" I asked. I pulled the truck to the edge of the field, into the shade of a few aspen that drooped over the fence.

"Better believe it," he said. He smiled. His front teeth were white and square, his grey eyes cool and friendly.

"I'm Mariel," I said.

It was two years ago that we began shooting. It was a way for us to be alone. Rand's wife was from the East and did not like guns. My daddy says I started shooting while I was still in my playpen. Rand, in another life, once trained as a police officer. I've never been a target shooter. He teaches me gun handling, safety, by what he calls police methods.

Rand pulls the truck into the empty parking lot of the firing range. Gravel cracks ominously under the tires. The October sun is gold and red like the leaves still clinging to the white-stalked birch that shade the tiny trailer that serves as a clubhouse.

All the way out here the words "A good day for dying" keep threading through my mind, piercing like tines of sunlight. Was it Hemingway who said that? It must have been.

I can smell the leather of Rand's vest. I light a cigarette, inhale deeply. Rand glances across at me. I've been sitting against the passenger door, punishing him, letting him see how sullen I am. In happier times, I'd be crowded against him, our hands entwined. I'd have my face against his chest, breathing in his odours, my hand between his legs, feeling the hardness of him beneath the denim. The corners of Rand's eyes crinkle as a smile begins.

A good day for dying.

We get out of the truck. There is a faint smell of burning leaves, of sunshine, of winter hiding just beyond the mountains. I inhale again. There is something so thrilling about smoking a cigarette in the crisp outdoors.

Rand leans over and unlocks the sheet-metal trunk that is welded into the box of the pick-up. I stand back a few paces, cigarette in my left hand, right hooked in the watch pocket of my Levi's. With the toe of my right boot, I toy with fragments of crushed rock. The trunk has three locks, for it is filled with Rand's guns. I wait for him to pull out the .22 pistol, extend it my way, handle first.

I'm preparing my argument. I am going to insist on using a heavier gun today.

Pick a fight if I have to. I remember the weight of the .44, the rush of the discharge, the thrilling tingle up my arms. A good day for dying.

"You've been shooting pretty well the last couple of weeks," Rand says, holding the lid of the trunk open, staring inside, speaking over his shoulder in my direction.

A good day for dying.

"I think you should shoot something larger today. You've earned it. Climb up here and take your choice."

I draw heavily on my cigarette. Rand wants me to quit smoking, but not really. He thinks it is really sexy. He kisses me like I have diamonds hid in my mouth. I toss the cigarette onto the gravel, rub it under my boot. My heart is melting, my insides aquiver. I feel such a sense of tenderness towards Rand. I place my hands on the tailgate of the truck, vault into the box. My murderous ways waft off like the smoke I have just exhaled. I reach into the trunk for the heaviest gun.

CHICK RICE

EVELYN LAU was born in 1971. She is the author of *Runaway: Diary of a Street Kid* (HarperCollins, 1989), *Fresh Girls and Other Stories* (HarperCollins, 1993), and three poetry collections. Her first novel, *Other Women*, will be published by Random House in Fall 1995.

First Sight, A Love Story

Evelyn Lau

Jodie is standing at the balcony railing, away from the party. When she turns to look inside the apartment, the layers of her chiffon dress blow around her body, as if she is at the end of a tunnel or before a door that opens into space.

When she turns, she sees a man across the room. He has a handsome face, a wedding band around his finger. They look at each other. Only for a moment, about as long as it takes to tear a small rent in a piece of fabric. Then Jodie walks towards the man. She walks through the open french doors, past the leather couches and the urn full of dried flowers attached to wire stems. Each step elongates the tear. The knowledge that she cannot retrace her steps cuts through her like a physical pain. She cannot go back to the moment before she saw him, when she was looking out on black water lapping the beach. *Too late*, her high-heeled shoes seem to tap, *too late, too late*. In this way, in this rhythm, she arrives in front of him.

The man glances at Jodie's breasts, signifying his interest. She feels his glance graze her skin and she understands his capacity for betraying the woman he first loved. It is then she shakes his hand, says her name.

He opens the hotel room door and she slips inside like a fish between two waves, it's so easy, how he opens his arms then and hugs her as if she were a friend. The door pulls shut behind them and the hallway vanishes. Its mirrors, its antique end tables, its Oriental vases full of wildly curling exotic flowers and grasses. In the sitting room she slips to her knees and takes his naked feet in her hands. He lifts her onto the couch beside him; he lifts her from the floor.

He opens his hand to cup her breast, kisses her with his tongue, his teeth. It is not sex, he has not yet betrayed anyone. If his wife were to ask, he could stare at her and say, *What are you talking about. I have not been having an affair.* He squeezes Jodie's breast as if only to test his grip. She undresses him, covers his genitals with her right hand. He takes her other hand then and holds it fast, against his hip, and winds his fingers through hers. She kneels once more and approaches him. His body is the brightest thing in the room. His body seems to rise even as she anchors him with her mouth.

He holds his breath as if by doing so he can maintain his precarious balance on the boundary between fidelity and betrayal. Minutes pass. The man stands with his legs apart, his breath held, and then he thinks of his wife. If she were to walk down the hallway in her beige leather pumps, if she were to stand in the doorway now. Would her mouth open in pain, as if she were being whipped? Would the sunlight rebounding from the office windows across the street flash for an instant on the diamond on her finger, the circle of gold? Her hands would relax in shock, and he would never forget the widening of her eyes.

The man lets out his breath and says, "Stop."

Jodie lets him go, and puts her cheek against his thigh which smells and feels like a marble surface in indirect sunlight. She sits back on her heels until he raises her and they embrace with bits of clothing caught between them, the man rocking the woman who cries in his arms.

Months pass. A year. He lays her upon the floor, kisses her belly, puts his fingers inside her. Once he knelt before her body and dug his thumb into the flesh of her right breast until a yellow bruise spread beneath the pressure.

There are whole nights where she lies with her mouth pressed against his shoulder.

These nights are rare and when they happen she does not let herself sleep, so she will not lose time with him.

When he goes home to his wife, Jodie does not leave her bare white apartment. She runs her fingers along the bedspread, sits in the chair where he sat, sits with her hands in her lap, drowns in the thought of him.

He calls to say goodbye; he is going on vacation with his wife.

"I think I've cut myself," Jodie says.

She crouches in a corner of her bedroom and waits for him, as he waited for her in a dozen hotel rooms, his feet naked on the floor.

"I can't be responsible for this," he says when he sees her.

He grabs her hands and holds them up so that the blood runs back down the insides of her arms.

"I didn't do this to you," he says, "you did this to yourself."

He is wearing a costly suit that drapes his body loosely as curtains. She turns her wrists outwards and wipes them on this suit as if it is a towel or perhaps a mirror upon which she needs to leave an urgent message. She sobs when the wool fibres catch upon the cuts in her arms; it hurts in a way that clears the haze in front of her eyes, reminding her of another kind of pain, the one she was trying to draw out of her body with the pointed razor.

Jodie turns from the railing on the balcony and spreads her arms out on either side of her body. Her red chiffon sleeves blow around her wrists. The night air smells of cologne, perfume, the dark ocean. When she sees the man she walks inside the apartment, where music is playing and bodies are mingling. Along the way she recognizes her host, who is wearing a black shirt and a knit tie; he detaches himself from a group of people near the door.

"Are you having a good time," he mouths at her.

She nods, smiles, keeps walking towards her destiny. She walks right up to the man standing next to a glass-and-metal bookcase, who staggers back as his suit is streaked copper by the wet arms of this woman he has never met before.

He holds her crossed wrists in his hands the way she once held his naked feet in hers, and pushes them underneath the tap, water splashing salmon-coloured against the porcelain basin in the bathroom. When she looks up, she sees their faces reflected side by side in the bathroom mirror. Without the pain, the panic, they might be the reflections of a husband and wife standing next to each other on a weekday morning, he fixing his tie and she her mascara, before picking up their briefcases and meeting for a departing kiss at the door. She sees this with a sudden, brilliant clarity. For a moment she even thinks he will meet her eyes in the mirror, and in a relaxed gesture of tenderness lift her hair off her neck, brush his lips against the nape.

Instead he fumbles for a towel from the rack, and curses under his breath as a fresh spurt of blood splashes the side of the sink.

"I love you," she says.

"No," he says, stiffening. He moves away from her where she sits at the foot of the bed, her bandaged wrists propped upon her thighs. "No, you shouldn't say that. I've told you, I love my wife."

"But," she says. "This past year."

She is thinking particularly of how he held her hand like a boyfriend or a husband, while they talked or watched television. She's thinking about his habit of gently touching her arm or her shoulder to emphasize a point in conversation. And how he raised her from her knees, his penis brushing her bare belly like an absolution.

"I know. I'm sorry. I shouldn't have."

But this was not what she wanted to hear. She didn't want him to be sorry about those things. Those were the things he should have been glad about. It was his wife he should be apologizing to, his wife whose face should be erased by pain.

"Of course I thought about it," he says. "I thought about leaving my wife. I love her, Jodie. I wouldn't survive hurting her. There'd be nothing of me left if I did that."

"But you're hurting me. Doesn't that mean anything?"

"Oh God," he says. He shakes his head as if to shut out the sound of her voice. "I made a commitment to her. Can't you understand that?"

"No," she says. She rises from the bed, stands against the wall. "I don't understand. You are hurting me so much."

He takes a deep breath, lets it out.

"I've decided to stay with her," he says. "No matter what happens between us. You can't change that."

* * *

I can, thinks the woman leaning against the balcony railing, I can change everything now.

She watches the man through the door of glass. It is all there in her hands, what she
can do now. Inside the apartment husbands and wives wearing suits and gold-buttoned
dresses drink white wine and give each other reassuring glances, and in the hallway by
the bathroom a cluster of young, glassy-eyed professionals tilt their heads back and sniff
ostentatiously. She walks into the cradle of light and sound, towards the man she loves.

"It's me. Isn't it," she says sadly.

"How can you say that! It's not you!"

He is shouting, furious at seeing the guilty happiness of the past year spill
through his fingers like the beads of a broken necklace. He wants her to stop talking before everything is lost.

"Please," he begs. "Try to understand."

He wraps his hands around her shoulders and pushes her against the wall. Her
shoulder blades dig into the wood as though he is trying to make an outline of her
there, a snow angel, on the bedroom wall. For a moment she wishes he would hurt
her. She wants him to give her bruises and scars so she can wear them like other
women wear wedding rings, proof of a man's devotion.

"Oh baby," he says, letting go too soon, reaching up to take her face between his
hands, rubbing at her cheeks with his thumbs as though she is clay and he is stroking
her into the shape he sees in his mind. "Believe me, it's not you, you're perfect."

"Then why can't you leave her," she says.

He drops his hands, shakes his head and walks out of the bedroom. He made a
mistake, he's apologized — what more can he do? He never said he would leave his
wife, or that he loved Jodie, or even that she meant anything to him, although of
course she did. But it's over. This has happened before, and he has returned to his
wife. Once, five years ago, he had an affair which almost destroyed his marriage. The
woman was a famous young singer, seductive as a cat. Once, hand in hand, they had
gone for a drink in a hotel lounge. She was recognized, and his wife informed. Her
eyes had widened in pain and disbelief. In almost having lost her he had realized how
important she was to him, and he devoted himself to her until the night Jodie turned
and looked at him from the balcony.

Now he stands at the living-room windows, looking out. Jodie watches him from the bedroom doorway. He has taken off his suit jacket and she can make out the line of his back, the definition of musculature, through the white shirt. After a moment she goes into the kitchen with its shining surfaces — the polished counters, the new appliances. She is the sort of woman who cleans and shops when she is most unhappy.

"You can't leave me," she says. She is talking into the hair that falls across her face as she bends over a drawer and reaches inside. "You can't," she says again, but he doesn't hear her voice. It is not until she comes up behind him and he turns around that he understands something is happening.

He turns and she stabs him. He turns and she pushes the knife into him. Around them people are laughing and shaking hands and women are kissing each other hello and goodbye. He turns and when he looks into Jodie's eyes he has the sensation that he is falling. He takes her proffered hand and shakes it, he says his name and smiles to cover his confusion. Then he glances at her breasts, and when he looks back up into her face it is to hear her say, "I love you, I love you."

Is this happening? He turns from the window and she raises the knife and stabs him. At first when he feels the impact he thinks she has punched him in the chest. He reaches up to hold her wrists, aware of her wounds; in trying to be gentle his fingers fail to gain a purchase on the bandages, and she punches him again. The sharp object in her fist enters him, parts him again.

Her hair is drifting around her shoulders the way it did that night when she stood on the balcony and looked at him as though she knew everything about him. Her mouth is open and she is saying something which is lost to him, as he feels himself fall.

Jodie sees the surprise on his face when she puts her fist between their bodies and stabs him. It is the same look of surprise he would wear if she had just given him something he had not expected, a ring, a book, a wrapped box. He puts his hands out as if to receive her gift, and when he sees the blood he doesn't know if it is his own, or if she is bleeding through her bandages, or if he is confusing this with her red chiffon sleeves which float between them as he falls.

* * *

He reaches behind him to put his wineglass on the bookshelf as the woman on the balcony steps through the french doors and walks towards him, holding her hand out and saying her name. And then it seems she is saying "I love you," and heads are turning in the room, the music from the CD player is drifting audibly over the silence that settles. It is an aria from an opera he has heard a dozen times before, some tragic love story the title of which he can't recall, as he staggers back against the bookshelf which breaks beneath his weight. Someone in the hallway lets out a long scream that could be laughter. Someone is always screaming at a party, he thinks, this happens all the time. He looks at Jodie's breasts and imagines her red mouth around his penis and that he will feel peaceful when this happens. He wouldn't want that feeling of peace to ever end.

He turns from the window and she walks into him with her clenched fist. He slips to his knees, pressing his hand to his heart and trying to hold back the blood that seeps through his fingers from the holes she has made in him. "No," he says to the woman standing above him, but in a growing corner of his mind he suspects it is too late. Already he feels faint, like a man who suddenly discovers he has fallen in love.

LEON ROOKE is a novelist, short story writer and dramatist. His novels include *Shakespeare's Dog*, which won the Governor-General's Award for Fiction in 1983, *The Magician in Love* and *Fat Woman*. Among his short story collections are *Last One Home Sleeps in the Yellow Bed*, *Vault*, *The Broad Back of the Angel*, *The Love Parlour* and *Death Suite*. Born in rural North Carolina, he now lives in Ontario.

THE YALE CHAIR

LEON ROOKE

One Foot and I and our beset tribe found ourselves on the lam through the Dakotas, and many yesteryears removed from those encounters here I am alone floating upriver on the Nile. The Nile? They said it was the Nile and took my passage money with nothing back. At night this was, off a black pier. You walked a shaky plank and hoped it was a boat at the end. Stay in line, they said. No bickering. Yes, Princess, I will assist you with that trunk. You don't mind I drag the bitch?

The riverbanks were a dark entanglement, as I remembered, but in fact you do not see much when you are slung over the deck and sick to your very footsoles still from the crossing. Down below this was, where you could see nothing of what might be out there, including entanglements.

Some wondered what we would do, what would happen to us when we landed, and where we might land — the captain being vague, in fact silent on this issue, though I did not inquire myself, being more the willy-nilly type who goes where gunshots, fate, or romance decrees she must. My main concern was my wardrobe, and for that matter it still is, so long as I have my head, because my wardrobe with my tattered princess dress is all I have brought with me from my marriage to One Foot in the Water.

One Foot. Oh, One Foot! One Foot is in retreat from civilization's memory now, but once he was the famous leader of his people and husband married to the beautiful princess in her boned and beaded dress. I say this proudly. A certain dispersement of beings brought him all the way to Yale University on a professorship, which by one measure was that point in our lives where ascent and descent, happiness and unhappiness, had their bridge. A Chair this was called, the Jefferson Chair! But the hellhag bride was discovered aswim in her princess dress on the savage's arm and every weathercock and slubbergut mobbed the streets and we were shouldered back to the train. Scat! Never let us see your faces again! Or else!

Which was how we found ourselves again in aim for the Dakotas, our entire tribe in the meanwhile out there in a state of collapse and desuetude without their leader One Foot to harangue them or muzzle the extreme faction bent on the suicidal cause.

But all this trading of the aged news is discouraging to me now, as it might have been then, for we were both without our sap and listing in the wind after our long flight from the Chair zealots.

Our child arrived during the return journey from Yale and the commotion surrounding this natural event put great strain on every person in the six cars constituting that train, especially following an episode with a man who called himself Luther. This man flung burning fuel at my husband — this in the form of a torch that some attested appeared flaming from his very mouth — and did his best to slit our throats during the conflagration and hubbub, with everyone shouting and sliding fast as they could through the windows of the train which was hurtling at topmost raucous speed across the continent.

It was the swaying of these cars, I believe, and the constant clickety-clack, the heavy air, the stink of boots, which brought on our child's early birthing. I was already sore from the sticks hurled at us at Yale and hearing so often the Whiffinpoof song in rendition by groups of boys assembled on each street corner, and confused from the beginning by the endless talk of the Chair, the Chair.

Oh, I can make light of it now. Now that I am ten thousand miles removed from those shores and am beginning to breathe the sweet moisture of home. Usumbura we passed yesterday. Ruana Urundi tomorrow. They can't fool me. It is something in the blood.

My husband, pursued by these Chair forces through the Dakotas over the span of three summers and winters, repeatedly had sent word to Yale's tireless posse that he had no interest in their Chair, or in the wealth that accompanied this appointment, as Jeffersonian democracy was neither his specialty nor a concept in total arrangement with his liking.

I would not recommend acceptance of this Chair, should the offer come your way.

I would be wary of any invitation to show yourself upon New Haven's public green.

Avoid the whole of this uneasy state, if you are able.

My husband told the Chair's emissaries that he under no circumstances could accept the Chair, even a Roving Chair, or ambassadorship, and in reaction to this sentiment we were ordered out of the Dakotas, advised that we must not step foot into any adjacent state or territory, nor think that we might take leave by water, for that ocean was under sovereign jurisdiction as well.

So all right, I lie. I veer from strict truth.

But we were on the lam through the Dakotas for some many seasons, the Chair's supporters in hot pursuit and our tribe decimated and factions arising at every turn, since none of us knew that much about why it was that such hordes of influential and moneyed people were willing to sacrifice so many lives or effect such widespread deprivation all in order to bring about One Foot's ensconcement in the deplorable Chair.

A council of elders was called and in one voice, after but a few minutes' deliberation, they summoned us before them and said, "One Foot in the Water, take the Chair."

Take it before all our people are dead and only our bones are left to rattle through these Dakotas.

Off we went to Yale for receipt of this honour.

Until our arrival that rain-soggy day, we had not known even of the existence of violent and powerful forces simultaneously at work to prevent just this occurrence.

Yet also at Yale, in the president's house where we were in the initial days lodged, some kind and consummately patient person sewed score upon score of roses onto the lining of my princess dress. These were of the old York variety, with each thorn carefully removed and fine invisible mending done on the hem, where my heels back in the Dakotas had time and time again caught the beaded and boned fringe.

Every bead polished, every bone wiped, our bedcovers folded back, and the pillows bestrewn with further displays of these blossoms.

Two bleached antelope shin-bones also crossed over my pillows, which sign made me tremble, for they spoke of home. Decades in the flow since and me but a nippling when uprooted.

I wore these petals next to my skin and wept, for it had been a long time since we had enjoyed privilege or mercy of any kind.

One Foot cried, to see me bathe, these lovely petals at float on the scented water.

Our bed and the floor about that bed ablaze with York blossom, and the air afire with the airy petals as we loved. Us little expecting these times to be our last hours of bliss in each other's embrace.

At five the butler's bell rang and we passed down the stairs to a gay reception and dinner.

"Perhaps you will get accustomed to sitting in this Chair," I said to my husband.

"Good bed," he said. "I like beds." And went on to explain his view that the entire westward expansion owed everything to the presence of these eastern beds. So I saw he was putting good face on this Chair issue, and thinking better of Jeffersonian principles in the aftermath of our couplings.

A stone occasionally strikes the deck of this boat, and skids off into water. We are told black infidels are ashore in the bush, tracking our passage, and to be watchful for poisoned arrows, though I have yet to see any proof of this menace. Only these small bouncing stones or harmless splats of mud which a child might mindlessly fling.

A crew-member sent by the captain stands solemnly beside me and after a long interval presses a warm glass in my hands. I drink its contents without inquiry, and return the glass to him. He does not quit my side.

"What was in the glass?" I ask.

He cocks his head indifferently, standing close by on spread legs.

"A soporific," he says.

"It had the taste of rum."

"A soporific, Princess. With rum, to settle the stomach."

He smells of monkey. I have seen any number of these animated creatures at swing in the wheelhouse or scampering along the deck. But I will not satisfy him by stirring even one inch, and my little knife as always is at the ready. I have stuck it through tougher beings than this one man.

"The captain wishes I should report to you that your trunk is secured."

Although he smiles, I am not deceived. He would pitch me overboard and be done with me, without the smallest qualm.

"It is in the wheelhouse?"

"Yes, Princess. Padlocked under heaviest chain." He bows witlessly and tosses the glass my lips have touched into the Nile.

"Then how am I to have ready bargain with my clothes?"

He does not reply.

I thank him and at last, reluctantly, he goes.

I hang over the deck again, retching into black water, as night-birds thrash and squawk in the trees.

Curiously, our train-car had palest-blue balloons in danglement from every inch of ceiling, these aloft at a level equal to the heads of those men and women standing in tight press along the aisles. Each few seconds a smoker's cigar would burst one or another of these, and each man in the vicinity grabbed for his blade or handgun. One Foot could not remove his gaze from this display of dancing blue balloons, the presence of which puzzled him greatly and elicited endless whispered commentary into my ear. He sought to find messages in this armada of balloons as he did in the night's sing of stars, and was vexed by his inability to conjure same, although he laughed mightily each time a balloon popped from the ceiling and on its own accord shot at dazzling speed its wild orbit above our heads.

The child was coming; I was in considerable torment and retained my composure, I hope, although One Foot was sorely incensed that no one in the packed car would surrender his seat or even squirm so much as an inch to right or left. But he was already hobbled in one leg from the fray on the public green at Yale, plus suffering dog bite which now was festering, plus carrying in addition deep wounds in his side from his youthful wars.

He could do little to right the matter beyond arranging some little rope's length of comfort for me in that space on the cold floor beneath the gentlemen's feet. I lay on this slab of grit and boots and food spat from the traveller's mouth, shuddering with the clickety-clack of iron against iron and in the grip of deepest anxiety and pain, for this child was my first and coming early and my attendants all scattered in result of the fray at Yale.

Pity me, to have been so senseless as to wear my princess dress.

It worried me that my dress should not survive the ordeal, or that my child might not, and between bursts of pain and the dizziness of balloons, I had mind to consider my great wardrobe of seven steamer trunks long-since reduced to the one, and One Foot's worry that he could no longer provide for me. It is a pitiful thing to see this recognition sap a prideful man, and I wept bitter tears for his misery and for my own and my labouring child.

These gentlemen pressed their boots about my head and chest and limbs through the entire birthing process, their cigars in ceremonious toil and their ash in steady cascade about my face. Their boots kicked and prodded my flesh at every turn, some perhaps unconsciously, to render them that justice. My floorspace smelt of pigshit and piss and the eastern civilizations enough to make me gag. Soldiers in attendance to see to our safety were at cards, or bent with drink and frivolity, or such obscenity as betokens handshake with the uniform. They lifted not the one hand, but instead inflamed the matter, which did not in the least surprise us, given the discord in surround of the Jefferson Chair.

Oddly, a gentleman sharing our cramped compartment sat in study of an Eastern paper through near the whole of my birthing throes, often kicking his boots against my head and body in his excitement as he discoursed upon the rights and wrongs of the Jefferson Chair, and its rich endowment, which investment seemed to his mind to exist in contrary fashion to the democratic ideals the Chair's very creation was meant to promulgate.

Mr. Jefferson had never been a piece of God's creation that he could champion, he said, and had Mr. Hamilton shot the rascal, as so often had been his desire, the country would have been saved much grief.

There was something cunning under way with this business, he said, and it was his guess that European monarchists were behind the whole of it; they had put up the coin, no doubt about that, he said, and duped the intelligentsia at Yale, which institution had sorely declined since its removal from old Saybrook. But what could you expect, given the tenor of these times. A great debauchment of the people's trust was in the wind now that the laws of entail and primogeniture were at lapse. Much claptrap, he said, was being put about with regard to the requirements of education for the poor and uncivil, with slave and red man and pickpocket rising to assail one at every turn. Women strutted in secret, arrogant rule up and down every corridor of power from the Potomac to Yale, and the country would suffer calamitously if the citizenry did not soon come to its senses and cast off the foreign yoke. Hang the scoundrels at home, who knew not where their bread and butter did come. Cast off this puerile exercise in free-thinking, which rewarded only free-loading rodent, chimney-sweep, and slubberdegullion. The country must forsake its restless clamouring for art and the snooty ideal and the luxurious life for every upstart or fieldhand with tongue to flap or arsehole to fart it out of.

A great boomswell of "ayes" sounded in aftermath of this speech, and heavy trampling of boots where I lay in dire sweat, huffing and puffing, with thrusting pelvis, my water sloshing beneath me and the flesh of poor One Foot's palm between my teeth chewed into rag.

"Aye!" they said. "All the evils of this nation's business can be seen in this episode of the Chair!"

"Aye, the Chair, heaven help us!"

But now my husband forced some little extraction of space between my legs and slung my limbs high upon his shoulders, for he took news from my shrieks and thrusts that the child was in its daylight chamber and he must be my woman and my midwife now.

The gentlemen through some precious moment or two fell silent, and stayed their feet.

I shrieked anew to see my heels at lock about my lover's neck and to glimpse his bloodied hands at work between my naked legs. Sweat roiled upon our skins and the jolting pain now was without surcease. I closed my eyes and locked my teeth on whatever came between them, as for instance the toe of the talkative gentleman's boot. But he grappled this away from me, with a show of bad humour which found release in a stream of lurid comment upon the vileness of travel in this ignorant age.

With each new siege my feet thrashed against my husband's face and chest, my great belly heaving and my buttocks at slushy romp, until at last he was made to force them into the grip or brace of whatever man of quality would consent.

The men, at crowd upon us, by and large, seemed bored with our activity, or assumed attitudes in antipathy with our goals, and soon went on again with their scholarly perquisites.

"Women should not ride the train," one of these said, "and there's the proof."

Another chorus of "Ayes" sounded, and much toasting to this chap.

The man with the newspaper announced that he held exalted status with the Halls of Transport and Railroads, and that he normally would be found riding in the owner's caboose, with mugs of hard cider in each hand and comely Chinee wenches in slit red dresses showing ample ankle or even garter belt to see to his every need. There followed a great tipping of hats and a flood of inquiries about the availability within that office of other exalted jobs.

On this occasion, the man said, the caboose had been turned over to that Chair savage from the Dakotas who had incited the riot at Yale and trampled innocent children underfoot. Yes, thanks to government intervention and outright laxitude, lawless, irreligious hordes could usurp a fine man's seat anywhere in the land, and it was high time a Cotton Whig took hold of the realm and hung this lowlife from a tree, wherever they be found.

Yes, yes, the savage was riding this very train, he said, and likely coupling this very minute on the owner's divan with his black princess who, as was well known, had cavorted shamelessly with a thousand men away there in the Egyptland she hailed from.

"Aye, aye!" the others said. "'Tis well known."

There's some as should hold the line, he said, as to which raw whore they'll take aboard a good slave ship.

"Aye!"

Profit or not, there's principles at stake here!

"Aye! We ought to go ourselves and plug the bitch!"

But at this moment the vulgarian's attention was drawn to One Foot, as if he had but just noticed my husband's presence for the first time. He offered his fatted hand for shaking, and for some protracted seconds that hand hung at mean jiggle above my eyes, One Foot's own hands being at busy engagement between my legs.

"And what is your opinion on these matters, sir?" this magpie asked One Foot. "Do you have views, I mean, as a redman and savage, on this treasonable business with the Chair?"

At this very moment my child's head slipped loose of all encumbrances, sorely irritating this unsavoury clown. I strained and huffed, certain I was being torn apart limb by limb. One Foot planted his legs anew, forcing my legs wider yet; a snarl was fixed upon his lips and glitter showed in his eyes and for an instant his sight locked with mine. "Push, bitch," I heard someone growl; One Foot's fingers probed inside me deep as a barge pole; he spat and yanked as I howled; I was aware of a great sucking, slurpish sound which seemed to arise from the entire car, and my guts ripping, then a swoosh, and then a great vacuum or hole suddenly opened inside my womb; this emptiness swept onwards and in the instant took hold upon my brain. My very bones seemed to have been scoured. Heaven help me, yes. My eyes opened and I saw the newborn gliding smoothly upwards, flowing like a skein of syrup between my bloodied legs into One Foot's nimble, fraught embrace.

"Aye, duckie!" someone said. And henhouse cackles all around.

My husband held the child high in the one hand, smacking rump.

"Sir?"

One Foot's hand at last shot out and shook Big Mouth's lingering paw.

"Indeed, sir," One Foot said to him. "Indeed I have views."

I arose — "You will move the buttocks, sir" — and took back my seat.

But that our child was a beauty to behold and born in perfect health despite the setting I have described, I leave to more proper and learned annals in our history to chronicalize in detail.

We named her Oryxes II, in my tongue, and Foot of the Dogs, in our shared language, with more than a few exchanges between ourselves of the mirthful code.

Some little aftermath of tranquillity must have followed this birthing, for I do recall I was asleep when this Luther person disconnected himself from that throng of travellers occupying each dot and parcel of seat and aisle. My eyes blinked, I mean to say, and in the next moment I felt the crush of One Foot's body slung across mine and our child's, though not before I saw the flaming torch in arched flight upon our very selves. And every man and woman screaming and trampling away from the fire's orbit, without regard for neighbour or friend.

From this attack I suffered a few unremarkable burns, together with nose bleed from one or another wild elbow, plus tintinnabulation, plus gore everywhere, and nothing to do with that dress except fling it at the first bush. But later I gave this decision second thinking and coerced myself into reclaiming the garment with a good wash, plus tincture of lye, plus needle and thread. Oryxes was unharmed, and One Foot's diminishment only the little greater, though the nature of his disfigurations in body and spirit did have weight upon me wearisome unto my depths. His mind was in deep cogitation of these Jeffersonian principles thrust upon him, and this study tired him mightily. What had seemed obvious now seemed arguable, he told me, and the vice versa. Each simple issue or statement of plain truth now arrived in his mind with interminable codicil, or long-winded preface, with gazette and appendices, or contrary council and allegation, and footnotes that went on into eternity. He feared his new scholar's mind was now in session with the full academic committee, and it tired him, it tired him, *it lays me low, my darling.*

Through the oily, coal-dusted windows could be seen vultures at glide with our traffic. They gobbled flesh as they sailed. When morsels fell from their beaks, crows swooped in from nowhere, with raucous chatter, to claim what was theirs.

At Yale, a woman wearing a scarlet bonnet had asked my husband which of these many eastern inventions he was witness to had most impressed him.

"The hammock," he said.

The president of that institution had taken us aside and said how sad he was that Meriwether could not be with us to celebrate my husband's ascension to the Chair. "Villains struck him down, you know. Years ago. On the Natchez Trace."

"Yes. My princess and I were much enriched by our association with him during the Expedition, as with our correspondence through the years."

"I understand you were most helpful to him during those difficult Louisiana years."

"Princess was."

The president bowed and kissed my hand. "We have much to learn," he said. "I understand your lineage can be traced as far back as the Middle Empire's Amenchet." I bowed to him, fluttering an impervious hand.

"Mr. Clark, alas, is also in the grave," he said to my husband. My husband fidgeted. He regretted Mr. Clark's demise, but had never forgiven him his decisions in the nasty Black Hawk affair.

"What do you hear of Sacajawea?" he asked us.

Ah, I thought: dear old Sacajawea. Even Whig bankers loved Sacajawea.

"She is toothless now," I said. "Though still the charmer. Her grandchildren are strung throughout the Dakotas and Wyoming. They are all great warriors."

He sniffed. "I smell roses," he said.

At that minute a rock crashed through the window; agitators were assembling on the lawn.

The captain's man again appears by my side. A monkey clambers about on his shoulder. The monkey regards me with merry, attentive eyes, looking over my attire to determine if I possess anything that can be put to its own use.

"The captain regrets the food aboard-ship is all contaminated," the man says. "It is all at rot."

"Your captain has never heard of salt?" I ask. "Of smoke?"

"Unfortunately, the pineapple does not smoke. Regrettably, the orange does not salt."

He scratches the monkey's belly. The monkey gyrates on his shoulder, then produces an orange.

I snatch at this fruit and have my teeth sunk into it almost before it has left the monkey's hand.

"To your health, Princess," the man says. He spins on his heels, the monkey chatters, and both are gone.

This man is not so bad after all.

Juice drips from my mouth. I have not eaten in a month.

Minutes later, the monkey returns. He hops about in noisy agitation at my feet, making horrendous noise. But he loses not a drop of what he has brought. A rum bottle bobs atop his head. He settles the rum glass in my hand, pours from the bottle, dances about once more, then rolls away like a wheel.

I hear gee-gaws of muffled laughter from the wheelhouse, and smile my own appreciation into the dark.

I mean not to dwell on my vicissitudes, being not the whiner type and finding such a parade of memories repellent to my nature, as earlier said. But there it is: history must be composed, if lessons are to be extracted and life ever improved and the winds again to sing.

All history, I mean to say, is not written in blood. To cite an example, I will mention the Night of the Trees. Soon after our train had crossed the border into Canada, it braked to sudden, lurching stop, and steam and dust engulfed us all. Urgent whistles rent the air and the very earth shook. The next moment passengers of every description were surging forth, the cars all but instantly emptying. Up and down the track people by the hundreds poured into the darkness, as though possessed by some claim of enthusiasm or madness beyond our normal call. Before one could make account for this, large beds of fire ba-roomed into being, these flaming campfires or outposts of light spreading far almost as the eye could encompass; in the shadows of these great flames an incalculable array of bodies swarmed this way and that, each man, woman, or child among them, it seemed, hastening to his or her objective as by some predetermined course and cause. Their heads and shoulders, sometimes the whole of their bodies, were soon obscured by their loads: massive trees, shrub plants, and flowering bush of every variety. These bodies in phantomish assembly, silhouettes at flow in graceful symmetry beneath the blackened sky. Others roved about in mysterious dialogue with pick and shovel, while numerous wagons pulled by horses barely larger than dogs arranged themselves in strange procession over the barren, ghostly plain, each of these instruments of transport piled high with mounds of black earth. In this rich cargo blinked pinpricks of mirrors all at steady flash, mica-chips, my husband observed, and over these wagon loads rode a latticework of cages big and small. An extraordinary convergence of wild, plumed birds were at flutter within these cages; birds swayed upon the creaking carts with their heads under wing, or held forth as statuesque sentinels transcribing shrieks and clucks and throaty, rapturous song into the dark, implausible night. Still other conveyances arrived, some as though dropped from the starry sky. In these prowled a montage of beasts large and small, many of a species heretofore unseen in the new world, you would think; these beasts arranged either in quiet curiosity as to what mercies it was that awaited them, or in wild roar of outrage at what travesty already had ensnared them. Men and women of Oriental cast were everywhere to be seen, come from nowhere to sound out their strange tongue to one another while applying tong and hammer to some spot immediately beneath where they stood. Transforming that spot in the instant and moving on decisively and with fierce muttering of excitement to the next chosen place; and the whole of this teeming terrain lit, as I say, by moonlight and torch — this flood of souls released to some higher plain of endeavour.

Oryxes nursed, cutting her eyes to right and left.

The night wore on. The mysterious work on the great plain beyond our windows continued without let-up.

Six white butterflies hovered at my window. They disappeared the instant my eyes claimed them. Scant seconds later they were at soft circling wing in the air above my child's head. As one, they descended, settling on the baby's brow. I sped them away with a wave of hands, but the second my hands stilled they again dropped as one upon the child's brow.

"She will live sixty years," my husband said.

Or die, I thought, in six days.

One Foot grasped my wrists to hold them quiet.

"Six days or sixty years," he said. "Do not wage war against the stars."

I watched the butterflies traverse my newborn's face.

At this point in our journey we were days from even the smallest hamlet or outpost and indeed knew not where we were, or were bound; in the darkened coach, with all this before us, my husband's spirit had revived; he sucked at my one breast as Oryxes suckled the other.

"You will bring great scope to the assignment," I told him. "You will bring honour to us, and to Yale, and to the Jefferson Chair. In the spring I will take Oryxes home and walk with her among our pyramids."

So much was the sense of goodness upon us that we swore anew our vows, pledging a strengthened loyalty to all in nature that was tranquil and harmonious.

Through the night the army worked beyond our windows, and at daybreak when the great fires were nothing more than ashen piles a great virgin forest stood in seemingly endless stretch towards the horizon; the arid plain was no more. Birds were in bivouac in the trees, or in summit each to each, and beasts and fowl at roam among the foliage and dazzlement of blossoms.

Something unyielding in the heart had finally yielded, I thought, and created this amazing oasis.

In the distance one could hear mighty waterfalls, and witness their wet haze in the clouds.

Morning, now.

Those who had disembarked came on again as the sun rose. They wore their previous composure now, and showed no evidence of toil; they were eastern loudmouths in suit-coats and boots, in quaint round-topped hats and string ties. They were demure ladies in unsoiled travellers' dress, in high-top shoes that still carried shine; they were strutting schoolboys and young gentlemen in apprenticeship to a latitude of professions and trades. Boisterous soldiers, as drunk or obscene as they had been earlier, trooped in noisy combat or comradeship up and down the aisles, to fling themselves into whatever empty seat or lap their province of thought led them. Old men and women hobbled aboard, as bent by ache and disfigurement as when they had disembarked. Hardly the crew, you would think, to have wrought what they had wrought through this wondrous night.

The fat impresario of the railroad swung elbows, fitting himself again beside me into his old seat. His bloated, immaculate hand thrust itself One Foot's way.

"Now," he said. "You were saying. As a red man and savage, and one who has known the unblessed life, what might be your thoughts about that infernal Yale Chair? Every scalawag and dog to have his day? Is that your tune?"

"Them coolies," I heard one woman whisper to another, passing along the aisle. "I couldn't make out the single word! Must we have ignorant foreigners in pigtails building our railroads?"

Our boat chugs on through the night, aimless as a plank tossed into water. Our stomachs have soothed and we repose on the deck like bundles of hay dropped haphazardly over the rail. Wind rakes at old cuts in the flesh, and my bones acknowledge their age. The sky has blackened, we can see nothing. Our boat scrapes bottom, brushes invisible foliage, and one can feel the lean of a thousand trees; we lift uncertain hands to dislodge drooping vines. One hears an occasional splash in the water, nearby or in the distance, and the heart quivers: is it fish or one of our own, sliding away into the black mystery?

The captain's man again returns, on shoes as silent as the evening's character.

"A pillow, Princess? The captain desires you should be comfortable."

Something else scrabbles across the deck, approaches me; already I have raised my knife. What does it want?

"It is only the monkey," the man tells me. "Come with a blanket."

Indeed, it is the monkey. I can smell now the raw smell. I can hear the monkey scratching its fur.

"Cover the princess," the man says. The monkey chatters a polite reply. I see the waves of yet a blacker darkness, and cool air, and the blanket settling lightly over my legs. The hair on the monkey's hands brushes my face.

"No rum?" I ask.

The rum glass finds my fingers. I hear the slosh of liquid in the glass. I drink.

"Tell the monkey thank you," I say to the captain's man.

"No need to," he says. "You already have. You could talk that Egyptian tongue, he'd likely understand that too."

They start to go.

"Should be quite the show," the man says. "Quite the celebration. Whole country at fever-pitch. You're coming home, Princess."

It seems to me I can feel some timid increase in the boat's speed. Some added play in the waves. Some extra force in the breeze.

It occurs to me that I must have the captain's monkey. I must walk through the capitals of Europe, Asia, and the Far East. Through this continent and back again in the New World. I in my princess dress and the monkey at my side, our hands intertwined.

Oryxes the First, I seem to recall, had monkeys and birds sealed with her in her golden tomb.

The railhead at Winnipeg, where we took on the cattle and into whose terminus we had been rerouted, was not an improvement, although it was here a man named Riel, said to be a rabble-rouser and menace to the earth's inner-tuning, furtively boarded and sat with us and recited his name. He spoke into his chest, although his eyes darted everywhere. He was an outlaw, on the run. Branded a traitor. His friends dead. So many of his people homeless, on their knees, or dead. Gutted end to end. The Great White Father was The Snake With One Belly and Two Heads. One head lived on the Potomac, the other up here. The snake's belly was fat with the dead. It liked the lard. The two heads saw little of each other. They did not need to. Such brains as the snake possessed were located in the belly. Or were up its arse-hole, forgive me, princess.

Riel wore a bell on a rawhide cord looped around his neck. He drew back his coat to show us this. A handgun hung by the same cord. He had never fired this weapon, he said, without first ringing the bell. The ringing bell made him feel easier about the matter. It soothed his conscience and brought peace to the swans at swim in his head.

"What was decided with the Chair?" he asked.

Yes, he had been approached in the early days. The offer had chagrined him; he had believed himself unworthy. He was too angry. Although in those days he had trod about with six bells round his neck, and no handgun, or even a knife or stone in his pockets.

"'Try One Foot,' I told them. 'He's the bigger fool.'"

We shook with laughter at this.

"What news of Sacajawea?" he asked. "She always excited my blood, though her own ever ran clear. She was ever trimming my nails, inserting sticks into my hair or slapping tree bark onto my face. Correcting my French. I see her now, walking Paris streets under a gay umbrella, white poodles dogging her heels. Quite the savage, eh? Sacajawea could read one page of Latin in Clark's book, and thereafter speak the tongue with a sauciness and grandeur the match of Cicero."

Ah, we all thought. The old days.

"Where do you go now?" we asked.

He laughed, and waggled his head.

The baby wriggled on my lap, wanting to join in.

"A child shall lead them," Riel said. "Onwards into light." He tickled the infant's chin. "Never fall asleep on a tree's mossy side."

A man stalking the aisle paused at our chairs and leaned his face into Riel's. Riel tinkled his bell. The man straightened and hastened on.

"And what news," he asked me, "of the empire? Of the darker continent? How fares the princess, her heels raw from the Dakotas' lam? So far from home, and for so long?"

"Upriver, slave ship oars thump out the iambic beat. More and more vessels thicken the water. High tide is ever higher."

He withdrew a white handkerchief, and with it daubed his sugar under my eyes.

"Downriver, there's talk of a canal."

"Ah," he said. "The innocent life."

For a time within his environment our spirits lifted; we smoked and spat and dwelled on the eternities and toasted the baby.

He slipped away, and our train rattled on, again in ungainly lurch towards the Dakotas.

A night and a day passed. The vultures once more plied commerce with our route, gliding calmly by like gulls at a seaport.

Three days, four days, five.

Then there was this same Luther underfoot again and the train at crash against a boulder set up across the rails. By Plum River this was, and it engorged, and somehow in the stew of this my newborn's throat being had at, plus Luther's gang at pile between my legs.

You can see here my sketchiness, for I have little stomach for the chronicle. A body tires, it wants relief, and the mind, too, desires the pruning.

Then this mucous scampering away into grass.

But One Foot was wounded and his head a hollow bell and his eyes sightless in the aftermath.

"More rum, princess?"

"I thank you, yes."

"More?"

"Yes."

"To the top?"

"Yes."

We survived in these conditions and made on again, on foot now and following a path of stars, accompanied by the maddened cadenza of wolves at rove on the plain. Some two hundred of Luther's sordid fireboilers drove in hot pursuit, as we nightly reconnoitred the matter from our moonward levels. This, thanks to a scurrilous document nailed to tree stump and post by our enemies, affirming that the Chair brigade had under face of darkness routed that institution called Yale, murdering every woman and child while they slept and leaving in their wake naught but the stench of rotting flesh in which maggots of a special Egyptian-Injun variety were at swim, with the whole of civilization now at peril. And these blackguards now loose in unprejudiced liberty through the continent, with more of their infamy to follow. And all this at the will of a moneyed claimant to the French throne, in conspiracy with the English Influence along the Potomac — and many a decent kettle-tender, pig-swiller, blackie or red man the dupes of these knaves who dared make use of the Jeffersonian name. These despoilers of his hand-writ Constitution and defilers of the *of, by, and for,* who would usurp our land's very foundations.

"More rum, Princess?"

"Dispatch the monkey for another keg."

"He's asleep, princess. Between yer legs."

We reside now in the wheelhouse, our features at dance under the globe of yellow lanterns. I sit on the captain's stuffed horsehair sofa, cold inside my bones, mindlessly rubbing the monkey's scalp. The monkey groans in his sleep; he has the sound of one grown weary and old from the drone of my voice.

The captain is attentive to the wheel and only intermittently shows notice of me. He cares for his boat and would have nothing harm her on this journey. "Yer has the mission, yer takes it," he has told me. "Yer hopes to effect no damage to yer vessel what brings yer to or from it."

"Yer does?"

"Yer. Yer does."

I have been here the past hour, the pair of us saluting ourselves with each drink we pour down our gullets.

"*Skaal!*"

"*Skaal!*"

"*Prosit!*"

"*Prosit!*"

"To yer nanny."

"To yer nanny!"

"*Pura quanzu!*"

"*Pura quanzu!*"

"*A votre santé!*"

"*A votre santé!*"

"Down the hatch!"

"Down the ruddy hatch!"

The captain is a piece of cloth new to my experience. I cannot make him out.

"I told yer," he says. "Yer takes on a mission, yer . . . "

Another lantern illuminates the boat's bow and some few feet of grey water. It illuminates the captain's weathered confederates. Ropes are entwined about their torsos as they dig in their heels, as they sway and pull. We are in shallow water; this tub is scraping bottom.

"We'll get yer through," the captain says. "No problem."

The monkey yawns, stretching his limbs. The right foot jiggles as he sleeps.

"I meant to ask," says the captain. "How's that Sacajawea? There were a woman could come at yer like oyster on the half-shell."

"You knew Sacajawea?"

"Why, my Lord yes. Like this us were."

He snaps his fingers behind his back, his torso at lean through a window. "Onward, boys," he shouts. "Another league onwards!"

It sounds silly. I help the monkey scratch at fleas, thinking that this monkey and I are walking down a Paris street. We are creating the sensation, and why should we not? I shall not let the lowlife deter me. Go away, I will say. You with your small minds. Who else will flap warm blankets over me when I am cold? I will sit on a bench and debate with the monkey Jeffersonian ideals and the Napoleonic Code.

"That Riel fella were hanged, yer know. Captured at Batoche and strung up." The captain pauses to gnash the gears, to kick at some hum of engine irregular to his ears. "Oh, not so long ago. Quite a fella. Yer. My old sidekick, in my rough-and-ready days."

He turns and looks at me. It is the first time I have seen his face near a lantern, in good light. He face shows the cascades of a thousand years.

"Didn't know yer husband. Knew his father, though. Old Two Foot, yer know. Two Foot in the Water. Now there were a man could chew yer up and spit yer out. Yer give him cause. Not the man for that Chair, though. Not a Jefferson man. The way yer husband was."

Beneath the wheel, where the captain rests his leg, is my chained steamer trunk. I started with seven, and now am returning with one. I have gone up and gone down.

I root a finger into the monkey's ear; I ream the knobby flesh.

"Yer can go on with yer tale, yer know," the captain says. "Anytime yer like."

Yer. My infant daughter ripped from my chest and flung into the Plum, even as these same tormenters tore away my dress and dropped down astride me. Shouting insane currency in my ears. Another of Luther's gang standing by at the ready. *"We'll show you democracy!"* My child at squall in rapids and no shriek too many to proclaim the atrocity.

Jackals at gnaw upon our bones.

Later on, my child at float, head down and much bloated. I pushed the swollen child along in the tide. Go, I said. Why do you tarry?

I observed her spirit rove ashore some further distance along; it arose sprightly, and joy flooded my heart. But then her legs kimbered and the arms spun as in a cripple's dance and the head sailed loose of her frame and one arm spiralled east-ward and the other westward and in the sky I saw lips nose eyes and ears all disas-sembled and whirling in wind and the next moment the form that remained in the water toppled backwards and sank into the fathomless bottom.

"Ujiji," the captain says. "Kigoma. Yer. By daylight. Then only three thousand more miles. Yer see slave ships in yer mind, Princess?"

Yer. And the cry of the birds when their wings are axed and the sky is no longer theirs and the slave ships slip away with the bird wings stacked one upon the other and the night of all nights has come down.

"Yer. I thought yer was."

We are entering a lake mouth. A soft rain is falling; the leaves are dripping.

"More rum, Princess?"

I think not.

A hush of people, come from nowhere, are lining the bank.

"Yer dress, Princess? Yer think?"

Already he has unlocked and opened my trunk.

"Yer are their princess too, yer know. Yer are the Chair."

Yer. My bones, my beads, my princess dress. Sticks in the hair. My face painted. Yer.

VI
THE LUST FOR ACTION

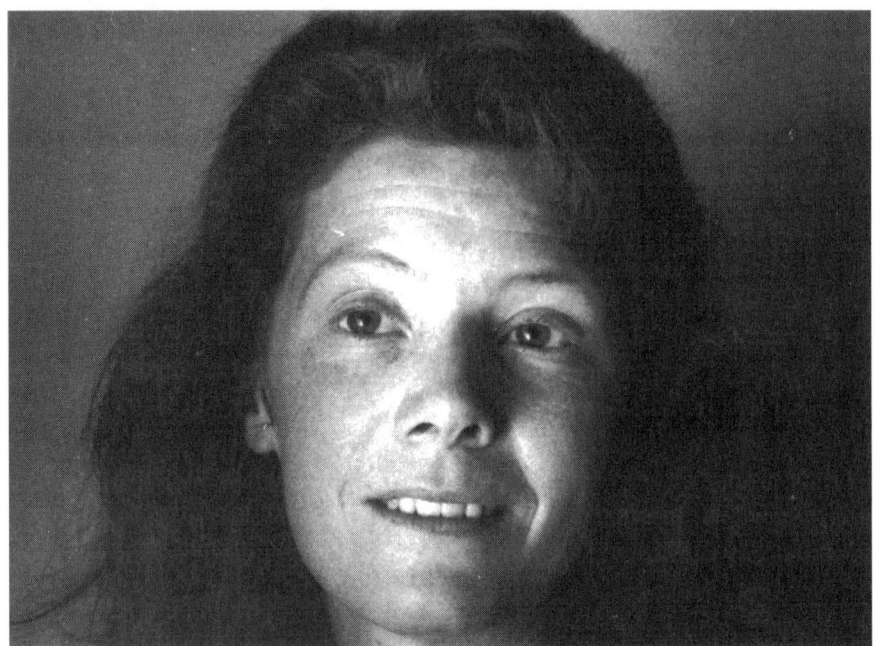

HELEN HUGHES

LAKE SAGARIS (born in Montreal, 1956) has lived in Chile since 1981, writing for media in Canada, the U.S.A., Chile, and Britain. She is currently the Santiago correspondent for *Newsweek*, the *Miami Herald*, and the *Times Educational Supplement*. She has published three books of poetry and edited two anthologies of Canadian writing (in Spanish). Her stories of life under the military, *After the First Death: A Journey Through Time, Place, Minds*, is forthcoming from Somerville House (Toronto) in January 1996.

"I Roar Through All Creation Like the Wind"[1] (Because I Have No Time To Take Things Slowly): Writing/Mothering

Lake Sagaris

I sit down to write this with a hunger for space and the crushing knowledge that time is short and although ideas often leap like water over rocks, sometimes they stagnate, deep and green, or build destructive energy pent up behind a dam and I have only this instant to catch them and throw them on to you. What if I miss? What if we miss each other?

---

[1]The goddess Vac, in a song of the Vedic nature-religion of India. Rosalind Miles, *A Woman's History of the World*, p. 40.

I have jotted these notes down on napkins and fax tags, working backwards through the notebooks where I'm also scrawling the words that will earn me money, leaping up from dinner or scribbling in the dark after all the lights are out. I have done all this with the full knowledge that I will never finish a thought, that as soon as I sit down at the computer two-year-old Danny will bash open my door like a drunk staggering into a saloon and demand "Animals! I want the animals!" or "Airplanes!" or "Coloured Pens!" Sure enough this happens. These paragraphs are already marked by two such interruptions.

What does mothering have to do with writing? Why write about the two in one breath? Or gasp? Or long sigh of longing? A lot has been written about how mothering and writing are mutually exclusive, the contradictions, how one makes it hard (some have said, impossible) to do the other. But what happens if you stubbornly demand to have your children and books too, insist on combining Mothering and Writing?

Shakespeare was not a mother and to my knowledge neither was Virginia Woolf. Mothering is what a nun like Sister Juana of Mexico had to avoid to become a great writer, part of our Old/New World heritage and the complex, colonial schizophrenia of our being. Although, it must be said, the Catholic hierarchy got her and destroyed her anyway.

Mothering and writing are often compared. Some women have children. Others have books. Some treat books as substitutes for children. Marge Piercy writes:

> My children are my books
> that I gestate for years,
> a slow-witted elephant
> eternally pregnant, books
> that I sit on for eras like the great
> auk on a vast marble egg . . .
>
> People take them in and devour them.
> People marry them for love.
> People write me letters and tell me
> how they are my children too.

I have children whose languages
rattle dumbly in my ears like gravel,

children of the wind that blows
through me from the graves of the poor
and brave who struggled all their short
throttled lives to free people
whose faces they could not imagine.
Such are the children of my words.[2]

Surely mothering is at least part of what drove Sylvia Plath to suicide. Watching the mountainous structure of your thoughts reduced to rubble by the endless screaming of a child turns even Sisyphus's punishment into, well, child's play.

But like alcohol or drugs, mothering can be both destructive and revealing, a tension, a delirium, a tugging on your sleeve when you most desire peace, a forcing your feet back into contact with the earth, whether you want it or not. Dealing with the constant interruptions sharpens your concentration, your ability to grab the broken bone of conversation and splint it back together, to pull an idea out of thin air as you break an egg and fry it up for dinner. You make the most of every moment, like this one.

It's also a test — if your compulsion to write survives the demands of mothering, you must do both, even if that means pinning junior to one knee as you tap away at the keyboard, getting down one last idea before all hell breaks loose.

Writers, in some cases, give mothers and writers good advice. In fifteenth-century Italy, Christine de Pisan said: "Gather what little drops of learning you can, and consider them a great treasure." In twentieth-century Canada, Gwendolyn MacEwen put it this way: "When you want to travel very far, do as the Bedouin do/ Drink to overflowing when you can,/ and then/ Go sparingly between wells." Both mothering and writing are journeys.

Mothering, that most idealized, uplifted and mythified activity, is a lesson in self-obliteration — whether you want one or not. You suffer the torture of years of sleep deprivation (the Nazis experimented with this stuff). No matter how important

---

[2]*My Mother's Body*, p. 72.

your regular job is or how many people must take your orders or at least listen to your opinion, at home with children you face constant humiliation, kneeling before the tiny squalling lord or empress, the tyrant whose shit you must clean, whose bath you must draw, whose back you must scratch and clothe and cool and caress and, eventually, wave goodbye to. Smiling.

The contradictions faced mostly alone can fill you with self-doubt, a useful filter, if something makes it to the other side.

This all makes mothering a lesson in extremes. It places women in the position where we're everything from the lowest slave to the Mother Goddess herself, the full range. It gives us a whole keyboard to tickle, pound and throw out the window when the occasion warrants it, and sometimes when it doesn't. That's useful too.

I'm not recommending it. Nor speaking against it. But I am snatching at this space to meditate upon what it all means, this combination of writing/mothering. I'm not talking about "fathering," a word with entirely different meanings according to time and place, nor that neutral, "non-sexist" (possibly non-existent) concept, parenting. Nor am I proscribing or prescribing.

So, what is it?

My computerized (to help overcome one handicap of mothering) *American Heritage Dictionary* gives me: *moth · er · ing n. The nurturing and raising of a child or children by a mother:* "Because they are involved in careers and mothering, many women lead exhausting lives," adds David E. Bloom, a candidate for the understatement-of-the-century award.

I also get the word "mother":

1. A woman who conceives, gives birth to, or raises and nurtures a child.

That doesn't sound so hard.

2. A female parent of an animal.

Simple biology, right?

3. A female ancestor.

Hmmm. This could go off in many directions.

4. A woman who holds a position of authority or responsibility similar to that of a mother: a den mother.

Sounds sinister, as in lion's den. To me.

5. Roman Catholic Church. a. A mother superior. b. Used as a form of address for such a woman.

Not a superior mother. It's all in the order.

6. A woman who creates, originates, or founds something: "the discovery of radium, which made Marie Curie mother to the Atomic Age" (Alden Whitman).

Great.

7. A creative source; an origin: Philosophy is the mother of the sciences.

Mmm-hmmm.

8. Used as a title for a woman respected for her wisdom and age.

All right.

9. Maternal love and tenderness: brought out the mother in her.

That knife cuts both ways. As the next definition shows.

10. Vulgar Slang. Something considered extraordinary, as in disagreeableness, size, or intensity.

Then we get the adjective:

1. Relating to or being mother.
2. Characteristic of a mother: mother love.

And mother hate? Where's that? It certainly exists, both ways. There are moments when we hate our mothers — sometimes long ones. And moments where we, as mothers, hate, if not our children, our own identity as mothers.

In *A Woman's History of the World*, Rosalind Miles says that "over-emphasis on the good mother, procreative and nurturing also denies the bad mother, her dangerous, dark and destructive opposite." She exists, however, in mythology (a term which is reduced to meaning "lies" too often these days) where, for the Greek, the dead were "Demeter's people," and for the Hindu religion she's the Kali-Ma, Black Mother, with blood-red hands and glaring eyes, huge pointed breasts, gore-stained hair, a "garland of skulls about her neck," her earrings "the images of dead men" and her girdle a "chain of venomous snakes." There are moments when I can definitely relate to that.

But the dictionary also gives us:

3. Being the source or origin: the mother church.
4. Derived from or as if from one's mother; native: one's mother language.

Mother language. Mother tongue. Yes. That adjective might seem a mere formality, a mere synonym for first, but it's not. In a paper on developing bilingual, intercultural curricula that recognize and build upon Native American cultures and languages rather than crushing them under the rush of so-called progress, Francesco Chiodo asks, "Why is the child's language called mother to differentiate from the other learned later on?" And answers:

> The mother tongue is the language that the child learns during the first years of life, while with the mother. A mother language or maternal tongue is essential, intimate, charged with emotional values, that is: "a cultural element that ties, like an umbilical cord, the individual to the mother, relatives, fore-bears, tradition."[3]

---

[3]Francesco Chiodi, "*Hacia un curriculum intercultural bilingüe.*" He quotes Lanternari, 1985: 15.

Ah. So somehow here's a link between mothering, the action and the tongue, and the carrying on and transmission of culture, writing. Many ancient myths confirm this connection. The goddess Vac, of Indian mythology, from whose song I borrowed for the title of this essay, is language itself, "personifies the birth of speech, and is represented as a maternal mouth-cavity open to give birth to the living word."[4] In other myths, women invent writing as well as language. In fact, my own personal nemesis, Medusa, gave the alphabet to Hercules. If I'd only known this, when I wrote my book *Medusa's Children*. But I must have sensed it, because it's part of what the book is about.

As writers / mothers we could well begin each work session with the Hindu prayer to the mother of Krishna, Devaki: "Goddess of the Logos, Mother of the Gods, One with Creation, thou art Intelligence, the Mother of Science, the Mother of Courage . . ." It takes all these to carry on.

Learn to talk your children's tongue. Listen.

Almost inevitably, theirs is the language of metaphor, the empirical knowledge of the world that comes only through tasting, touching, counting, testing every element, every moment, every drop, lick, suck on the breast and what comes after. (And that sucking experience is the first training the child's tongue and lips and teeth receive in preparation for talking, language, writing.)

This child's view of the world through metaphor is part of the language that makes writing good, partly a way of seeing with the new eyes of the child.

Let us pause here, deliberately, for once. For an interruption. A scratch on my attempt at a smooth surface for this writing. A scar. Let us go back to the beginning of mothering. And writing. Inside.

Seventeen extra kilos on, my body lumbered and groaned. I wanted a block and tackle to roll over in bed. My feet ached more than the mermaid's (I'm sure) after walking even fifteen minutes. It was easy to pop off into an altered state of consciousness, to see dots before my eyes or feel like something strange was about to happen to me, right there on the street, under the Carabineros' watchful eyes, walking past the Moneda to the post office. Out of my way! Can't you see? I felt knocked about, even when no one touched me.

---

[4]Rosalind Miles, *A Woman's History of the World*, p. 128.

Yet, I felt untouched so often, as if it were me floating in the amniotic sac, water muffling voices, the wind's soft touch, the warmth of fingers up my legs. Sex. Yes. Pregnancy and sex. The last taboo? The weight and volume on my vagina and the steady pulse of all that extra blood, those taut nerves ringing with sensation, echoes spreading in concentric circles through the towering hollows of the pelvis.

The beginning of mothering, when Inside is inside me, when I seem to shrink into myself. Where we city dwellers are inside all the time, yet still deny what's inside us, our own biological reality, the animal that bleeds and sweats and smells and gives us pleasure. The sense and sexuality of mothering, transformed into language, informs writing. The limits we cling to elsewhere don't exist. Forget about "pure," asexual motherhood. It's a lie. Sexuality is in the way we touch our children, where and how they touch us, for the simple reason that there is no limit between touch and feeling. Rationality comes later.

Then there's the place where inside and outside meet. Writing. Birth.

The feeling that something inside/outside of me, huge, powerful as a waterfall had grabbed my belly and was pushing me inside out. A feeling of power I couldn't completely control — the white water when you hit it in the canoe and all you can do is dig your paddle in, swishing it from side to side without time for thought or talk, hoping your partner in the stern is doing the same, in time, coordinated enough to keep you going. Hitting white water is fear and exhilaration, panic and energy, my own wit-strength, pulling me through and out of there.

Afterward I would have got up and danced. The baby on my chest while Nino stitched up another long episiotomy. I didn't care. As long as the baby was there I literally felt no pain. Just the joy of his arrival and my own return to lightness, my body coming back to me. I loved him then. His separation from me.

Now we begin to separate. To be. Me again. You for the first time. I knew we would get along not like fetus and womb strung together by blood and nerves, but like two planets rotating in reference to each other, complex and whole. Free. Relatively.

After birth, spending a month at a wild cabin in the Andes, I realize that in the city, even the space outside our homes has become another kind of inside, insulating us from the natural world, from our own fears and smallness and doubts about our place on the planet. To walk outside at night is to walk into fear itself, darkness engulfing, unravelling all our explanations, making them insufficient. Like waterlogged trunks they don't sustain us when darkness closes over our heads.

Inside the cabin, light creates a barrier, makes windows opaque. They lie, shooting back images of the kitchen, the stove, the lamp, instead of revealing what hides outside. We're taught that mothering is an inside job (like writing). But mothering is a journey that can take you anywhere. Mothering is standing between the baby, inside, and whatever's out there in the dark. Mothering (and writing) is learning to face your own fears and do something with them.

To venture out you need names for things, rituals for protection insiders lack. What if we go so far inside we forget the way back, how to live in/with the outside?

Because, with all our modern gadgets, computers, switches, explanations, it's not that we have overcome our fear of the dark. No. With our bright neon lights, electric undercurrents, we've murdered the dark, pushed it under a bright marble stone of artificial daylight, and with it, the dreams that frighten us, the dreams that comfort us, the dreams that might lead us onward into unknown patches of ourselves, as individuals or members of communities, strange territories, changed worlds.

Either way, in writing or in life, we start inside. In darkness. Then comes a peal of laughter or pain as we are born. The word. As I discovered once, writing a poem, that word is mother, not God. But this is the child's view.

With the baby's birth, the mother discovers play, the writer plays out different roles, explores the game, the myth, the world, the imagination maps. Another scratch. Or scar.

There are times when only the knowledge that my four-month-old baby will one day be a four-year-old boy keeps me going. I am sitting in my cabin in the middle of the forest on top of a mountain with my computer plugged into a car battery. What more should I need to produce pages and pages of wonderful writing? Well, someone to do the laundry would help. And feed the baby. And change him and rock him and sing and talk to him when the muse has me by the horns. He's a lovely baby, probably the only person in the world who appreciates my gift for humour. He chuckles merrily at my antics as I fire spoonfuls of pablum at him, skillfully duplicating the sound of a missile slicing the sky. And he laughs outright as the spoon hits target in his mouth, a reaction which never fails to scatter pablum in every direction.

He also loves to hear me sing, being the only person in the world who listens with genuine enjoyment as I absentmindedly switch from one song to another, forgetting to change key, in fact, forgetting the key completely and growing more and more out of tune as my enthusiasm soars.

Danny really appreciates me. And that helps. Because his needs have changed an absent-minded writer worried about where the next meal's coming from into dancer, comedian and housekeeper. Not a mean feat. I think longingly of my first baby, now a delightful, stubborn, seven-year-old. Nowadays he rocks the baby around the clock, or at least the living room, as I desperately pump away at one breast or the other, trying to get the baby's lunchtime pablum prepared before one or other explodes.

He shoots baby in baby-chair all over the floor, firing real soccer balls through imaginary goal posts. While this has meant some expense on household repairs, I am destined to be eternally grateful for the few minutes of peace, defined as absence of tearful howling, that he's bought me.

Every day, my children remind me of where I come from, everything that I've forgotten. And we do forget. Time, to a very large extent, is amnesia.

We forget the power of words. We who wield them, pinch them into bloom and prod them into movement, forget their power even as we convoke it, handle them carelessly, mutter counterspells even as we chant our spells, hopefully, building our Spanish castles, our worlds of air that smell of blood, of thyme, of fresh wind blowing through the illusions we've shaped so lovingly, homes we expect others to share.

Danny turns two and learns to say "Come." When I stop dead on my way out of his room, turn around, walk back to him, he tastes a power he's wanted his whole short life. The day he learns to say "No" and his father pleads with him, while his brother explains that you can't go out without your shoes on, and he shouts No and NO and NOO and NOOO and NOOOO until he has the whole family crowded around him, pleading and pushing, then trying to distract him, then angry, then walking away, then running back. No *quiele*, he says. I don't want. Me gusta. I like.

I want shorts. I want the car. I want the plaza. I want milk — WARM milk. He shapes the words clumsily between tongue and teeth and lips, pushes them out. Most of the time he gets what he wants.

We learn to speak, we grasp the world, through metaphors. Then why are we so quick to desert them?

Poetry is as undervalued as babytalk, as commonplace, as pure and thick as raw honey, and as difficult to extricate from the bees that protect it. Poetry is a voice speaking, as Tom Wayman once said, "in a world full of people talking," words that "put down roots in someone's mind/ so that he or she likes to have them here—/ these words no one was paid to write/ that live with us for a while/ in a small container/ on the ledge where the light enters."

Unless you're Neruda or at least a university prof or a novelist as well, poetry may not enhance your reputation, and it will certainly distract you from success, especially in the monetary sense. But that's irrelevant. Once you start, poetry, writing generally, ceases to be an option, becomes a compulsion, an addiction, a drug. Unless treated with a certain ritual respect, the craving it teases into being can destroy you. But when you're on it, nothing else matters. There's strength and nourishment in the freedom it provides.

It won't feed your children, but it will teach you to listen to them with more respect. And they will teach you to write better.

As children struggle to combine the right words, form thoughts, make sense of their world (and isn't that what we, as writers, do?), they use metaphors to join what they've figured out, inside, with what goes on around them, outside, the birth of character. They speak and poetry is their first language.

"The moon is a father," Camilo told me when he was three. "That's why all the stars crowd around him." "The rain pecks at the pavement," he discovered one fall day. Once he asked me, seriously, "Who turns the day on and off?"

(All these percolate through my writing.)

With the word, or shortly thereafter, comes voice. The child's voice turns slowly on the wheel of her or his words, starting thick and unformed, a lump of almost shapeless sound, a wind blowing through trees that slowly becomes music flowing from a flute.

Every writing has a voice, many voices. Listen. Dorothy Livesay once wrote: "All the people I have known intimately, loving or hating, are [in my writing]. They have acted as catalysts. But there seems to be another source of poetry, quite outside one's conscious experience. . . . What happens is that one is 'taken over' by other voices. . . . the poet is the mouth through which the voices speak."

Just as the child crawls, staggers, strides, words, voice, language stand up and walk us into our culture, our society. Francesco Chiodi says, "It is the learning of the mother language that permits knowledge of the world, providing a way of seeing and understanding things. When a child enters school, everything he or she knows and can say is tied to the mother language."

Chiodi adds that language registers and codifies a people's cultural experience, is "the most intimate and exclusive belonging of a people. A child becomes a member of a social community by entering into communication with it." And he emphasizes that children cannot come to understand the cosmovision that forms the framework of their culture in a foreign language, but only their mother tongue.

In a world where we generally work for money instead of the common good, consume instead of create, writing is action, steering our own boat, and that is, perhaps, as close to freedom as we'll get.

Nevertheless, like the air we fill with smog and the water we pile with waste, this raising, this writing, have no value in our neo-liberal, market-driven world. Mothers, or writers, or native cultures that have by some miracle survived: we all face a world that measures value by the number of dollars earned or spent, rather than the number of minds changed or opened, or comforted. When the men, and occasional woman in power, decide to send people off to wars (internal or otherwise), throwing them away like pennies, the nights spent rocking a howling child count for nothing.

In many ways, those of us who can't measure what we do by the salaries that we earn are fighting an unequal war to hold a worthwhile place in this merciless world. Suicide can seem like a logical out. Within this context, our "useless" occupations of mothering/writing, children can hold us to life in our most desperate moments, even as they drive us to desperation.

Danny is at the totem-spirit stage. After a hot bath, he wraps himself in a towel with a huge and vivid tiger face emerging from among leaves, puts on his tiger slippers and prowls around the house. He growls when crossed and can be dangerous. Hauled off to bed he inflicts deep scratches and bites his would-be captors. This world is as real to him as any other and it's a world where he wields genuine power.

This enables him to build and fight and grapple with more in his daily life. His world of magical powers is like the one I enter when I write, rotating next to his, a place where I could say, as Isis did,

> . . . mistress of every land. I laid down laws for all, and ordained things no one may change . . . I divided the earth from heaven, made manifest the paths of the stars, prescribed the course of the sun and the moon . . . I brought together men and women . . . What I have made law can be dissolved by no man.[5]

Ursula K. Le Guin says that "To learn to speak is to learn to tell a story." To mother then, is, can, should be, to teach, to tell a story. To learn the language all over again, to question received beliefs, the way our children do. To ask, why? Over and over again. That, too, is writing.

Another interruption. Danny bangs open the door and stomps in, chewing on a piece of pâté-smeared bread.

"Plant!" he says.

"What plant? Where?" I ask.

"PLANT!" he shouts. Is this a reference to a vegetable type existence or an order like "Go forth and multiply"? I wonder. In the meantime, I'm reduced to shouting back.

"PLANT?"

"YES. PLAAANNNNTTTT!" he hollers, then stomps back out.

He leaves me with the knowledge that this day, this precious space in my life for my own writing, is coming to a close. Outside the yellow blinds, a grim grey day has darkened and the mercury lamps glow orange among the acacia trees. Inside/outside haunts me for an instant.

I know that this writing is shorter than I would have liked, longer than I hoped, both broken and perhaps enriched by the interruptions that have marked this day, the doubts that will come tomorrow. When I reread, rewrite, correct this later on, I know it will not live up to all my expectations, but I hope I'll find a few surprises.

---

[5]John Langdon-Davis, quoted in Rosalind Miles, *A Woman's History of the World*, p. 55.

I know that it will drive me crazy with frustration. But it will also drive me on. And that, dear reader, writer, fellow, mother, friend, is all that matters in the end. Isn't it?

Originally from Calgary, ERIN MOURÉ lived in Banff, Edmonton, and Vancouver before moving to Montreal in 1985. Her books of poetry are: *Empire, York Street, Wanted Alive, Domestic Fuel, Furious* (all Anansi), *WSW* (*West South West*) and *Sheepish Beauty, Civilian Love* (both Véhicule). Her selected poems, *The Green Word*, appeared from Oxford Canada in late 1994.

Parts of a Clock, or Asthma

Erin Mouré

(Two years into the Bosnian civil war, on February 5, 1994, a mortar shell fired into Sarajevo market killed 68 Saturday shoppers.)

The poem is not a
cute thing. Thousands of us have vanished into there.
Perished. Or.

A woman has come to sell parts of a clock. A small
ramshackle table is set up where she waits with the clock piece.

A description of attire. Who is wearing what
in this picture. Where the black leather coat is. The
dream of -------- this Saturday before the shell hit.

Killing 68*. The poem is not a cute
thing. Wearing the "manteau de voyage."

The available supply of goods diminished

2) FATTY-ACID

A defect in fatty-acid metabolism
leaves us fearful. The woman is not in the market

a hole in the buildings opposite. Trailers of goods exist in the
head where they rumble at the border check-points

priests counting the alcohol. "Their yellow beards
are long & the drivers are cold, waiting."
This is what the woman's head is saying in the market,
so alive, a conscious spark or glow in the universe
this living

Or a hot firefly over the hay fields of Garthby Québec could be
as nuanced, as fine

An investment in emerging Latin markets over the next 2-3

3) CHEST-LEVEL

An examination of the shell crater leaves us wondering.
The northeast hills it came from, killing 68*.
Its gentle nose, they said, struck

the market table, exploding in mid-air at chest-level, the iron
sleeve shattering with the charge & propelling shards
at rocket-speed, still audible,

shearing the bodies. A clock broken is these pieces. Some clocks still
for sale here. The never-ending repetition of markets.
Someone needs what someone else might have,
or we exchange nothings. Circulation in the broken stands.

The crucible. We meant to

Increased consumption is possible in a zero-based

4) Description of Asthma

A metabolic cue or error. Her endometrium
concentrates arachidonic acid. The woman dreams of

bread & laughs, secretly. Who are we apart from this inner spark
whose neural screen or glow makes "bread"? The wounds
in the buildings & towers she walks thru.
Opens the blood supply of the organism,
irrevocably.

Others bring the found jacket to the market,
the old piece of iron, someone can boil it, or shoes.
A woman wants to bargain these old clock parts of time for

shorn at chest-level. 68 minus 1. An end to it here*

~~Recurrent attacks of shortness of breath, cough & expectoration of tenacious mucoid sputum~~

In the long term, market corrections are largely irrelevant to

TIMOTHY FINDLEY, a former actor, is now an award-winning author of novels, short-fiction collections, plays, and a memoir, and a writer of dramas and documentaries for radio, television, and film. His work has been translated into fifteen languages. He is an Officer in the Order of Canada and from 1986 to 1987 was president of English Canada P.E.N.

MARTHA AND THE MINDER

TIMOTHY FINDLEY

To the artist, freedom of expression is vital.

And yet, such freedom is being denied by censorship — even by imprisonment.

Martha and the Minder is dedicated to those whose freedom is yet to be won, and to those who help them win it by adopting prisoners of conscience. This process begins with letters written to and in behalf of the prisoner. Those who write these letters are known as *minders*. Making and maintaining contact is often painfully frustrating, since there is not always evidence the letters are being received.

EPISODE ONE

There are two lecterns, one on either side of the stage, each with a microphone and each capable of being lit by a spotlight. MARTHA is stage right; MINDER is stage left. Both begin in darkness.

MARTHA:

Someone? (PAUSE) Someone? (PAUSE) Please? Someone?

LIGHT BEGINS TO RISE ON MARTHA STAGE RIGHT

Hello? Hello? Hello! (PAUSE) Isn't there someone there? Anyone? Anywhere?

MINDER:

Yes?

MARTHA:

Oh . . . .

MINDER:

Did someone speak?

MARTHA:

Yes. I did.

MINDER:

Who are you? Where are you?

MARTHA:

I'm in prison. My name is Martha.

SILENCE

Hello?

LIGHT BEGINS TO RISE ON MINDER STAGE LEFT

MINDER:

Yes? What?

MARTHA:

Who are you? Tell me your name.

MINDER:

Minder.

MARTHA:

How do you do, Mister Minder?

MINDER:

I'm well — but please don't call me Mister. Call me Minder. (BEAT) May I call you . . .

MARTHA:

Martha. That's the only name I have that I can give you.

MINDER:

I see. (PAUSE) Why are you in prison?

MARTHA:

I don't really know. Something I said — or something I wrote. Well — no. It was definitely something I wrote.

MINDER:

You mean it was censored?

MARTHA:

Yes. Well — no. Not what I wrote — but me. *I'm* in prison. Not my words. (LAUGHS) And I'd like not to be. (SOBER) Trouble is, there's no one out there who knows I'm in here. Except you — whoever you are. And — now that you know, do you think you could help me?

SILENCE

Do you? Hello? (ANGRY) Hello, for god's sake!

MINDER:

Yes? What?

MARTHA:

Where did you go?

MINDER:

Nowhere. I'm standing right here.

MARTHA:

Well — you might have answered.

MINDER:

Answered what?

MARTHA:

My question. I asked you a question.

MINDER:

I didn't hear you. What did you want to know?

MARTHA:

I wanted to know . . . . (BEAT) How do I know I can trust you?

MINDER:

You don't. But you'd better.

MARTHA:

What makes you say that?

MINDER:

Well — you said yourself I was the only one who knew you were in there. . . .

MARTHA:

Yes.

MINDER:

So. What was your question?

SILENCE

Martha? Please answer.

SILENCE

MARTHA:

Minder? Are you there?

SILENCE

No. So it's true. You can't trust anyone. Oh, god — why did he even bother to answer? (SHOUTS) Why did you bother? You son of a bitch! It isn't fair!

MINDER: (NOT HEARING HER)

Well. The only thing to do, I guess, is to go on speaking . . .

MARTHA: (CAN'T HEAR: SHOUTS)

How dare you do this to me! . . .

MINDER:

She is there. I know that . . .

MARTHA:

. . . Raise my hopes and dash me down again!

MINDER:

. . . I heard her . . .

MARTHA:

You bastard, Minder!

MINDER:

. . . at least once.

PAUSE

MARTHA: (QUIET)
All right. The only thing to do . . . is to go on speaking. . . .

MINDER: (FORMAL)
"Excellency — I join with International P.E.N. in appealing to your honour. . . ."

LIGHTS BEGIN TO FADE ON MARTHA STAGE RIGHT

MARTHA: (AS BEFORE)
Someone ? . . .

MINDER:
" . . . to reconsider the situation . . ."

MARTHA:

. . . please ? . . .

MINDER:

" . . . of the imprisoned writer, Martha . . ."

MARTHA:

. . . Someone ? . . .

MINDER:

". . . We wish for her to be . . ."

MARTHA:

. . . Hello ? . . .

MINDER:

". . . reunited with her children . . ."

MARTHA: (NOW IN GHOST-LIGHT)
. . . Hello! Hello! . . .

MINDER:

". . . and to be granted (HE WAITS) her freedom."

PAUSE: LIGHTS BEGIN TO FADE ON MINDER STAGE LEFT

It's so ironic . . .

MARTHA:

Minder ? . . .

MINDER:

. . . just when she finally catches someone's attention . . .

MARTHA:

Minder?

MINDER:

. . . she disappears.

MARTHA:

HELP!!

TOTAL BLACKOUT

EPISODE TWO

LIGHTS UP

MINDER:

Well, Martha, we have waited now two years with no further word of you. We think perhaps you have been moved to another prison, but we have no way of knowing. At any rate, I will go on writing and so will others. Because it seems the only sane thing to do.

MARTHA:

Not a word. And, of course, I have no way of communicating with the out-side world. The only money I have, I must spend on food. No one out there understands that. Prisons here don't feed you. Or clothe you. Or anything. All they do is keep you. And if I could afford some writing paper, I couldn't afford the postage. And even if I could afford the postage — they wouldn't pass it through the system. Two whole years in silence. They want the world to think I'm dead — and they want me, too, to think the world is dead. And I — right now, I'm quite prepared to believe it.

MINDER:

When we were children, my brother and I would write our names on pieces of paper — and we would write the word "hello" and put the pieces of paper into bottles and seal the bottles and throw them into the sea. Well — here comes another bottle with another note. Hello, Martha. Hello.

MARTHA: (HAS NOT HEARD HIM)

I need a bottle of aspirin. I need a bar of soap. I need a package of toilet paper. I need disinfectant. I need vitamins. I need bread. I need tea. I need a lemon — one lemon. I need clean underwear. I need a pair of shoes. I need a box of tampons. I need a ball of string. I need money. I need news. I need my chil-dren . . . please.

MINDER: (HAS NOT HEARD HER)

It is winter here, now — and coming on to Christmas. Snow — have you ever seen snow? Martha?

MARTHA: (HAS NOT HEARD HIM)
(PUTTING HER OTHER NEEDS ASIDE) I need one card — one stamp

— an envelope. Thank you. Now — I will see if the world is still there. And if it remembers me.

MINDER:

Oh — my — (OPENS ENVELOPE) Oh — my — god! (HOLDS UP CARD)

MARTHA:

Merry Christmas. Love. Martha.

MINDER:

She's alive.

BLACKOUT

EPISODE THREE

MARTHA and MINDER share microphone, stage left. LIGHTS UP.

MINDER:

This morning, I went shopping with my friend. The store clerk didn't know what to make of us, though it began innocently enough.

MARTHA: (STORE CLERK)

Good morning, gentlemen.

MINDER:

Good morning.

MARTHA:

Is there something I can do for you?

MINDER:

Yes. We want to buy some clothing.

MARTHA:

I see. You realize, of course, you're in the wrong department. Men's clothing is . . .

MINDER:

No, no. It's women's clothing we're looking for.

MARTHA:

Oh, I see. Yes. Well. What did you have in mind?

MINDER:

Bottoms.

MARTHA:

Bottoms.

MINDER:

Yes. And tops.

MARTHA:

Tops . . . and bottoms?

MINDER:

Yes.

MARTHA:

What of?

MINDER:

Well . . .

MARTHA: (STARING AT HIM)

I know you, don't I?

MINDER:

No. I don't think so.

MARTHA:

Yes. I do. I know you. I've seen you on television. . . .

MINDER:

Well . . .

MARTHA:

And in the papers.

MINDER:

I . . .

MARTHA:

You're that gay writer, aren't you.

MINDER:

Well . . .

MARTHA:

The one with all the opinions.

MINDER:

Could we get the tops and bottoms, please?

MARTHA:

I suppose this gentleman with you is your . . . friend.

MINDER:

Yes. He is my friend. Now . . .

MARTHA:

What sort of tops and bottoms had you in mind? We never did get to that, did we?

MINDER:

No — we didn't.

MARTHA:

Are they for him — or for you?

MINDER:

Please, madame, we just want . . .

MARTHA:

I suppose you'll want to try them on.

MINDER:

No . . .

MARTHA:

I can't, of course, let you anywhere near the lingerie. That's not allowed.

MINDER:

We don't . . .

MARTHA:

Even in the men's department, it is absolutely forbidden. Customers are not allowed to test drive the underwear.

MINDER: (SHOUTS)

We don't want underwear! We want tops and bottoms!

MARTHA:

Yes, sir.

MINDER:

For a friend!

MARTHA:

Ladies' tops and bottoms for a friend . . .

MINDER:

Yes.

MARTHA:

This friend here?

MINDER:

No! For a friend in prison!

MARTHA:

I see. You want ladies' tops and bottoms for a friend in prison.

MINDER:

Yes.

MARTHA: (PAUSE)

What size is he?

BLACKOUT

EPISODE FOUR

MARTHA stage right, MINDER stage left. PARTIAL LIGHTING only, stage left. THE LIGHTS grow hotter stage right around MARTHA as she speaks.

MARTHA:

Are you there?

MINDER:

Yes.

MARTHA:

The clothing arrived.

MINDER:

Oh, yes?

MARTHA:

Blue is my favourite colour.

MINDER:

Blue is the colour of hope.

MARTHA:

Yes. Well — It's that time of year again. September.

MINDER:

September. Yes.

MARTHA:

This is the month of pardons — of amnesty — forgiveness — freedom.

MINDER:

Yes.

MARTHA:

In September of every year, they come through that gate — and they choose
twelve people — and they set them free.

MINDER:

Yes.

MARTHA:

I have been here, now, nine Septembers.

MINDER:

Eight. This one is not yet over.

MARTHA:

Yes. It is not yet over. But it is still number nine. (BEAT) What are you doing today, I wonder.

MINDER:

Sitting in the shade.

MARTHA:

Oh, Minder! You sound so weary of it all. I'm sitting in the sun. I love the sun. It is spring here, now, you see. Spring — and the month of pardons.

MINDER:

We're thinking of you, Martha — all of us — and praying.

MARTHA: (PAUSE)

When they come through the gate, you never know. I mean — they come for you, and sometimes, it is not an amnesty. Sometimes it is not a pardon. And it is never forgiveness. Never. (BEAT) Thank you for writing — all these years. Just in case. (BEAT) Some people . . . sometimes, they come through the gate and they choose you — and you disappear. People disappear. It is not always a good thing — to be chosen.

MINDER:

We are with you, Martha.

MARTHA:

On the other hand — a person can be set free. Pardoned. Hah! Pardoned! How dare they "pardon" me. I did nothing wrong. Only what I believed was right. And I will believe it was right to the day I die, Minder. Yes. To the day I die. (BEAT) Are you afraid of death, Minder?

MINDER:

Yes.

MARTHA:

So am I. And here I sit — waiting for the gate to open. (BEAT) If it opens to an amnesty, I will see my children.

MINDER:

Yes.

MARTHA:

Well — Minder — here they come. Goodbye.

MINDER:

I won't say goodbye. I can't. (HE TURNS UPSTAGE, BECOMING ANOTHER PERSON) *MAR-THA!*

MARTHA:

Yes. That is me. (SHE TURNS UPSTAGE, AND SLOWLY WALKS INTO THE WINGS)

PAUSE

MINDER: (TURNING FRONT)

Ladies and gentlemen — after almost ten years, Martha was released from prison — and reunited with her children. And here she is.

Enter MARTHA KUMSA, no longer imprisoned in Addis Ababa, but living in Toronto with her children.

She was welcomed with a loud and prolonged standing ovation which caused her young son in the audience to ask: *Why is everyone standing up?*

Prisons around the world still hold those whose words, written or spoken, have cost them their freedom. We must not give up the struggle to set them free; and they must not give up hope.

This dramatization, Martha and the Minder*, was written especially for presentation at a gala for P.E.N. International, produced in December 1991 at the Winter Garden Theatre in Toronto. It was performed by Judith Thompson as* Martha *and Timothy Findley as* Minder.

The four episodes were performed at intervals throughout the evening. The final episode was the culmination of the whole gala.

KAREN MULHALLEN is editor-in-chief of *Descant* magazine which she has edited for most of its twenty-five years. She is the author of three volumes of poetry, *Sheba and Solomon* (1984), *Modern Love* (1990), and *War Surgery* (1996), and of the prose travel-fiction-memoir *In The Era of Acid Rain* (1993). She co-edited *Tasks of Passion: Dennis Lee at Mid-Career* (1982), and edited *Views from the North, An Anthology of Travel Literature* (1984). She is the former arts features editor of *The Canadian Forum* magazine, on which she worked for fourteen years, as well as the author of numerous articles and reviews on the arts. She teaches in Toronto where she is Professor of English at Ryerson Polytechnic University.